HANDBOOK OF RADIO COMMUNICATIONS AND ENGINEERING

HANDBOOK OF RADIO COMMUNICATIONS AND ENGINEERING

Volume 2

James Stewart
Addison Grant

Kruger Brentt
Publishers
2026

Kruger Brentt Publishers UK. LTD.
Company Number 9728962

Regd. Office: 68 St Margarets Road, Edgware, Middlesex HA8 9UU

ISBN: 978-1-78715-673-9 (Vol. 2)

For information on all our publications visit our website at http://krugerbrentt.com/

PREFACE

Radio communications form the backbone of modern telecommunication systems, enabling wireless connectivity across vast distances and supporting applications ranging from mobile networks and satellite communications to emergency services and defense systems. As technology advances, the field of radio communications continues to evolve rapidly, integrating new methodologies, devices, and signal processing techniques.

Handbook of Radio Communications and Engineering provides a comprehensive reference for students, engineers, and researchers in the field of wireless communications and radio engineering. The book covers fundamental principles, modern technologies, system design, and practical applications, offering a detailed exploration of both theoretical and applied aspects. Topics such as modulation techniques, antennas, wave propagation, RF circuits, signal processing, and emerging technologies are addressed in depth to provide a well-rounded understanding of the field.

The text aims to bridge the gap between foundational knowledge and practical engineering solutions, making it a valuable resource for academic study, research, and professional practice. It emphasizes problem-solving, design considerations, and real-world applications to equip readers with the tools required for effective communication system development and analysis.

James Stewart

Addison Grant

CONTENTS

VOLUME 2

20 Chapter

THROUGHPUT-ENHANCED COMMUNICATION METHODOLOGY FOR SUBSCRIBER STATIONS IN IEEE 802.16 POINT-TO-MULTIPOINT NETWORKS

1. INTRODUCTION: AN OVERVIEW

The IEEE 802.16 standard for wireless metropolitan area networks (WMANs) aims to meet diverse requirements for high capacity, elevated data rates, and sophisticated multimedia services (Abichar et al., 2006). The medium access control (MAC) layer of IEEE 802.16 networks facilitates both point-to-multipoint (PMP) and mesh configurations for packet transmission (IEEE Std. 802.16-2004, 2004). According to the application criteria, the standard recommends that only one mode may be utilized by the network components at the specified time intervals, with the PMP mode being regarded as the most widely accepted option. In the PMP mode, a base station (BS) orchestrates packet transmission, managing communication with numerous subscriber stations (SSs) in both downlink (DL) and uplink (UL) directions. Traffic within an IEEE 802.16 PMP network can be classified into two categories: inter-cell traffic and intra-cell traffic. In inter-cell traffic, the source and destination of each traffic flow are situated in distinct cells. Conversely, intra-cell traffic is described as occurring when entities are located within the same cell. The inefficiency in the PMP mode arises when two SSs attempt to transmit packets, specifically regarding intra-cell traffic between the SSs. The base station must forward data packets between the subscriber stations, even if the stations are next to one another. The packet rerouting procedure results in lost communication bandwidth, hence increasing the packet-rerouting latency.

To mitigate the disadvantages arising from indirect transmission, a direct communicable method between SSs should be implemented in IEEE 802.16 networks. Various direct communication methodologies have been suggested for diverse network types. The Direct-Link Setup (DLS) protocol is codified in the IEEE 802.11z draft standard to provide direct communication between two station systems (SSs) in wireless local area networks (IEEE P802.11zTM/D5.0, 2009). The

DLS protocol functions as a contention-based method, lacking the assurance of direct link establishment and data exchanges between two SSs. The dynamic slot assignment (DSA) scheme for Bluetooth networks is suggested in Zhang et al. (2002) and Cordeiro et al. (2003), principally implemented based on the characteristics of the Bluetooth standard. Due to the differences in frame structures and medium access procedures among various wireless communication technologies, neither the DLS protocol nor the DSA scheme can be directly implemented in IEEE 802.16 networks.

This chapter proposes a point-to-point direct communication (PDC) method for facilitating direct transmission between two SSs. The PDC methodology is formulated as a versatile and contention-free framework specifically for time division duplexing in IEEE 802.16 PMP networks. The BS is organizing and scheduling particular time periods for the two SSs engaged in packet transfer. The relative positions and channel conditions between the base stations and subscriber stations are employed as criteria to ascertain if direct communication should be implemented. The benefit of utilizing the PDC strategy is that it can substantially decrease both the necessary bandwidth for packet transmission and the packet rerouting latency for intra-cell traffic. The efficacy of the proposed PDC approach is evidenced by the simulation results, which indicate that the PDC approach surpasses the traditional IEEE 802.16 transmission mechanism for user throughput.

2. IEEE 802.16 PMP NETWORKS

The PMP mode is considered the well-adopted network configuration in IEEE 802.16 net- works wherein the BS is responsible for controlling all the communication among SSs. Two duplexing techniques are supported for the SSs to share common channels, i.e., time division duplexing (TDD) and frequency division duplexing. The MAC protocol is structured to sup- port multiple physical (PHY) layer specifications in the IEEE 802.16 standard. In this book chapter, the WirelessMAN-OFDM PHY, utilizing the orthogonal frequency division multi- plexing (OFDM), with TDD mode is exploited for the design of the proposed PDC approach. Both the frame structure and packet transmission mechanism of IEEE 802.16 PMP networks are described in the following subsections.

2.1 Frame Structure

Fig. 1 illustrates the schematic diagram of the IEEE 802.16 PMP OFDM frame structure with TDD mode. It can be observed that each frame consists of a DL subframe and a UL subframe. The DL subframe contains only one DL PHY protocol data unit (PDU), which starts with a long preamble for PHY synchronization. The preamble is followed by a frame control header (FCH) burst and several DL bursts. A DL frame prefix (DLFP), which is contained in the FCH, specifies the burst profile and length for the first DL burst (at most four) via the information element (IE). It is noted that each DL burst may contain an optional preamble and more than one MAC PDUs that are destined for the same or different SSs. The first MAC PDU followed by the FCH is the DL-MAP message, which employs DL-MAP IEs to describe the remaining DL bursts. The DL-MAP message can be excluded in the case that the DL subframe consists of less than five bursts; nevertheless, it must still be sent out periodically to maintain syn- chronization. A UL-MAP message immediately following the DL-MAP message denotes the usage of UL bursts via UL-MAP IEs. An interval usage code, corresponding to a burst profile, describes a set of transmission parameters, e.g., the modulation and coding type, and the for- ward error correction type. The DL interval usage code (DIUC) and UL interval usage code (UIUC) are specified in the DL channel descriptor (DCD) and UL channel descriptor (UCD) messages respectively. The BS broadcasts both the DCD and UCD messages periodically to define the characteristics of the DL and UL physical channels respectively.

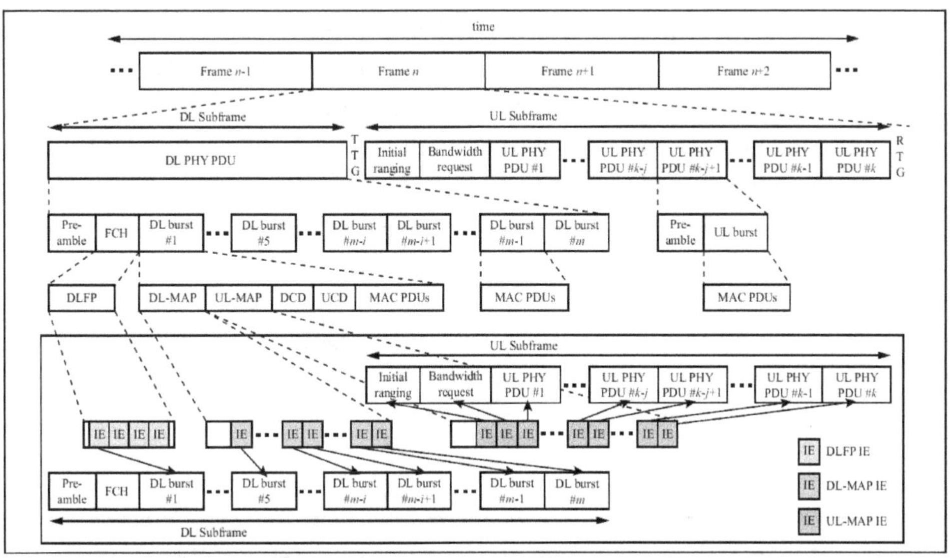

Fig. 1. Schematic diagram of IEEE 802.16 PMP OFDM frame structure with TDD mode.

On the other hand, as can be seen from Fig. 1, the UL subframe starts with the contention intervals that are specified for both initial ranging and bandwidth request. It is noted that more than one UL PHY PDU can be transmitted after the contention intervals. Each UL PHY PDU consists of a short preamble and a UL burst, where the UL burst transports the MAC PDUs for each specific SS. Moreover, a transmit-to-receive transition gap (TTG) and a receive- to-transmit transition gap (RTG) are inserted in between the DL and the UL subframes and at the end of each frame respectively. These two gaps provide the required time for the BS to switch from the transmit to receive mode and vice versa.

2.2 Packet Transmission Mechanism

A connection in IEEE 802.16 PMP networks is defined as a unidirectional mapping between the BS and an MS, which is identified by a 16-bit connection identifier (CID). Two kinds of connections, including management connections and transport connections, are defined in the IEEE 802.16 standard. The management connections are utilized for delivering MAC manage- ment messages; while the transport connections are employed to transmit user data. During the initial ranging of a SS, a pair of UL and DL basic connections are established, which be- long to a type of the management connections. It is noted that a single Basic CID is assigned to a pair of UL and DL basic connections, which is served as the identification number for the corresponding SS. Thus the SS uses the individual transport CID to request bandwidth for each transport connection while the BS arranges the accumulated transmission opportunity by addressing the Basic CID of the SS.

An exemplified network topology that consists of one BS and two neighboring SSs is shown in Fig. 2. Two types of traffic exist in the network: inter-cell traffic and intra-cell traffic. For the inter-cell traffic, the source and the destination for each traffic flow are located in different cells, e.g., the traffic flow of SS2 for accessing the Internet. On the other hand, the intra-cell traffic is defined while the source and destination are situated within the same cell network,

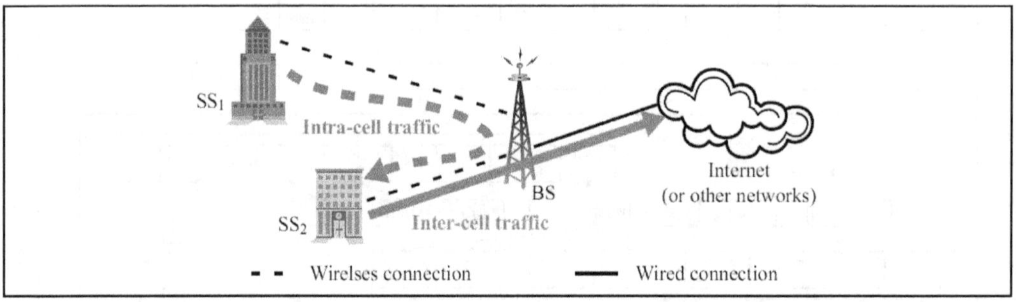

Fig. 2. Example of IEEE 802.16 PMP network topology.

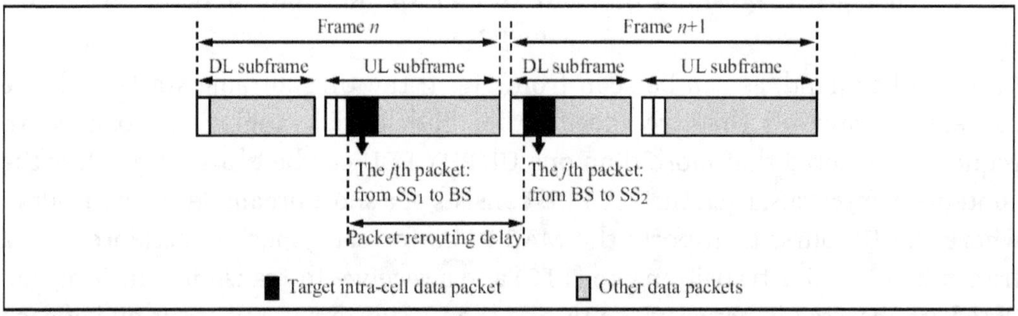

Fig. 3. Schematic diagram of IEEE 802.16 packet transmission mechanism in time sequence.

such as the traffic flow between SS1 and SS2 in Fig. 2. Considering the scenario that SS1 intends to communicate with its neighboring station SS2, two transport connections are required to be established via the service flow management mechanism for the intra-cell traffic, i.e., the UL transport connection from SS1 to the BS and the DL transport connection from the BS to SS2. Fig. 3 illustrates the conventional transmission mechanism of IEEE 802.16 PMP networks in time sequence. In the most ideal case, the jth intra-cell packet, transmitted from SS1 to the BS in the nth frame, will be forwarded to SS2 in the (n+1)th frame by the BS. The rerouting process apparently requires twice of communication bandwidth for achieving the intra-cell packet transmission, which consequently increases control overhead by duplicating the corresponding data packet. Moreover, the delay time for packet-rerouting can be more than one half of a frame duration

3. POINT-TO-POINT DIRECT COMMUNICATION (PDC) APPROACH

The objective of the proposed PDC approach is to provide a directly communicable mecha- nism for SSs within IEEE 802.16 PMP networks such that both the communication bandwidth and packet-rerouting delay of intra-cell traffic are reduced. The PDC approach is designed as a flexible and contention-free scheme wherein the establishment of direct link is conducted along with packet transmission. Based on the channel conditions among the BS and SSs, the BS coordinates and arranges specific time intervals for the two SSs that are actively involved in packet transmission. It is worthwhile to mention that the PDC approach is carried out after the establishment of the original transmission path, which is compatible and can be directly integrated with the existing protocols defined in the IEEE 802.16 standard. In the following subsections, the proposed architecture and management structures will be described in Sub- section 3.1; while an admission control scheme for direct link establishment is explained in Subsection 3.2. The direct communication procedures of the PDC approach are given in Sub- section 3.3.

3.1 Architecture and Management Structure

For the purpose of providing time intervals for direct transmission between SSs, a point-to- point direct link (PDL) subframe is proposed in the PDC approach. A PDL subframe that consists of one or more PDL PHY PDUs is designed as a subset of a DL or UL subframe. Each PDL PHY PDU starts with a short preamble followed by a PDL burst, which is designed to transport the MAC PDUs for each specific SS. Furthermore, in order to be compatible with the existing IEEE 802.16 standard, three categories of management structures are proposed, which are detailed as follows:

- ***DL-PDL IE and UL-PDL IE:*** The proposed DL-PDL IE and UL-PDL IE are designed to depict burst profiles and lengths of their corresponding PDLs in the DL and UL sub- frames respectively. The DL-PDL IE is a new type of the extended DIUC dependent IE within the OFDM DL-MAP IE; while the UL-PDL IE is a new type of the UL extended IE that is contained in the OFDM UL-MAP IE. It is noted that the formats of both the proposed DL-PDL IE and UL-PDL IE are designed to conform to the formats of the DL-MAP dummy IE and UL-MAP dummy IE, specified in the IEEE 802.16 standard, respectively.
- ***PDL Subheader:*** The PDL subheader is designed for implementing the request, re- sponse, announcement, and termination of the direct communication. It is a new type of per-PDU subheader, which can be inserted in the MAC PDUs immediately followed by the generic MAC header in both the DL and UL directions. For different purposes, the DL subheader carries various types of information, including MAC addresses, CIDs, and location information.
- ***PBPC-REQ and PBPC-REP Messages:*** In the IEEE 802.16 standard, the adaptive mod- ulation and coding (AMC) is exploited as the link adaption technique to improve the network performance on time-varying channels. The BS selects an adequate modula- tion and coding scheme (MCS) for a SS based on the reported signal-to-interference and noise ratio (SINR) value. Moreover, the BS permits the changes in MCS that are sug- gested by the SS via the burst profile change request message. Similarly, both the pro- posed PDL burst profile change request (PBPC-REQ) and response (PBPC-REP) mes- sages are designed to change the MCS applied in a direct link. The PBPC-REQ message is utilized to request the adjustment of assigned MCS for PDL burst. The BS will re- spond with the PBPC-REP message for either confirming or denying the alternation in the suggested MCS.

3.2 Admission Control Procedure

In the PDC approach, some criteria should be exploited to determine the execution of direct communication between two SSs. A two-tiered admission control scheme for a BS and two at- tached SSs is presented in this subsection. In wireless communication system, the data trans- mission range for each station is proportional to its corresponding transmission power. In order to avoid potential interference introduced by adopting the PDC approach, the distance factor is considered as the first-tiered constraint (C1), which is defined as

$$C1 : D(SSs, SSd) \le D(SSs, BS),$$

where D(x, y) denotes the relative distance between x and y; while the source SS and desti- nation SS of a intra-cell traffic is represented as SSs and SSd respectively. In other words, the transmission power utilized by SSs for achieving direct transmission is adjusted to be equal to or less than that as specified in the conventional IEEE 802.16 mechanism.

On the other hand, for the purpose of enhancing the efficiency for data transmission, channel conditions among the BS and (SSs, SSd) pair should be taken into account. Different MCSs associated with various number of data bits are adopted for data transmission under different channel conditions. Based on channel states and the corresponding MCSs, the second-tiered constraint (C2) is defined as

$$C2 : TPDC (SSs, SSd) \geq TConv (SSs, SSd),$$

where T(SSs, SSd) represents the raw user throughput defined as "number of bits per second that is received by the destination SSd while the source is SSs". In other words, the raw user throughput resulted from the PDC approach (TPDC) should be at least equal to or higher than that from the conventional IEEE 802.16 mechanism (TConv). The values of both TPDC and TConv are derived as the description in the following paragraph.

Table 1. OFDM Modulation and Coding Schemes

MCS index	Modulation	Coding rate	Coded block size (byte)	Receiver SNR (dB)
0	BPSK	1/2	24	3.0
1	QPSK	1/2	48	6.0
2	QPSK	3/4	48	8.5
3	16-QAM	1/2	96	11.5
4	16-QAM	3/4	96	15.0
5	64-QAM	2/3	144	19.0
6	64-QAM	3/4	144	21.0

Table 1 shows the supported MCSs that are specified within the IEEE 802.16 standard. In the considered OFDM system, the raw data rate Rd of a MCS with index ξ is represented as

$$R_d[\xi] = \frac{B_u[\xi]}{T_s}, \tag{1}$$

where Ts is the OFDM symbol duration. The notation Bu [ξ] indicates the number of uncoded bits per OFDM symbol of a MCS with index ξ, which is obtained as

$$Bu [\xi]= Nd \cdot \log2 M \cdot Rc [\xi], \tag{2}$$

where Nd denotes the number of data subcarriers and Rc [ξ] is the coding rate of a MCS with index ξ. The value of the parameter M depends on the adopted MCS, i.e., M = 2 for BPSK, M = 4 for QPSK, M = 16 for 16-QAM, and M = 64 for 64-QAM. Moreover, the OFDM symbol duration Ts can be acquired as

$$T_s = T_b + T_g = T_b + G \cdot T_b = \frac{1+G}{\Delta f}, \tag{3}$$

where Tb and Tg represent the useful symbol time and the cyclic prefix (CP) time respectively. The notation G denotes the ratio of Tg to Tb. The subcarrier spacing Δf is obtained as

$$\Delta f = \frac{F_s}{N_s} = \frac{8000}{N_s} \cdot \left\lfloor \frac{n \cdot BW}{8000} \right\rfloor, \tag{4}$$

where Ns indicates the number of total subcarriers. The notation Fs represents the sampling frequency with its value specified by the IEEE 802.16 standard as in (4), where n is the sam- pling factor and BW is the channel bandwidth. By substituting (4) into (3), the OFDM symbol time can be approximated as

$$T_s = \frac{N_s}{F_s} \cdot (1+G) \approx \frac{N_s}{n \cdot BW} \cdot (1+G). \tag{5}$$

With (2) and (5), the raw data rate Rd of a MCS with index ξ in (1) becomes

$$R_d[\xi] \approx \frac{N_d \cdot \log_2 M \cdot R_c[\xi] \cdot n \cdot BW}{N_s \cdot (1+G)}. \tag{6}$$

Based on (6), the raw user throughput by adopting the PDC approach is acquired as

TPDC (SSs, SSd)= Rd [ξ(s,d)], (7)

where ξ(s,d) represents the index of a MCS that will be assigned to the direct link of the (SSs, SSd) pair. On the other hand, the raw user throughput in the conventional IEEE 802.16 mech- anism is constrained by the two-hop transmission, i.e., from SSs to BS and from BS to SSd. Thus the TConv can be obtained as

$$T_{Conv}(SS_s, SS_d) = \frac{1}{2} R_d[\phi_{(s,d)}], \tag{8}$$

where

φ(s,d) = min ξ(s,BS), ξ(BS,d) . (9)

The notation ξ(s,BS) denotes the index of the MSC utilized in the link between the SSs and BS; while that is assigned to the link between the BS and SSd is represented as ξ(BS,d).

3.3 Direct Communication Procedures

Based on the aforementioned management structures and admission control scheme, the di- rect communication procedures of the PDC approach are explained in this subsection. Con- sidering a basic IEEE 802.16 PMP network that consists of a BS and two SSs, an intra-cell traffic flow is existed between the SSs. Two transport connections are established for packet transmission, i.e., a UL transport connection from the source station SSs to the BS and a DL transport connection from the BS to the destination station SSd. The initialization of direct communication is achieved by conducting the link request and information collection. The source-destination pair (SSs, SSd) anticipating to establish the direct link are required to pro- vide their location information and channel conditions to the BS. The collected information is utilized in the admission control scheme mentioned above.

Fig. 4 illustrates an exemplified message flows of the SS-initiated procedure for direct commu- nication. In the case that SSs intends to conduct direct communication with SSd, it attaches a PDL subheader to a data packet that will be delivered to the BS; meanwhile, the location information of SSs will be filled into the PDL subheader.

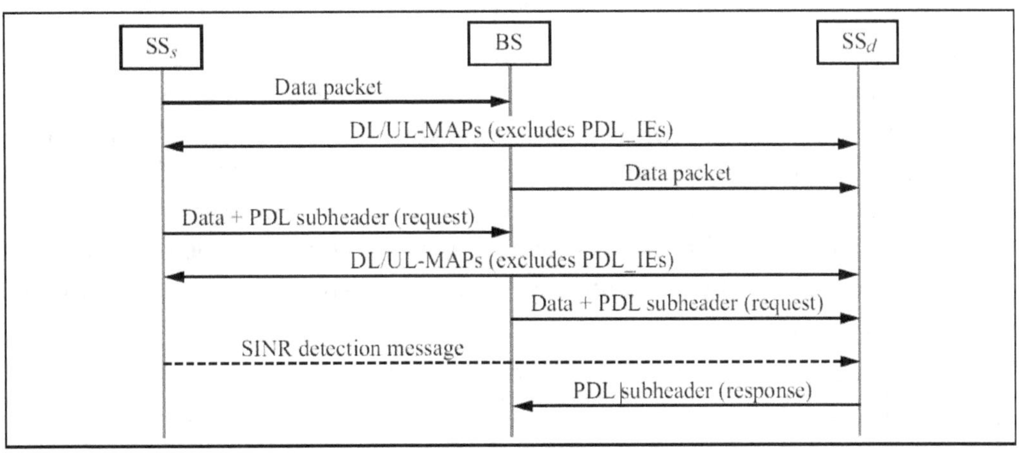

Fig. 4. Schematic diagram of SS-initiated procedure for direct communication.

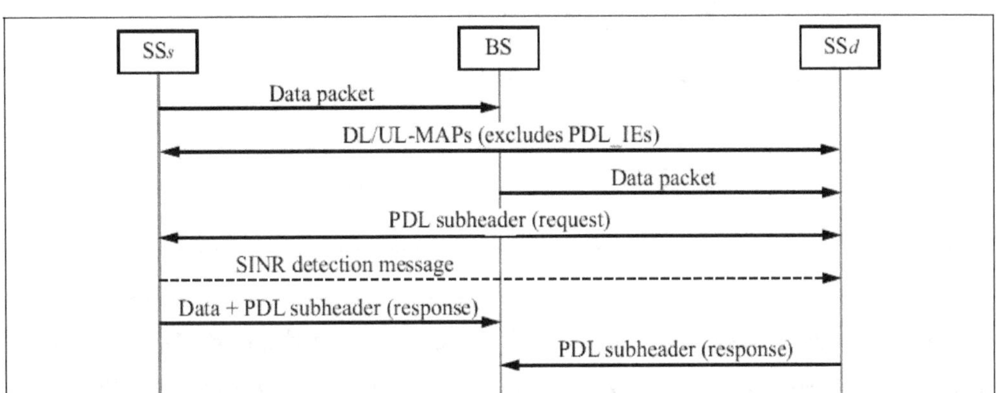

Fig. 5. Schematic diagram of BS-initiated procedure for direct communication.

As the BS receives the request PDL subheader from the SSs, the BS will attach a PDL subheader to the data packet and conduct the transmission to SSd. Moreover, the

BS will arrange a DL burst for SSs with the assignment in the corresponding DL-MAP message. SSs will transmit an SINR detection message to SSd with the BPSK 1/2 MCS for estimating the channel state of the direct link. After receiving the PDC subheader and the SINR detection message from the BS and SSs respectively, SSd will transmit a response PDL subheader associated with the calculated SINR value. It is noted that the location information of SSd is carried in the response PDL subheader if it is required by the BS. On the other hand, the BS-initiated direct communication procedure is shown in Fig. 5. Contrary to the SS-initiated procedure, the BS actively announces the link request along with the PDL subheader to the specific SSs, i.e, SSs and SSd. As SSs receives the requesting PDL subheader from the BS, it will utilize the response PDL subheader to provide the location information that is requested by the BS. The remaining steps of the BS-initiated procedure are similar to that of the SS-initiated case, such as the SINR detection and SSd response.

The BS executes the admission control procedure after it received the response PDL subheader transmitted from SSd. Based on the collected information, the aforementioned two-tiered control scheme is exploited by the BS to either confirm or deny the direct communication request between SSs and SSd. If the request is rejected, the BS will broadcast a denying announce- ment along with the PDL subheader. On the other hand, a confirming announcement will be transmitted if the request is granted. Consequently, the BS will arrange the PDL bursts for the direct link in the subsequent frames.

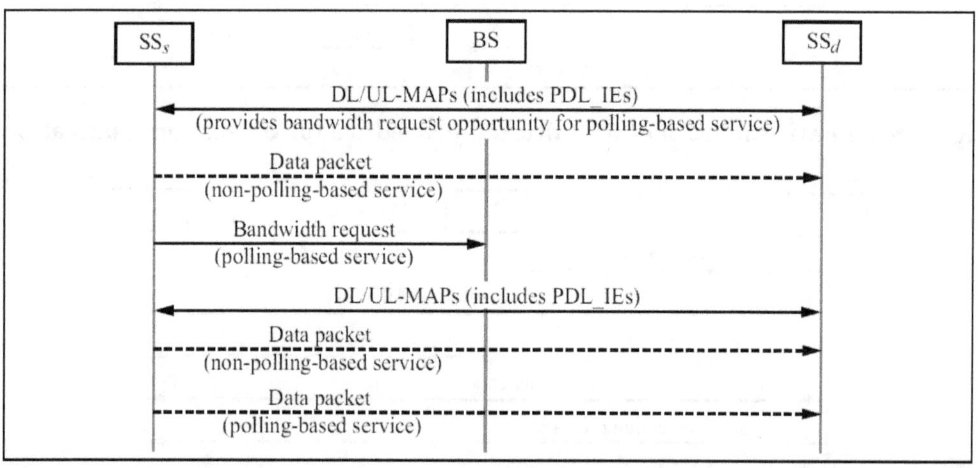

Fig. 6. Schematic diagram of bandwidth request procedure in PDC approach.

After receiving the confirmation announcement, the considered SSs will activate the procedure of direct communication. According to the received MAPs associated with the PDL IEs, SSs will conduct packet transmission directly to SSd within the PDL bursts. Moreover, SSd will continuously observe and evaluate the cannel condition for the direct link with the adaptation to an appropriate MCS. The calculated

SINR is compared with the receiver SNR range of the current MCS (as listed in Table 1) by SSd. If the existing MCS is observed to be improper for the current channel condition, SSd will initiate a PBPC-REQ message to the BS for suggesting an appropriate MCS. Consequently, the BS will respond a PBPC-REP message with a recommended MCS.

It is worthwhile to mention that bandwidth requests are conducted by an SS based on individual transport connection; while bandwidth grants from the BS is executed according to the accumulated requests from the SS. In other words, the bandwidth grant is addressed to the Basic CID of the corresponding SS, not to the individual transport CIDs. As a result, the CID specified for the PDL burst becomes the Basic CID of SSs. Furthermore, in order to integrate with the existing specification, the procedures of bandwidth requests and allocations specified in the IEEE 802.16 standard are implemented within the proposed PDC approach. Fig. 6 illustrates the bandwidth request procedure while the PDC approach is adopted. It can be observed that the BS preserves the PDL burst for non-polling based service periodically. Furthermore, the BS will continue to provide unicast bandwidth request opportunity for the polling-based services based on the original transport CIDs of SSs. The unicast bandwidth grant of those services will consequently be assigned to the PDL burst based on the Basic CID of SSs.

The procedure for the link termination occurs as one of the following two conditions is satisfied: (i) the channel condition of the direct link is becoming worse than that from the indirect channels (i.e., via the BS); (ii) the direct communication is determined to be ceased. It is noted that the link termination can be initiated by either the BS or SS. In the SS-initiated termination procedure, the SS will transmit a termination PDL subheader to the BS. As the message is received by the BS, it will broadcast an announcement along with a PDL subheader to both SSs and SSd regarding the termination of the direct link. On the other hand, for the BS-initiated termination procedure, the termination information is actively announced by the BS. As a result, the BS and the associated SSs will return to adopt the original packet transmission mechanism as defined in the IEEE 802.16 standard.

4. PERFORMANCE EVALUATION

The performance of the proposed PDC approach is evaluated and compared with the conventional packet transmission mechanism in IEEE 802.16 PMP networks via simulations. A single BS with 12 SSs uniformly distributed within the BS's coverage are considered as the simulation layout. The OFDM modulation and coding schemes listed in Table 1 are adopted in the simulation. The occurring frequencies for both inter-cell traffic and intra-cell traffic are considered uniformly distributed. The packet lengths are selected to follow the exponential distribution; while the Poisson distribution is adopted for packets arrival time. Since scheduling algorithm is not specified in the IEEE 802.16 standard, the direct round robin (DRR) (Shreedhar & Vargh- ese, 1996) and weighted round robin (WRR) (Katevenis et al., 1991) algorithms are selected as the BS's DL and UL schedulers respectively. The DRR algorithm is also utilized by the SS to share the UL grants that are provided by the BS among their connections. The parameters adopted in the simulations are listed in Table 2.

Table 2. Simulation Parameters

Parameter	Value
Channel bandwidth (BW)	7 MHz
Number of total subcarriers (N_s)	256
Number of data subcarriers (N_d)	192
Sampling factor (n)	8/7
Sampling frequency (F_s)	8 MHz
Useful symbol time (T_b)	32 μs
CP time (T_g)	2 μs
The ratio of CP time and useful time (G)	1/16
OFDM symbol duration (T_s)	34 μs
Maps modulation	BPSK
Data modulation	QPSK, 16-QAM, 64-QAM
Frame duration	5 ms, 10 ms
SSTTG/SSRTG	35 μs
Initial ranging interval	5 OFDM symbols
Bandwidth request interval	5 OFDM symbols
Average packet size	200 bytes
Simulation time	1 sec

Fig. 7 shows the comparison of the user throughput with an increasing number of intra-cell traffic flows ranging from 10 to 100 (frame duration = 5 and 10 ms). As can be expected that the user throughput increases as the number of intra-cell traffic flows is augmented. It can be observed that the proposed PDC approach outperforms the conventional IEEE 802.16 scheme with higher user throughput under different frame durations. In the conventional mechanism, it is required for the intra-cell traffic to be forwarded by the BS. Consequently, more than twice of the communication bandwidth is necessitate for the packet transmission. By adopting the proposed PDC approach, the intra-cell traffic can be directly transmitted from the source station to the destination station, which resulted in saved bandwidth. Moreover, the longer frame duration can achieve higher user throughput owing to the reason that less control overheads are required within the transmission. The comparison of the user throughput under differ- ent traffic load (λ) is illustrated in Fig. 8, wherein there are 50 intra-cell traffic flows. Similar performance benefits can be observed by adopting the proposed PDC approach.

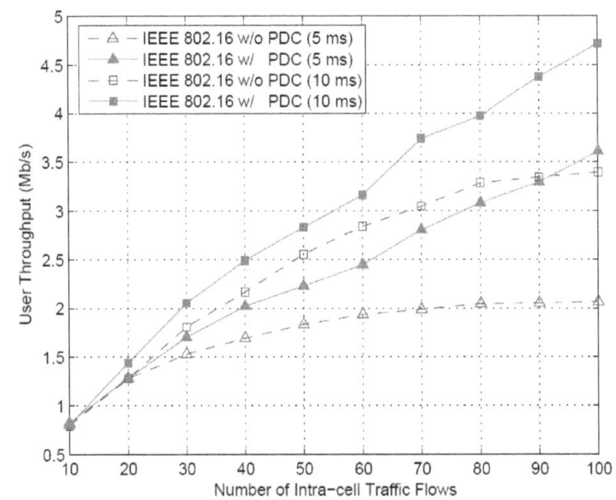

Fig. 7. Performance comparison: user throughput versus number of intra-cell traffic flows.

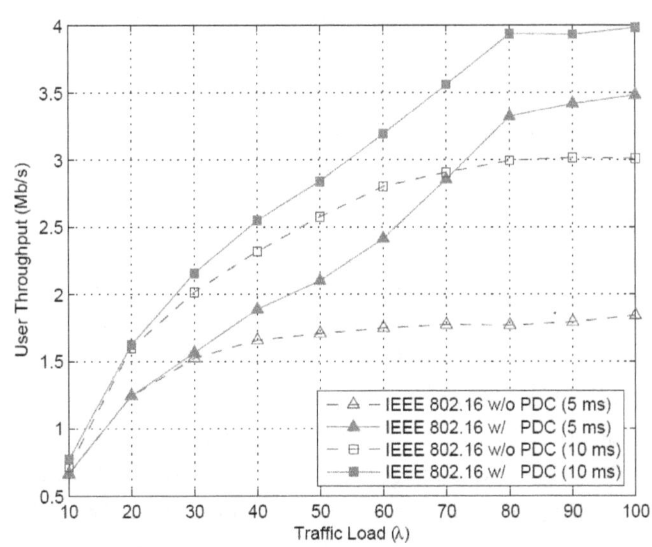

Fig. 8. Performance comparison: user throughput versus traffic load.

In order to evaluate the influence from the inter-cell traffic, the user throughput with an increasing number of inter-cell traffic flows ranging from 10 to 100 is shown in Fig. 9 (with the number of total traffic flows is equal to 100). It is noticed that the inter-cell traffic can be considered as a particular type of direct communication within the cell since the packets are passed from the BS to SS directly. Consequently, the user throughput is decreased as the percentage of the intra-cell traffic is augmented since there are increasing amounts of indi- rect links within the network. Nevertheless, the PDC approach can still provide comparably higher user throughput under different percentages of intra-cell traffic flows. The merits of the proposed PDC scheme can be observed.

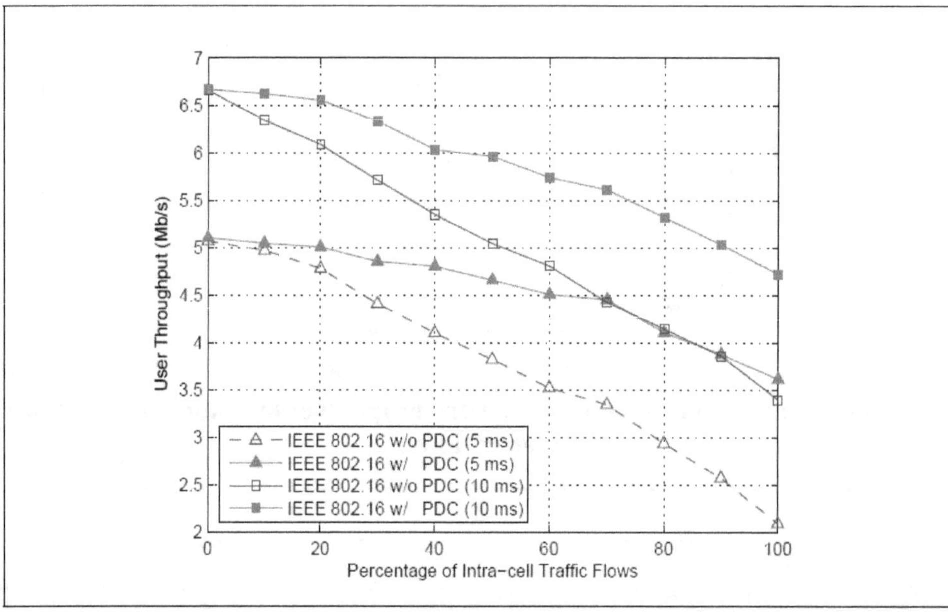

Fig. 9. Performance comparison: user throughput versus percentage of intra-cell traffic flows.

5. CONCISE SUMMARY

This chapter proposes a flexible, contention-free point-to-point direct communication (PDC) method to facilitate direct transmission between SSs in IEEE 802.16 PMP networks. A two-tiered admission control mechanism is presented to establish a direct link between the SSs in the PDC approach, taking into account the relative positions and channel conditions of both the BS and SSs. In implementing the PDC technique, the BS designates specified time intervals for the two SSs engaged in direct transmission. The benefit of utilizing the PDC strategy is that it can substantially decrease both the necessary bandwidth for packet transmission and the packet rerouting latency for intra-cell traffic. Moreover, the PDC approach's design is compatible and may be seamlessly integrated with the protocols established in the IEEE 802.16 standard. The efficacy of the proposed PDC approach is evidenced by the simulation results, which indicate that the PDC approach surpasses the traditional IEEE 802.16 transmission mechanism for user throughput.

REFERENCES

1. Abichar, Z., Peng, Y. & Chang, J. M. (2006). WiMAX: The emergence of wireless broadband, IEEE IT Prof. 8(4): 44–48.
2. Cordeiro, C., Abhyankar, S. & Agrawal, D. P. (2003). A dynamic slot assignment scheme for slave-to-slave and multicast-like communication in Bluetooth personal area net- works, Proc. IEEE Global Telecommunications Conf. (GLOBECOM), San Francisco, CA, pp. 4127–4132.
3. IEEE P802.11zTM/D5.0 (2009). Draft Standard for Information Technology-Telecommunications and information exchange between systems- Local and metropolitan area networks- Specific requirements- Part 11: Wireless LAN Medium Access Control (MAC) and Physical Layer (PHY) specifications, Amendment 6: Extensions to Direct Link Setup (DLS), IEEE, 3 Park Avenue, New York, NY 10016-5997, USA.
4. IEEE Std. 802.16-2004 (2004). IEEE Standard for Local and Metropolitan Area Networks- Part 16: Air Interference for Fixed Broadband Wireless Access Systems, IEEE, 3 Park Avenue, New York, NY 10016-5997, USA.
5. Katevenis, M., Sidiropoulos, S. & Courcoubetis, C. (1991). Weighted round-robin cell multi- plexing in a general-purpose atm switch chip, IEEE J. Sel. Areas Commun. 9(8): 1265– 1279.
6. Shreedhar, M. & Varghese, G. (1996). Efficient fair queueing using deficit round robin, IEEE/ACM Trans. Netw. 4(3): 375–385.
7. Zhang, W., Zhu, H. & Cao, G. (2002). Improving Bluetooth network performance through a time-slot leasing approach, Proc. IEEE Wireless Communications and Networking Conf. (WCNC), Orlando, FL, pp. 592–596.

21 Chapter

METHODS FOR DELAYING THE START OF THE IEEE 802.16 MESH MODE IN MULTIPLE-HOP WIRELESS MESH NETWORKS

1. INTRODUCTION: ANOVERVIEW

Multi-hop wireless mesh networks (M-WMNs) [Akyildiz, I. F., 2005] are a fundamental aspect of beyond 3G systems due to their adaptability and cost-effective implementation. To date, the majority of known research on multi-hop wireless mesh networks has been conducted utilizing the IEEE 802.11 ad hoc mode. The IEEE 802.16 working group established the IEEE 802.16-2004 standard in October 2004, which delineated two operational modes: point-to-multi-point (PMP) mode and mesh mode. The IEEE 802.16 mesh standard delineates three strategies for scheduling data transmission: centralized scheduling (CSCH) [Morge, P. S., 2007], coordinated distributed scheduling (C-DSCH) [Morge, P. S., 2007], and uncoordinated distributed scheduling (Un-DSCH). In the IEEE 802.16 mesh mode utilizing the CSCH, C-DSCH, and Un-DSCH, multi-hop communication is feasible among nodes, including mesh base stations (MeshBSs) and mesh subscriber stations (MeshSSs), as all nodes function as peers, enabling each node to serve as a router for multi-hop packet forwarding. Specifically, in the IEEE 802.16 mesh mode utilizing the C-DSCH, each node contends for channel access through a distributed election algorithm (DEA) that relies on the scheduling data of extended neighborhoods (one-hop and two-hop neighbors) in a fully decentralized manner. Nodes reserve radio resources via a three-way handshaking protocol, wherein they request, grant, and confirm available radio resources using the mesh distributed scheduling (MSH-DSCH) message. The IEEE 802.16 mesh mode with the C-DSCH offers significant flexibility and scalability, making it an appropriate alternative medium access control (MAC) protocol for the establishment of M-WMNs. The protocol architecture for M-WMNs must prioritize high network throughput to function as a wireless network infrastructure. In the IEEE 802.16 mesh mode utilizing the C-DSCH, after a node has occupied radio resources, it is prohibited from transmitting any MSH-DSCH messages for a designated holdoff period to facilitate resource sharing with other nodes in the M-WMN. In a densely saturated network scenario, if nodes are assigned a brief holdoff period, competition among them will intensify, resulting in prolonged contention times prior to securing radio resources. On the other hand, if nodes get a long holdoff time in a lightly loaded network situation, radio resource will be wasted unnecessarily. Like this, network throughput has a close relationship with the performance of holdoff algorithm.

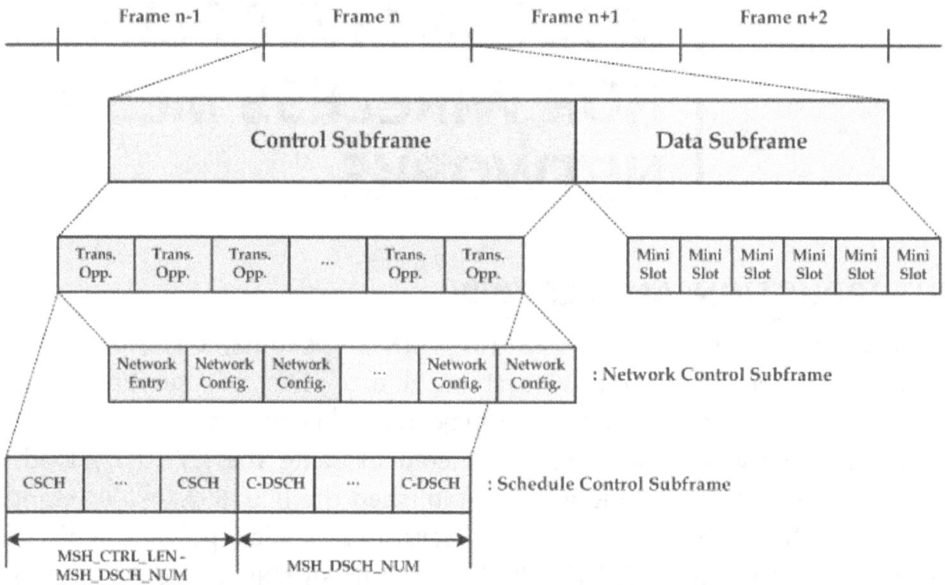

Fig. 1. Frame structure of IEEE 802.16 mesh mode

2. OVERVIEW OF IEEE 802.16 MESH MODE WITH C-DSCH

In this section, the overview of the IEEE 802.16 mesh mode with the C-DSCH is given in four aspects: frame structure, MSH-DSCH message format, bandwidth reservation by three- way handshaking, and distributed election algorithm.

2.1 Frame structure of IEEE 802.16 mesh mode

Figure 1 shows the frame structure of the IEEE 802.16 mesh mode. As shown in the figure, the frame of the IEEE 802.16 mesh mode is based on the time division multiple access (TDMA) frame structure and consists of the control and data subframes.

The data subframe is used to transmit data packets and the control subframe is used to transmit MAC management messages. The control and data subframes are composed of multiple transmission opportunities (TOs) and minislots, respectively. As one of network parameters, the number of TOs consisting of the control subframe (MSH_CTRL_LEN) is set to one value between 0 and 15. Each TO in the control subframe consists of seven OFDM symbols and can carry only one MAC management message.

The control subframe consists of two types of subframes: the network control subframe and the schedule control subframe. The network control subframe enables new nodes to join mesh network. In a mesh network, nodes broadcast network entry and network configuration information and this enables a new node to get synchronization and initial network entry into the mesh network. The schedule control subframe is used to transmit MAC management messages in order to reserve minislots in the data subframe and it is divided into two parts, as shown in Fig. 1. The first part is used for the MSH-CSCH and MSH-CCFG messages transmissions in the CSCH mechanism and the second part is used for the MSH-DSCH message transmission in the C-DSCH mechanism.

The number of TOs (MSH_DSCH_NUM) consisting of the C-DSCH part is selected in a range between 0 and 15 and thus, the length of the CSCH part is equal to MSH_CTRL_LEN – MSH_DSCH_NUM.

2.2 MSH-DSCH message format

In this chapter, because we focus on holdoff algorithms for the IEEE 802.16 mesh mode with the C-DSCH, only the MSH-DSCH message format related with the C-DSCH is given in detail. Every node sends its available resource information to neighbor nodes via MSH- DSCH messages. The request, grant, and confirmation of resource are also accomplished by exchanging the MSH-DSCH messages between a pair of nodes.

Syntax	Size
MSH-DSCH_Message_Format() {	
Management_Message_Type = 41	8 bits
Coordination Flag	1 bit
Grant/Request Flag	1 bit
Sequence Counter	6 bits
No. Requests	4 bits
No. Availabilities	4 bits
No. Grants	6 bits
reserved	2 bits
if(Coordination_Flag == 0)	
MSH-DSCH_Scheduling_IE()	variable
for (i = 0; I < No_Requests; i ++)	
MSH-DSCH_Request_IE()	16 bits
for (i = 0; I < No_Availabilities; i ++)	
MSH-DSCH_Availability_IE()	32 bits
for (i = 0; I < No_Grants; i ++)	
MSH-DSCH_Grant_IE()	40 bits
}	

Fig. 2. MSH-DSHC message format

As shown in Fig. 2, in the C-DSCH, the MSH-DSCH message contains the following information elements (IE): [Morge, P. S., 2007]

- MSH-DSCH_Scheduling_IE includes the next MSH-DSCH transmission times and holdoff exponents of a node and its neighbor nodes.
- MSH-DSCH_Request_IE is used by a node to specify its bandwidth demand for a specific link.
- MSH-DSCH_Availability_IE is used by a node to convey its own status for individual minislots to its neighbors.
- MSH-DSCH_Grant_IE is used by a node to send bandwidth grant in response to a bandwidth request as well as to send a grant confirmation for a received bandwidth grant.

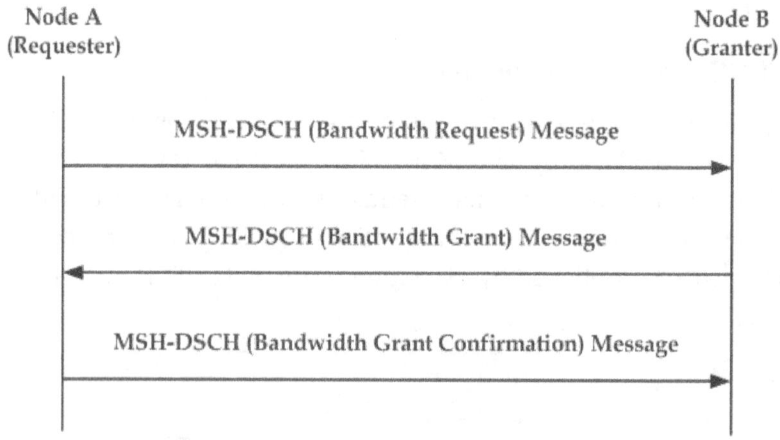

Fig. 3. Three-way handshaking

2.3 Bandwidth reservation by three-way handshaking

Based on the four IEs above, in the C-DSCH, nodes perform the bandwidth reservation process by three-way handshaking: bandwidth request, bandwidth grant, and bandwidth grant confirmation, as shown in Fig. 3.

In the bandwidth reservation procedure, node A (requester) uses the Link ID to uniquely indentify a link for which node A needs bandwidth, and it sends an MSH-DSCH message that contains a set of MSH-DSCH_Request_IEs and a set of MSH-DSCH_Availability_IEs. The MSH-DSCH message with an MSH-DSCH_Request_IE is received by all the neighbors around node A. After receiving the bandwidth request message, node B (granter) looks up the set of available minislots in order to select a subset of minislots that is available for data receptions from node A. Node B chooses an available range of minislots for a bandwidth grant and sends the MSH-DSCH message with the MSH-DSCH_Grant_IE, which contains the set of minislots for the bandwidth grant. All the neighbors around node B receive the bandwidth grant message and they update their availability status by reflecting the scheduled data reception specified in the bandwidth grant message.

In the bandwidth grant confirmation, node A transmits an MSH-DSCH message with the MSH-DSCH_Grant_IE in order to inform all the neighbors around node A of the scheduled data transmission information. The neighbors update their availabilities by reflecting the newly scheduled data transmission. Data transmission is accomplished only over the reserved minislots, after the successful transmission of the bandwidth grant confirmation message.

2.4 Distributed election algorithm

In the three-way handshaking process, nodes independently select their own transmission times of MSH-DSCH messages using the distributed election algorithm. The DEA enables nodes to forward MSH-DSCH messages in an M-WMN in a completely distributed manner. A node can transmit an MSH-DSCH message without message collision at a selected transmission time by the DEA. In the C-DSCH, the transmission time corresponds to a specific TO in the schedule control subframe shown in Fig. 1. In the DEA, a node performs two functions: collecting the next transmission times (Next_Xmt_Times) of all nodes within its extended neighborhood (one-hop and two-hop neighbors) and selecting its Next_Xmt_Time.

Collecting the Next_Xmt_Times of all nodes within extended neighborhood: to select a collision- free TO for the MSH-DSCH transmission, every node should collect the Next_Xmt_Times of all nodes within its extended neighborhood. So, every node must inform its neighbors of the next MSH-DSCH transmission time of its neighbors as well as itself. In the DEA, nodes broadcast not an exact Next_Xmt_Time but the next transmission time interval (Next_Xmt_Time_Interval) information, which is expressed by two parameters of next transmission maximum (Next_Xmt_Mx) and transmission holdofff exponent (Xmt_Holdoff_Exp) as follows:

$$2^{Xmt\_Holdoff\_Exp} * Next\_Xmt\_Mx < Next\_Xmt\_Time < 2^{Xmt\_Holdoff\_Exp} * (Next\_Xmt\_Mx + 1) \quad (1)$$

The Next_Xmt_Time_Interval is a series of one or more C-DSCH TOs. Every node broadcasts MSH-DSCH message containing the next transmission time interval information (Next_Xmt_Mx and Xmt_Holdoff_Exp) of its one-hop neighbors as well as itself. Using the next transmission interval information received from neighbors via MSH-DSCH messages, every node can calculate the Next_Xmt_Time_Intervals of all nodes within its extended neighborhood. In the IEEE 802.16 mesh standard, a node first selects its own Next_Xmt_Time at a current MSH-DSCH transmission time (Current_Xmt_Time) and then, it calculates a Next_Xmt_Mx value using equation (1) and a current Xmt_Holdoff_Exp value. Next, the node broadcasts an

MSH-DSCH message containing the Next_Xmt_Mx and Xmt_Holdoff_Exp, which represents its Next_Xmt_Time_Interval, in order to inform neighbors of its next transmission time information.

Selecting a Next_Xmt_Time: in the IEEE 802.16 mesh standard, after an MSH-DSCH message transmission, a node is not eligible to transmit an MSH-DSCH message for transmission holdoff time (Xmt_Holdoff_Time) in order to share radio resource with other nodes in an M-WMN. Therefore, when a node selects a Next_Xmt_Time in the DEA, it first sets the temporary transmission time (Temp_Xmt_Time) as follows:

$$\text{Temp\_Xmt\_Time} = \text{Current\_Xmt\_Time} + \text{Xmt\_Holdoff\_Time} + 1 \quad (2)$$

Next, the node should determine the set of eligible competing nodes related to the Temp_Xmt_Time from its neighbor table. This set will include neighbors that meet at least one of the following conditions: [Bayer, N., 2006]

- The Next_Xmt_Time_Interval of neighbor includes the Temp_Xmt_Time,
- The earliest subsequent transmission time (Earliest_Subsequent_Xmt_Time) of neighbor is equal to or smaller than Temp_Xmt_Time, or
- The Next_Xmt_Time of neighbor is not known.

In the conditions above, the Earliest_Subsequent_Xmt_Time is the earliest time that the node is eligible to transmit a MSH-DSCH message after the Next_Xmt_Time, as shown in equation (3):

$$Earliest\_Subsequent\_Xmt\_Time = Next\_Xmt\_Time + Xmt\_Holdoff\_Exp + 2^{Xmt\_Holdoff\_Exp} * Next\_Xmt\_Mx \quad (3)$$

The DEA is performed based on this set of eligible competing nodes. With this set, a node checks whether any competing nodes do not use a specific TO corresponding to the Temp_Xmt_Time, or not. If any competing nodes of the node do not use the specific TO, the node is the winner of the distributed election and the Next_Xmt_Time is set equal to the Temp_Xmt_Time. If a node does not win the distributed election, the Temp_Xmt_Time is set to Temp_Xmt_Time + 1 and the above process is performed again in order to select a collision-free Next_Xmt_Time.

3. HOLDOFF ALGORITHMS FOR IEEE 802.16 MESH MODE

In the IEEE 802.16 mesh standard with the C-DSCH, a node is not eligible to transmit any MSH-DSCH messages for at least holdoff time after an MSH-DSCH message transmission. The reason to stop an MSH-DSCH message transmission for a holdoff time is for nodes to share radio resource with other nodes in M-WMN. However, a holdoff mechanism can result in resource waste by holding MSH-DSCH message transmission even in a lightly loaded network situation. Some holdoff algorithms have been proposed for the IEEE 802.16 mesh mode with the C-DSCH in order to improve the network throughput and to share the radio resource.

3.1 Static holdoff algorithm

In the IEEE 802.16 mesh standsard, the Xmt_Holdoff_Time is calculated based on the static Xmt_Holdoff_Exp and Xmt_Holdoff_Exp_Base values, as shown in equation (4):

$$\text{Xmt\_Holdoff\_Time} = 2(\text{Xmt\_Holdoff\_Exp} + \text{Xmt\_Holdoff\_Exp\_Base}) \quad (4)$$

The IEEE 802.16 mesh standard defines static holdoff algorithm. In the static holdoff algorithm, the Xmt_Holdoff_Exp_Base is fixed to 4 for resource sharing between nodes in an M-WMN. The Xmt_Holdoff_Exp is also set to a specific value between 0 and 7 in initial node configuration procedure. That is, all nodes in M-WMN have an identical transmission holdoff time regardless of current network situation. Thus, when Xmt_Holdoff_Exp = 0, the competition between nodes happen severe and a node experiences long contention times before reserving resource. On the other hand, as the Xmt_Holdoff_Exp value increases, the contention between nodes becomes less competitive; however, nodes get a longer holdoff time and thus transmission interval becomes longer [Cao, M., 2005]. In particular, if the Xmt_Holdoff_Exp is set to an unnecessarily large value in a lightly loaded network situation, the waste of resource happens. Hence, the static holdoff algorithm can result in network throughput degradation regardless of an assigned Xmt_Holdoff_Exp value.

3.2 Dynamic holdoff algorithm

In [Cao, M., 2005], the authors performed the modelling and performance analysis of distributed scheduler in the IEEE 802.16 mesh mode, and they concluded that the capacity of IEEE 802.16 mesh network can be optimized by assigning appropriate Xmt_Holdoff_Exp values to nodes in the network.

In [Bayer, N., 2007], the dynamic exponent (DynExp) algorithm was proposed. In the DynExp algorithm, nodes that are currently not sending, receiving, or forwarding data packets use large Xmt_Holdoff_Exp values and thus get large Xmt_Holdoff_Time values. Nodes that transmit, receive, and forward data packets or nodes that have been selected by the routing protocol as potential forwarding nodes use small Xmt_Holdoff_Exp values and thus get small Xmt_Holdoff_Time values. For this purpose, nodes are classified as follows:

- Mesh base station (M-BS) is a normal mesh base station.
- Active node (ACT) is a node that is part of an active route and sends, receives, or forwards data packets.

- Sponsor node (SN) is a node that is not part of an active route but has been selected as a potential forwarding node by at least one of its neighbors.
- Inactive node (IN-ACT) is a node that is not part of an active route and does not send, receive or forward data packets.

According to the node types above, different Xmt_Holdoff_Exp values are defined as follows:

$$0 < Xmt\_Holdoff\_Exp_{M\text{-}BS} < Xmt\_Holdoff\_Exp_{ACT} < Xmt\_Holdoff\_Exp_{SN} < Xmt\_Holdoff\_Exp_{IN\text{-}ACT}'$$

By using different Xmt_Holdoff_Exp values according to current node types, the DyExp algorithm improves network capacity. However, because the operation of DynExp algorithm depends on information from the routing layer, the DynExp algorithm cannot be operated independently without cooperation with routing layer.

3.3 Adaptive holdoff algorithm

In this section, we propose an adaptive holdoff algorithm. In the adaptive holdoff algorithm, nodes adaptively adjust the Xmt_Holdoff_Exp value according to current node state.

3.3.1 Definitions

Before proposing the adaptive holdoff algorithm, the neighbors of a node are classified into four types: tx-neighbor, rx-neighbor, tx/rx-neighbor, and null-neighbor. Each classification is defined as follows:

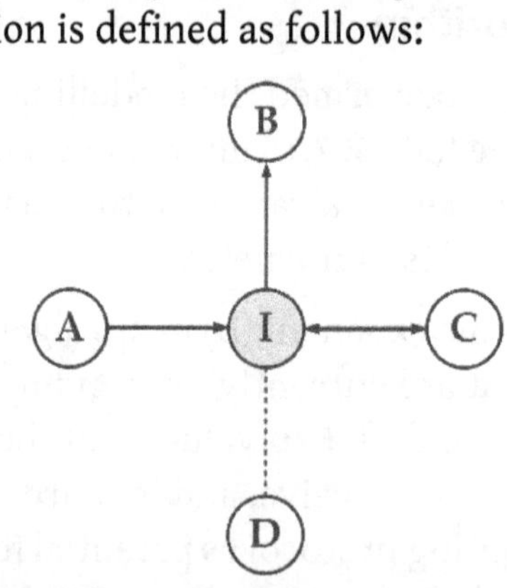

Fig. 4. Classification of neighbor nodes: A solid line between a pair of nodes indicates that there is at least one data packet to transmit between the two nodes, with an arrow showing the direction of the pending data transmission. A dotted line indicates that there is no data waiting for transmission between the pair of nodes

- A tx-neighbor of a node is a neighbor that has a data packet to send to the node.
- An rx-neighbor of a node is a neighbor to which the node has a data packet to send.
- A tx/rx-neighbor of a node is a neighbor that is both tx-neighbor and rx-neighbor of the node.
- A null-neighbor of a node is a neighbor that has no data packet to send to or receive from the node.

In Fig. 4, node I has four types of neighbors. Nodes A, B, C, and D correspond to the tx-neighbor, rx-neighbor, tx/rx-neighbor, and null-neighbor of node I, respectively.

3.3.2 Adaptive holdoff algorithms based on node state

In this section, an adaptive holdoff algorithm based on node state is presented. The adaptive holdoff algorithm does not depend on information from higher layer such as routing layer and it operates independently. In addition, it maintains backward compatibility with the IEEE 802.16 mesh standard.

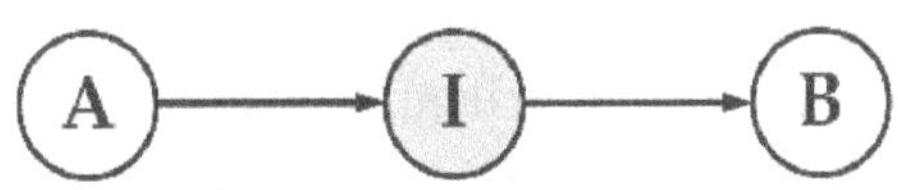

Fig. 5. Example topology: A solid line between a pair of nodes indicates that there is at least one data packet to transmit between the two nodes, with an arrow showing the direction of the pending data transmission

In Fig. 5, node I has two links (Links 1 and 2) for communication with nodes A and B, respectively. As shown in Fig. 5, node I should reserve each minislot for data reception from node A and data transmission to node B. On the other hand, node A needs to reserve only minislots for data transmission to node I, and node B needs to reserve only minislots for data reception from node I. Therefore, node I should be able to access schedule control subframe at a higher rate than nodes A and B in order to prevent node I from being a bottleneck.

Node_ID	Type_Tx	Type_Rx	Expire_Tx	Expire_Rx	Expire
A	1	0	nonzero	0	nonzero
B	1	0	nonzero	0	nonzero
C	1	1	nonzero	nonzero	nonzero
D	0	0	0	0	nonzero

Fig. 6. Neighbor table of node I in Fig. 4

Based on the features above, the Weight of a node is first defined for the adaptive holdoff algorithm as follows:

$$\text{Weight} = \text{tx\_exist} * 1 + \text{rx\_exist} * 2 \quad (5)$$

In equation (5), the tx_exist represents whether a node has at least one tx-neighbor or not. And, the rx_exist indicates whether a node has at least one rx-neighbor or not. Because a node transmits only one MSH-DSCH message (bandwidth grant message) to tx-neighbor over the TO of the schedule control subframe during the three-way handshaking, the tx_exist is multiplied by 1 in equation (5). On the other hand, because a node transmits two MSH-DSCH messages (bandwidth request and bandwidth grant confirmation messages) to rx-neighbor during the three-way handshaking, the rx_exist is multiplied by 2. In addition, as shown in Fig. 2, the MSH-DSCH message can contains multiple MSH- DSCH_Request_IE()s, MSH-DSCH-Availability_IE()s, and MSH-DSCH_Grants_IE()s at one time. Namely, a node can simultaneously request, grant, and confirm resources for multiple links via only one MSH-DSCH message. Therefore, the Weight depends on only the tx_exist and rx_exist in equation (5).

Next, a neighbor table is presented in order to explain how to obtain the Weight of a node. In the adaptive holdoff algorithm, nodes store neighbor information in their neighbor table, as shown in Fig. 6. Each entry in the neighbor table contains Node_ID, Type_Tx/Rx, Expire_Tx/Rx, and Expire. Node_ID denotes the identifier of a neighbor. Type_Tx/Rx is used to distinguish the neighbor types: tx-neighbor, rx-neighbor, tx/rx-neighbor, or null- neighbor. Expire_Tx/Rx indicates the expiration time of a neighbor as a tx-neighbor or as an rx-neighbor. Expire represents the expiration time of a neighbor table entry.

In the adaptive holdoff algorithm, the neighbor table is managed in the following way:

1. **Setting Type_Tx/Rx, Expire_Tx/Rx, and Expire:** Whenever a node sends or receives a data packet to or from a neighbor over minislots of data subframe, it sets the values of Type_Tx/Rx, Expire_Tx/Rx, and Expire in the neighbor table entry for the neighbor. When a node receives a data packet from a neighbor, it finds the neighbor table entry for that neighbor in its neighbor table and sets the values of Type_Tx, Expire_Tx, and Expire as follows: the Type_Tx is set to 1. The Expire_Tx and Expire are set to EXPIRE_TIME, which is a pre-defined constant value. When a node sends a data packet to a neighbor, it finds the neighbor table entry for that neighbor in its neighbor table and sets Type_Rx, Expire_Rx, and Expire as follows: the Type_Rx is set to 1. The Expire_Rx and Expire are set to EXPIRE_TIME.
2. **Maintaining/removing neighbor table entries:** Maintenance and removal of a neighbor table entry is performed using the neighbor

timer. The neighbor timer expires periodically; when this occurs, a node compares the current time with each values of Expire_Tx/Rx and Expire in a neighbor table entry and updates Type_Tx/Rx, Expire_Tx/Rx, and Expire in the following way: if the values of Expire_Tx/Rx are higher than the current time, the values of Type_Tx/Rx and Expire_Tx/Rx are not changed; otherwise, they are set to 0. If the value of Expire is less than the current time, the neighbor table entry is removed; otherwise, the value of Expire is not changed. This procedure is repeated for all the entries in the neighbor table.

According to the neighbor table management above, node I in Fig. 4 has the neighbor table as shown in Fig. 6. In the adaptive holdoff algorithm, a node can calculate its Weight using its neighbor table. For example, node I can calculate the Weight by checking the values of Type_Tx/Rx in its neighbor table entries as follows: if a node has at least one neighbor entry with the Type_Tx value of 1 in its neighbor table, the tx_exist is set to 1; otherwise, the tx_exist is set to 0. In a similar way, if a node has at least one neighbor entry with the Type_Rx value of 1 in its neighbor table, the rx_exist is set to 1; otherwise, the rx_exist is set to 0. Therefore, node I in Fig. 4 has the Weight value of 3 (= 1 * 1 + 1 * 2).

In the adaptive holdoff algorithm, the Weight of a node represents its access rate required to reserve a shared resource for data transmission or reception. Therefore, a node with a large Weight value should be able to access the TOs of the schedule control subframe at a high rate, and a node with a small Weight value should access the TOs of the schedule control subframe at a low rate.

To achieve this goal, in the adaptive holdoff algorithm, current transmission holdoff exponent (Cur_Xmt_Holdoff_Exp) is defined as follows:

$$\text{Cur\_Xmt\_Holdoff\_Exp} = \text{Max\_Xmt\_Holdoff\_Exp} * (1 - \text{Weight} / 3) \qquad (6)$$

In equation (6), the Max_Xmt_Holdoff_Exp is the maximum value of transmission exponent. The Max_Xmt_Holdoff_Exp of a node is set to a constant in initial node configuration process.

And then, a node selects its Xmt_Holdoff_Time as follows:

$$\text{Xmt\_Holdoff\_Time} = 2(\text{Xmt\_Holdoff\_Base} + \text{Cur\_Xmt\_Holdoff\_Exp}) \qquad (7)$$

Algorithm 1 shows the operation of the adaptive holdoff algorithm. In Algorithm 1, it is assumed that the Xmt_Holdoff_Exp_Base is set to 4 and the Max_Xmt_Holdoff_Exp to 3.

As shown in Algorithm 1, if a node has a large Weight value, the small Xmt_Holdoff_Time value is obtained by setting the Cur_Xmt_Holdoff_Exp to a small value. Thus, the node can access the TOs of the schedule control subframe for resource reservation at a high rate. On the other hand, if a node has a small Weight value, the large Xmt_Holdoff_Time value is obtained by setting the Cur_Xmt_Holdoff_Exp to a large value. Thus, the node can access the TOs of the schedule control subframe for resource reservation at a low rate. In this way, nodes can adjust their access rate to the TOs of the schedule control subframe according to their current state.

Algorithm 1 Adaptive Holdoff Algorithm based on Node State

Notations Used:

tx_exist = indicate whether a node currently has at least one tx-neighbor rx_exist = indicate whether a node currently has at least one rx-neighbor Weight = access rate of a node

Current_Xmt_Holdoff_Exp = current transmission holdoff exponent Xmt_Holdoff_Exp_Base = transmission holdoff exponent base (= 4) Max_Xmt_Holdoff_Exp = maximum value of transmission holdoff exponent (= 3) Xmt_Holdoff_Time = transmission holdoff time

01: Set the tx_exist by cheking the Type_Txs of neighbor table entries 02: Set the rx_exist by cheking the Type_Rxs of neighbor table entries 03: Compute Weight = tx_exist * 1 + rx_exist * 2

04: if (Weight == 0)

05: Current_Xmt_Holdoff_Exp = Max_Xmt_Holdoff_Exp; 06: end if

07: else

08: Current_Xmt_Holdoff_Exp = Max_Xmt_Holdoff_Exp * (1 - Weight / 3); 09: end else

10: Compute Xmt_Holdoff_Time = 2(Xmt_Holdoff_Exp_Base + Current_Xmt_Holdoff_Exp)

4. SIMULATION EVALUATION

Computer simulations were performed to evaluate the performance of the holdoff algorithms. To show the importance of adjusting holdoff time according to current network situation from the perspective of performance improvement, the performance of the adaptive holdoff algorithm based on node state (AHA) is compared with that of the static holdoff algorithm (SHA), which is described in the IEEE 802.16 mesh standard.

4.1 Simulation environments

NCTUns-4.0 [Wang, S. Y., 2007-(a)], [Wang, S. Y., 2007-(b)], [Wang, S. Y., 2007-(c)] is used to evaluate the performance of the holdoff algorithms for the IEEE 802.16 mesh mode with the C-DSCH. Table 1 shows the parameters used in the simulation. For all other parameters, the default values provided in NCTUns-4.0 are used.

Figure 7 shows the network topology used to evaluate the performance of the holdoff algorithms. The network consists of 16 nodes. Among 16 nodes, one node acts as MeshBS and the others as MeshSSs. Node 11 corresponds to the MeshBS and other nodes to MeshSSs. All nodes remain stationary for a simulation time of 300s. The number of traffic flows is varied from 1 to 6 to investigate the performance variation in different offered loads. Each traffic source generates user datagram protocol (UDP)-based data packets with the size of 512 bytes at a rate of 2Mbits/s.

Table 1. Simulation parameters for holdoff algorithms

Parameters	Value
Max. transmission range	MeshSS: 400m, MeshBS: 400m
Bytes per OFDM symbol	108 (64-QAM_3/4)
Xmt_Holdoff_Exp_Base	4
Xmt_Holdoff_Exp	3 (only static holdoff algorithm)
Distance between MeshSSs	300m

Simulations are performed in two scenarios: multi-hop peer-to-peer and multi-hop Internet access scenarios. Figure 8 shows traffic flows in the multi-hop peer-to-peer scenario. The multi-hop Internet access scenarios are classified into upload and download patterns. The traffic flows for upload and download patterns are shown in Figs. 9 and 10, respectively.

To evaluate the performances of two holdoff algorithms (SHA and AHA), the following performance metrics are used:

- The average per-flow throughput is the average packet throughput at a receiver.
- The total network throughput is the sum of the average packet throughputs at all receivers.

4.2 Simulation results

In the multi-hop peer-to-peer scenario where traffic is distributed throughout entire network, the performance of AHA is compared with that of SHA. The average per-flow throughput and total network throughput are shown in Figs. 11 and 12, respectively. In the SHA, because all nodes have an identical Xmt_Holdoff_Exp value (= 3), they have an identical holdoff time regardless of their current state. However, in the AHA, because nodes adjust their Xmt_Holdoff_Exp in a range between 0 and 3 according to their current state, the radio resource can be used efficiently.

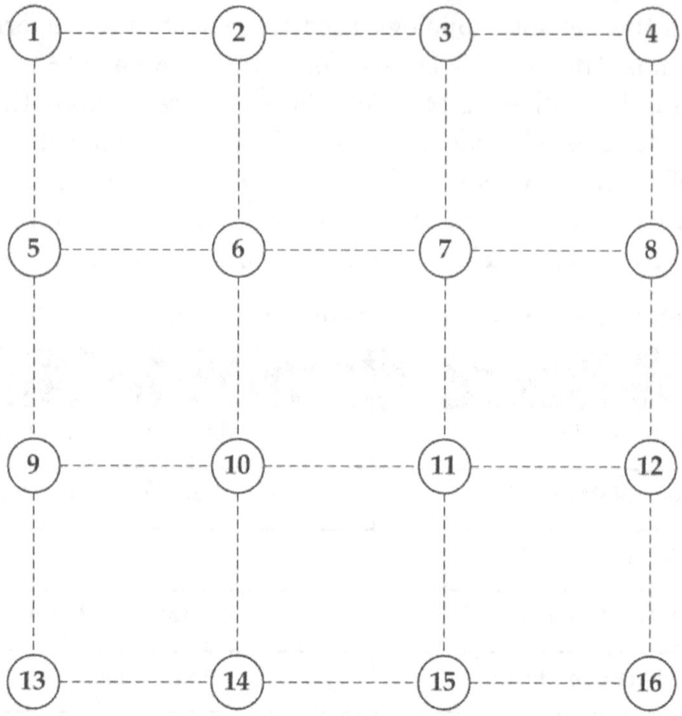

Fig. 7. Simulation network topology

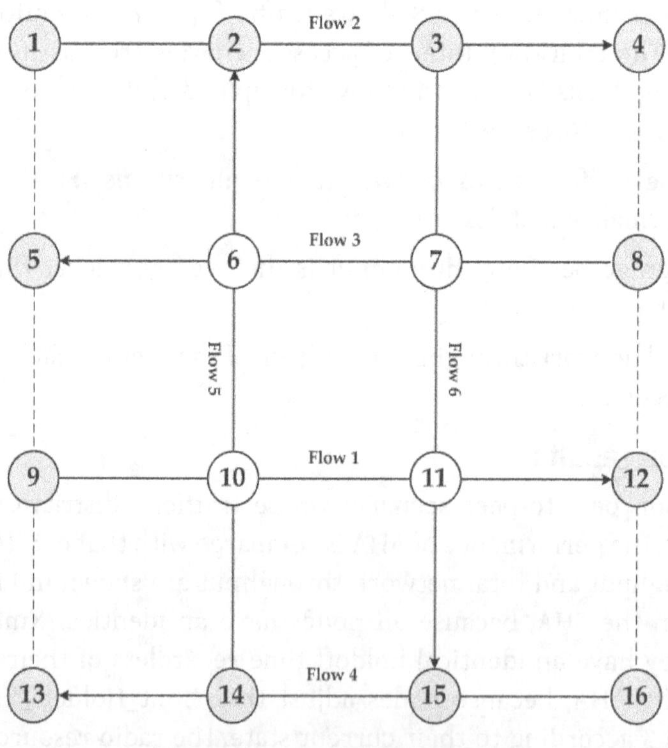

Fig. 8. Multi-hop peer-to-peer

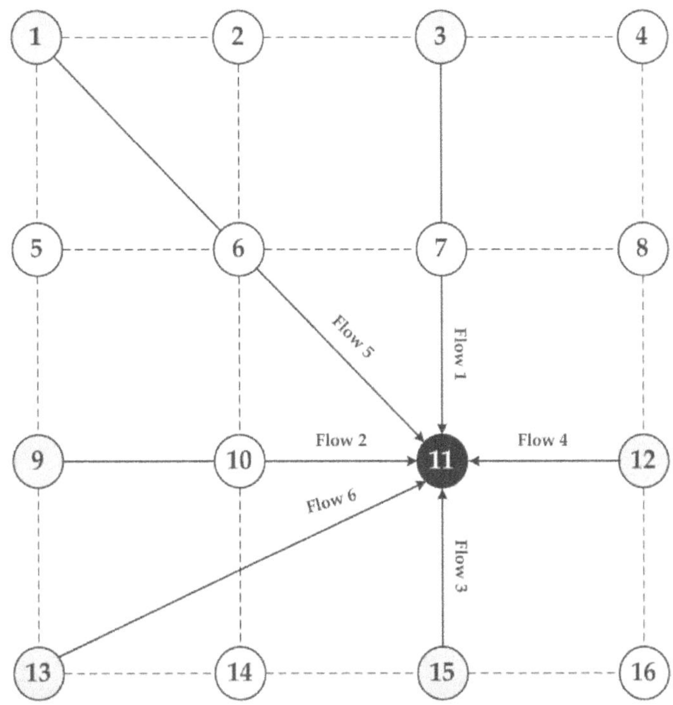

Fig. 9. Multi-hop Internet access with upload pattern

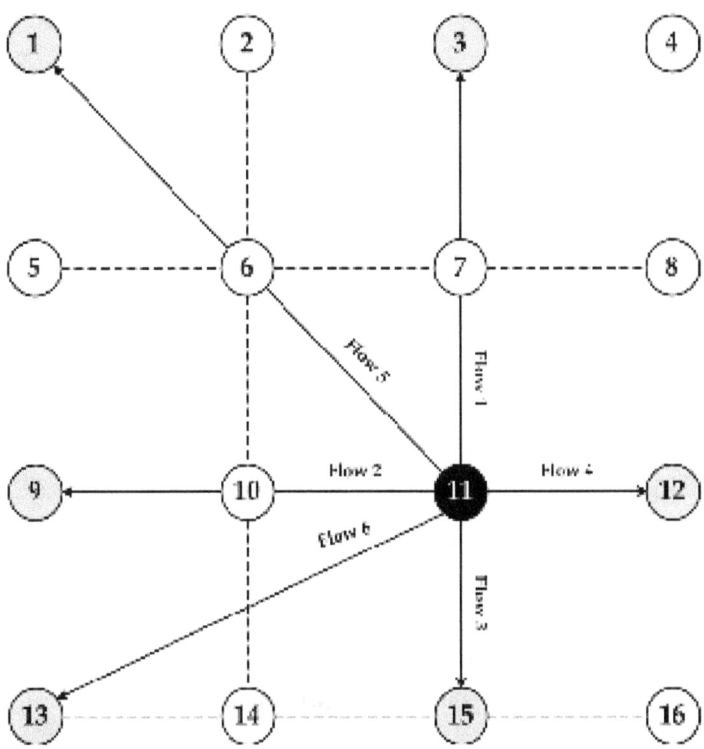

Fig. 10. Multi-hop Internet access with download pattern

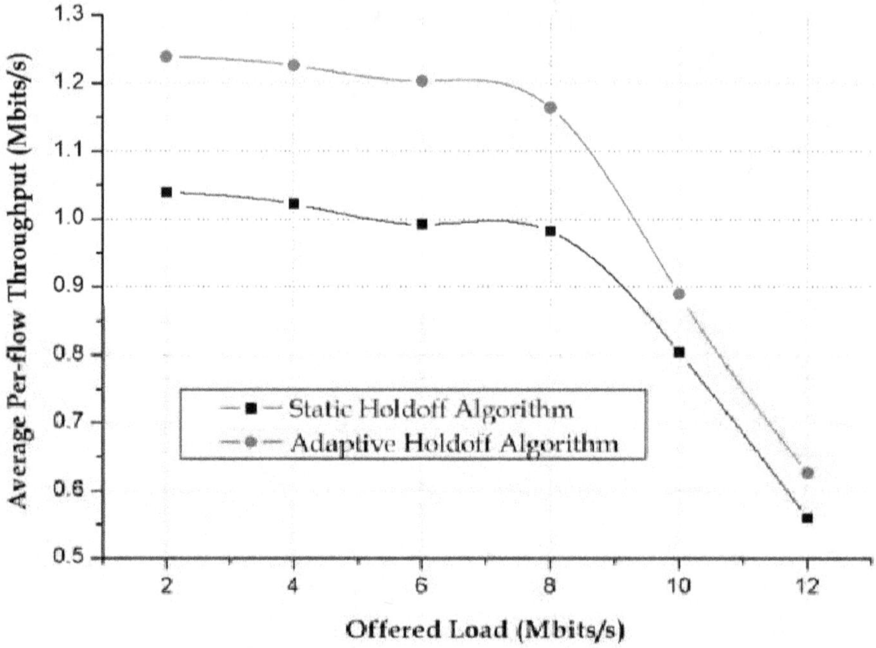

Fig. 11. Average per-flow throughput in multih-hop peer-to-peer

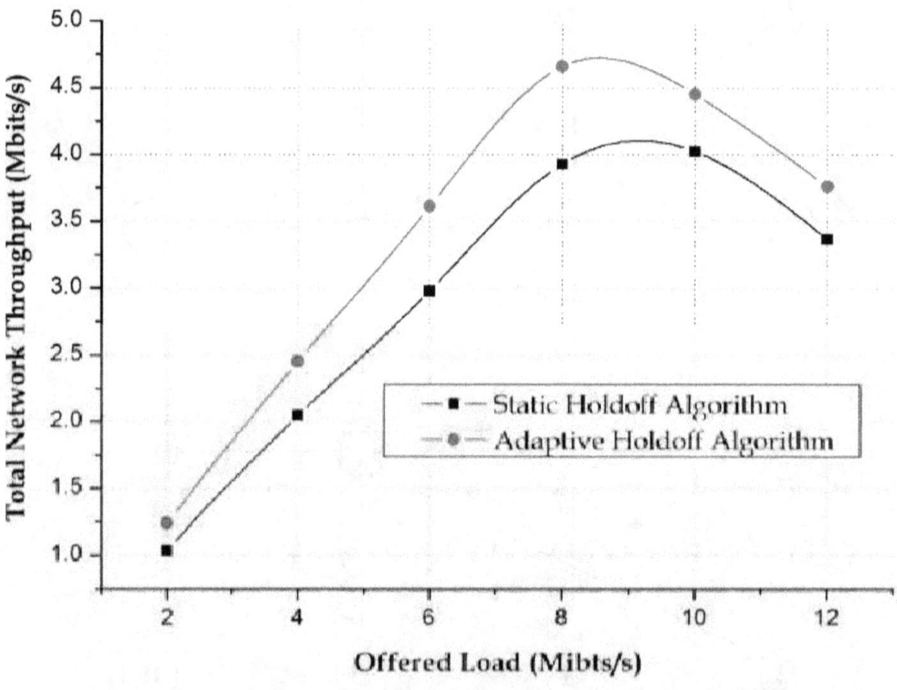

Fig. 12. Total network throughput in multi-hop peer-to-peer

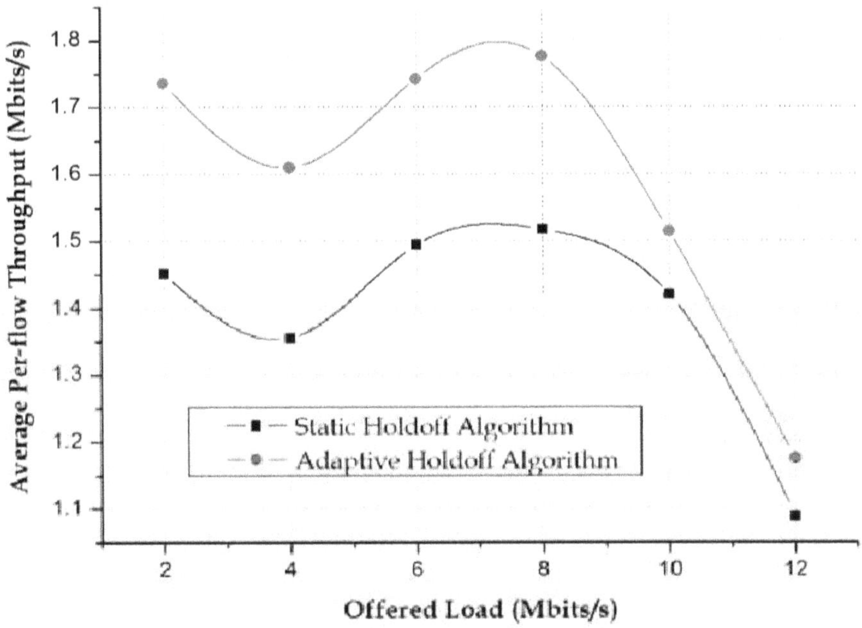

Fig. 13. Average per-flow throughput in multi-hop Internet access - upload

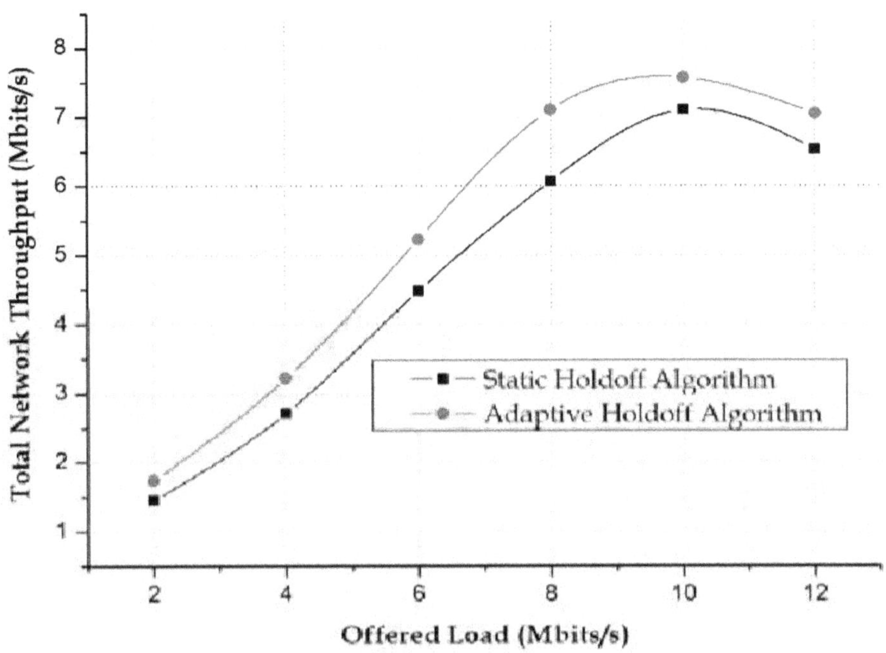

Fig. 14. Total network throughput in multi-hop Internet access - upload

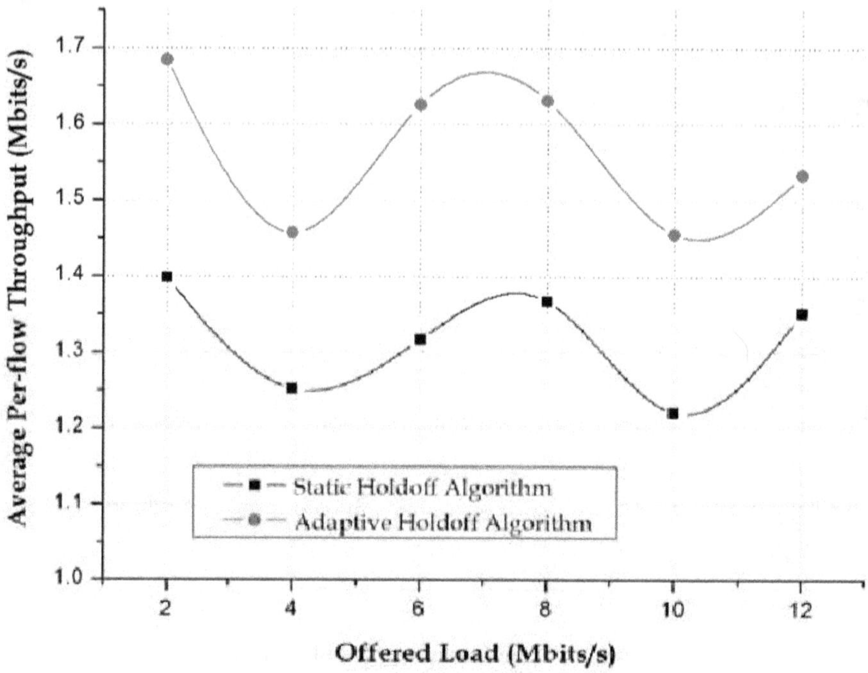

Fig. 15. Average per-flow throughput in multi-hop Internet access - download

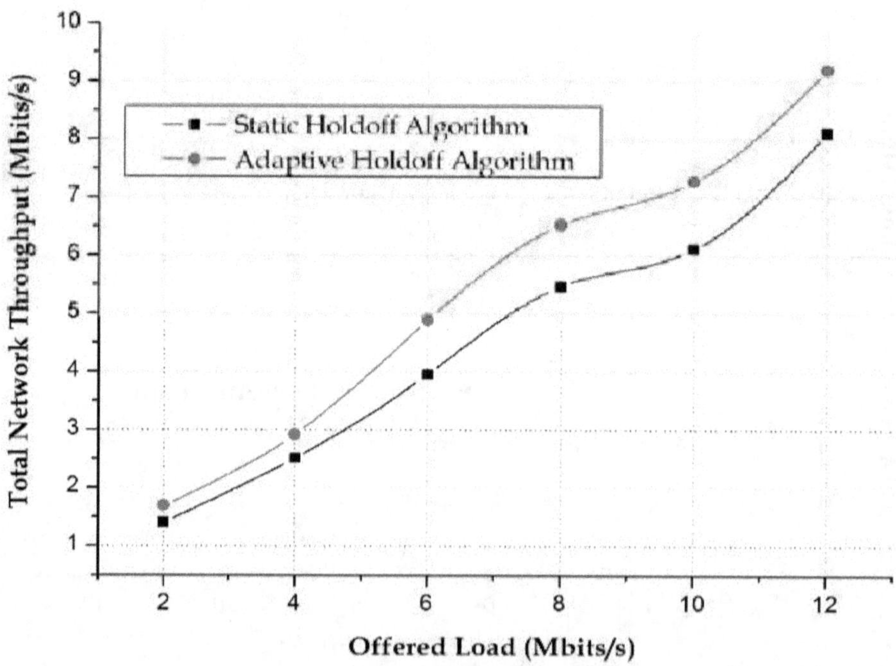

Fig. 16. Total Total network throughput in multi-hop Internet access - download

For example, because a node with the Weight = 0 currenlty has no data communication with neighbors, even though the node uses the Xmt_Holdoff_Exp of 3 in the holdoff process, the communication problem does not happen. Furthermore, that a node with a small Weight value reduces the access rate to the schedule control subframe enables other nodes with a large Weight value to access the schedule control subframe at a high rate.

A node with the Weight = 3 can access the schedule control subframe at a high rate by setting the Xmt_Holdoff_Exp to 0. By adaptively adjusting the Xmt_Holdoff_Exp value according to the current node state, the AHA performs better than the SHA in terms of average per- flow throughput and total network throughput, as shown in Figs. 11 and 12.

In general, access to the Internet through MeshBS is desirable for MeshSSs to obtain necessary service. In the multi-hop Internet access scenario, it frequently happens that MeshSSs upload files to Internet through MeshBS and MeshSSs download files provided in the Internet through MeshBS. As illustrated in Figs. 9 and 10, computer simulations are also performed in the multi-hop Internet access scenario with upload and download patterns. Figures 13 and 14 show the average per-flow throughput and total network throughput in the multi-hop Internet access scenario with upload pattern, respectively. In addition, Figs. 15 and 16 show the average per-flow throughput and total network throughput in the multi- hop Internet access scenario with download pattern, respectively. In the multi-hop Internet access scenario, it frequently happens that nodes act as one of sender or receiver. For example, node 12 serves only as sender in Fig. 9, and only as receiver in Fig. 10. In the AHA, because nodes set their Xmt_Holdoff_Exp to an appropriate value according to their current role, the AHA outperforms the SHA, as shown in Figs. 13, 14, 15, and 16.

5. CONCISE SUMMARY

Multi-hop wireless mesh networks are a fundamental characteristic of beyond 3G systems due to its adaptability and cost-effective implementation. The IEEE 802.16 mesh mode utilizing the C-DSCH has recently surfaced as an alternate MAC protocol for the establishment of M-WMNs. For the IEEE 802.16 mesh mode to function as a MAC protocol for M-WMN, it must achieve elevated network throughput. The holdoff mechanism of the IEEE 802.16 mesh standard imposes a limitation on the performance enhancement of M-WMN. This chapter examined existing holdoff algorithms, including the static and dynamic holdoff algorithms, and outlined their shortcomings. Furthermore, we introduced an adaptive holdoff technique predicated on node status for the IEEE 802.16 mesh mode utilizing the C-DSCH. The adaptive holdoff method designates a suitable Xmt_Holdoff_Exp value based on the prevailing network conditions while ensuring backward compatibility with the

IEEE 802.16 mesh standard. Simulation results indicate that nodes must adaptively modify their holdoff time based on prevailing network conditions to enhance the performance of an IEEE 802.16 mesh system.

FOOTNOTES

1. This work was performed while the first author was a Ph.D. student.

REFERENCES

1. Han, B., Jia, W., and Lin, L. (2007). Performace Evaluation of Scheduling in IEEE 802.16 based Wireless Mesh Networks, Elsevier Computer Communications, Vol. 30, No. 4, Feb. 2007, pp. 782-792, ISSN 0140-3664
2. Akyildiz, I. F., Wang, X., and Wang W. (2005). Wireless Mesh Networks : A Suervey, Elsevier Computer Networks, Vol. 47, No. 4, Mar. 2005, pp. 445-487, ISSN 1389- 1286
3. IEEE Std. 802.16-2004 (2004). IEEE Standard for Local and Metropolitan Area Networks: Part 16: Air Interface for Fixed Broadband Wireless Access Systems, Oct. 2004
4. Cao, M.; Ma, W.; Zhang, Q.; Wang, X. & Zhu, W. (2005). Modeling and Performance Analysis of the Distributed Scheduler in IEEE 802.16 Mesh Mode, Proceedings of ACM MobiHoc, pp. 78-89, ISBN 1-59593-004-3, Urbana-Champaign, May 2005, ACM, Illinois, USA
5. Bayer, N.; Xu, B. ; Rakocevic, V. & Habermann, J. (2007). Improving the Performance of the Distributed Scheduler in IEEE 802.16 Mesh Networks, Proceedings of IEEE VTC Spring, pp. 1193-1197, ISBN 1-4244-0266-2, Burlington Hotel, Apr. 2007, IEEE, Dublin, Ireland
6. Bayer, N. ; Sivchenko, D.; Xu, B.; Rakocevic, V. & Habermann, J. (2006). Transmission Timing of Signaling Messages in IEEE 802.16 based Mesh Networks, Proceedings of European Wireless, ISBN 978-3-8007-2961-6, National Technical University of Athens, Apr. 2006, Athens, Greece
7. Morge, P. S.; Hollick, M. & Steinmetz, R. (2007). The IEEE 802.16-2004 MeSH Mode Explained Technical Report, KOM-TR-2006-08, Feb. 2007
8. Wang, S. Y.; Huang, C. H.; Lin, C. C.; Chou, C. L. & Liao, K. C. (2007-(a)). The Protocol Developer Manual for the NCTUns 4.0 Network Simulator and Emulator, July 2007.
9. Wang, S. Y.; Chou, C. L. & Lin, C. C. (2007-(b)). NCTUns Hompage. [Online]. Available: http://nsl10.csie.nctu.edu.tw/
10. Wang, S. Y.; Chou, C. L. & Lin, C. C. (2007-(c)). The GUI User Manual for the NCTUns 4.0 Network Simulator and Emulator, July 2007

22 Chapter

ADMISSION CONTROL ALGORITHMS UTILIZING RANDOM WAYPOINT MOBILITY FOR IEEE 802.16E NETWORKS

1. INTRODUCTION: AN OVERVIEW

The next-generation network WiMAX (Worldwide Interoperability for Microwave Access) is synonymous with the IEEE 802.16 Wireless Metropolitan Area Network (MAN) air interface standard. The initial edition of the 802.16 standard focused on applications inside licensed bands spanning the 10 to 66 GHz frequency range. Subsequent updates have broadened the 802.16 air interface standard to encompass non-line of sight (NLOS) applications throughout licensed and unlicensed frequency bands ranging from 2 to 11 GHz. The 802.16 networks can deliver high data speeds and are ideally based on Orthogonal Frequency Division Multiple Access (OFDMA) for non-line-of-sight (NLOS) applications (Piggin, 2004). In OFDMA, modulation and/or coding can be selected variably for each sub-carrier and may also fluctuate over time. In the IEEE802.16 standard, coherent modulation methods range from low-efficiency modulations (BPSK with a coding rate of 1/2) to high-efficiency modulations (64-QAM with a coding rate of 3/4), contingent upon the Signal-to-Noise Ratio (SNR). Research indicates that systems employing adaptive modulation have superior performance compared to those with fixed modulation and coding (Yaghoobi, 2004). Adaptive modulation enhances data transmission capacity and system dependability by employing varying constellation sizes across different sub-carriers.

Peyre et al. (2008) present a novel Quality of Service (QoS) framework for real-time calls within the IEEE802.16e Multi-class Capacity, incorporating an Adaptive Modulation and Coding (AMC) scheme and QoS Differentiation for Initial and Bandwidth Request Ranging (Seo et al., 2004). The Quality of Service (QoS) established in this study aims to sustain a consistent bit rate for real-time calls, regardless of the user's location within the cell. The authors employ a Discrete Time Markov Chain (DTMC) to model the system within a breakdown of the IEEE802.16e cell.. The authors took account the mobility of users among the regions of the cell. So, the analysis of wireless systems, as IEEE802.16e WiMAX, often requires to model the effect of user mobility. The mobility model is a critical element for any study about the radio communications. Therefore we choose to use the Random Waypoint (RWP) mobility model. This model have been studied largely in Ad-hoc networks (Johnson & Maltz, 1996) and briefly in wireless networks (Hyyti & Virtamo, 2007). In particular we consider (Johnson & Maltz, 1996), wherein the authors introduced the RWP mobility model to find the mean arrival and departure rates into a concentric cell as well as the mean sojourn time in the cellular networks.

Admission Control systems are crucial in the management of radio resources (Kobbane et al., 2007; Ibrahimi et al., 2008; Ibrahimi et al., 2009). Their objectives are to uphold an acceptable Quality of Service (QoS) for various calls by restricting the number of concurrent calls in the system, reducing call blocking and dropping probabilities, while simultaneously optimizing the utilization of available resources (Niyato & Hossain, 2005). Our research aims to identify the optimal Connection Admission Control (CAC) in IEEE 802.16e WiMAX for both real-time (RT) and best-effort (BE) traffic, addressing intra- and inter-cell mobility challenges in the downlink via Adaptive Modulation and Coding (AMC) techniques. Utilizing the RWP mobility model for an IEEE802.16e cell, we represent the system capacity via a Continuous Time Markov Chain (CTMC). Consequently, we propose to examine two promising CAC algorithms that ensure Quality of Service (QoS). Our ideas enable Internet Service Providers (ISPs) to select a CAC based on their network management objectives.

2. FRAMEWORK

2.1 IEEE802.16 basis principles

The IEEE802.16e Physical layer uses an OFDMA sub-carrier allocation policy for the data transmission. The uplink and downlink sub-frames divide the time and frequency space into sub-carriers. The minimum frequency-time unit of sub-channelization is one slot, and a frame is constructed by a number of slots. Different sub-carriers are allocated to a mobile transmission in function of the resource requested by the mobile. Moreover, a sub-channel can be used periodically by different mobiles due to theirs classes of traffic. Once a mobile is granted to transmit by a bandwidth response in the DL-MAP, base station assigns one or more subcarriers and hence defines the sub-channels that the mobile will be able to use for its data transmission.

An IEEE802.16e cell is organized in region. Each region use specific modulation and coding technics. Users belongs to a region in function of theirs Signal-to-Noise Ratio SNR. The number of subcarriers allocated to a mobile directly depends on the available modulation, the type of traffic and the requested bandwidth.

2.2 System description

In this paper we consider a continuous time performance model for a single IEEE802.16e cell. The cell is decomposed into several regions. Mobiles are uniformly distributed on the whole cell. The cell population is dispatched between the regions according with theirs area coverages. Each region is characterized by the modulation used for data transmissions. Due to the AMC scheme described in the previous section, the calls use a modulation chosen in function of the receiver SNR. We consider the Adaptive Modulation and Coding (AMC) with pathloss only, consequently, the SNR depends only on the distance between the base station and the calling mobile. The four classes of services defined in the standard are:

- Unsolicited Grant Service (UGS) that caters for real-time, fixed-size data packets with constant bit rate (CBR). This service is granted at regular time intervals without a request or polls.
- Real-Time Polling Service (rtPS) that caters for real time data packets that vary in size generated at periodic intervals, such as MPEG video and VoIP with silence suppression, where packet sizes are variable.
- Non-Real-Time Polling Service (nrtPS), designed for connections that do not have delay requirements. nrtPS is similar to BE. It only differs from BE in that it guarantees a minimum bandwidth, e.g., FTP.
- Best-Effort (BE) that service makes no guarantee of service. To guarantee a minimum bandwidth the connection must subscribe to the nrtPS service, e.g., web browsing data.

We gather these classes of traffic into two types: Real Time (RT), corresponding to UGS or rtPS classes, and Best Effort (BE), corresponding to classes nrtPS and BE. Thus the RT class gathers the non delay-tolerant calls.

The calls can change of roamed region on the basis of the Random Waypoint (RWP) model. We use the RWP model to determine the mobility behavior of a call over a convex area. This area (i.e. the cell) is decomposed into several concentric regions. The RWP model helps us to determine the incoming/migrating rates for each region (intra-mobility). Moreover we extends our theoretical results to obtain the handover rate to/from external cell (inter- mobility).

2.3 Connection Admission Control

In Fig. 1, we describe the first CAC algorithm for a new call of class-c. In this first algorithm, the calls receive the same bit rate depending on its type of traffic (without the priority between RT and BE calls). Consequently, the system allocate a number of subcarriers in function of the location of the call. A new class- c call arriving in region i is accepted if the required resources are available for it. Else, the call is blocked. If a call did not finish its\ service in the region i and moves to the neighbor region j = i ± 1, the call is accepted in region j if the system accepts its modulation changing. The available resources of the system could be not enough to accept a bandwidth increase. In this case, the migrating call is dropped.

The Fig. 2 represents our last CAC algorithm for a new call of class- c . In this other CAC algorithm the BE calls have no bandwidth requirement. Since the BE calls tolerate throughput variation, they will use the sub-carriers left by the RT call occupancy. In fact, the BE calls are never blocked and received the same resources according with the Processor Sharing (PS) (Benameur et al., 2001). Thus, the bit rate of a BE call depends on its region (i.e modulation). For the RT calls only, the CAC algorithm follows the same scheme than previously: a new RT call arriving in region i is accepted if enough resources are available for it. And since a RT call did not terminate its service in region i before migrating to a region j , j = i ± 1, the call will be able to remain in the system if enough resources are available to afford the modulation change.

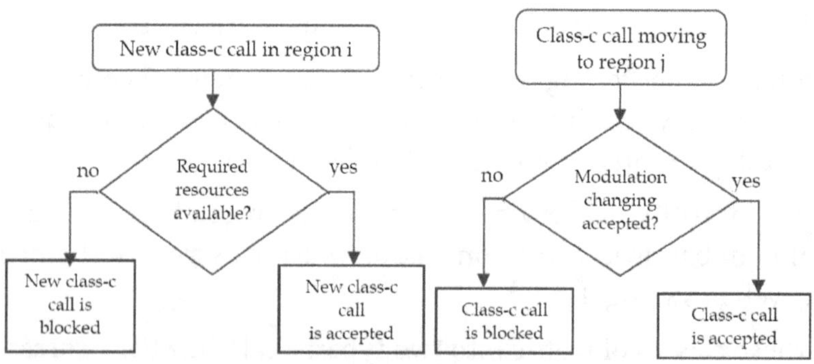

Fig. 1. First CAC Algorithm decision.

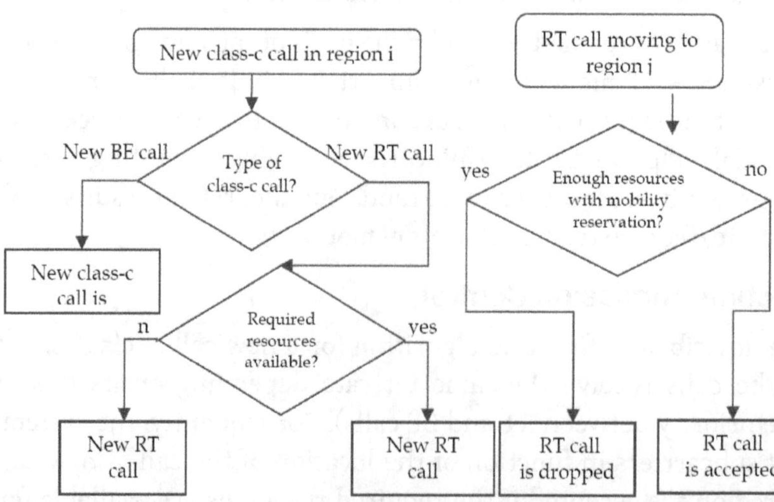

Fig. 2. Second CAC Algorithm decision.

Finally, remarks that for both CAC algorithms, the RT calls are independent of the consume resources: the RT-call remaining-time only depends on the behavior of the user. Conversely the BE calls remain in the system in function of the consumed resources: the more sub- carriers a BE call have, the faster it leaves the system.

In addition, our CAC algorithms seek to reduce the dropping probability: the probability that an on-progress service is dropped due to its mobility. As explained above, the call consumes bandwidth in function of the used modulation. By migrating to an outer region, a call may require additional resources. Thus, this call might undergo a drop due to lack of available resources. To prevent from these drops, our CAC algorithms introduce a reserved part of bandwidth. This reservation aims to satisfy the need of additional resources demanded in case of outer migration.

3. MODEL

3.1 Cell decomposition and instantaneous throughput

We consider without loss of generality, the Adaptive Modulation and Coding (AMC) with pathloss only. Then, the OFDMA cell is decomposed into r regions according to the AMC value corresponding to a certain value of SNR as depected in Fig. 3. Let Ri (i=1, ...,r) be the radius of the i-th region and Si represents the corresponding surface. Each region corresponds to a specific modulation order (see Table 1). In OFDMA scheme, the total number N of sub- carriers is divided into L sub-channels (or groups) each containing k sub-carriers, such k=N/L. In our study, we consider the multi-services WiMAX/OFDMA system with two types of traffics real-time (RT) and best-effort (BE). Also, we define the instantaneous bit rate (radio interface rate) for a call of class-c located in the region i as follows:

$$d_c^i = L_c^i \times k \times B \times e_i, \qquad (1)$$

where K is the number of sub-carriers assigned to each sub-channel; B is the baud rate (symbol/sec); ei is the modulation efficiency (bits/symbol) and Lci is the sub-channels allowed for class-c call in region i . The above bit rate can be degraded by the error channel due to collision, shadow fading effect, as defined in (Tarhini & Chahid, 2007),

$$R_c^i = d_c^i \times (1 - BLER_i), \qquad (2)$$

where BLERi is the BLock Error Rate in region i. The Table 1 indicates the modulations and codings used in a IEEE802.16e cell as function of the user SNR. The SNR requirement for a BLER less than 10-6 depends on the modulation type as specified in the standard (Standard IEEE802.16, 2004). Then, we have γ1= 24.4 dB, γ2= 18.2 dB, γ3= 9.4 dB, γ4= 6.4 dB and γ0 =∞.

Table 1. IEEE802.16e AMC settings.

Modulation	Coding rate	Received SNR (dB)	Cell ratio (%)
64-QAM	3/4	$[\gamma 1, \gamma 0)$	1.74
16-QAM	3/4	$[\gamma 2, \gamma 1)$	5.14
QPSK	1/2	$[\gamma 3, \gamma 2)$	20.75
BPSK	1/2	$[\gamma 4, \gamma 3)$	39.4

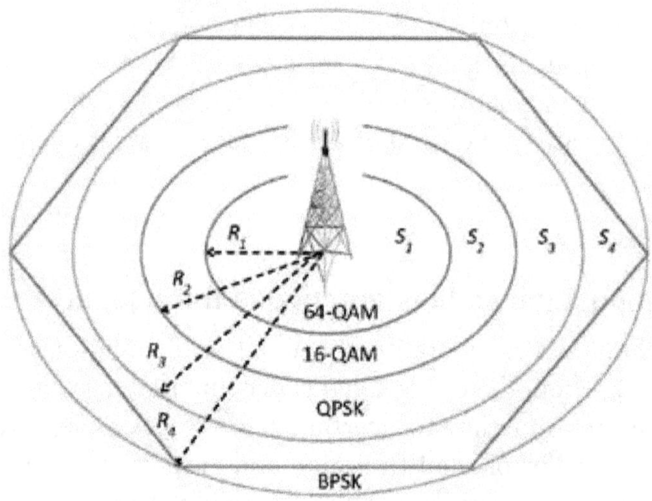

Fig. 3. OFDMA Cell decomposed into concentric regions.

3.2 System state and transitions

Our model of the system is based on the Continuous Time Markov chain (CTMC) technic. The different transition rates within the space of feasible states defined in the next sections are caused by one of the following events: arrival of a new call of class-c to region i; migration of an ongoing call of class-c from region i to j; termination of an ongoing call of class-c in the region i. Furthermore, we consider in our analysis the following assumptions:

1. The arrival process of new calls of class-c in region i is Poisson with rate λ 0 ;
2. The service time of a class-c call is exponentially distributed with mean 1/ μc;
3. The mean dwell time or sojourn time in region i is exponentially distributed with mean 1/ Γi ;
4. The mean arrival rate of migrating call of class-c from the region i to region j is λ i, j .

Let $n_c^i(t)$ be the number of calls of class-c in progress at time t in region i. The state of the system at time t is defined by: $\vec{n}(t) = (n_{RT}^1(t), \ldots, n_{RT}^r(t), n_{BE}^1(t), \ldots, n_{BE}^r(t))$. Then, we model the process $\{\vec{n}(t), t > 0\}$ as 2r-dimension quasi-birth and death Markov chain. In the steady-state it has an unique stationary distribution, with:

$$\vec{n} = (n_{RT}^1, \ldots, n_{RT}^r, n_{BE}^1, \ldots, n_{BE}^r).$$

3.3 User mobility behaviour

We compute the arrival migration rates using RWP model. In the RWP model a node moves in a convex domain Ω ⊂ R2 along a straight line segment from one waypoint to another.

The waypoint, denoted by Pi, are uniformly distributed in Ω, Pi U(Ω). Transition from Pi-1 to Pi is referred to as the i-th leg, and the velocity of the node on i-th leg is given by random variable vi. In particular in the RWP model, it is assumed that Pi and vi are all independent and vi are uniformly distributed. Here, the domain Ω corresponds to one cell and leg to path between both waypoints Pi and Pi-1. Also, the node corresponds to a mobile or user moving in the cell. With this notation the RWP process (for a single node) is defined by an infinite sequence of triples (Bettstetter et al., 2004), {(P0 , P1, v1), (P1, P2 , v2), }.

We note that the process RWP is time reversible. This means that the arrival rates across any line segment or border are equal in both directions. In other words, the average rates of calls moving from region i to region j per time unit is equal to the number of calls moving from region j to region i per time unit, i. e., λi, j = λ j,i as proved in (Norris, 1999).

Our aim is to compute the migration rates λi, j . As the velocity of the user (node) is assumed to have an uniform distribution from vmin, (vmin>0) to vmax, denoted by fv(v), where

$$f_v(v) = \begin{cases} \dfrac{1}{v_{\max} - v_{\min}}, & if\ v \in [v_{\min}, v_{\max}]; \\ 0, & otherwise. \end{cases}$$

Let T_i denote the transition time on i-th leg (path) defined as $T_i = \dfrac{l_i}{v_i}$, where $l_i = |P_i - P_{i-1}|$. The variables l_i and v_i are independent random variables. The average time from one waypoint to another is given by:

We consider the area Ai of each concentric cell of radius Ri as a convex disk of same radius in which the mobiles move according to the RWP model. Our aim is to compute the arrival rate into a cell of radius Ri-1 . As introduced in (Hyyti & Virtamo, 2007), let a1 = a1 (Ri-1,φ) denote the distance from point Ri-1 =| (0, Ri-1) |∈ Ai to the border of Ai in direction φ (angle anti-clockwise away from the tangent at point Ri-1 =| (0, Ri-1) |). a2 = a1 (Ri-1,φ + π) denotes the distance to the border in the opposite direction (see Fig. 4). Also, we note the specific flux at Ri-1 in direction φ by

$$\psi(R_{i-1},\phi)=\frac{1}{2C_v}.a_1a_2(a_1+a_2), \tag{4}$$

where $C_v=\bar{l}A_i^2.E[1/v]$. We recall that the $i-th$ disk surface is $A_i=\pi R_i^2$ and the mean length of a leg in this disk is

$$\bar{l}=\frac{1}{\pi R_i^2}\int_0^{\pi}a_1a_2(a_1+a_2)d\phi. \tag{5}$$

According with the RWP model developed in cellular network context (Hyyti & Virtamo, 2007) , the arrival rate for one user to region i -1 over all contour of disk of the radius Ri-1 is given by

$$\lambda(R_{i-1})=2\pi R_{i-1}\int_0^{\pi}\sin(\phi)\psi(R_{i-1},\phi)d\phi. \tag{6}$$

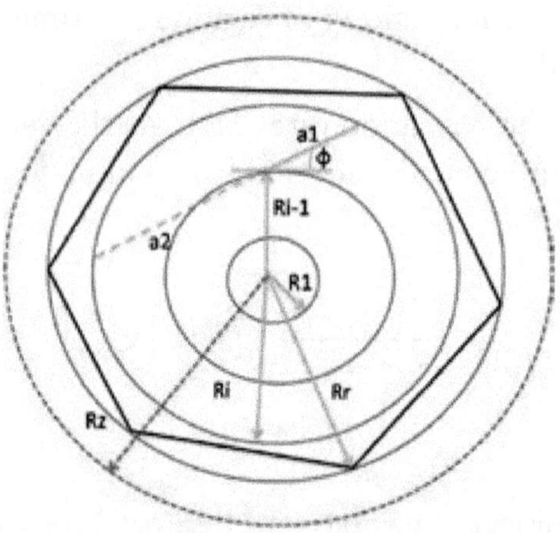

Fig. 4. RWP domains (disk of radius Ri) and Rz=2Rr-Rr-1.

From the Fig. 6, we deduce easily the distances a1 and a2 as follow:

$$a_1(R_{i-1},\phi)=\sqrt{R_i^2-R_{i-1}^2\cos^2(\phi)}-R_{i-1}\sin(\phi),$$

$$a_2(R_{i-1},\phi) = \sqrt{R_i^2 - R_{i-1}^2\cos^2(\phi)} + R_{i-1}\cos(\phi).$$

As the user mobility behaviors are independent, the total migration rate from region i (i = 1,•, r) to region j (j = i ±1) of class- c is given by

λi, j = λ (Rj).nic . (7)

Finally, the handover arrival rate is given by

$$\lambda_c^{ho} = \lambda_c^{r+1,r} = \lambda(R_r).n_c^r. \tag{8}$$

Now we can compute the mean sojourn time Γi of one mobile that proceed to class-c call in region i . This mobile can arrives from region j with rate λ j,i (i = j ±1) or from outside as new call with rate λ 0. Let i be the probability of finding a call of class-c in region i(i = 1,•, r). Then the mean sojourn time is given by (Hyyti & Virtamo, 2007):

$$\Gamma_c^i = \frac{p_c^i}{\lambda_c^{i+1,i} + \lambda_c^{i-1,i} + \lambda_{c,i}^0}, \quad with \quad \lambda_c^{0,1} = 0, \tag{9}$$

where

$$p_c^i = P(n_c^i(t) \geq 1) = \sum_{\vec{n}, n_c^i \geq 1} \pi_k(\vec{n}). \tag{10}$$

where πk is the probability distribution computed in the next system analysis and k=1, 2.

4. SYSTEM ANALYSIS FOR THE FIRST CAC ALGORITHM

4.1 Bandwidth occupancy

As described above in the Fig. 1, the interest QoS is to guarantee for a call of class-c a same bit rate independently of its position in the cell. In fact, we allocate to it the needed sub- channels by using equation (2) as

$$L_c^i = \frac{R_c}{k \times B \times e_i \times (1 - BLER_i)}. \tag{11}$$

We recall that the mean call duration of BE calls in the system depends on the transmitting payload in bits, i.e., $\mu_{BE} = \frac{R_{BE}}{E(Pay)}$, where E(Pay) is the mean file size (Downey, 2001). Thus, we define the space of the admissible states as follows

$$E = \{\vec{n} \in N^{2r} \mid \sum_{i=1}^{r} \{n_{RT}^i L_{RT}^i + n_{BE}^i L_{BE}^i\} \leq L\}. \tag{12}$$

Let Lm be the reserved capacity for migrating or handoff calls of class-c and L0 denotes the remaining capacity given by when system state is n , with L0 = L - Lm . Let $B_1(\vec{n})$be the occupancy bandwidth when system state is n , with

$$B_1(\vec{n}) = \sum_{i=1}^{r} \{n_{RT}^{i} L_{RT}^{i} + n_{BE}^{i} L_{BE}^{i}\}. \tag{13}$$

4.2 Equilibrium distribution

The call of class-c can come as new call or migrating/handoff call in region i of the cell. For n the current system state, we define the arrival rate of call in region i , as

$$\lambda_c^i(\vec{n}) = \begin{cases} \lambda_{c,i}^0 + \lambda_c^{i-1,i} + \lambda_c^{i+1,i}, & \text{if } B_1(\vec{n}) < L_0; \\ \lambda_c^{i-1,i} + \lambda_c^{i+1,i}, & \text{if } L_0 \le B_1(\vec{n}) < L. \end{cases} \tag{14}$$

We have two classes of services RT and BE. Each class-c call in region i (i = 1, 2,..., r) requires the effective bandwidth Li . Then, we have 2r classes in the cell and the equilibrium distribution is given by BCMP theorem (Chao et al., 2001) for multiple classes with possible class changes, with $\rho_c^i = \frac{\lambda_c^i(n)}{\Gamma_c^i + \mu_c}$ as

$$\pi_1(\vec{n}) = \frac{1}{G} \prod_{i=1}^{r} \frac{(\rho_{RT}^i)^{n_{RT}^i}}{n_{RT}^i!} \frac{(\rho_{BE}^i)^{n_{BE}^i}}{n_{BE}^i!}, \tag{15}$$

where $\vec{n} \in E$ and G is the normalizing constant given by

$$G = \sum_{\vec{n} \in E} \prod_{i=1}^{r} \frac{(\rho_{RT}^i)^{n_{RT}^i}}{n_{RT}^i!} \frac{(\rho_{BE}^i)^{n_{BE}^i}}{n_{BE}^i!}.$$

So, this probability depends of the mean sojourn time i which depends itself on the probability pci in equation (10). Also the latter depends of the above distribution and vice versa. We can use the fixed point theorem to resolve this problem as follow:

Algorithm : Probability convergence algorithm

1: Initialize the probability in (9): pi c,old = pic = 0.1.

2: Compute the mean sojourn time in (9).

3: Calculate the steady-state probability π1(n) from (15).

4: Derive the new value of probability from (10), denoted by $p^i_{c,new}$.

5: Check the convergence of the probability between the old and the new values. if | pi - pi |< ξ , where ξ is a very small positive number, then the new probability is c,new c,old used to compute the performance metrics. Otherwise, go to step 2 with new value as initial value. The iterations are continued until to reach the convergence of probability.

5 SYSTEM ANALYSIS FOR THE SECOND CAC ALGORITHM

5.1 Bit rates per class and feasible system states

Here, we consider the CAC algorithm follows the scheme described in the Fig. 2. Consider there is a minimum capacity reserved for BE calls denoted by LBE and reserved LmRT sub- channels for RT calls mobility. We denote by LRT the remaining capacity for RT calls given by:

$$L_{RT} = L - L_{BE} - L_{RT}^{m}. \tag{16}$$

Let B2 (n) RT BE RT be the bandwidth occupied by RT calls when system sate is n , with

$$B_2(\vec{n}) = \sum_{i=1}^{r} n_{RT}^{i} L_{RT}^{i}, \tag{17}$$

where

$$L_{RT}^{i} = \frac{R_{RT}}{k \times B \times e_i \times (1 - BLER_i)}.$$

In this section, we guarantee for RT calls a QoS in terms to maintain a same bit rate everywhere in the covered area by the cell. Whereas a BE call receives the instantaneous bit rate denoted by RiBE in region i . The dynamic capacity $C(\vec{n})$ shared fairly among all BE calls simultaneously in progress in the system is

$$C(\vec{n}) = \begin{cases} L - B_2(\vec{n}) - L_{RT}^{m}, & if\ B_2(\vec{n}) < L_{RT}; \\ L_{BE}, & otherwise. \end{cases} \tag{18}$$

The BE calls share the reserved capacity with PS manner. The number of sub-channels LiBE allocated to a BE call in region i with PS policy is

$$L_{BE}^{i}(\vec{n}) = \left| \frac{C(\vec{n})}{\sum_{i=1}^{r} n_{BE}^{i}} \right|, \tag{19}$$

where $\lfloor x \rfloor$ indicates the largest integer that is less than or equal to x. Then the BE call receives in region i the bit rate $R^i_{BE}(\vec{n}) = L^i_{BE}(\vec{n}) \times k \times B \times e_i \times (1 - BLER_i)$. Therefore, the mean BE call duration is given by $\mu^i_{BE} = \dfrac{R^i_{BE}(\vec{n})}{E(Pay)}$. Since the system accept without limit the BE calls, the space of admissible states is

$$F = \{\vec{n} \in N^{2r} \mid \sum_{i=1}^{r} n^i_{RT} L^i_{RT} \leq L_{RT}\}. \tag{20}$$

We define the indication function as

$$\delta(X) = \begin{cases} 1, & \textit{if } X \textit{ is true;} \\ 0, & \textit{otherwise.} \end{cases}$$

5.2 Transition rates

The transition rates from the state $\vec{n}$ to other ones are introduced as described in the sequel. Let $\vec{n}^c_{i+}$ be the state when a new class-c call is arrived and we denote this transition by $q_{(\vec{n},\vec{n}^c_{i+})}$. Let $\vec{n}^c_{i-}$ be the state when a class-c call in region i terminates its service or changes

its modulation order and we denote this transition by $q_{(\vec{n},\vec{n}^c_{i-})}$. Let $\vec{n}^c_{i,j}$ ($j = i \pm 1$) be the state when a class-c call in region i moves to the neighbor region j and we denote this transition by $q_{(\vec{n},\vec{n}^c_{i,j})}$. Then, we have

$$q_{(\vec{n},\vec{n}^{RT}_{i+})} = \delta(B_2(\vec{n}) + L^i_{RT} \leq L_{RT})\lambda^0_{RT,i},$$

$$q_{(\vec{n},\vec{n}^{BE}_{i+})} = \lambda^0_{BE,i},$$

$$q_{(\vec{n},\vec{n}^{RT}_{i,j})} = \delta(B_2(\vec{n}) + \Delta^{i,j}_{RT} \leq L_{RT} + L^m_{RT})\lambda^{i,j}_{RT},$$

$$q_{(\vec{n},\vec{n}^{BE}_{i,j})} = \lambda^{i,j}_{BE},$$

$$q_{(\vec{n},\vec{n}^{RT}_{i-})} = n^i_{RT}(\mu_{RT} + \Gamma^i_{RT}),$$

$$q_{(\vec{n},\vec{n}^{BE}_{i-})} = n^i_{BE}(\mu^i_{BE}(\vec{n}) + \Gamma^i_{BE}),$$

where Γ_c^i is computed in Algorithm 1 by replacing the the probability π_1 by π_2, and $\Delta_{RT}^{i,j} = L_{RT}^i - L_{RT}^j$.

Let Q be the matrix of the possible transitions, where $Q = (q_{(\vec{n},\vec{n}')})$ for $\vec{n} \in F$ and $\vec{n}' \in F$. The transition rate from state $\vec{n}$ to $\vec{n}'$ is denoted by $q_{(\vec{n},\vec{n}')}$. Its value must be obtained as the sum of all terms in each line in matrix Q is equal to zero for RT call and BE one as well as $i = 1,\ldots,r$.

5.3 Steady-state distribution

Now, we recall that $\pi_2(\vec{n})$ denotes the steady-state probability when system is in the state $\vec{n}$ ($\vec{n} \in F$) and by $\vec{\pi}$ the steady-state distribution vector, where $\vec{\pi} = \{\pi_2(\vec{n}) \mid \vec{n} \in F\}$. The steady-state probability vector is solution of the following system of equations:

$$\vec{\pi} Q = \overline{0}, \tag{21}$$

$$\vec{\pi} \overline{1} = 1. \tag{22}$$

where $\overline{1}$ is a column vector of ones and $\overline{0}$ is a row vector of zeros.

6. PERFORMANCES METRIC

Once the equilibrium distribution probabilities 4.2 and 5.3 are calculated, we compute many interesting metrics of the system. In this section, we provide explicit expressions for various metrics like dropping probabilities, blocking probabilities, average sojourn time and average throughput.

6.1 First scheme

6.1.1 Blocking probabilities

A new call of class-c in region i is blocked with probability:

$$B_c^i = \sum_{\vec{n} \in E_c^i} \pi_1(\vec{n}), i = 1,\ldots,r, \tag{23}$$

where $E_c^i = \{\vec{n} \in E \mid B_1(\vec{n}) + L_c^i > L_0\}$.

6.1.2 Dropping probabilities

Migrating call dropping probability in region i . The migrating call of class-c from region i to region j is dropped with probability

$$D_c^i = \sum_{\vec{n}\in E_c^{i,j}} \pi_1(\vec{n}), i = 2,\ldots,r, \tag{24}$$

where $E_c^{i,j} = \{\vec{n} \in E \mid B_1(\vec{n}) + L_c^j - L_c^i > L\}$.

6.1.3 Average throughput

The average throughput in the system is

$$Th_1 = \sum_{\vec{n}\in E} \pi_1(\vec{n}) \sum_{i=1}^{r} (n_{RT}^i R_{RT} + n_{BE}^i R_{BE}). \tag{25}$$

6.2 Second scheme

6.2.1 Blocking probabilities

A new call of class-RT in region i is blocked with probability

$$B_{RT}^i = \sum_{\vec{n}\in F_{RT}^i} \pi_2(\vec{n}), i = 1,\ldots,r, \tag{26}$$

where $F_{RT}^i = \{\vec{n} \in F \mid B_2(\vec{n}) + L_{RT}^i > L_{RT}\}$.

6.2.2 Dropping probabilities

Migrating call dropping probability in region i . The migrating call of class-RT from region i to region j is dropped with probability

$$D_{RT}^i = \sum_{\vec{n}\in F_{RT}^{i,j}} \pi_2(\vec{n}), i = 2,\ldots,r, \tag{27}$$

where $F_{RT}^{i,j} = \{\vec{n} \in F \mid B_2(\vec{n}) + \Delta_{RT}^{j,i} > L_{RT} + L_{RT}^m\}$.

6.2.3 Average throughput

The average throughput in the system is

$$Th_2 = \sum_{\vec{n}\in F} \pi_2(\vec{n}) \sum_{i=1}^{r} (n_{RT}^i R_{RT} + n_{BE}^i R_{BE}^i(\vec{n})). \tag{28}$$

7. NUMERICAL APPLICATIONS

The following parameters and assumptions are used in our numerical applications. Considering OFDMA cell system with an FFT (fast Fourier transform) size of 2048 sub- carriers. The cell is decomposed into two regions (r = 2), R1 = 300 m and R2 = 600 m with AMC scheme: 16-QAM 3/4 (e1 = 3 bits/symbol) and QPSK 1/2 (e2 = 1 bit/symbol). The baud value B = 2666 symbols/sec, BLERi = 0, and K = 48. These parameters correspond to the transmission modes with conventionally coded modulation (Liu & Zhou, 2005); The bit rate RRT is equal to 128 Kbps and RBE is 384 Kbps (Tarhini & Chahed, 2007); The total bandwidth L is 10 sub-channels; The mean call duration for RT calls is equal to 120 sec and the download of files with mean size for BE calls is equal to E(Pay) = 5 Mbits. We assume a mobile moves according to the RWP model on a convex disk of radius Rz = 900 m. It randomly chooses a new speed in each waypoint from an uniform distribution between [vmin, vmax], where vmin=3km/h (low mobility) or vmin = 20km/h (high mobility), vmax = 90 km/h.

7.1 Impact of first scheme

The Fig. 5 presents the blocking probabilities for each burst profile (i.e. modulation) in terms of reserved resources for mobility.

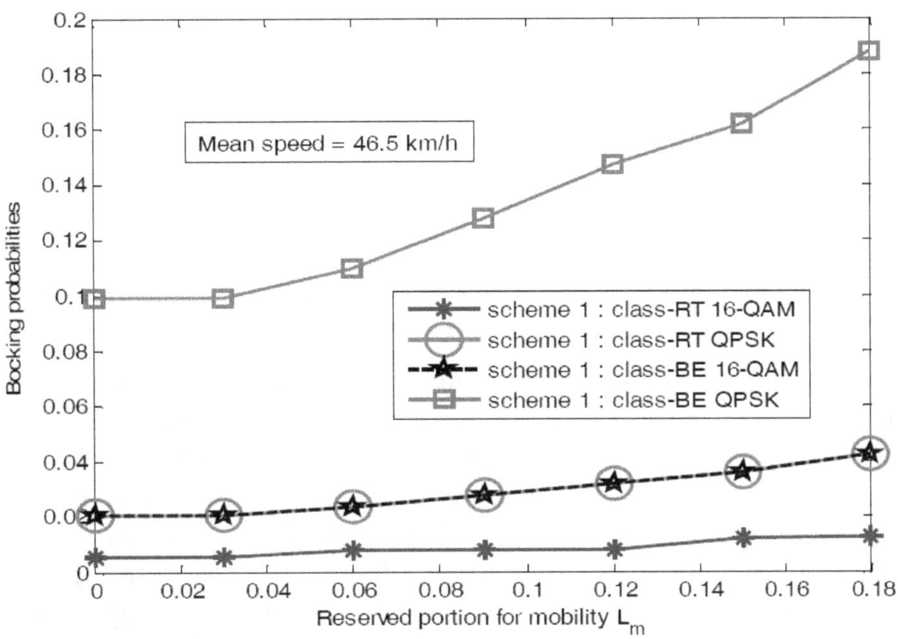

Fig. 5. Blocking probabilities versus threshold Lm and mean speed for RT λ0 = BE ,i λ0 = 0.3 call/sec

As expected, the probabilities increase as the reserved threshold Lm increases and the modulation efficiency decreases. Moreover, an appreciable difference exists between class RT and class BE blocking probability. This is due to the required capacity per class type, the BE class call in our numerical environment requires more bandwidth than the RT class call. So, when threshold increases, the blocking probability increases due to the CAC mechanism which gives the priority to migrating/handoff call than the new call. So the blocking probability mainly depends on the required bandwidth associated with the call modulation efficiency. We also observe that as the reserved bandwidth Lm increases, the calls are more blocked as the incoming region is away from the base station and as the calls demand an high bandwidth. In particular, we observe on the figure the blocking probabilities for two type of arrivals : BE calls in 16QAM and RT calls in QPSK. The blocking probabilities are exactly the same because the product between the required bandwidth and the modulation efficiency are the same for both.

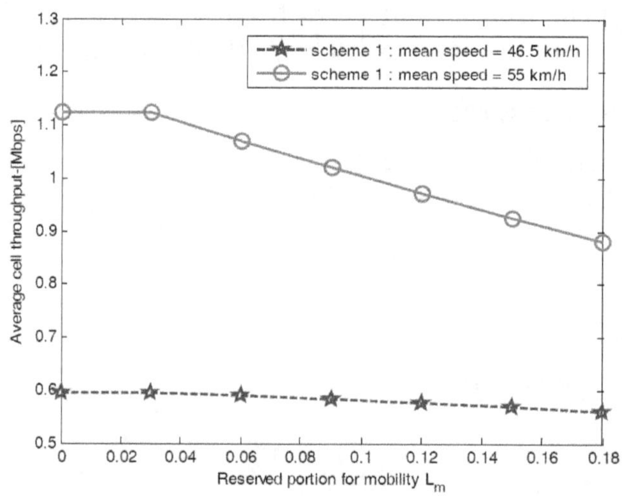

Fig.6. Blocking probabilities versus threshold Lm and mean speed for $\lambda^0_{RT,i} = \lambda^0_{BE,i}$= 0.3 call/sec.

The Fig. 6 shows the average throughput of the whole cell versus the reserved threshold mobility. On this figure two singular behaviors have to be studied. The first main observation deals with the throughput increasing because of an higher mobility. As a mobile moves faster, it increases its probability to change region (and thus modulation) per unit of time. This fact implies also more calls dropped due to lack of resources. In fact the system will implicitly coerce the system calls to use better modulations. This last deduction explains how an higher mobility allows to reach a better throughput. Note that this remark is confirmed in (Peyre & Elazouzi, 2009) and also observed for the ad-hoc networks (Grossglause & Tse, 2002). Moreover, we can criticize on the Fig. 6, the impact of resource reservation to ease the call mobility. For any mobility behavior, the average cell throughput decreases as the reservation share increases. But the throughput fall depends on the mobility behavior. In fact, by introducing a resource reservation, we helps more and more migrating calls to remain in the border regions. Theses calls use more subchannels to reach the same bit rate than previously. Consequently, the system reaches a lower throughput by prioritizing the user mobility management.

The Fig. 7 represents the dropping probabilities versus reserved threshold Lm . We plot the results for both types of traffic in the border region (i.e. QPSK modulation), and for two mobility behaviors. The figure helps to appreciate the great impact of the resource reservation on the mobility management efficiency. Concerning the real-time traffics, we observe that an higher mobility causes an twenty-times dropping increase. To fight against this effect, our CAC algorithm permits to tune the resource reservation in order to decreases the call drops under a desired value. For examples, a reservation lower than ten percents of the total bandwidth decreases the number of dropped calls under a one-percent probability. For the Best Effort traffic, we observe exactly the same behavior. Nevertheless, the dropping probability for the BE traffic remains higher than for the RT because the BE calls require an higher bit rate. As they ask for more bandwidth, they undergo more drops. For this type of traffic, our CAC allows also to greatly reduce the dropping probability of the BE calls by increasing the resources reservation Lm .

7.2 Impact of second scheme

The Fig. 8 shows the blocking probabilities for the RT traffics in both regions versus the bandwidth reservation for the Best Effort call. We plot the results obtained for two resource reservation profiles for the user mobility management. This figure clearly shows the impact of LBE and on the blocking probabilities experienced in each region. In general, the blocking probabilities are heavily increased by the BE bandwidth reservation. In addition, this drawback is amplify by the increase of the mobility management resource reservation.

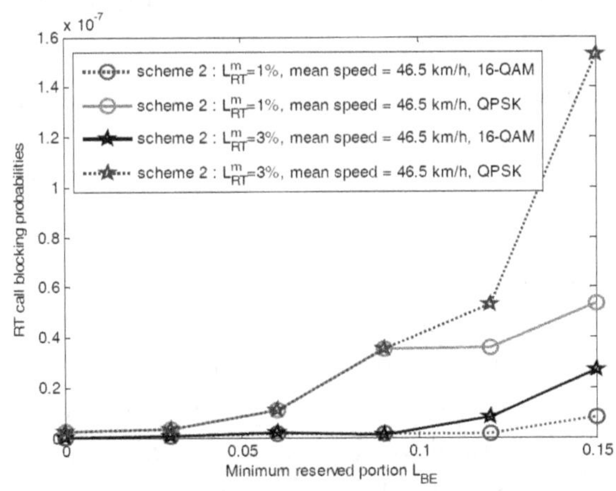

Fig. 7. Blocking probabilities versus threshold Lm and mean speed for $^{\lambda 0}$RT,i = $^{\lambda 0}$ BE,i = 0.3 call/sec.

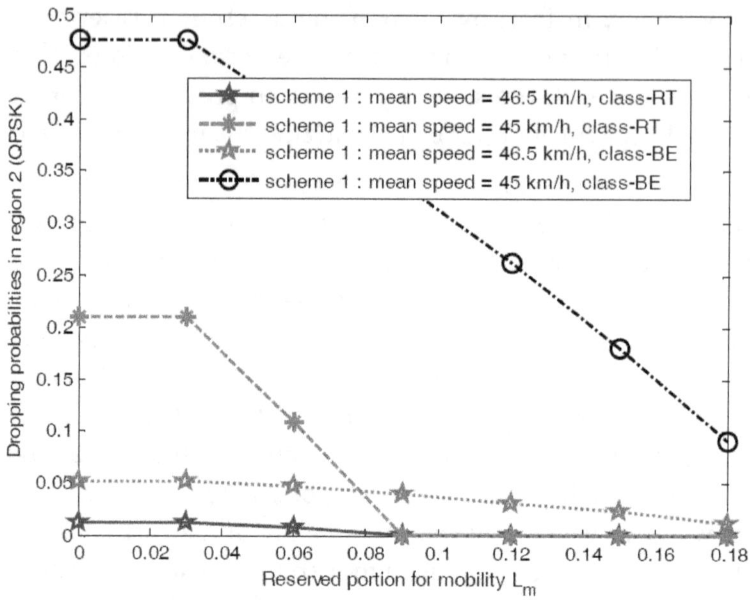

Fig. 8. Dropping probabilities versus threshold L and Lm for $^{\lambda 0}$RT,i = $^{\lambda 0}$ BE,i = 0.3 call/sec.

From this statement, we could compute the the value ranges for LBE and m which satisfy a maximum blocking probability threshold.

The Fig. 9 shows the dropping probabilities for the RT traffics in the border region versus the bandwidth reservation for the Best Effort call. We plot the results obtained for two resource reservation profiles for the user mobility management. The figure shows how the resource reservation m fights against the dropping due to the BE bandwidth reservation.

On this figure, the dropping probability is reduced as the BE reservation is greater than ten percents. So we can determine the possible values for dropping probability. m from a desired maximum.

The Fig. 10 shows the total cell throughput. This figure presents the impact of the different bandwidth reservation to increase the BE call throughput and to ease the call mobility. On the Fig. 10 we can appreciate the great impact of the BE bandwidth reservation LBE .

Indeed, by reservation 15% of the total bandwidth, we double the total cell throughput. In addition, to increase the mobility-purpose reservation slightly decrease the total throughput. This observation leads to think that a small quantity of subchannels for Best effort calls allows to reach very higher throughput. In fact, this by reserving few subchannels to the BE calls, we also increase the blocking and dropping probabilities for the RT calls. Therefore, these amount of resources freed by the dropped call or let free by the blocking one allow to the BE calls to use even more resources.

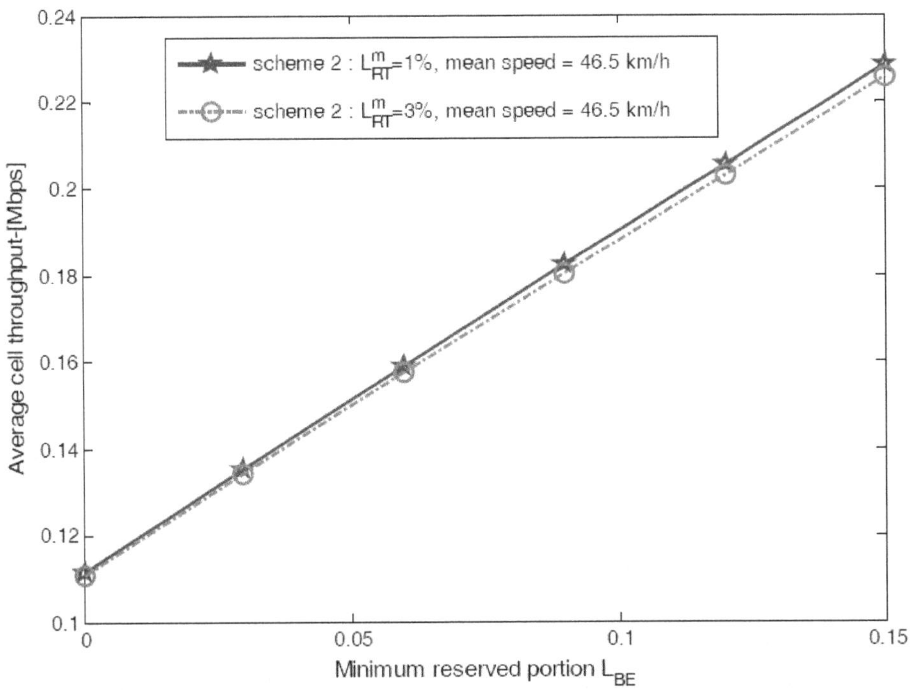

Fig. 9. Mean throughput versus L and L for$^{\lambda0}$RT,i = $^{\lambda0}$ BE,i = 0.3 call/sec.

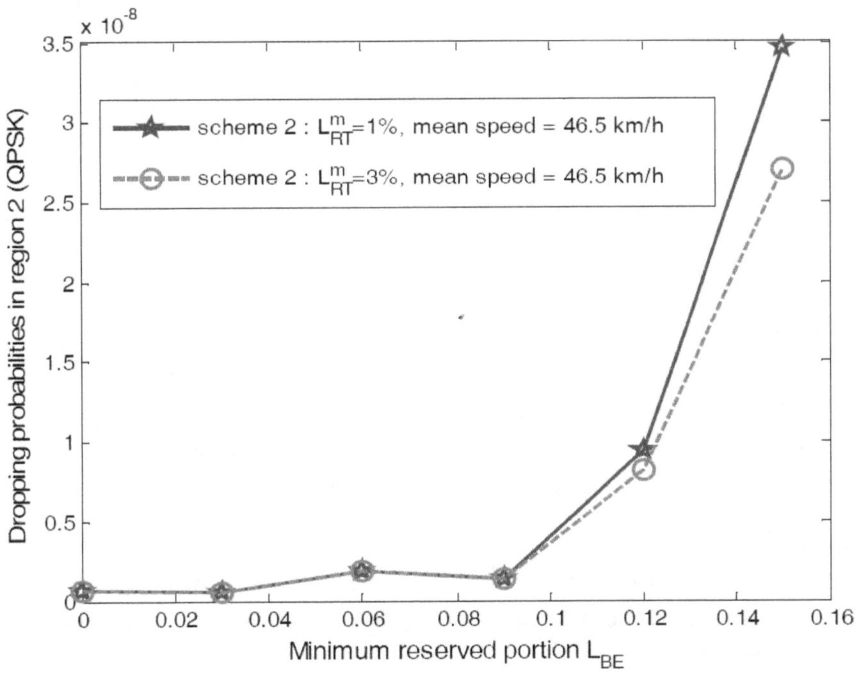

Fig. 10. RT dropping probabilities versus threshold BE L and m RT L for $^{\lambda0}$RT,i = $^{\lambda0}$ BE,i = 0.3 RT i BE i call/sec.

8. CONCISE SUMMARY

Recently, numerous studies have been conducted to analyze WiMAX performance to enhance certain Quality of Service (QoS) for customers. In this regard, our effort enhances the quality of service for users. By analyzing both RT and BE traffic, we offered two methodologies for QoS management. The initial definition establishes constant bit rates (CBR) for real-time (RT) and best effort (BE) communications. We also implement a resource reservation to facilitate user mobility. The second system substitutes the CBR policy for Best Effort calls with a Processor Sharing (PS) approach, and incorporates an additional bandwidth reservation to enhance the minimum throughput of Best Effort calls. Furthermore, we establish a pragmatic mobility model utilizing the precise Random Waypoint model. Utilizing these assumptions, we construct a continuous-time Markov chain that ascertains the system's steady state. We offer an extensive array of performance metrics derived from the model. We end our investigation by critiquing the influence of each CAC algorithm setting on system performance. By consolidating our data, we can readily select one of the two proposed CAC algorithms to align with the required traffic prioritizing policy. Furthermore, we examined potential methods to adjust the parameters of each CAC algorithm to delineate the primary thresholds (average throughput, blocking, and dropping probabilities). In future endeavors, we aim to incorporate cognitive intervals into our RWP model. Our primary purpose is to enhance the CAC algorithms by identifying the optimal method for directing mobile users to a location, based on their speed and the anticipated duration of stay in the subsequent region.

FOOTNOTES

1. This work was supported by a research contract with Maroc Telecom R&D No. 10510005458.06 PI.

REFERENCES

1. Benameur, N.; Ben Fredj, S.; Delcoigne, F.; Oueslati-boulahia, F.; Roberts, J. W.; & Moulineaux, I. L. (2001). Integrated admission control for streaming and elastic traffic. Journal Lecture Notes in Computer Science, Vol. 2156, (February, 2001), pp. 69- 82, ISSN 0302-9347.

2. Bettstetter, C.; Hartenstein, H. & Perez-Costa, X. (2004). Stochastic properties of the random waypoint mobility model. ACM/KluwerWireless Networks: Special Issue on Modeling and Analysis of Mobile Networks, Vol. 10, No. 5, (September, 2004).

3. Chao, X.; Miyazawa, M.; Pinedo, M. & Atkinson, B (2001). Queuing networks: Customers, signals and product form solutions. The Journal of the Operational Research Society, Vol. 52, No. 5, (May, 2001), pages number (600-601).

4. Downey, A.B. (2001). The structural cause of file size distributions. IGMETRICS/ Performance, Vol. 29, No. 1, (June, 2001), pages number (328–329), ISSN 0163-5999.

5. Grossglauser, M. & Tse, D. (2002). Mobility increases the capacity of ad-hoc wireless networks. IEEE/ACM Transactions on Networking, Vol. 10, (August, 2002) pages number (477-486), ISSN 1063-6692.

6. Hyyti, E. & Virtamo, J. (2007). Random waypoint mobility model in cellular networks. Wireless Network, Vol. 13, No. 2, (Avril, 2007), pages number (177-188), ISSN 1022- 0038.

7. Ibrahimi, K.; El-Azouzi, R.; & Bouyakhf, E.H. (2008). Uplink Call Admission Control in Multi-services W-CDMA Network. Proceedings of 13th IEEE Symposium on Computers and Communications (ISCC'08), July 2008, Marrakech, Morocco.

8. Ibrahimi, K.; El-Azouzi, R.; S.K. Samanta; & Bouyakhf, E.H. (2009). Adaptive Modulation and Coding scheme with intra- and inter-cell mobility for HSDPA system. To apear in the Sixth International Conference on Broadband Communications, Networks, and Systems (IEEE/ICST BROADNETS), Septembre 2009, Madrid, Spain.

9. Johnson, D.B. & Maltz, D.A. (1996). Dynamic source routing in ad hoc wireless networks. In the book Mobile Computing, pages number (153–181). Kluwer Academic Publishers.

10. Kobbane, A.; El-Azouzi, R.; Ibrahimi, K. & Bouyakhf, E.H (2007). Capacity Evaluation of multi-service W-CDMA : A Spectral Analysis Approach. Proceedings of the Sixth IASTED International Conference on Communication Systems and Networks, CSN, August 2007, Palma of Mallorca, Spain.

11. Liu, G.O. & Zhou, Z. (2005). Queuing with adaptive modulation and coding over wireless links: Cross-layer analysis and design. IEEE TRANSACTIONS ON WIRELESS COMMUNICATIONS, Vol. 4, No. 3, (May 2005).

12. Niyato, D. & Hossain, E. (2005). Call admission control for qos provisioning in 4G wireless networks: issues and approaches. IEEE Network, Vol. 19, No. 5, (2005) pages number (5–11), ISSN 0890-8044.

13. Norris, J.R. (1999). Markov chains. Cambridge University Press, ISBN = 0-521-68181-3.

14. Peyre, T. & El-Azouzi, R. (2009). IEEE802.16 multi-class capacity including AMC scheme, mobility and QoS differentiation for initial and bandwidth request ranging. To appear in the proceedings of WCNC, Hungary, April 2009, Budapest.

15. Peyre, T.; Ibrahimi, K. & El-Azouzi, R. (2008). IEEE802.16 multi-class capacity including AMC scheme and QoS differentiation for initial and bandwidth request ranging. Proceedings of Valuetools, Greece, October 2008, Athens.
16. Piggin, P. & Depth, W. (2004). Broadband wireless access. IEEE Communications Engineer, Vol. 2, Issue 5, (Octobre 2004), pages number (36-39).
17. Seo, H.H.; Ryu, B.H.; Hwang, E.S.; Cho, C.H. & Lee, N.W. (2004). A study of code partioning scheme of efficient random access in OFDMA-CDMA ranging subsystem. Proceedings of JCCI, pages 262, April 2004.
18. Standard IEEE802.16. (2004). IEEE standard for local and metropolitan area networks, part 16: Air interface for fixed broadband wireless access systems, New York, USA.
19. Tarhini, C. & Chahed, T. (2007). On capacity of OFDMA-based ieee802.16 WiMAX including adaptative modulation and coding and inter-cell intereference. Proceedings of the 15th IEEE Workshop on Local and Metropolitan Area Network (LANMAN), Princeton NJ, June 2007, USA.
20. Yaghoobi, H. (2004). Scalable OFDMA physical layer in IEEE 802.16 Wirelessman. Intel Technology Journal, Vol. 8, (August 2004), pages number (201–212).

23
Chapter

ANALYSIS OF IEEE802.11 WIRELESS LANS UTILIZING QUEUEING MODELS FOR NON-SATURATED NODES

1. INTRODUCTION: AN OVERVIEW

The IEEE 802.11 protocol has achieved significant adoption as a standard MAC-layer protocol for wireless local area networks (WLANs). The IEEE 802.11 standard characterizes the Distributed Coordination Function (DCF) as a contention-based MAC protocol, without quality-of-service (QoS) capabilities. The IEEE 802.11 standard group has sanctioned the 802.11e standard, which introduces MAC layer QoS improvements to the original 802.11 standard, wherein the Enhanced Distributed Channel Access (EDCA) function of 802.11e serves as a QoS enhancement of the Distributed Coordination Function (DCF).

Despite the IEEE 802.11e's assertion of Quality of Service (QoS) support, numerous significant challenges persist in accommodating real-time applications with stringent QoS demands. Within the DCF framework, real-time bidirectional applications such as Voice over IP (VoIP) are unable to effectively leverage the bandwidth of WLANs. The suboptimal bandwidth utilization is primarily attributed to the uplink/downlink unfairness issue in WLANs (Cai et al., 2006). The DCF allocates an equal number of access chances to each mobile terminal and the access point (AP); nevertheless, each mobile terminal manages a single uplink flow, whilst the AP must accommodate all downlink flows. Consequently, a downlink flow inherently receives somewhat less bandwidth than an uplink flow. The disparity between uplink and downlink flows likely exacerbates queue accumulation at the access point (AP) and results in packet loss for downlink flows, even under moderate load, when unused bandwidth persists for uplink flows in a WLAN. This suggests that, with the implementation of bidirectional apps, the access point is likely to become a performance bottleneck compared to regular WLANs. The occupancy of the AP buffer is significantly influenced by the WLAN throughput, which determines the rate at which the AP can effectively transmit frames across the WLAN. Consequently, the efficacy of bidirectional applications over WLANs must be assessed by considering both the occupancy of the access point buffer and the throughput of the IEEE 802.11 Distributed Coordination Function (or Enhanced Distributed Channel Access).

This article introduces a mathematical model for assessing MAC-layer performance, including per-flow throughput, and network-layer performance, specifically packet loss at each station. Our idea integrates a Markov chain model to assess the throughput of the IEEE 802.11 DCF with a queueing model to evaluate the network-layer performance of each station. Our proposal's Markov chain model is fundamentally derived from Malone's model (Malone et al., 2007), enabling the analysis of IEEE 802.11 throughput under unsaturated nodes. However, we have significantly extended their model to account for the impact of incoming IP packets being queued in a station's buffer while the station has frames ready for transmission. To evaluate the performance of the network layer, we utilize the GI/M/1 model, wherein the service time reflects the MAC-layer packet service duration, defined as the period from when a packet arrives at the front of the queue to when it is successfully transmitted. Zhai et al. (2004) demonstrated that the exponential distribution effectively approximates the MAC-layer packet service time, the mean of which can be assessed by the analysis of the IEEE 802.11 DCF. Through comprehensive simulations utilizing the ns2 simulator, we demonstrate that our model can precisely forecast the number of VoIP calls that can be multiplexed across a WLAN without any packet loss. Our model enables the assessment of the IEEE 802.11 DCF with contention window (CW) differentiation, a service differentiation mechanism offered by EDCA. This article examines how the differentiation of contention windows (CW) could enhance bandwidth efficiency by reducing the AP's contention window compared to that of mobile terminals..

2. RELATED WORK

The performance of the IEEE802.11 has been widely studied in the literature. Bianchi (Bianchi, 2000) proposed a two-dimensional Markov chain model to analyze the performance of the IEEE 802.11 DCF under the so-called saturation condition, in which all stations always have data to send. Robinson et al. (Robinson & T.S.Randhawa, 2004) and Xiao (Xiao, 2005) extended Bianchi's DCF model to analyze the performance of the EDCA function of IEEE802.11e under the saturation condition.

Since persistent saturation continues only during a short time period in actual operation, it is important to evaluate the performance of IEEE 802.11 under non-saturation conditions. Ergen et al. (Ergena & Varaiya, 2005) proposed an extension of the Bianchi's DCF model by introduc- ing additional states to the Bianchi's Markov chain to represent idle states of a station. Malone et al. (Malone et al., 2007) developed a different extension of the Bianchi's DCF model; their model allows stations to have different packet-arrival rates. Daneshgaran et al. (Daneshgaran et al., 2008) proposed an analytical model for non-saturated conditions in order to account for packet transmission failures due to errors caused by propagation through the channel. Foh et al. (Foh et al., 2007) proposes to use a queueing model to evaluate the performance of IEEE 802.11 under non-saturated conditions. In their queueing model, customers in the system represent active stations, where being "active" means having frames to send. The Zhao et al. (Zhao et al., 2008) proposed approximating the attempt rate, at which a station attempts to send a frame, in non-saturated setting by scaling the attempt rate of saturated setting with the probability that a packet arrives.

As we have explained, in the use of bidirectional applications, packets are likely to be delayed and dropped in the buffer of the AP. The queueing delay and the packet loss in the buffer of the AP would largely affect the performance of real-time applications. All of the studies mentioned in the above, however, could not analyze the queueing delay and the packet loss at the buffer of the AP or each station. Several proposals have been made to conduct cross- layer analysis where the performance of the network layer such as queueing delay or packet loss at stations is jointly evaluated with the MAC-layer performance such as the throughput (Cheng et al., 2007; Tickoo & Sikdar, 2004; Xiang et al., 2007; Zhai et al., 2004). For example, Zhai et al. (Zhai et al., 2004) integrated the Bianchi's Markov-Chain with a queueing model. Tickoo et al. (Tickoo & Sikdar, 2004) proposed a similar model where a simplified Bianchi's model was used. The proposal by Xiang et al. (Xiang et al., 2007) corresponds to the exten- sion of the Zhai's model to non-saturated conditions. The existing proposals concerning the cross-layer analysis approximate the Bianchi's Markov-chain by a simplified model. Our ana- lytical model, which is categorized into the cross-layer analysis, attempts to directly integrate Bianchi's (or Malone's) Markov-chain with the queueing model.

3. MODEL OF NON-SATURATED STATIONS

In this section, we present a bi-dimensional Markov model for evaluating the performance of IEEE 802.11 DCF under non-saturated conditions. We represent the state of each station by a pair of integers (s(t), b(t)), where s(t) and b(t) respectively denote the back-off stage and counter of a given station (say station A) at time t. We also let $\{t1, t2, \ldots, \}$ denote state transition instants of station A. Note that $\{(s(t), b(t)), t \geq 0\}$ is not a continuous-time Markov process because the inter-state-transition time is not exponentially distributed. The state at state-transition instants $\{(s(tn), b(tn)), n \geq 1\}$, however, would define a Markov chain, where $\{tn\}n \in N$ form imbedded Markovian points. In the following, we focus on the state transitions on imbedded Markovian points and simply represent the state of a station by (s, b), omitting the time parameter t.

3.1 Per-station Markov Model

Assume that there are n stations (one access point and n 1 terminals) in the system. The back-off stage starts at 0 at the first attempt to transmit a packet and increases by 1 every time a transmission attempt results in a collision up to the maximum value. We denote the maximum back-off stage of station l (l = 1, . . . , n) by ml . The maximum back-off stage is related to CWmax through 2ml W0 = CWmax + 1 where W0 = CWmin + 1. The probability that a transmission attempt of station l results in a collision is assumed to be pl . The back-off stage is reset at 0 after a successful transmission. At the back-off stage s, the back-off counter is initially chosen uniformly between [0, Ws – 1], where Ws = 2sW0. The counter decreases by one at the start of every time slot when the medium is sensed idle. Note that the back-off counter is suspended when the medium is busy due to the transmission (or collision) by other stations. When the back-off counter reaches zero, the station attempts to transmit a frame at the start of the next time slot.

When the back-off stage of station l reaches the maximum value ml , it remains ml even if the station consecutively fails to send frames. Note that the frame is discarded and the back-off stage is reset at 0 when the number of consecutive-frame-retransmission exceeds the retry limit. In this article, however, we do not consider the influence on the frame discard due to consecutive transmission failures because the frame discard due to the consecutive retrans- mission failures rarely occur in usual cases. This simplification was also used in Bianchi (Bianchi, 2000) and Malone (Malone et al., 2007).

In non-saturated conditions, a station may not have a frame to transmit just after transmitting a frame and resetting the back-off stage and timer. In this paper, such a station is referred to as being "post-backoff". As used in Malone (Malone et al., 2007), we introduce notation (0, k)e for k ∈ [0, W0 - 1] to represent a post-backoff station with back-off timer k. A station in state (0, k)e makes a transition into (0, k - 1) at the start of the next time slot if (at least) one frame has arrived during the current time slot; otherwise it enters (0, k – 1)e. We assume that the transition probability from state (0, k)e to state (0, k – 1) of station l is ql .

A station in state (k, 0) (0 ≤ k ≤ ml) attempts to transmit a frame at the beginning of the next time slot. In the case of a successful transmission, it makes a transition into one of post- backoff states ((0, k)e, k = 0,. . ., W0 – 1) with probability 1 – rl , and it makes a transition into one of backoff states with stage 0 ((0, k), k = 0,. . ., W0 – 1) with probability rl . In the case of a collision, it enters one of states with back-off stage k + 1 (when 0 ≤ k < ml) or ml (when k = ml). More precisely,

$$\begin{aligned} P[(0,l)_e|(k,0)] &= (1-r_l)(1-p_l)/W_0, \\ P[(0,l)|(k,0)] &= r_l(1-p_l)/W_0, \\ P[(k+1,l)|(k,0)] &= r_l(1-p_l)/W_{k+1}, \quad \text{for } 0 \le k < m_l \\ P[(m,0)|(m,0)] &= r_l(1-p_l)/W_{m_l}. \end{aligned} \tag{1}$$

Parameter rl is the probability that station l has at least one frame after frame transmission. If the back-off counter of the station in post-backoff state reaches 0 but it has no frame, it remains in post-backoff state (0, 0)e. A station in state (0, 0) e receives at least one frame with probability ql during the current time slot. If it receives at least one frame during the current time slot and the medium is sensed idle, it attempts to transmit a frame at the start of the next time slot. In the case of a successful transmission, it makes a transition into one of post- backoff states ((0, k)e, k = 0, . . . , W0 – 1) with probability 1 – ql , and it makes a transition into one of backoff states with stage 0 ((0, k), k = 0, . . . , W0 – 1) with probability ql . In the case of a collision, it enters one of states with back-off stage 1. If a station in state (0, 0)e receives a frame during the current time slot but the medium is sensed busy at the start of the next time slot, it enters one of backoff-states with stage 0. More precisely,

$$\begin{aligned} P[(0,0)_e|(0,0)_e] &= 1-q_l+\frac{q_l(1-p_l)P_{idle}}{W_0}, \\ P[(0,k)_e|(0,0)_e] &= q_l(1-p_l)P_{idle}/W_0, \quad \text{for } k>0 \\ P[(0,k)|(0,0)_e] &= q_l(1-P_{idle})/W_0, \quad \text{for } k \ge 0 \\ P[(1,k)|(0,0)_e] &= q_l p_l P_{idle}/W_1, \quad \text{for } k \ge 0. \end{aligned}$$

3.2 Analysis of the Markov Chain

Figure 1 shows the state transition diagram of the Markov chain. Fortunately, the stationary distribution of the Markov chain can be analytically obtained (see Appendix A). To show this, let b(i, k) denote the stationary probability of being in state (i, k), and let b(i, k)e denote the stationary probability of being in (i, k)e. We can show that the stationary distribution of the state (0, 0)e, b(0, 0)e, is given through the following equation:

$$\begin{aligned} 1/b(0,0)_e = 1-q_l &+ \frac{q_l(W_0+1)}{2(1-r_l)}\left(\frac{q_l W_0}{1-(1-q_l)^{W_0}}\right. \\ &\left. +(1-P_{idle})(1-r_l)-r_l P_{idle}(1-p_l)\right) \\ &+\frac{p_l q_l^2}{2(1-p_l)(1-r_l)}\left(\frac{W_0}{1-(1-q_l)^{W_0}}-\frac{P_{idle}(1-p_l)r_l}{q_l}\right) \\ &\times\left\{1+2W_0\frac{1-p_l-p_l(2p_l)^{m-1}}{1-2p_l}\right\}, \end{aligned} \tag{2}$$

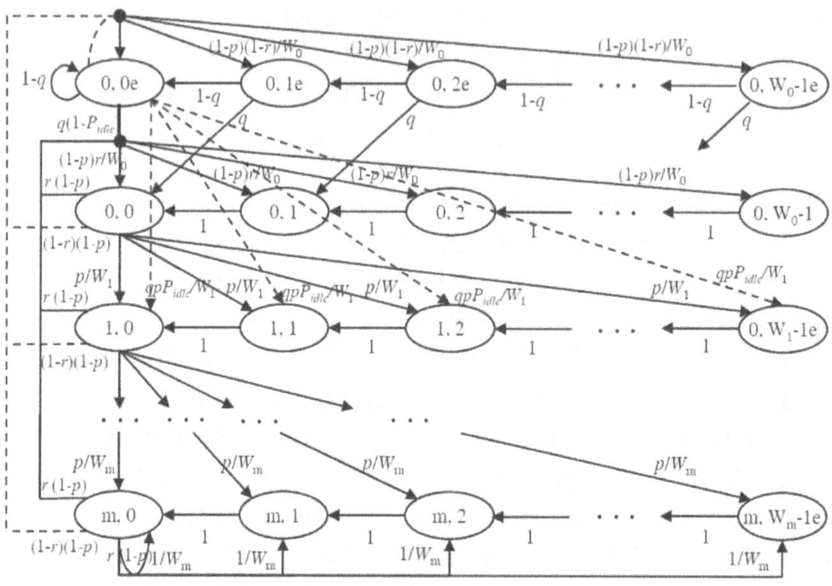

Fig. 1. State transition diagram.

where Pidle is the probability that the medium is idle when the station in state (0, 0)e attempts to transfer a frame. Malone et al. assumed that Pidle = 1 – pl , and we use this assumption in this article. We can explicitly obtain the stationary distribution of other states.

A station in state (k, 0) (0 ≤ k ≤ m) attempts to transmit a frame when the medium is idle at the beginning of the next time slot. A station in state (0, 0)e also attempts transmission at the beginning of the next time slot if (at least) one frame arrives during the current time slot. The probability that station l attempts transmission, Tl , is then given by

$$\tau_l = q_l P_{idle} b(0,0)_e + \sum_{i \geq 0} b(i,0)$$
$$= b(0,0)_e \left(\frac{q_l^2 W_0}{(1-p_l)(1-r_l)(1-(1-q_l)^{W_0})} - \frac{q_l r_l P_{idle}}{1-r_l} \right). \quad (3)$$

As shown in (2), the stationary distribution of each state contains unknown parameter pl , ql , and rl . If packets arrive at station l according to a Poisson process with mean rate λl , we can estimate pl and ql through the following equations:

$$p_l = 1 - \prod_{j \neq l} (1-\tau_j),$$
$$q_l = \left(\prod_j (1-\tau_j) \right) (1-e^{-\lambda_l T_s}) + \left(1 - \prod_j (1-\tau_j) \right) (1-e^{-\lambda_l T_c}). \quad (4)$$

To obtain rl , we assume that the station l can be modeled as a queue with infinite-buffer, and observe that the mean inter-arrival time of packets at station l should be equal to the mean frame-transmission interval of station l if the queue is stable. Now assume that a station enters one of post-backoff or backoff states via absorbing state (0, 0)a after successful frame transmission. (The sojourn time in (0, 0)a is assumed to be zero.) Note that the mean return time to (0, 0)a is equal to the mean frame-transmission interval. With denoting Es the expected time spent per state, it follows from the fact b(0, 0)a = Tl (1 - pl) that

$$\text{mean frame-transmission interval} = \frac{E_s}{b(0,0)_a} = \frac{E_s}{\tau_l(1-p_l)}.$$

Since the mean inter-arrival time of packets is 1/λ,

$$\frac{1}{\lambda} = \frac{E_s}{\tau_l(1-p_l)}, \tag{5}$$

from which we obtain

$$r_l = \left\{1 - q + \frac{q_l(W_0+1)(1-P_{idle})}{2} + \frac{T_F - 1/\lambda_l}{E_s}\frac{q_l^2 W_0}{1-(1-q)^{W0}}\right\} \Big/ \left\{1 - q + \frac{q_l(W_0+1)(1-P_{idle})}{2} + \frac{T_F - 1/\lambda_l}{E_s}(1-p)qP_{idle}\right\}, \tag{6}$$

where TF is the mean MAC-layer packet service time, which is defined as the time interval between the instant that a packet reaches the head of the queue and the instant that the packet is successfully transferred, and it is approximately represented by (8). If the right hand side of (6) exceeds 1, we set rl = 1. Note that the right hand side of (6) exceeds 1 only when station l is congested and thus the frame loss frequently occurs due to the buffer overflow at station l. The expected time spent per state Es is given as follows:

$$E_s = \left(\prod_i (1-\tau_i)\right) T_s + \left(1 - \prod_i (1-\tau_i)\right) T_c,$$

where Ts is the length of time slot, and Tc is the expected time taken for a collision. In this article, we assume that RTS/CTS is disenabled and thus

$$T_c = \frac{\mathrm{ACK} + 2 \times \mathrm{PHY}}{R_b} + \frac{DATA}{R_d} + \mathrm{SIFS} + \mathrm{DIFS},$$

where

- SIFS: SIFS duration
- DIFS: DIFS duration

- ACK: length of ACK frame (without physical header)
- PHY: length of physical header
- DATA: length of date frame (without physical header)
- Rb: basic rate
- Rd: data rate

Equations (3), (4), and (6) are simultaneous equations concerning pj, qj, rj, Tj for j = 1, . . . , n which can be numerically solved by iterative substitution.

Remark 1. The difference between our model and the model by Malone et al. (Malone et al., 2007) is in (1) where Malone et al. assumes rl = ql but our model does not. Parameter ql is the probability that at least one frame arrives at station l during a time slot while rl is the probability that station l has at least one frame after successful frame transmission. Since rl is almost equal to the probability that at least one frame arrives during the mean MAC-layer packet service time, rl is usually larger than ql and both parameters are the same only when station l has no buffer. In this sense, rl = ql is equivalent to the buffer less model where each station is able to have at most one frame.

3.3 Throughput and MAC-layer packet service time

The throughput of a flow is the ratio of the length of a data frame to the inter-frame- transmission time; that is,

$$\text{throughput} = \frac{DATA}{E_s/b(0,0)_a} = \frac{(1-p_l)\tau_l DATA}{E_s}. \tag{7}$$

The MAC-layer packet service time is the interval between the instant that the station enters one of back-off state and the instant that it successfully transmits a frame. The MAC-layer packet service time can be approximated by the interval between the instant entering state (0, 0) and the instant of successful frame transfer, and its mean is given as follows:

$$T_F = \left(\frac{1 + p_l W_0 (2p_l)^m}{2(1-p_l)} + \frac{W_0(1-(2p_l)^{m+1})}{2(1-2p_l)} \right) E_s. \tag{8}$$

4. QUEUEING MODELING FOR IP LAYER ANALYSIS

At mobile terminals, the network layer receives packets from the transport layer. At the AP, network layer receives packets from mobile terminals or a router connected via wired line. Received packets make a queue in the buffer and are sequentially delivered to destinations via the IEEE 802.11-MAC layer. The queueing analysis is required to evaluate the queueing delay in the buffer or the packet loss due to buffer overflow, which have large impact on the end-to-end quality of service of applications. In this section, we show how we could evaluate these performance metrics by the queueing analysis.

4.1 Evaluation of GI/M/1/K+1 model

A queueing model is mainly characterized by the arrival process and the service time distribution. In the current model, the service time corresponds to the MAC-layer packet service time. It was reported in (Zhai et al., 2004) that the exponential distribution is a good approximation for the MAC-layer packet service time, and thus in this article we use this approximation. The exponential distribution is fully characterized by the mean value, which is given by (8). To evaluate the performance under constant-bit-rate traffic like VoIP, we assume that packets arrive according to a renewal process at each station. Under the renewal-process arrival and the exponential service distribution, the queueing behavior of each station is modeled as a GI/M/1/K + 1 model, where the system is able to have at most K + 1 customers (one is server and other K customers in the buffer). Note that it is not difficult to extend the analysis under renewal arrivals to that under some non-renewal (correlated) arrival processes including Markov Modulated Arrival Process (MMPP) or Markovian Arrival Process (MAP) (Neuts, 1981).

The analysis of GI/M/1/K + 1 model is often conducted by the imbedded Markov-Chain technique (Gross & Harris, 1998), where customer arrival instants form imbedded Markovian points. Let πj denote the steady state probability that j customers (packets) stay in the system at arrival instants, and let P = {pij} represents the transition probability matrix:

$$pij = P[Xn{+}1 = j|Xn = i],$$

where Xn denotes the number of customers (frames) in the system at the nth arrival instant. The balance equation is π = πP where π = (π0,. . ., πK+1). We define

$$\beta_K \stackrel{\text{def}}{=} \int \frac{(\mu T)^k}{k!} e^{-\mu x} A(dx),$$

where A(x) is the distribution function of the inter-arrival time. Note that βk is the probability that n customers departs from the queue during the inter-arrival time. It is easy to see that

$$P = \begin{pmatrix} 1-\beta_0 & \beta_0 & 0 & \cdots & 0 & 0 \\ 1-\beta_1-\beta_0 & \beta_1 & \beta_0 & \cdots & 0 & 0 \\ \vdots & \vdots & \vdots & \vdots & \vdots & \vdots \\ 1-\sum_{j=0}^{K-1}\beta_j & \beta_{K-1} & \beta_{K-2} & \cdots & \beta_0 & 0 \\ 1-\sum_{j=0}^{K}\beta_j & \beta_K & \beta_{K-1} & \cdots & \beta_1 & \beta_0 \\ 1-\sum_{j=0}^{K}\beta_j & \beta_K & \beta_{K-1} & \cdots & \beta_1 & \beta_0 \end{pmatrix}.$$

It follows from the balance equation that for j ≥ 1

$$\pi_j = \sum_{k=0}^{K+1-j} \beta_k \pi_{k+j-1} + \beta_{K+1-j} \pi_{K+1},$$

from which

$$\pi_{j-1} = \frac{1}{\beta_0} \left\{ \pi_j - \sum_{k=1}^{K+1-j} \beta_k \pi_{k+j-1} - \beta_{K+1-j} \pi_{K+1} \right\}. \tag{9}$$

Observe that the right-hand-side of the above equation is represented in terms of {πj,. . . , πK+1 }, which enables us to recursively obtain the steady state distribution.

4.2 Average Delay and Loss Ratio

Once we obtain the steady state distribution at arrival instants {πj}K+1, we can evaluate the queueing delay and the loss ratio. For example, the average queueing delay E[D] is given by

$$E[D] = \frac{1}{\mu} \sum_{j=1}^{K+1} k\pi_j.$$

The distribution function of the queueing delay is

$$\begin{aligned} P[D \le x] &= \sum_{j=0}^{K+1} P[D \le x|k] \pi_j \\ &= \sum_{j=0}^{K+1} \left(1 - \sum_{k=0}^{j-1} e^{-\mu x} \frac{(\mu x)^k}{k!} \right) \pi_j. \end{aligned} \tag{10}$$

The packet loss ratio is equal to π_{K+1}.

Table 1. DCF parameters used in the numerical examples

Basic rate	1Mbps
Date rate	11Mbps
PHY header	192bits
MAC header	288bits
ACK length	112bits + PHY header
SIFS	10μs
DIFS	50μs
Slot time	20μs

5. NUMERICAL EXPERIMENTS: EVALUATION OF THE ADMISSIBLE LIMITS OF VOICE FLOWS

5.1 Conditions of Numerical Experiments

In this section, we see the accuracy of the proposed analytical model by comparing numerical analysis and computer simulation results. We used network simulation tools ns2 to obtain simulation results. In the simulation, there were n mobile terminals in an IEEE 802.11b-based wireless LAN. Each mobile terminal conducted a bidirectional voice conversation through the AP with a node outside the WLAN, and thus there were n uplink and n downlink voice flows under n mobile terminals. Each voice flow generated G.711-codec traffic; 200 byte packets (160-byte data and 40-byte RTP/UDP/IP header) were generated every 20 ms in a voice flow. The parameters of the DCF used in the numerical examples is depicted in Table 1. The buffer- sizes of the AP and mobile terminals were all set at 30 in packet.

In the experiments, we evaluated the throughput and packet-loss ratio of each flow. We also investigated how many voice conversations could be multiplexed in the wireless LAN with- out having packet loss, which we refer to as the "multiplexable limit of voice conversations" and denote by Nmax in this article. As mentioned in Section 1, the uplink/downlink unfair- ness in WLANs makes the AP the performance bottleneck under the standard IEEE 802.11 DCF. The CW differentiation between the AP and mobile terminals would provision a fair resource sharing between the uplink and downlink traffic. In the experiments, we investigate how much the CW differentiation enhances the multiplexable limit of voice flows.

5.2 Results of Numerical Experiments

5.2.1 Throughput

We first evaluated the throughput of uplink and downlink voice flows when the contention window parameters of all stations were set at (CWmin, CWmax) = (31, 1023), which are the default setting of the IEEE 802.11. Figure 2 compares analytical and simulation results con- cerning the total throughputs of uplink flows as well as the total throughputs of downlink flows. For reference, we also show the results evaluated by the analytical model of Malone (Malone et al., 2007). The result was given in terms of application level throughput defined by (7), where we exclude the lengths of PHY, MAC, IP, UDP, and RTP headers from the length of data frame. The throughput estimated by our analytical model agrees well with simulation results. Figure 2 shows that the uplink flows obtained larger throughput than the downlink, indicating that the AP was the performance bottleneck.

Figure 3 shows the result when the contention window parameters of the AP were set at (CWmin, CWmax) = (7, 1023). Note that parameter setting (CWmin, CWmax) =

(7, 1023) gives higher priority to the AP over mobile terminals and thus, under this parameter setting, the unfairness between uplink and downlink flows should be improved. Actually, the differ- ence between uplink and downlink flows in the total throughput became smaller than the case when (CWmin, CWmax) = (31, 1023). The throughput estimated by our analytical model agrees well with simulation results when the number of mobile terminals was less than 13, but some discrepancy was observed when the number of mobile terminals was larger than 15. This discrepancy may come from (5) where we neglect the packet loss at the buffer of stations. We also evaluated the throughput when the contention window parameters of the AP were set at (CWmin, CWmax) = (3, 7). The results are shown in Figure 4. In this parameter setting, the downlink flows obtained larger throughput than the uplink, indicating that mobile terminals were the performance bottleneck.

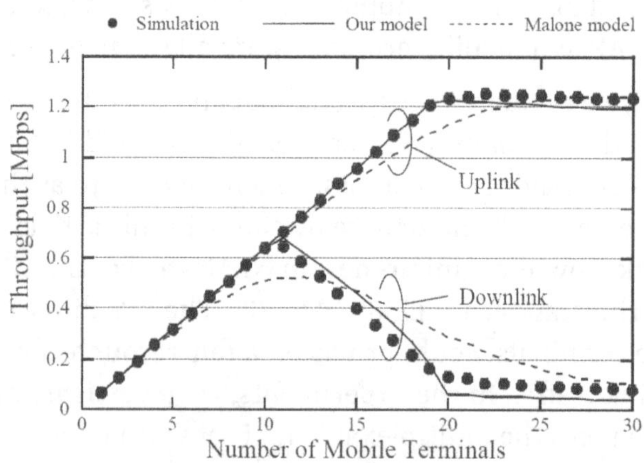

Fig. 2. Throughput versus the number of voice flows: (CWmin, CWmax)= (31, 1023) at the AP.

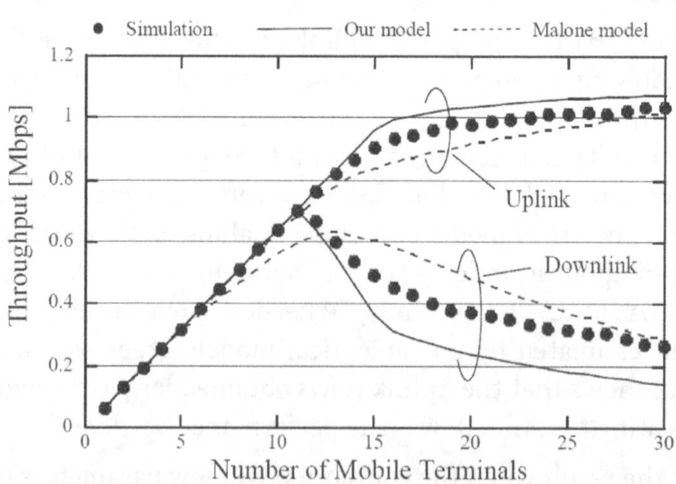

Fig. 3. Throughput versus the number of voice flows: (CWmin, CWmax)= (7, 1023) at the AP.

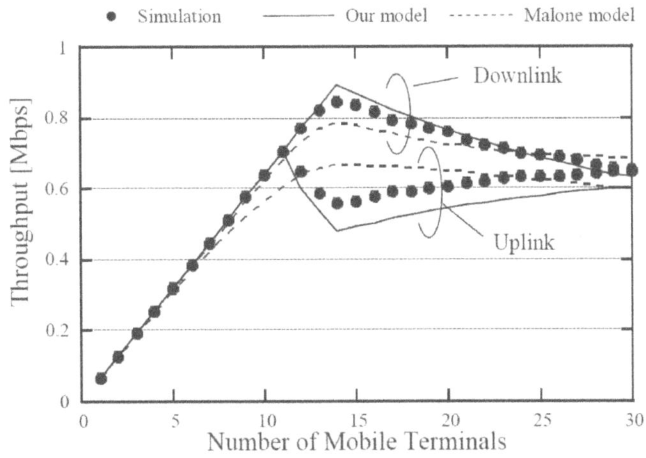

Fig. 4. Throughput versus the number of voice flows: (CWmin, CWmax)= (3, 7) at the AP.

5.2.2 Multiplexable limit of voice conversation

From the total throughput of uplink or downlink flows, we see whether the AP or mobile terminal is overloaded or not. To explain this, let Tup and Tdown respectively denote the total throughput of uplink and downlink flows. Since one voice flow generates 64kbps traffic, if

$$\text{Tdown} = n \times 64\text{kbps} \quad (11)$$

is not satisfied, then the sufficient throughput for downlink flows is not obtained and thus the AP is overloaded, while if

$$\text{Tup} = n \times 64\text{kbps} \quad (12)$$

is not satisfied, then mobile terminals are overloaded. We define the multiplexable limit for downlink (uplink) flows by the maximum number of voice flows satisfying (11) ((12)) and denote it by N↓ max (N↑ max). The multiplexable limit of voice conversation Nmax is equal to min{N↓ max , N↑ max}.

Table 2. Multiplexable limit of voice conversation.

(CWmin, CWmax) of the AP	(31, 1023)			(7, 1023)			(3, 7)		
	N↓ max	N↑ max	Nmax	N↓ max	N↑ max	Nmax	N↓ max	N↑ max	Nmax
Simulation	10	15	10	11	11	11	12	11	11
Our model	10	19	10	11	15	11	13	11	11
Malone model	1	1	1	1	1	1	1	1	1

Table 2 summarizes the multiplexable limits of voice conversations under three different com- binations of congestion window parameters of the AP. The congestion window parameters of mobile terminals were all set at (CWmin, CWmax) = (31, 1023). For all cases, the multi- plexable limits of voice conversations Nmax estimated by our model agreed with the simulation results although some discrepancy was observed in the estimation of Nm↓ ax or Nm↑ ax .

Under the analytical model by Malone et al. (Malone et al., 2007), (11) and (12) were not satisfied when more than one voice conversation were multiplexed. Thus, according their model, Nmax = Nm↑ ax = Nm↓ ax = 1, which was far from the simulation results.

The unbalance between Na↓d and Na↑d when (CWmin, CWmax) = (31, 1023) comes from the uplink/downlink unfairness in WLANs. The table shows that the discrepancy was resolved as the congestion window parameters of the AP became smaller. The multiplexable limit of voice conversation, however, did not increase so much even when the uplink/downlink unfairness was improved.

5.3 Packet Loss Ratio

We also evaluated the packet loss ratios of uplink and downlink voice flows by our analytical model and simulation. Results were depicted in Figure 5 when the contention window pa- rameters of the AP were (CWmin, CWmax) = (31, 1023), in Figure 6 when (CWmin, CWmax) = (7, 1023), and in Figure 7 when (CWmin, CWmax) = (3, 7). These figures indicate that results by our analytical model agree well with the simulation results. The discrepancy between ana- lytical results and simulation may come from that assumption that the mobile terminals have large buffer to temporarily keep frames, which is not satisfied in the setting of ns2.

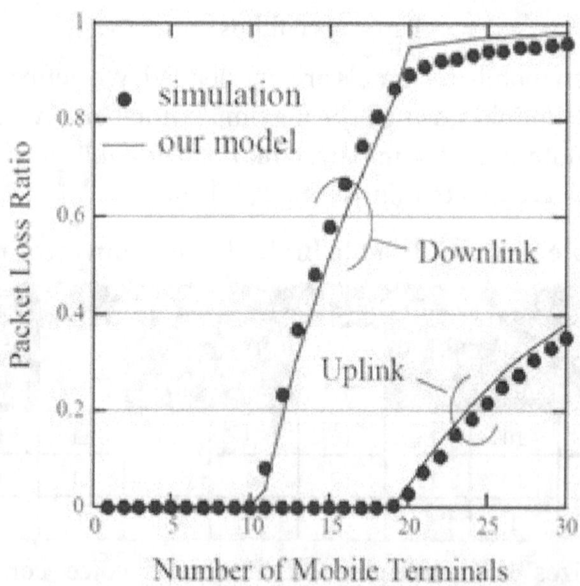

Fig. 5. Packet loss ratio: CWmin=31, CWmax=1023.

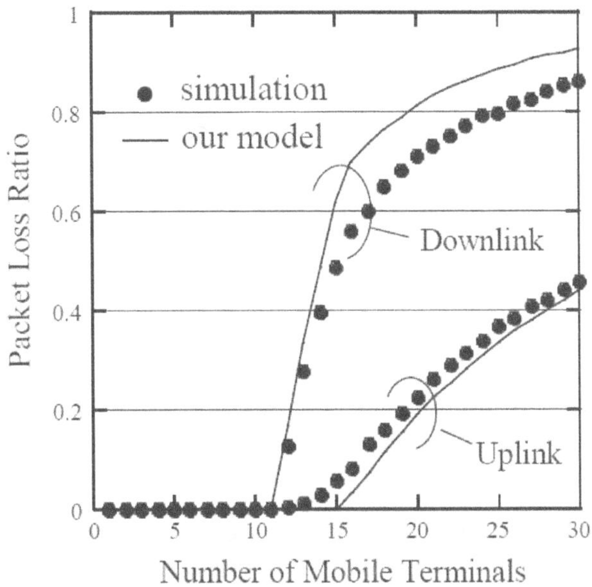

Fig. 6. Packet loss ratio: CWmin=7, CWmax=1023.

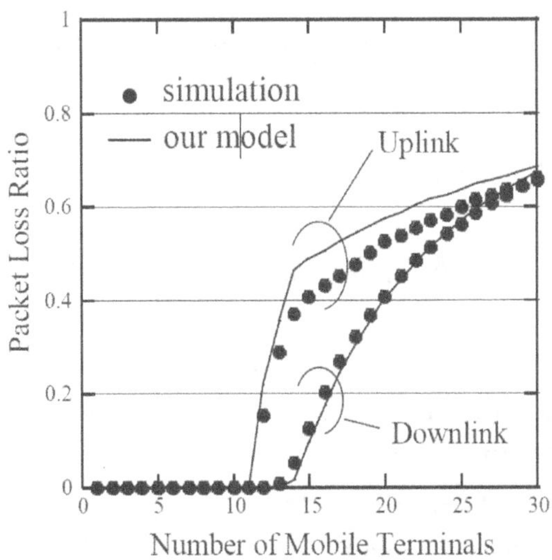

Fig. 7. Packet loss ratio: CWmin=3, CWmax=7.

6. CONCISE SUMMARY

This chapter presents an analytical model for the concurrent assessment of the IEEE 802.11-DCF MAC layer and the network layer performance. Our model effectively assesses the per-flow throughput and packet loss ratio when several uplink and downlink voice flows are multiplexed across a WLAN. A mismatch emerges between the predictions of our model and the simulation results, particularly when the number of multiplexed speech flows is substantial. The cause of the discrepancy requires more investigation. The existing model does not account for frame loss resulting from surpassing the retry limit, which is likewise designated for future development.

REFERENCES

1. Bianchi, G. (2000). Performance analysis of the IEEE802.11 distributed coordination function, IEEE Journal on Selected Areas in Communications 18(3): 535–547.
2. Cai, L., Shen, X., Mark, J., Cai, L. & Xiao, Y. (2006). Voice capacity analysis of wlan with unbalanced trafic, IEEE Trans. Veh. Technol 55(3): 752–761.
3. Cheng, Y., Ling, X., Song, W., Cai, L., Zhuang, W. & Shen, X. (2007). A cross-layer approach for WLAN voice capacity planning, IEEE J. Select. Areas Commun. 25(4): 678–688.
4. Daneshgaran, F., Laddomada, M., Mesiti, F. & Mondin, M. (2008). Unsaturated throughput analysis of IEEE 802.11 in presence of non ideal transmission channel and capture effects, IEEE Trans. Wireless Communications 7(4): 1276–1286.
5. Ergena, M. & Varaiya, P. (2005). Throughput analysis and admission control in IEEE 802.11a, Mobile Networks and Applications 10(5): 705–716.
6. Foh, C., Zukerman, M. & Tantra, J. (2007). A Markovian framework for performance evalua- tion of IEEE 802.11, IEEE Trans. Wireless Communications 6(4): 1276–1285.
7. Gross, D. & Harris, C. (1998). Fundamentals of Queueing Systems, 3rd Ed., John Wiley & Sons.
8. Malone, D., Duffy, K. & Leith, D. (2007). Modelling the 802.11 distributed coordination function in non-saturated heterogeneous conditions, IEEE/ACM Trans. Networking 15(1): 159–172.
9. Neuts, M. (1981). Matrix-Geometric Solutions in Stochastic Models: An Algorithmic Approach, The Johns Hopkins University Press.
10. Robinson, J. & T.S.Randhawa (2004). Saturation throughput analysis of IEEE802.11e enhanced distributed coordination function, IEEE J. Select. Areas Commun. 33(5): 917–928.
11. Tickoo, O. & Sikdar, B. (2004). Queueing analysis and delay mitigation in IEEE802.11 random access MAC based wireless networks, IEEE INFOCOM, pp. 1404–1413.
12. Xiang, B., Yu-Ming, M. & Jun, X. (2007). Performance investigation of IEEE802.11e EDCA un- der non-saturation condition based on the M/G/1/K models, IEEE ICIEA, pp. 298– 304.

13. Xiao, Y. (2005). Performance analysis of priority schemes for IEEE802.11 and IEEE802.11e wireless LANs, IEEE Trans. Wireless Communications 4(4): 1506–1515.

14. Zhai, H., Kwon, Y. & Fang, Y. (2004). Performance analysis of IEEE 802.11 MAC protocols in wireless LANs, Wireless Communications and Mobile Computing 4: 917–931.

15. Zhao, Q., Tsang, H. & Sakurai, T. (2008). A simple model for nonsaturated IEEE 802.11 DCF networks, IEEE Communication Letters 12(8): 563–565.

A. Analysis of the Markov chain of Figure 1

Since b(i + 1, 0)= pb(i, 0) for i ≥ 1 and b(1, 0)= b(0, 0)p + b(0, 0)eqpPidle, we obtain

$$\sum_{i\geq 1} b(i,0) = \frac{b(1,0)}{1-p} = \frac{b(0,0)p + b(0,0)_e qpP_{idle}}{1-p}. \tag{13}$$

The balance equation concerning state $(0, W_0 - 1)_e$ yields

$$b(0,W_0-1)_e = b(0,0)_e \frac{q(1-p)P_{idle}}{W_0} + \frac{(1-p)(1-r)}{W_0}\sum_{i\geq 0} b(i,0).$$

Substituting (13) into the above yields

$$b(0,W_0-1)_e = b(0,0)_e \frac{q(1-rp)P_{idle}}{W_0} + b(0,0)\frac{1-r}{W_0}. \tag{14}$$

From the balance equation concerning state (0, k)e, we have

$$\begin{aligned} b(0,k)_e &= (1-q)b(0,k+1)_e + b(0,W_0-1)_e, \quad \text{for } W_0-1>k>0, \\ qb(0,0)_e &= (1-q)b(0,1)_e + b(0,W_0-1)_e, \end{aligned} \tag{15}$$

from which for k > 0

$$b(0,k)_e = b(0,W_0-1)_e \frac{1-(1-q)^{W_0-k}}{q}, \tag{16}$$

and

$$qb(0,0)_e = b(0,W_0-1)_e \frac{1-(1-q)^{W_0}}{q}. \tag{17}$$

Substituting (14) into (17) yields

$$\frac{b(0,0)_e}{b(0,0)} = \frac{1-r}{q}\frac{1-(1-q)^{W_0}}{qW_0 - P_{idle}(1-rp)(1-(1-q)^{W_0})}. \tag{18}$$

It follows from (16) and (17) that

$$\sum_{k=1}^{W_0-1} b(0,k)_e = b(0,0)_e \left\{ \frac{W_0 q}{1-(1-q)^{W_0}} - 1 \right\},$$

and thus

$$\sum_{k=0}^{W_0-1} b(0,k)_e = b(0,0)_e \frac{W_0 q}{1-(1-q)^{W_0}}. \tag{19}$$

Next we consider the stationary probability of state (0, k). The balance equation concerning state (0, W0 – 1) yields

$$\begin{aligned} b(0,W_0-1) &= \sum_{k\geq 0} b(k,0)\frac{(1-p)r}{W_0} + b(0,0)_e \frac{q(1-P_{idle})}{W_0} \\ &= \left\{ b(0,0) + \frac{b(0,0)p + b(0,0)_e qpP_{idle}}{1-p} \right\} \frac{(1-p)r}{W_0} + b(0,0)_e \frac{q(1-P_{idle})}{W_0} \\ &= \left\{ \frac{b(0,0) + b(0,0)_e qpP_{idle}}{1-p} \right\} \frac{(1-p)r}{W_0} + b(0,0)_e \frac{q(1-P_{idle})}{W_0} \\ &= b(0,0)\frac{r}{W_0} + b(0,0)_e \frac{q}{W_0}\{1-(1-pr)P_{idle}\}. \end{aligned} \tag{20}$$

It comes from the balance equation concerning state (0, k) that for W0 – 1 > k ≥ 0

$$\begin{aligned} b(0,k) &= b(0,k+1) + b(0,W_0-1) + qb(0,k+1)_e \\ &= b(0,k+1) + b(0,W_0-1) + b(0,W_0-1)_e(1-(1-q)^{W_0-k-1}) \\ &= (W_0-k)b(0,W_0-1) + b(0,W_0-1)_e \sum_{n=1}^{W_0-1-k} \{1-(1-q)^n\} \\ &= (W_0-k)(b(0,W_0-1) + b(0,W_0-1)_e) - b(0,W_0-1)_e \frac{1-(1-q)^{W_0-k}}{q}. \end{aligned} \tag{21}$$

Combining (14), (20), and (21) yields

$$\begin{aligned} \sum_{k=0}^{W_0-1} b(0,k) &= b(0,0)\left\{ \frac{W_0+1}{2} - \frac{1-r}{q} + \frac{(1-q)(1-(1-q)^{W_0})(1-r)}{q^2 W_0} \right\} \\ &+ b(0,0)_e \left\{ \frac{q(W_0+1)}{2} - (1-rp)P_{idle} + \frac{P_{idle}(1-q)(1-rp)(1-(1-q)^{W_0})}{qW_0} \right\} \end{aligned} \tag{22}$$

By representing b(0, 0) in (22) in terms of b(0, 0)e through (18), we obtain

$$\begin{aligned} \sum_{k=0}^{W_0-1} b(0,k) = b(0,0)_e \frac{q}{1-r}&\left\{ \frac{qW_0}{1-(1-q)^{W_0}} - P_{idle}(1-rp) \right\} \\ &\times \left\{ \frac{W_0+1}{2} - \frac{1-r}{q} + \frac{(1-q)(1-(1-q)^{W_0})(1-r)}{q^2 W_0} \right\} \\ &+ b(0,0)_e \left\{ \frac{q(W_0+1)}{2} - (1-rp)P_{idle} + \frac{P_{idle}(1-q)(1-rp)(1-(1-q)^{W_0})}{qW_0} \right\} \end{aligned}$$

$$= b(0,0)_e \left[1 - q - \frac{qW_0}{1-(1-q)^{W_0}} + \frac{q(W_0+1)}{2(1-r)} \times \left(\frac{qW_0}{(1-(1-q)^{W_0})} + (1-P_{idle})(1-r) - rP_{idle}(1-p) \right) \right]. \tag{23}$$

Since b(i, k)= (Wi - k)/Wib(i, 0) for i > 0, it follows that

$$\sum_{k=0}^{W_i-1} b(i,k) = b(i,0)\frac{W_i+1}{2},$$

from which we have

$$\begin{aligned}\sum_{i=1}^{} \sum_{k=0}^{W_i-1} b(i,k) &= \sum_{i=1}^{m} b(i,0)\frac{W_i+1}{2} + \sum_{i=m+1}^{\infty} b(i,0)\frac{W_m+1}{2} \\ &= \frac{b(1,0)}{2}\left\{ \sum_{i=1}^{m} p^{i-1}(W_0 2^i + 1) + \sum_{i=m+1}^{\infty} p^{i-1}(W_0 2^m + 1) \right\} \\ &= \frac{b(1,0)}{2}\left\{ \frac{1}{1-p} + \frac{2W_0(1-(2p)^m)}{1-2p} + \frac{W_0(2p)^m}{1-p} \right\} \\ &= \frac{b(1,0)}{2(1-p)}\left\{ 1 + 2W_0\frac{1-p-p(2p)^{m-1}}{1-2p} \right\}. \end{aligned} \tag{24}$$

It comes from (13) and (18) that

$$b(1,0) = b(0,0)_e \frac{pq^2}{1-r}\left(\frac{W_0}{1-(1-q)^{W_0}} - \frac{P_{idle}(1-p)r}{q} \right). \tag{25}$$

By substituting (19), (23), (24), and (25) into the normalization condition

$$\sum_{i=0}^{} \sum_{k=0}^{W_i-1} b(i,k) + \sum_{k=0}^{W_i-1} b(0,k)_e = 1,$$

we finally have

$$\begin{aligned} 1/b(0,0)_e &= 1 - q + \frac{q(W_0+1)}{2(1-r)}\left(\frac{qW_0}{(1-(1-q)^{W_0})} + (1-P_{idle})(1-r) - rP_{idle}(1-p) \right) \\ &+ \frac{pq^2}{2(1-p)(1-r)}\left(\frac{W_0}{1-(1-q)^{W_0}} - \frac{P_{idle}(1-p)r}{q} \right)\left\{ 1 + 2W_0\frac{1-p-p(2p)^{m-1}}{1-2p} \right\} \end{aligned} \tag{26}$$

Once we have obtained b(0, 0)e, the stationary probabilities of other states are easy to calculate.

24 Chapter

EXTENDING CONNECTIVITY DURATION TO EXISTING 802.11 WIRELESS NETWORKS WHILE COMMUTING VIA SUBWAY

1. INTRODUCTION: AN OVERVIEW

Recently, a growing number of individuals access diverse material through the Internet utilizing a publish/subscribe service, such as podcasts. The standard use of these applications involves subscribing to numerous preferred sites and selectively enjoying the automatically downloaded latest episodes. Recently released portable multimedia players allow individuals to conveniently access downloaded video and audio content in diverse locations, while integrated communication features such as 3G or 802.11 facilitate the immediate retrieval of newly published episodes online.

Services such as podcasts are particularly advantageous for individuals commuting by subway, given their idle time on the train. As of December 2008, the majority of subway tunnels in Tokyo remain regrettably devoid of both 3G and 802.11 coverage. A wireless connection can be formed when a subway train is within coverage regions at a station; however, it will be consistently interrupted once the train traverses non-coverage areas in the tunnels during transit along the railroad. This interruption constrains the duration within coverage areas, hence diminishing the maximum potential connected time. This duration is further diminished due to the current solution inadequately using intermittent connectivity. This chapter examines 802.11 wireless connection management during subway transit because to its superior throughput, reduced subscription costs, and greater diversity of 802.11-enabled portable devices compared to 3G.

Our objective is to enhance the connectivity duration of existing 802.11 wireless networks for podcast-like applications while commuting on the Tokyo subway. To comprehend the target environment, we examined the commercial 802.11 HOTSPOT networks (NTT Communications HOTSPOT, [Online]) implemented in Tokyo Metro. One of the findings against the common belief regarding long distance mobility is that the main factor to the diminishment of available connected time is link layer connection management, not IP layer mobility support because of the deployed VLANs across the target networks. We present an efficient strategy for this subway setting to enhance connectivity by mitigating two specific types of delay. The delay occurs when establishing the wireless connection after exiting a non-coverage area in the tunnel, then again when transitioning the wireless connection to the subsequent access point while traversing overlapping coverage areas at stations.

Our approach minimizes the establishment latency by creating a connection between the last access point (AP) at the preceding station before the tunnel and the initial AP at the subsequent station after the tunnel, referred to as border APs in this chapter. By utilizing this chain when departing a station, a client can minimize the latency in establishing a connection by employing passive scanning exclusively on the channel associated with the forthcoming border AP. The switching delay is minimized by compiling a list of the access points (APs) accessible at each station for which a client possesses connection authorization, referred to as preferred APs in this chapter. By consulting this list when traversing overlapping coverage zones inside a station, a client can minimize connection-switching delays by employing unicast scans with Authentication Request frames directed at a select group of preferred access points. This is achievable by using the critical characteristics of the target environment: robust mobility patterns along a train and a restricted number of access points at each station. Our investigation reveals that the delay achieved by our method is 94.4% less than that of passive scanning for establishing terminated wireless connections, and 94.2% less than that of active scanning while transitioning wireless connections to the subsequent access point..

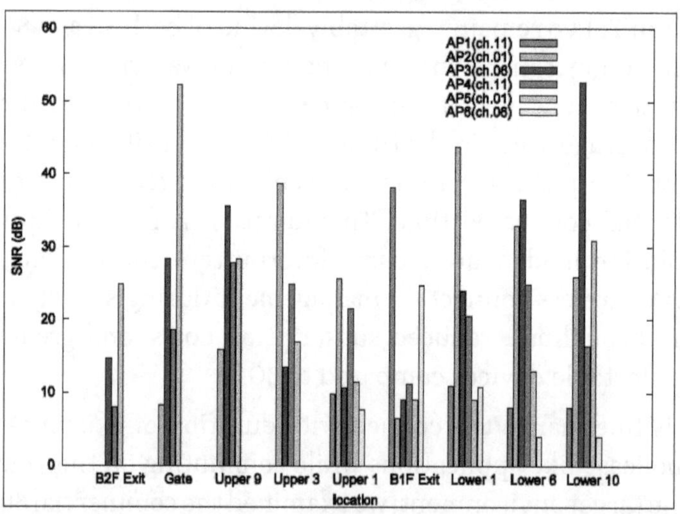

Fig. 1. Averaged SNR values of beacon frames measured at different locations in Waseda (T4) station. The names of location refer to Fig. 2.

2. TARGET ENVIRONMENT INVESTIGATION

In order to find out the factors that decrease the possible connected time, we investigate the commercial 802.11 HOTSPOT network in Tokyo Metro. All experiments were performed with a windows XP machine while walking at stations and moving by subway in November 2008. NetStumbler (NetStumbler, [Online]), Wireshark (Wireshark, [Online]), and built-in Wireless Auto Configuration were used to monitor beacon frames, analyze IP packets and manage 802.11 wireless network connections. The findings are classified by the points of our interest: link layer handoff, IP mobility support, and restrictions on application layer. This section discusses each of them in detail.

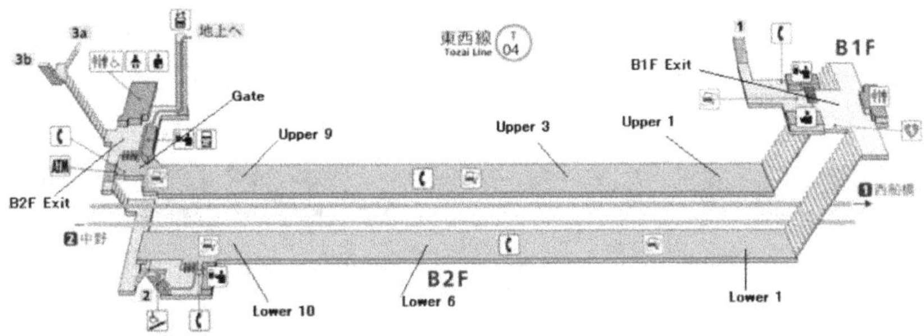

Fig. 2. Waseda (T4) station structure (Tokyo Metro, [Online]) There are six 802.11g APs installed on channel 1, 6 and 11 to collaboratively cover the station including entrances, ticket gates, platforms, etc.

2.1 Link Layer Handoff

To find the necessity of link layer handoff in 802.11 HOTSPOT3, we studied coverage areas at stations by measuring the averaged SNR values of beacon frames at different locations in 10 stations4 . In each station, multiple APs ranging from four to seven are installed to collaboratively cover entrances, ticket gates, platforms, passages for transfer, etc. Figure 1 shows an example of the measured results in Waseda (T4) station on Tozai line, whose structure is as shown in Figure 2. From the figure we observe that: 1) the coverage area of a single AP is not large enough to cover the entire station, and 2) each location is under coverage areas of multiple APs. Therefore, while a client moves around at stations, it is necessary to switch the wireless connection across overlapping wireless coverage areas. For example, let us assume that a subway train comes in from right in Figure 2. The clients in the train get associated to AP2 according to Figure 1. For some clients staying in the train, the established wireless connection will be switched from AP2 to AP3, when the train moves to the left for the next station. For others getting off the subway train at Lower 1 on the platform and walk out B1F Exit, the wireless connection will be switched from AP2 to AP1. Unlike stations with overlapping coverage areas, there are non-coverage areas in each tunnel between stations. To show non-coverage areas in tunnels, we measured the time stamps of received beacon frames while moving by subway through seven stations from Nihombashi (T10) to Waseda (T4) station on Tozai line. The measured results are shown in Table 1. From the table we observe that: 1) there exist non-coverage areas in each tunnel, and 2) the time length under non-coverage areas is approximately one third of the total moving time on a railroad. This is explained by different speeds of subway when passing above two areas: high speed within large non-coverage areas in the tunnels and low speed within small coverage areas in the stations. Though there is large period of time spent under coverage of 802.11 wireless networks even while traveling by subway, the wireless connection is repeatedly interrupted due to non-coverage areas in the tunnel. Therefore, it is necessary to establish disconnected wireless connection whenever the client enters the following coverage areas.

Table 1. Non-coverage areas in the tunnels

Station	Coverage Area	Non-coverage Area
Nihombashi (T10)	83 sec	20 sec
Otemachi (T9)	66 sec	56 sec
Takebashi (T8)	69 sec	36 sec
Kudanshita (T7)	70 sec	29 sec
Iidabashi (T6)	81 sec	53 sec
Kagurazaka (T5)	81 sec	55 sec

2.2 IP Mobility Support

To find the necessity of IP mobility support, we studied IP network configuration by dumping and analyzing IP packets. After a successful association using the proper ESSID (i.e., 0033) and WEP key, a global IP address is assigned via Dynamic Host Configuration Protocol (DHCP) (Droms, 1997). The DHCP server has multiple ranges of address pool. It is possible to have various addresses assigned with the same client and AP at different times. To show the range of DHCP address pool, we collected the obtained TCP/IP address configuration with a single AP at different times in Yoyogi-uehara (C1) station on Chiyoda line. Part of the collected information is shown in Table 2.

Table 2. The range of DHCP address pool

Host address	Subnet Mask	Default Gateway
210.162.9.65	255.255.254.0	210.162.9.1
211.0.159.54	255.255.254.0	211.0.159.1
61.127.100.37	255.255.254.0	61.127.100.1

Once an IP address is assigned in the beginning of a session, the same address is repeatedly assigned not only from different APs in the same station, but also from the APs in other stations by another DHCP request during the DHCP lease length. We confirmed this fact by starting a session at Yoyogi-uehara (C1) station, and receiving the same IP address from two different APs in the same station and also receiving it in other stations such as Yoyogi-koen (C2), Meiji-jingumae (C3), Omote-sando (C4), etc.

From above two experiments, we observe that HOTSPOT implements Virtual Local Area Network (VLAN) (IEEE Standard 802.1Q-2003, 2003) to accommodate multiple subnets in each physical LAN, and therefore, IP layer mobility support is unnecessary. The initially assigned IP address does not need to be changed, as long as it performs DHCP lease renewal every lease length (i.e., 5 minutes). In order to prevent DHCP renewal from failing in the non-coverage areas in the tunnels, it is necessary to perform DHCP renewal with a shorter interval: (lease length) - (the maximum time spent in the non-coverage areas). As shown in Table 1, the time spent in non-coverage areas in the tunnels are much shorter than the lease length, therefore, we can perform the DHCP discovery only once in the beginning of the session, and skip it later on by renewing DHCP with the above shorter interval.

2.3 Restrictions on Application Layer

NTT Communications HOTSPOT implements web-based authentication to complement the open system authentication. Despite a successful TCP/IP address configuration via DHCP, a client is unable to send and receive data traffic outside the network. To gain Internet access outside the network, users are required to enter a username and password in an authentication web page, to which the first attempt to access any web page after launching a web browser is automatically redirected. We also found that the web authentication expires when there is no traffic sent or received during DHCP lease length (i.e., 5 minutes). Again, as the time spent in non-coverage areas in the tunnels are much shorter than the lease length, it needs to be done only once in the beginning of the session in our subway mobility scenario. Moreover, a download manager such as DownThemAll (DownThemAll, [Online]) is necessary to automatically resume broken downloads due to the intermittent connectivity.

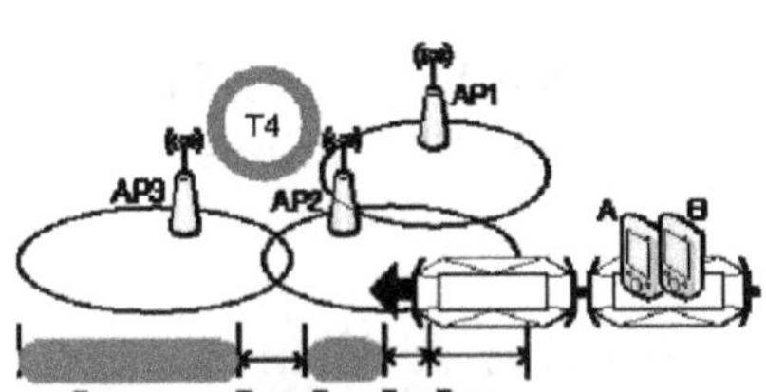

Fig. 3. Mobility scenario

3. INCREASING TIME CONNECTED WHILE TRAVELING BY SUBWAY

In this section, we describe our proposed method to increase the time connected to 802.11 wireless networks while traveling by subway. We look into the detailed composition of the main factor to the diminishment of available connected time, and propose a method to address them.

3.1 Problem Statement

To clarify the problems arising from utilizing 802.11 wireless connection while traveling by subway, consider the following scenario depicted in Figure 3. Assume that two clients (A and B) took a subway train in the previous T5 station downloading subscribed podcasts with 802.11-enabled portable devices. The wireless connection is terminated while passing through the non-coverage area in the tunnel. When the train is entering T4 station, the devices discover that they become under coverage area, scan available APs, and get connected to AP2. When the train stops at T4 station, client A gets off and walk to the coverage area of AP1, but client B stays in the train and moves to the next station passing through the coverage area of AP3.

Given that we do not modify the commercially deployed APs to enlarge coverage areas, the maximum connected time of devices passing through T4 station (e.g., client B) is limited shown in Figure 3, and only some parts Tdata of it is used to download subscribed podcasts. This limited time is also used to recognize the coverage area of the firstly appearing AP and establish link layer connection to it (Testablish), to check the availability of a previously used IP address via DHCP Request message (Tdhcp), and switch link layer connection to a closer AP (Tswitch). Since DHCP request can be skipped by DHCP renew with shorter interval as shown in the previous section, the main factor to the diminishment of available connected time is composed of Testablish and Tswitch for the link layer connection management.

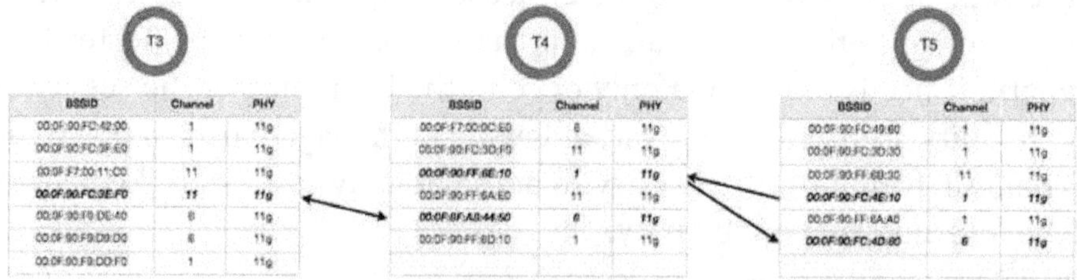

Fig. 4. An example of a chain of border APs and a list of preferred APs in T3, T4 and T5 stations

3.2 Proposed Method

In order to reduce the delay experienced when managing link layer connection, we take advantage of the following key attributes of the target environment: 1) strong mobility pattern along a railroad, and 2) limited number of APs at each station.

3.2.1 Fast Connection Establishment after Coming out of Non-coverage Areas

In order to reduce the delay experienced when establishing link layer connection (Testablish), a client needs to discover that it came out of non-coverage areas in the tunnel, and find the AP to associate to with less scanning delay. Because the standard does not define the behavior when no AP is found during scanning process, periodical active scanning is commonly implemented for a general purpose. For example, Wireless Auto Configuration in Windows XP, executes active scanning every 60 seconds (Microsoft Technet, [Online]) when no preferred AP is found during channel scanning phase. However, this periodic scanning makes Testablish up to in the magnitude of tens of seconds in subway mobility scenario due to this coverage area recognition delay. Therefore, it is necessary to perform channel scanning continuously, when no AP is found in the tunnel.

We reduce Testablish by continuously performing selective passive scan, which does not generate excessive management traffic under non-coverage area in the tunnel. Taking advantage of a strong mobility pattern along a railroad, we build a chain that links the last AP in the previous station before the tunnel with the first AP in the next station after the tunnel, called border APs. By referring to this chain when leaving a station, a client can reduce Testablish through the use of passive scan only on the channel corresponding to the upcoming border AP. For example, back in Figure 1, AP2 in T4 station is the border AP appearing at the end of non-coverage area in the tunnel from T5 station. A part of a chain of border APs regarding T3 (1 border AP), T4 (2 border APs), and T5 (2 border APs) stations is shown in Figure 4. The border APs are related by arrows with the information of BSSID, channel number, and PHY type.

The connection establishment process is performed in the following steps. When a client can not find any APs after being disconnected from a border AP (e.g., 00:0F:90:FC:4E:10 AP in T5 station), it assumes that it is passing through non-coverage area in the tunnel and looks up its chain of border APs to find next border AP (e.g., 00:0F:90:FF:6E:10 AP in T4 station). Then, it sets up its interface to the desired channel and PHY type (e.g., channel 1 and 11b/g), and waits for a beacon from the next border AP. If a beacon from the border AP arrives within the maximum time spent in the non-coverage area, a client executes authentication and association phase. Otherwise, standard active scan is excuted to handle this unexpected case where the pre-built chain of border APs can not reflect the real situation due to changes in infrastructure or unexpected non-coverage area, etc.

The delay of selective passive scan is as follows. Under the best case scenario the beacon arrives as soon as the device enters the coverage area, so the delay is 0. The worst case happens when the device just missed beacon when it enters the coverage area, so the delay is the same as beacon interval, 100 msec by default.

Therefore, the highest Testablish will be composed of one beacon interval for the selective passive scan, one RTT for authentication, and one RTT for association phase.

3.2.2 Fast Connection Switching across Overlapping Coverage Areas

In order to reduce the delay experienced when switching link layer connection Tswitch across overlapping coverage areas, a client needs to find the next AP to handoff with less scanning delay. Because a client has flexible mobility patterns in a station, referring to a chain of border APs can not tell clients staying in the train to go to next station from ones getting off to go to other direction, leading to executing active scan. Active scan takes long, because it tries to acquire the information about all nearby APs regardless of a client's connection authorization. Therefore, it is necessary to perform channel scanning only to the target APs that the client has connection authorization.

We reduce Tswitch by performing multiple open system authentication only to target APs at each station, called AuthScan (Ok et al., 2008). Taking advantage of limited number of APs at each station, we build a list of the APs available at each station for which a client has connection authorization, called preferred APs. By referring to this list when crossing overlapping coverage areas in a station, a client can reduce Tswitch through the use of unicast scan using Authentication Request frames to the limited number of preferred APs. For example, back in Figure 1, there are only six APs of which a client has connection authorization in Waseda (T4) station. A part of a possible preferred AP list regarding T3 (7 APs), T4 (6 APs), and T5 (6 APs) stations is shown in Figure 4. The information is composed of BSSID, channel number, and PHY type. In addition, other common beacon information such as capability information, SSID, supported rates, PHY parameter sets, and WPA parameters needs to be saved for the successful handoff completion.

The connection switching process is performed in the following steps. When detecting the need for switching the current link based on its policy (e.g. signal strength, transmission rate, missed beacon number, retransmission number, etc), a client looks up its preferred AP list and selects one except its currently associated AP in the same station as a target AP. Then, it sets up its interface to the desired channel and PHY type, transmits an Authentication Request frame to the target AP, and waits for an Authentication Response during MinChannelTime, a time parameter involved in active scan long enough to guarantee the reception of a Probe Response frame. This process is repeated for all the remaining APs in the list. After the next AP is selected by comparing the Received Signal Strength Indications (RSSIs) measured when receiving Authentication Response frames from each AP, a client executes authentication and association phase. The algorithmic flow of our system including selective passive scan and AuthScan is shown in Figure 5.

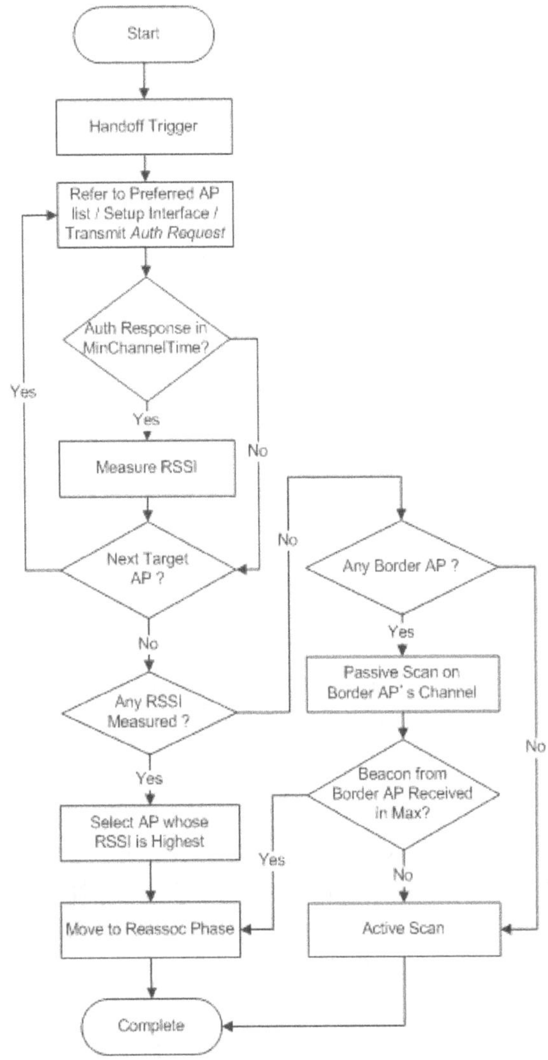

Fig. 5. The algorithmic flow of our system including AuthScan and selective passive scan

The delay of AuthScan is as follows. Assuming at least one of the target APs is available and can fulfill the handoff policy, it takes M * RTT + (N - M) * MinChannelTime, where N is the number of target APs that exclude the associated AP before handoff in the preferred AP list at each station, and M is the number of Authentication Response frames received. The total connection switching delay Tswitch will be composed of M * RTT + (N - M) * MinChannelTime due to the scanning process, one RTT for authentication, and one RTT for association phase. This achieves channel scanning with lowest delay among the approaches to work under subway's intermittent connectivity without modifying deployed APs as shown in the next section.

4. INCREASED CONNECTED TIME COMPARISON

In this section, we introduce the related work and analyze the increased connected time by our proposed method in a subway mobility scenario.

4.1 Limitations of Related Work

Many approaches have been proposed to address the channel scanning issues, and can be classified into two groups as below. The first group tries to eliminate the necessity for the channel scanning phase. Some approaches decouple the time-consuming channel scan from the actual handoff phase and scan earlier for maintaining a list of candidate APs with their handoff metrics before the connection to the current AP is terminated (Ramani & Savage, 2005; Wu et al., 2007). Other approaches enable scanning while communicating with the currently associated AP utilizing multiple NICs (Brik et al, 2005; Ok et al, 2007). Though the total handoff delay of these approaches in the first group is shorter than that of our proposed method, none of the above related work can be applied in our subway environment. (Ramani & Savage, 2005; Wu et al., 2007; Brik et al, 2005) can not generate a list of candidate APs with their handoff metrics before the connection to the current AP is terminated under subway's intermittent connectivity. (Ramani & Savage, 2005; Ok et al, 2007) require modification to APs, and (Brik et al, 2005; Ok et al, 2007) require extra hardware on a client.

The second group tries to improve the efficiency of the channel scanning phase. The first way to do this is to reduce the number of channels that are effectively going to be scanned by the client. This can be achieved through various methods such as a cache (Shin et al., 2004), Neighbor Graph (NG) (Mishra et al., 2004), sensor overlay network (Waharte et al., 2004), etc. Another way to improve the efficiency is by reducing the time waiting at each channel. In order to do this, a client is provided with an AP list, and only scans target APs in a unicast fashion to reduce the time to wait at each channel (Ok et al., 2008; Kim et al., 2004; Jeong et al., 2003; Huang et al., 2006). The performance of these approaches depend on the number of channels to scan or deployed APs, but this is not an issue in our target environment, where there are limited number of APs available. Among these, AuthScan achieves the lowest handoff delay, one RTT less than selective unicast scan (Kim et al., 2004) without modifying standard.

4.2 Performance Comparison

To show the increased connected time by our method, we estimate the interrupted time under coverage areas (Testablish and Tswitch) by various methods. Firstly, we compare Testablish of passive scan and selective passive scan, which do not generate excessive management traffic under non-coverage area in the tunnel. Assuming that a client starts to scan at the benining of coverage area, total delay to establish wireless connection of each method is as follows.

- Passive Scan: 185 * Beacon Interval + 2 * RTT
- Selective Passive Scan: 1 * Beacon Interval + 2 * RTT

For example, in the case of T4 station where a single border AP exists on channel 1, as depicted in Figure 3, Testablish of above two methods are compared in Table 3, where RTT is 0.6 msec, beacon interval is 100 msec.

Table 3. Connection establishment delay

Method	Testablish
Passive Scan	18 * 100 + 2 * 0.6 = 1801.2 msec
Selective Passive Scan	1 * 100 + 2 * 0.6 = 101.2 msec

Secondly, we compare Tswitch of active scan, selective active scan, selective unicast scan, and AuthScan, which expedite scanning process by generating extra management traffic across overlapping coverage area at station. Assuming that there are M target APs on N channels and all of them response to requests, total delay to switch wireless connection of each methods are as follows, where MaxChannelTime is a time parameter involved in active scan long enough to guarantee the reception of the Probe Response frames from multiple APs available in the same channel.

- Active Scan: MaxChannelTime * N + MinChannelTime * (18 - N) + 2 * RTT
- Selective Active Scan: N * MaxChannelTime + 2 * RTT
- Selective Unicast Scan: M * RTT + 0 * MinChannelTime + 2 * RTT
- AuthScan: M * RTT + 0 * MinChannelTime + 1 * RTT

For example, in the case of T4 station where five target APs exist on three channels as depicted in Figure 3, Tswitch of above four methods are compared in Table 4, where RTT is 0.6 msec, beacon interval is 100 msec, MaxChannelTime is 15 msec, and MinChannelTime is 1024 μsec (Jeong et al., 2003).

Table 4. Connection switching delay

Method	Tswitch
Active Scan	3*15+15*1.024+2*0.6=61.56 msec
Selective Active Scan	3 * 15 + 2 * 0.6 = 46.2 msec
Selective Unicast Scan	5 * 0.6 + 2 * 0.6 = 4.2 msec
AuthScan	5 * 0.6 + 1 * 0.6 = 3.6 msec

From the two tables, we can observe that the combination of selective passive scan and AuthScan achieves the lowest interrupted connection time. The delay obtained by selective passive scan is 94.4% smaller than the one obtained by standard passive scan when establishing terminated wireless connections. The delay obtained by

AuthScan is 94.2% smaller than the one obtained by active scan when switching wireless connection to the next AP. The increased connected time will become larger in proportion to the number of wireless connection establishment and switching while traving by subway. Besides the aforementioned parameters, there are hardware induced delays such as interface setup time. These delays are not considered in the previous analysis, because they vary from maker to maker and, therefore, are unsettled. In fact, the real delay observed in experiments is even larger than the values obtained in the analysis.

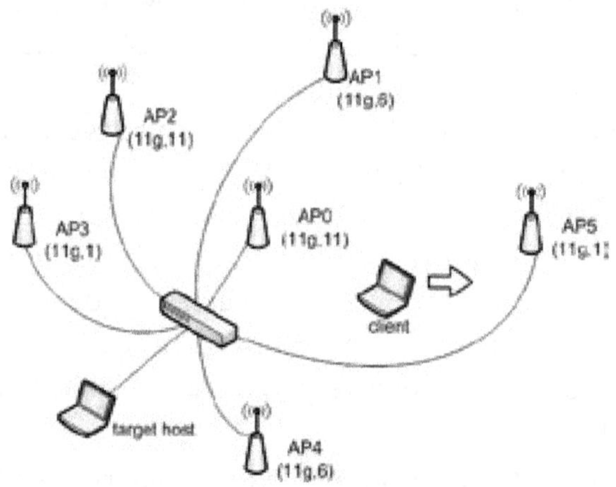

Fig. 6. Experimental setup

5. IMPLEMENTATION AND EXPERIMENTS

We have implemented a prototype of our proposed method on an IBM Thinkpad X31 (CPU Pentium M 1.7GHz, 1GB RAM) with an Atheros AR5212-based wireless interface. It runs Debian Linux 4.0 Etch with a 2.6.18-5 kernel, modified madwifi (MadWifi, [Online]) as the wireless interface driver, and modified wpa_supplicant (Linux WPA/WPA2/IEEE 802.1X Supplicant, [Online]) as the application software. We also implemented an active scan enabled client6 to scan all 18 channels in an active manner for a comparison purpose. Since the delay of selective passive scan in Testablish is probabilistically de termined between 0 and 100 msec as shown in Section 3, our experiments focus on the delay to switch wireless connection Tswitch of our prototype.

In order to evaluate the performance of our prototype in an actual network, we set up the following experimental environment. We build six overlapping BSSs in an office7: AP0(11g, ch.11), AP1(11g, ch.6), AP2(11g, ch.11), AP3(11g, ch.1), AP4(11g, ch.6), and AP5(11g, ch.1), as described in Figure 6. The APs and a target host (IBM Thinkpad X31) are connected by 100 Base-T cable, and all APs are working as a bridge between the wireless and wired network in link layer level under open system authentication.

We evaluate our prototype's performance by measuring 1) its average delay to switch wireless connection on the application level, and 2) RTTs during handoff in comparison with active scan in the following experiment scenario. A client with an IEEE 802.11 a/b/g NIC is associated to AP0. The client moves towards AP5 while using ping command to transmit ICMP Echo Request frames to the target host in the same subnet. We set the ICMP frame size as 480 bytes, and the interval between frames as 10 msec. Then, we reduce the transmission power of AP0, while increasing that of AP5 to emulate a mobility scenario in a limited space. As the client gets closer to AP5, the degradation of signal strength from AP0 triggers handoff to AP5. Figure 7 shows the average delay to switch wireless connection from ten runs of the handoff scenario since the sending of the Authentication Request frame to the first AP scanned (2AQ in the graph). The x-axis shows the steps in the authentication scanning process. They correspond to the sending of the Authentication Request frame (AQ), reception of the Authentication Response frame (AS), sending of the Reassociation Request frame (RQ) and reception of the Reassociation Response frame (RS). The number before each of them is the actual AP name being checked. The y-axis is the time delay in milliseconds measured in the application in order to get the handoff delay from the user's perspective. We added a checkpoint right before calling the driver ioctl, in the case of the AQ and RQ, and right after receiving the driver's informational event for the AS and RS.

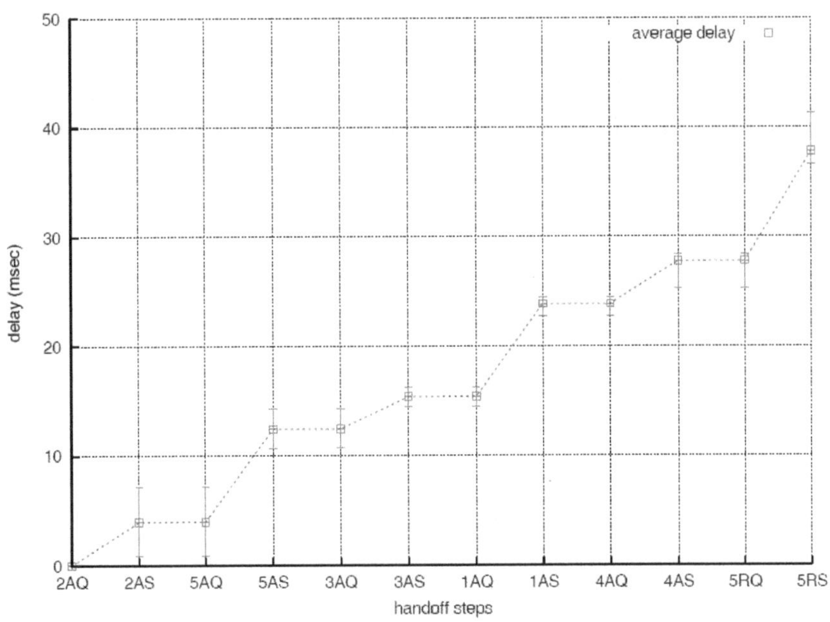

Fig. 7. The average handoff delay checking five APs

The total handoff delay in the application level obtained when checking five APs with open system authentication is 37.84 msec in average. This includes hardware induced delay such as interface setup time, delay introduced by system calls and events that flow between userland and kernel space, and 1 RTT for Authentication Request and Authentication Response. It takes 3.60 msec in average to check APs on the same channel (from AP 0 to AP2, from AP5 to AP3, from AP1 to AP4), while it takes 8.46 msec in average to check APs on the different channel(from AP 2 to AP5, from AP3 to AP1). Therefore, the AuthScan client saves 4.86 msec to setup the interface into the desired channel, each time checking APs on the same channel consecutively in our experiment.

Figure 8 shows one example of the way RTT changes during handoff from AP0 to AP5. The upper graph corresponds to one run by an AuthScan client, and the lower by an active scan client. The x-axis shows the ICMP sequence number and the y-axis shows the RTT in milliseconds. Handoff takes place between the 682nd and 686th frames (A) in the case of the AuthScan client (i.e., 3 frames dropped, 30 msec disrupted), and between the 3637th and 3924th frames (B) for the active scan client (i.e., 286 frames dropped, 2860 msec disrupted). Therefore, the AuthScan client drops approximately 98.95% fewer frames than the active scan client in the experiment.

6. CONCISE SUMMARY

To enhance connectivity duration with existing 802.11 wireless networks while traversing the Tokyo subway, we have devised a system featuring two scanning modes: 1) passive scanning on a designated channel, and 2) scanning with multiple open authentications. Our analysis and experiments demonstrate that our method enhances the duration of connectivity to 802.11 wireless networks by initiating a wireless connection upon exiting a non-coverage area in the tunnel and seamlessly transitioning the connection within overlapping coverage areas at the station with reduced latency.

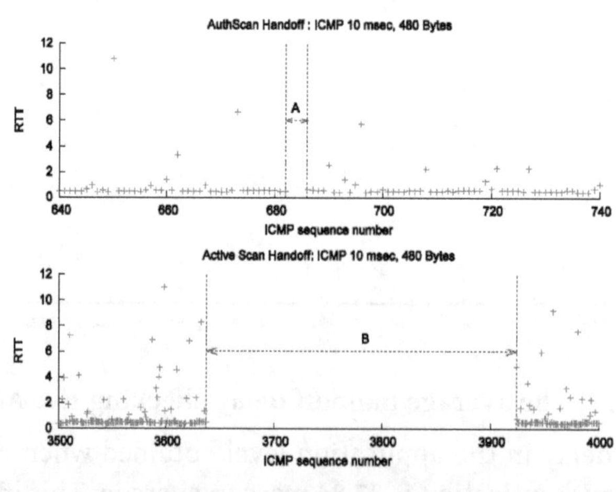

Fig. 8. Profile of RTTs during handoff from AP5 to AP0

The main contribution of this chapter is two-fold:

- We investigated the commercial 802.11 HOTSPOT wireless networks deployed in Tokyo Metro, and clarified the main factor to the diminishment of available connected time.
- We proposed an optimized solution for the subway's intermittent connectivity environment, and analyzed the increase connected time by our method. In addition, we showed the effectiveness of our system through experiments in comparison with standard active scan.

Our proposed technique will function effectively in analogous subway 802.11 wireless network conditions in other cities. Our future endeavors will focus on establishing a more advanced network of border access points and a catalog of favored access points. A series of border access points, including periods of inactivity in non-covered tunnel areas, can conserve energy by deactivating the interface prior to executing a selective passive scan. A compilation of recommended access points established for each access point at every station can further reduce unicast scanning duration.

FOOTNOTES

1. Tokyo Metro carries average 6.22 million passengers per day as of 2007 (Tokyo Metro, [Online])
2. In Tokyo, for example, approximately 97% of subway stations are densely covered by three different service providers as of December 2008 (NTT Communications HOTSPOT; NTT DoCoMo Mzone; NTT EAST FLET'S SPOT, [Online])
3. In Tokyo Metro, NTT Communications HOTSPOT provides 173 subway stations among 179 with IEEE 802.11 b/g wireless access service. (Tokyo Metro, [Online])
4. Yoyogi-uehara (C1), Yoyogi-koen (C2), Meiji-jingumae (C3), Omote-sando (C4), Takatanobaba (T3), Waseda (T4), Kagurazaka (T5), Kasumigaseki (M15), Ginza (M16), Tokyo (M17), and Otemachi (M18) station
5. Additional 4 channels (52, 56, 60, and 64ch) in 5.3GHz (W53) and 11 channels (100, 104, 108, 112, 116, 120, 124, 128, 132, 136, and 140ch) in 5.6GHz (56W) were added to the conventional 4 channels in 5.2 GHz (52W) for 11a in 2005 and 2007, respectively. Therefore, the total number of channels to scan sums up 33 channels. However, we focus on the conventional 18 channels, which most of devices in Japan support, in this
6. Because of regulatory reasons, wpa_supplicant is implemented to passively scan channel 12, 13, 14, 34, 38, 42 and 46.
7. There are 19 802.11 a/b/g APs on seven channels sharing the same medium with our experimental APs.

REFERENCES

1. Brik, V.; Mishra, A. & Banerjee, S. (2005). Eliminating handoff latencies in 802.11 WLANs using multiple radios: Applications, experience, and evaluation, Proceedings of ACM/USENIX IMC 2005, Berkeley, CA, October 2005
2. DownThemAll. [Online]. Available: http ://www.downthemall.net/
3. Droms, R. (1997). Dynamic Host Configuration Protocol, RFC 2131, Internet Society
4. Huang, P.; Tseng, Y. & Tsai, K. (2006). A Fast Handoff Mechanism for IEEE 802.11 and IAPP Networks, Proceedings of IEEE VTC 2006-Spring, Melbourne, Australia, May 2006
5. IEEE Standard 802.11. (1999). IEEE. Part 11: Wireless LAN Medium Access Control (MAC) and Physical Layer (PHY) Specifications
6. IEEE Standard 802.1Q-2003. (2003) IEEE Standards for Local and Metropolitan Area Networks, Virtual Bridged Local AreaNetworks
7. Jeong, M.; Watanabe, F. & Kawahara T. (2003). Fast active scan for measurement and handoff, Technical report, DoCoMo USA Labs, Contribution to IEEE 802, May 2003
8. Kim, H.; Park, S.; Park, C.; Kim, J. & Ko, S. (2004). Selective Channel Scanning for Fast Handoff in Wireless LAN using Neighbor Graph, Proceedings of ITC-CSCC 2004, Sendai, JAPAN, July 2004
9. Linux WPA/WPA2/IEEE 802.1X Supplicant. [Online]. Available: http://hostap.epitest.fi/
10. MadWifi - a Linux kernel device driver for Wireless LAN chipsets from Atheros. [Online]. Available: http://madwifi.org/
11. Microsoft Technet. [Online]. Available: http ://technet.microsoft.com/en-us/library/cc757419.aspx
12. Mishra, A; Shin, M. & Arbaugh, W. (2003). An Empirical Analysis of the IEEE 802.11 MAC Layer Handoff Process, ACM SIGCOMM Computer Communication Review, Vol. 3, April 2003, pp. 93-102
13. Mishra, A.; Shin, M. & Arbaugh, W. (2004). Context Caching using Neighbor Graphs for Fast Handoffs in a Wireless Network, Proceedings of IEEE INFOCOM 2004, Hong Kong, March 2004
14. NTT Communications HOTSPOT. [Online]. Available: http://www.hotspot.ne.jp/
15. NTT DoCoMo Mzone. [Online]. Available: http://www.nttdocomo.co.jp/service/data/mzone/

16. NTT EAST FLET'S SPOT. [Online]. Available: http://flets.com/spot/
17. NetStumbler. [Online]. Available: http://www.netstumbler.com/
18. Ok, J.; Morales, P.; Darmawan, A. & Morikawa, H. (2007). Using Shared Beacon Channel for Fast Handoff in IEEE 802.11 Wireless Networks, Proceedings of IEEE VTC2007- Spring, Dublin, Ireland, April 2007
19. Ok, J.; Morales, P. & Morikawa, H. (2008). AuthScan: Enabling Fast Handoff across Already Deployed IEEE 802.11 Wireless Networks Mobility, Proceedings of IEEE PIMRC 2008, Cannes, France, September 2008
20. Ramani, I. & Savage, S. (2005). SyncScan: Practical Fast Handoff for 802.11 Infrastructure Networks, Proceedings of IEEE INFOCOM 2005, Miami, FL, March 2005
21. Shin, S.; Forte, A. G.; Rawat, A. S. & Schulzrinne, H. (2004). Reducing MAC layer handoff latency in IEEE 802.11 wireless LANs, Proceedings of MobWiac 2004, Philadelphia, PA, September 2004
22. Tokyo Metro. [Online]. Available: http://www.tokyometro.jp/global/en/about/outline.html
23. Waharte, S.; Ritzenthaler, K. & Boutaba, R. (2004). Selective Active Scanning for Fast Handoff in WLAN using Sensor Networks, Proceedings of MWCN 2004, Paris, France, October 2004
24. Wireshark. [Online]. Available: http://www.wireshark.org/
25. Wu, H.; Tan K.; Zhang, Y. & Zhang, Q. (2007). Proactive Scan: Fast Handoff with Smart Triggers for 802.11 Wireless LAN, Proceedings of IEEE INFOCOM 2007, Anchorage, Alaska, May 2007

25 Chapter

ASYMMETRIC CARRIER SENSING IN DIVERSE MEDICAL NETWORK ENVIRONMENTS

1. INTRODUCTION: AN OVERVIEW

The integration of diverse wireless technologies is essential for transformative healthcare delivery in hospitals, minor clinics, residential care centers, and homes [1-4]. The medical environment is a multifaceted workspace that includes the patient admission process, examination, diagnosis, therapy, and management of these activities. The notion of a "wireless hospital" integrates all medical, diagnostic, and clinical data as required using wireless technology [4]. There is an intention to implement IEEE standards for wireless local area networks (WLAN) and wireless personal area networks (WPAN) technologies within the unlicensed industrial, scientific, and medical (ISM) bands as a unified communication infrastructure [2, 3]. WLAN technology is primarily employed for office-related applications and facilitating patient connectivity to external networks, whilst WPAN technology is generally utilized for wearable sensors that gather crucial data for pervasive healthcare services [2-6].

The employment of complementary heterogeneous WLANs and WPANs inside the common ISM band leads to coexistence, interference, and spectrum utilization challenges. The coexistence of wireless technology in the ISM band has been a prominent subject of discussion [6-9]. Adaptive frequency hopping was suggested for Bluetooth devices to mitigate interference from WLAN [7]. Howitt and Gutierrez [8] presented a methodology for evaluating the impact of 802.15.4 on the performance of 802.11b. The decline in WLAN performance is minimal due to the low activity of WPAN. The elevated duty cycle of WLAN traffic might significantly impair WPAN performance [6]. A distributed adaptation technique utilizing Q-learning for WPAN has been developed to mitigate the effects of interference from 802.11b [9]. Nevertheless, the topic of spatial reuse in heterogeneous networks has not garnered significant attention. Research indicates that spatial reuse and aggregate throughput in homogenous WLAN mesh networks are highly linked to physical channel sensing. Yang and Vaidya demonstrated that the overall throughput may experience considerable decline due to an unsuitable selection of carrier sense threshold [10]. Ma et al. utilized a Markov chain model to assess the impact of carrier sense threshold on throughput and packet collisions [11]. Zhai and Fang discovered that the ideal carrier sensing threshold for one-hop flows is ineffective for multihop flows [12]. Zhu et al. indicated that a modifiable sensing threshold can efficiently enhance spatial reuse, as evidenced by testbed measurements [13, 14]. In [15], Zhu et al. suggested a heuristic technique to adaptively adjust the carrier sense threshold to improve user throughput. Jamieson discovered that carrier sense can be ineffective at low data rates when the capture effect is most pronounced [16]. Ramachandran and Roy demonstrated a cross-layer dependency between carrier sensing and system performance [17]. Simulators commonly employed for performance assessment, such as NS-2 and OPNET, lack comprehensive physical layer modules, including carrier sense. Due to insufficient carrier sensing information between WPAN and WLAN, Golmie et al. simulated two scenarios: one in which the WPAN can solely identify its own packet type and another in which the WPAN can also detect WLAN transmissions, as part of their coexistence study for medical applications. [6].

In this chapter we study the coexistence issue in the heterogeneous medical networks environment from carrier sensing point. The remainder of the chapter is organized as follows. Section II briefly reviews various carrier sense methods and the considered WLAN and WPAN systems. In section III, a mathematical analysis of energy based carrier sense in both AWGN channel and fading channel is presented. Section IV describes the impact of asymmetric carrier sense in heterogeneous networks environment and presents a two-band carrier sense to combat the asymmetry. Section V finally concludes the chapter.

2. REVIEW OF SYSTEMS AND CLEAR CHANNEL ASSESSMENT

2.1 Wireless medical sensor networks

Wireless medical sensor networks can be considered as a special part of general wireless sensor networks (WSN), which are mainly implemented by low-rate WPAN technologies. As compared in Table I, both share some common features which include limited resources (e.g. computation power, memory, battery, bandwidth), low/modest duty cycle, energy efficiency, plug-and-play, diverse coexistence environments, and heterogeneous device ability. But we can also find significant differences between them in the sensor device, dependability, networking, traffic pattern and channel.

Firstly medical sensors consider safety, quality and reliability as top priority, while general WSN are cost sensitive for market reason. The safety to human/animal body is therefore the first factor taken into considered. Thus medical sensors must be conscious of specific absorption ratio (SAR) to protect human tissue. Wearable IEEE WPAN devices are suggested to be separated at least 30cm distance from human body. Safe to human is the top priority of medical sensors. The radio emission should be as weak as possible. And medical sensors should be lightweight and small to achieve non-invasive and unobtrusive monitor. This limits the available resource which includes memory, battery power and computation ability in the medical sensors. The requirement is more stringent than the general WSN. Secondly the medical sensor networks have more frequency bands to select than general WSN, which usually work in ISM band. Although the specific medical bands are less noisy, they are narrow band and conditional license. For example, the wireless medical telemetry service (WMTS) band can only be used in the licensed hospital and clinic, but not at home. On the contrary, the wideband ubiquitous ISM is somehow noisy since the frequency band should be shared with other systems.

Thirdly, the traffic pattern in medical sensor networks is featured by periodical real time data (e.g. EEG and ECG) and some top priority burst data (e.g. alarm and alert) [17]. In contrast, general WSN typically consider versatile traffic. The medical information, especially the alarm notification, have very strict requirement in terms of Quality-of-Service (QoS) since they are life critical. The transmission of vital signal has a life or dead meaning. This means more stringent QoS requirement than general WSN.

Fourthly, security of data is traditionally utmost important. Patient data needs to be protected in all stages of data acquiring, data transmission and data storage. It therefore importance to secure data at physical layer and MAC lay. However, security is not free, extensive sources are needed to secure data at the link layer. In the resource limited WSN, security becomes an overhead of existing network QoS. Because both of them are paramount in the healthcare service, the balance of security and QoS is a new issue. The general WSN do not require strict QoS and security simultaneously.

Fifthly, to improve reliability, general WSN tend to distribute redundant sensors as backup for sensing, transmission and forwarding. In contrast, there is little redundancy in medical WSN for medical reasons. For example, vital signals, like EEG (Electroencephalography) and ECG (Electrocardiogram), are location dependent and can only be measured by deterministic location. Therefore it is difficult to allocate redundant sensors in the limited area. Especially, it makes no sense to allocate sensors outside of the interest/effect area.

In summary, the lack of redundancy, priority traffic, dominant periodical data and balance of guaranteed QoS and security in versatile coexistence environment challenge the reliability design of wireless medical sensor networks.

Table 1. Comparison between wireless medical sensor network and general wireless sensor networks

	Medical wireless sensor networks	General wireless sensor networks
Common features	Limited resources: battery, computation, memory, energy efficiency Diversity coexistence environment low/modest data rate, low/modest duty cycle. Dynamic network scale, plug-and-play, heterogeneous devices ability, dense distribution	
Sensor/ actuator	Single-function device Fast relative movement in small range device lifetime, days, <10 years (implant sensor) Safe (low SAR) and quality first	Multi-function device Rare or slow movement in large range network lifetime and device lifetime, months, <10 years
Dependability	Reliability (first), guaranteed QoS Strongly security (except emergency)	Cost sensitive expected QoS, redundancy-based reliability Required security
Networking	Small scale star network No redundancy in device Deterministic node distribution	Large scale hierarchical network redundant distribution Random node distribution
Traffic	Periodical RT (dominant), burst (priority) Uni-directional traffic M:1 communication	Burst (dominant), periodical Uni-directional or bi-directional traffic M:1 or point-point communication
channel	Specific medical channel, ISM band. Body surface or through body	ISM band. Obstacle is unknown

2.2 Systems overview

We consider IEEE 802.15.4b and 802.11b as examples for the ubiquitous medical services [2, 3, 6]. The former is a good candidate technology for low data rate and low cost medical sensors. Both systems operate in the unlicensed 2.4GHz ISM band, and both are based on carrier sense multiple access with collision avoidance (CSMA/CA) protocol. Carrier sense is more generally known as clear channel assessment (CCA) in the standards. The physical CCA can be either energy based, or feature based, or a combination of two. As shown in Fig. 1, there are only 4 WPAN channels locate in the guard bands of WLAN. Table II lists the parameters of both systems [18, 19]. The bit error rate (BER) of WLAN systems with AWGN channel is give by [18]

$$BER_{11b} = \frac{128}{255} \times \sum_{l=1}^{6} M1_l \times \sqrt{Q(M2_l \times SNR)}, \qquad (1)$$

where SNR is the signal-to-noise ratio, Q(.) is Gaussian Q-function, M1=[24 16 174 16 24 1], and M2=[4 6 8 10 24 16]. The BER of WPAN systems is given by [19]

$$BER_{15.4b} = \frac{8}{15} \times \frac{1}{16} \times \sum_{k=2}^{16} -1^k \binom{16}{k} e^{20 \cdot SNR(1/k-1)}. \qquad (2)$$

The radio path loss for indoor channels in the working frequency band is given by

$$\begin{cases} pl = 40.2 + 20\log_{10} d & d \le 8 \\ pl = 58.5 + 33\log_{10}(d/8) & d > 8 \end{cases}, \qquad (3)$$

where d is separation distance between transmitter and receiver.

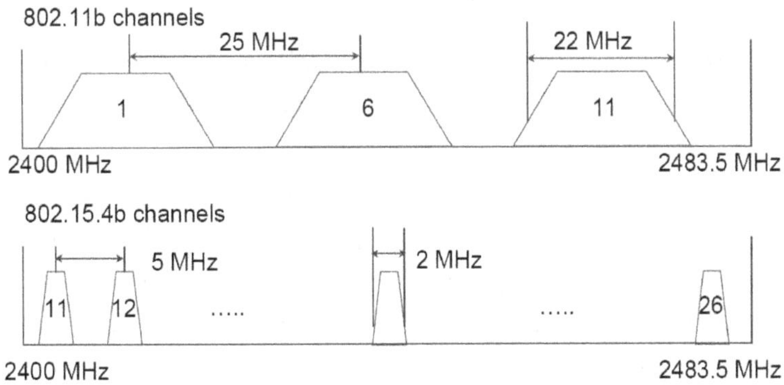

Fig. 1. Channel plan for IEEE 802.11b and 802.15.4b in 2.4GHz ISM band

Table 2. System parameters of IEEE WLAN and WPAN

Parameters	802.15.4b	802.11b
Transmission power (dBm)	0	16
Channel bandwidth (MHz)	2	22
Adjacent channel separation (MHz)1	5	25
Background noise (dBm) 2	-94.9	-84.6
Spread code (chips)	32/4 bits	11
Data rate (Mbps)	0.25	11
CCA window (μs)	120	15

2.3 Clear channel assessment

Several IEEE WLAN and WPAN standards adopt CSMA protocol for channel access. CCA is a physical layer activity and is an essential element of the CSMA protocol.

The concept of CCA was first proposed as an enhancement to the ALOHA protocol. The CCA detects an incoming packet and ensure a free medium before transmission. The CCA module processes received radio signals in a suitable time duration termed CCA window. It then reports the medium state, either busy or idle, by comparing the detection with a threshold. The energy based CCA integrates signal strength from radio front end during the CCA window. The feature based CCA looks for the known features, e.g. the modulation and spreading characteristics, of the signal over the channel. Modulated signals are in general coupled with sine wave carriers, pulse trains, repeating spreading, or cyclic prefixes, which result in built-in periodicity. This periodicity can be used to detect signal of a particular modulation type.

The feature based CCA performs far better than the energy based CCA. However, a prior knowledge of the signal characteristic is necessary. And the CCA module would need a dedicated detector for every potential coexistence signal class. The main advantages of energy based CCA are its simplicity, generality, and low power consumption. It is a universal mechanism that can be deployed in all systems. Unlike feature based CCA, there is no need for waiting time for the specific features of the signal and synchronization [17]. The downside of energy based CCA is that it is prone to false detection.

We applied energy based CCA to 802.15.4b and 802.11b systems to deliver ubiquitous healthcare service in this heterogeneous networks environment. There are several reasons for this. First, there have been nearly 10 wireless technologies with different modulations, band plans, and transmission powers in the 2.4GHz ISM bands due to its global availability.

These include WLAN (802.11, 802.11b, 802.11g and 802.11n), WPAN (Bluetooth, 802.15.3, 802.15.4b, and chirp spread spectrum PHY of 802.15.4a), and passive radio frequency identification etc. Significantly, some medical equipments like electric surgical knife, magnetic resonance imaging (MRI), heat treatment machines, and microwave ovens also use this frequency band. Different from the communication device, the medical equipments emit radio signals unintentional. All the communication device and medical equipments are expected to be collocated in the integrated medical environments. Secondly, a medical sensor based on 802.15.4b is unlikely to have all the knowledge. And feature based CCA is usually complex and power-hungry due to the waiting time and synchronization [17].

3. ENERGY BASED CLEAR CHANNEL ASSESSMENT IN HETEROGENEOUS NETWORKS

In mathematics, CCA is a test of two hypotheses:

$$\begin{cases} H_0 : y[n] = w[n] & \text{signal absent} \\ H_1 : y[n] = x[n] + w[n] & \text{signal present} \end{cases}, \tag{4}$$

'where x[n] is the targeted signal: w[n] is the white Gaussian noise with variance σ2; and n=1,...,N is the sample index in total N independent samples in the CCA window. Under common detection performance criteria, e.g. Neyman-Pearson (NP) criteria, likelihood ratio yields the optimal hypothesis testing solution. The CCA metric is compared to a threshold to make a decision. CCA performance is characterized by a resulting pair of detection and false alarm probabilities, (Pd and Pfa), which are associated with the particular threshold. For simplicity, we assume the energy based CCA is realized by a simple non-coherent module that integrates the square of the received signal and sums its samples in analog or digital domain. In particular, the energy detection consists of a quadrature receiver with yI and yQ representing samples of signals on the I (in-phase) and Q (quadrature) branches respectively. Figure 2 depicts a block diagram of energy based CCA.

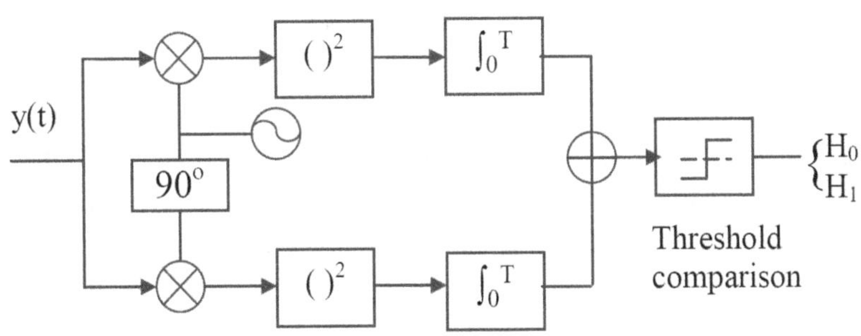

Fig. 2. Block diagram of energy based CCA detector

The energy based CCA metric can be given by

$$Y = \frac{1}{N}\sum_{n=1}^{N}\left(|y_I[n]|^2 + |y_Q[n]|^2\right), \tag{5}$$

where N is the number of independent samples in the CCA window. In an AWGN channel, each yI [n] and yQ [n] has a normal distribution with mean μ and variance σ2 and Y can be evaluated as generalized chi-square function Y ~ χ2 (λ,2N), where 2N is the degrees of freedom and λ = σ 2 + μ 2 . Under the H0 hypothesis, each normal distribution has μ=0. Thus, Y has a χ2 distribution. Under the H1 hypothesis in the present of signal with an signal-to-noise ratio (SNR) $\gamma = \frac{\mu^2}{\sigma^2}$, γ has a non-central χ2 distribution. We have mean and variance as follows [20, 21]

$$\begin{cases} H_0: \ \mu_0 = \sigma^2, \ \ \sigma_0^{\ 2} = \dfrac{2}{N}\sigma^4 \\ H_1: \ \mu_1 = \mu^2 + \sigma^2, \ \ \sigma_1^{\ 2} = \dfrac{2}{N}(2\mu^2 + \sigma^4) \end{cases} \tag{6}$$

When N is large, using central limit theory, the energy based CCA metric in Eq. (4) can be approximated as Gaussian random process. Then Pd and Pfa can be expressed in terms of Gaussian Q-function

$$P_d = Q\left(\frac{\frac{\Gamma}{\sigma^2} - (1+\gamma)}{\sqrt{\frac{2}{N}}(1+2\gamma)}\right), \quad P_{fa} = Q\left(\frac{\frac{\Gamma}{\sigma^2} - 1}{\sqrt{\frac{2}{N}}}\right), \tag{7}$$

where Γ is the decision threshold. Eq. (7) clearly shows that the decision threshold is related with noise level. If the noise is completely known, eliminating Γ in Eq. (7) gives

$$N = 2\left(\frac{Q^{-1}(P_{fa}) - Q^{-1}(P_d)\sqrt{1+2\gamma}}{\gamma}\right)^2, \tag{8}$$

where Q-1() is inverse Gaussian Q-function. The energy based CCA can meet any desired Pd and Pfa simultaneously by increasing the number of samples in the CCA window N. Given a limited N, the CCA ability is obviously determined by the SNR of the signal and noise variance σ2. There is an inherent tradeoff between Pd and Pfa. We define the CCA error floor at the optimal threshold, which can be found by equating 1-Pd and Pfa. Using Eq. (7), we obtain the CCA error floor

$$P_{CCA\_ef} = Q\left(\sqrt{N}\frac{\gamma}{1+\sqrt{1+2\gamma}}\right). \tag{9}$$

Note that the error floor depends on the number of symbol chips and the SNR. When SNR<<1, Eq. (9) can be approximated as

$$P_{CCA\_ef} = Q\left(\sqrt{N}\frac{\gamma}{2}\right). \tag{10}$$

A linear decrease in SNR requires a quadratic increase in N to maintain the same error floor.

3.1 Asymmetric energy based CCA

Table III lists the numbers of signal chips in the CCA windows of IEEE WLAN and WPAN. Figure 3 shows the CCA error floor in the heterogeneous networks environment when the noise is known. Per Eq. (9), the error floors decrease with increment in signal chips in the CCA window. Given the defined CCA windows, the CCA abilities, e.g. sensitivity and range, to determine the channel state are different, this is termed asymmetric CCA. Under the same SNR conditions, the lowest error floor is where WPAN is used to sense 802.11b signals; the highest error floor is where WLAN is used to sense 802.15.4b signals. The performance difference is nearly 10dB.

The CCA asymmetry can be attributed to differences in the underlying signals over channel (power, symbol rate and background noise) and CCA window. In physics, a higher data rate and a longer CCA window means more signal pulses in baseband can be collected. Better CCA performance is a natural result. Asymmetric CCA can be further reinforced by other factors. For example, the difference in transmission powers which is usually stronger for WLAN, and the difference in channel bandwidth, which are 22MHz and 2MHz for the WLAN and WPAN, respectively. For both WPAN and WLAN, the performances to detect the signal of its own type are similar. There is not big difference in the numbers of symbols in the CCA window.

Table IV compares communication with CCA when both have an error probability of 1‰ with AWGN channel. As expected, the CCA range is larger than the communication range. For WPAN, sensing 802.11b signals has 4dB greater link margin compared to sensing the signals of its own type. In contrast, for WLAN sensing 802.15.4b signals requires a 4.8dB higher SNR.

Asymmetric CCA makes channel sensing insensitive or oversensitive to other signals in the mixed WLAN and WPAN environment. The asymmetric CCA in the heterogeneous networks is different from the traditional "hidden node" or "exposed node" issues in the homogeneous network. In the homogeneous network, two devices belong to the same system are reciprocal in ability to sense each other (we do not consider the minor difference due to implementation.). However, in the heterogeneous networks, the sensing abilities of different systems are unequal and depend on the underlying signals over channel and the separation distances. As shown in Fig. 3, WLAN signals are well sensed by both of them, but WPAN signals could be ignored by the WLAN systems when they are separated by enough space.

Table 3. Number of signal chips in the CCA window

Sensed signals Device	802.15.4b signals	802.11b signals
802.15.4b	32*8	120*11
802.11b	15*2	15*11

Table 4. SNRs (dB) to achieve 1‰ communication BER and CCA error floors in AWGN channel

Devices Signal	802.15.4b	802.11b
Communication	-0.8	5.6
802.15.4b CCA	-3.2	2.6
802.11b CCA	-7.2	-2.2

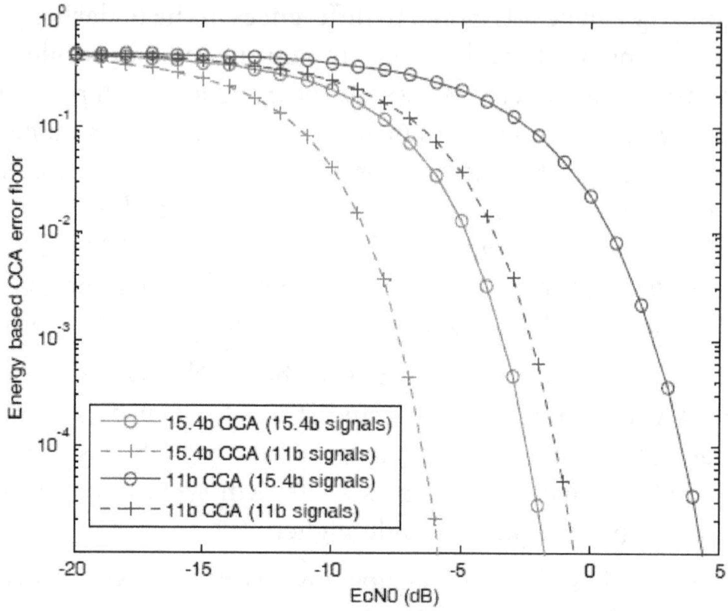

Fig. 3. Error floor of energy based CCA with AWGN channel in heterogeneous networks

Usually, NP criteria is adopted in CCA because a miss detection of a busy channel is riskier than a false alarm of a free channel. Eq. (7) can be re-written as

$$P_d = Q\left(\frac{Q^{-1}(P_{fa}) - \sqrt{2N\gamma}}{\sqrt{1+2\gamma}}\right). \tag{11}$$

As expected, Pf is independent of γ since there is no signal under H0. When the channel is varying due to fading and shadowing, Eq. (12) gives a CCA performance conditioned on the instantaneous SNR. The average CCA performance can be derived by averaging Eq. (11) over fading statistics

$$\overline{P_d} = \int_0^{\infty} Q\left(\frac{Q^{-1}(P_{fa}) - \sqrt{2N\gamma}}{\sqrt{1+2\gamma}}\right) f(\gamma)d\gamma, \tag{12}$$

where f (γ) is the probability of distribution function (PDF) of SNR under fading.

The medium-scale variance of SNR can be characterized by log-normal distribution [22]. The log-normal shadowing is usually described in-term of its dB-spread, σdB, which is related to σ by

$$\sigma = \sigma \text{ dB} \ln(10)/10. \tag{13}$$

Under Rayleigh fading, the SNR γ has an exponential PDF

$$f(\gamma) = \frac{1}{\bar{\gamma}} \exp(\frac{\gamma}{\bar{\gamma}}) \quad \gamma \geq 0, \tag{14}$$

where $\bar{\gamma}$ denotes to average SNR. If the SNR follows a Rician distribution, the PDF of γ becomes

$$f(\gamma) = \frac{K+1}{\bar{\gamma}} \exp(-K - \frac{(K+1)\gamma}{\bar{\gamma}}) I_0(2\sqrt{\frac{K(K+1)\gamma}{\bar{\gamma}}}) \quad \gamma \geq 0, \tag{15}$$

where K is the Rician factor and I0(.) is the modified Bessel function with order zero. Because it is difficult to have close-form expressions of Eq. (12) over fading channels, we evaluated them numerically in this chapter.

Figure 4 plots ROCs of energy based CCA over AWGN, log-normal shadowing, Rayleigh fading, and Rician fading channels. The asymmetric CCA abilities of WPAN and WLAN remain the same in fading channels. WLAN systems are insensitive to WPAN signals, while WPAN systems are oversensitive to WLAN signals. Comparing with the AWGN curves, we observe that channel fading degrades the performance of energy based CCA, and the degradations are closely related with the CCA parameters and SNR. In other words, meeting the desired performance demands a longer CCA window. Especially Rayleigh fading and Rician fading degrade the CCA performance of all systems significantly.

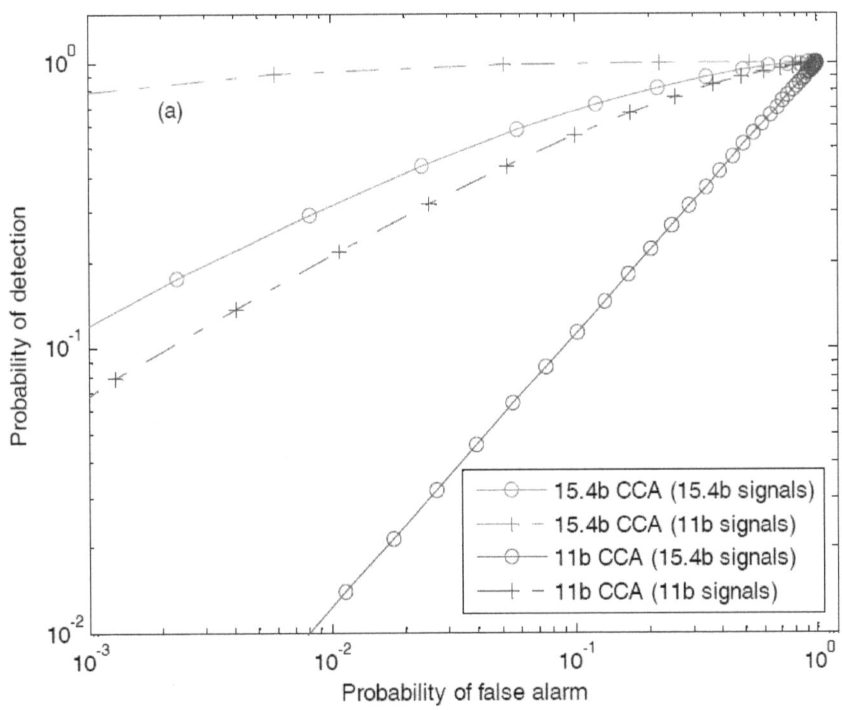

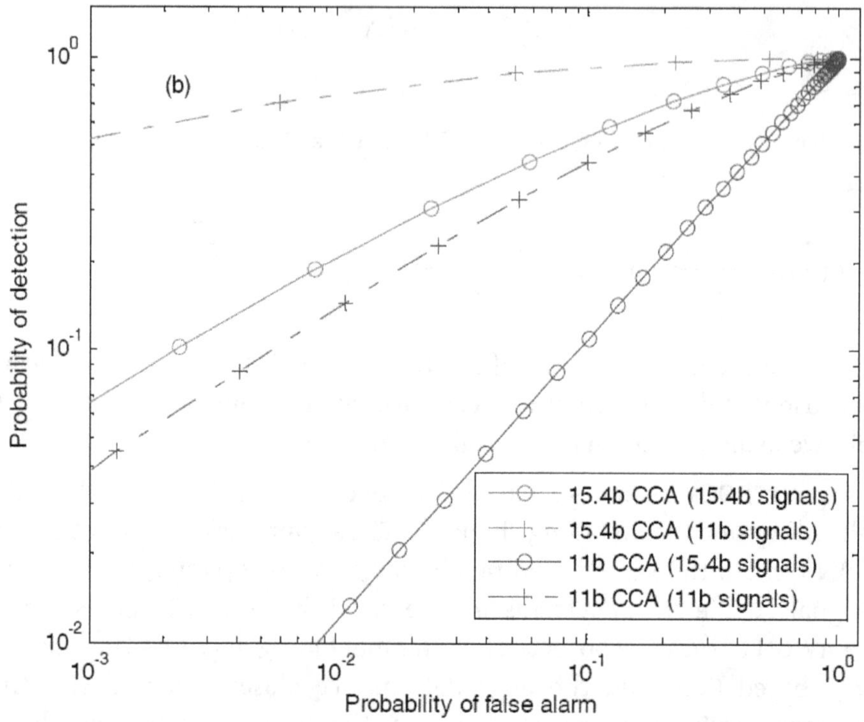
(b)
Probability of detection
Probability of false alarm
15.4b CCA (15.4b signals)
15.4b CCA (11b signals)
11b CCA (15.4b signals)
11b CCA (11b signals)

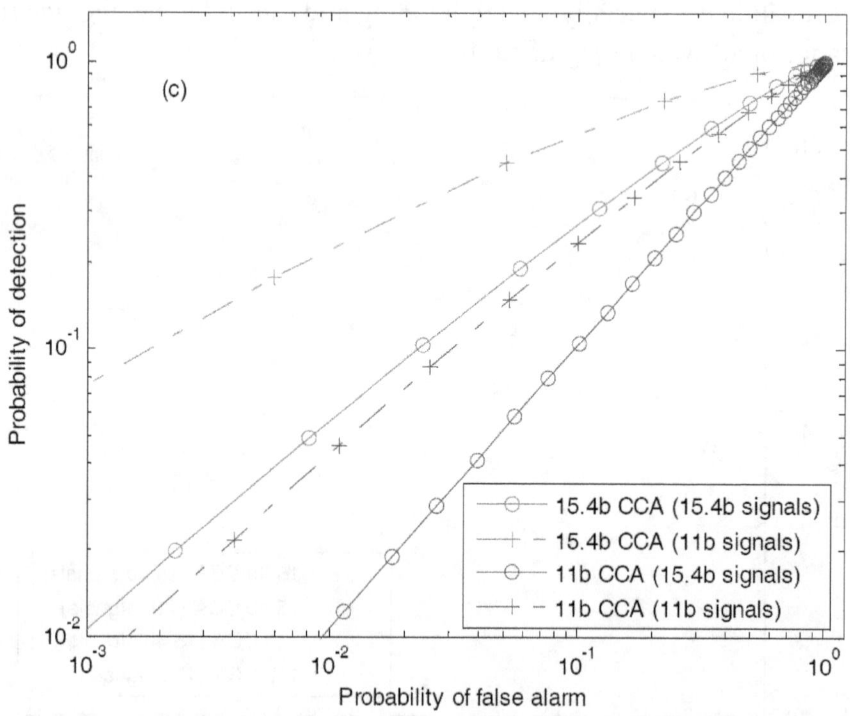
(c)
Probability of detection
Probability of false alarm
15.4b CCA (15.4b signals)
15.4b CCA (11b signals)
11b CCA (15.4b signals)
11b CCA (11b signals)

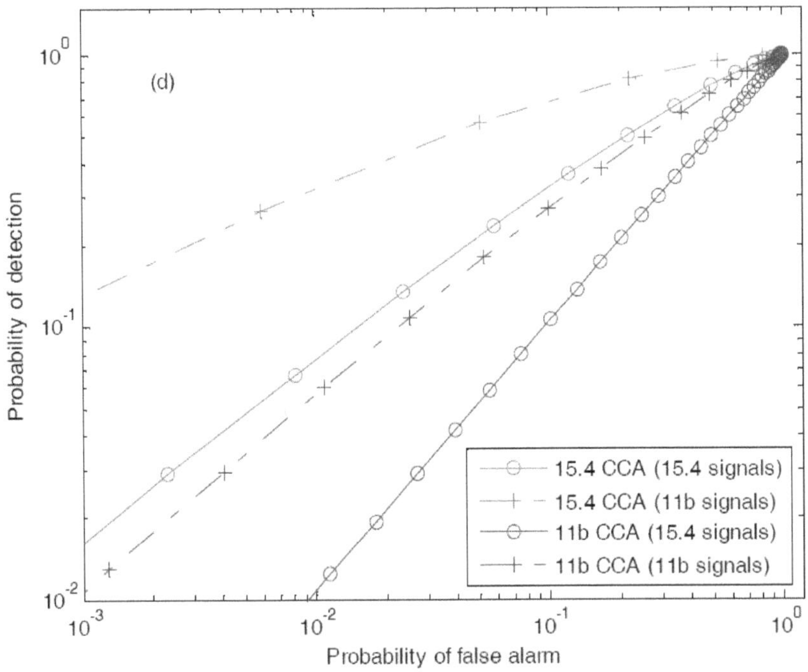

Fig. 4. ROC of energy based CCA in the case of SNR=-9.5 dB measured by WPAN over a) AWGN channel; b) log-normal shadowing (σdB= 6dB) channel; (c) Rayleigh fading channel, and d) Rician fading (K=1.5) channel.

3.2 Noise uncertainty

NP criteria requires a desired Pfa to determine the decision threshold. We can rewrite Eq. to have

$$\Gamma = \sigma^2 (1 + Q^{-1}(P_{fa})\sqrt{\frac{2}{N}}) \quad (16)$$

which shows the desired threshold should proportional to the noise energy. In practical, the noise power cannot be estimated accurately because of noise uncertainty [23].

The background noise power fluctuates from time to time due to changes of environment and mobility of device. Another source of uncertainty is the error in quantization which us usually implemented by A/D convertor. Assume the noise estimation is expressed as

$$\sigma 2 = k\sigma 2 , k \geq 0 . \quad (17)$$

When $0 < k < 1$, the noise is underestimated; when $k > 1$, it is overestimated. The Γ biases to the desired value due to error in noise estimation. An overestimation of noise decreases Pfa at expense of boosting Pd. It is vice versa for an underestimation of noise level. We can obtain the total CCA error approximated by $\begin{cases} 10*\lg(k) & 0<k\leq 1 \\ -10*\lg(k) & k>1 \end{cases}$ 1-Pd+Pfa using Eq. (7). Figure 5 shows the impact of noise uncertainty with 3 dB error. We used an 802.15.4 device to sense the 802.15.4 signals. The x-axis is the true SNR condition of CCA. As expected, both overestimation and underestimation deteriorate the CCA performance because of an un-optimal threshold. As shown in Fig. 5 and other numeric results, the performance loss of energy based CCA can be approximated as in both cases when SNR is high. In practical, we are usually more interested in noise underestimation. In order to guarantee the Pfa the Γ is purposely biased. This increases the probability of miss detection of CCA and therefore the probability of packet collision. In other words, the noise level estimation of free channel also plays an important role in the CCA operation.

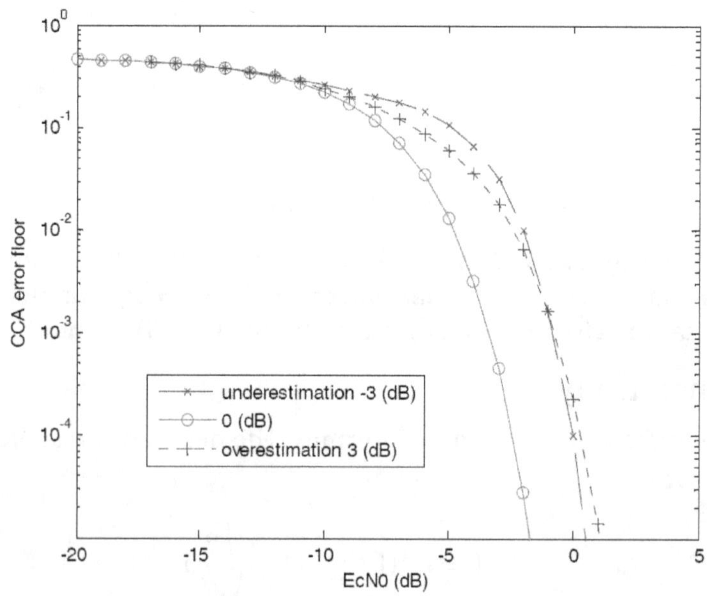

Fig. 5. Total error of energy based CCA with AWGN channel in the case of a 3dB noise uncertainty

4. TWO-BAND CLEAR CHANNEL ASSESSMENT

4.1 Impact of asymmetric CCA in heterogeneous networks

Table V lists the required minimum SNRs and their corresponding distances to achieve reliable energy based CCA (PFA<1% and PD>90%) over AWGN channel. The corresponding distances were computed using Eq. 1 to Eq. 3 and the parameters listed in Table I. For WPAN, the sensing of 802.11b signals is reliable at an SNR as low as -9.25dB. This SNR is 9.65dB lower than the critical SNR which is the least SNR to achieve BER<0.1‰ for communication. The CCA range is 180 meters longer than the communication range. In contrast, sensing 802.15.4b signal by WLAN requires a high SNR up to 9.75dB, which is 3.15dB more than the critical SNR for communication. The CCA range is 42 meters shorter than the communication range. In the fading channels, all distances decreases depending on the fading condition.

We can define a "heterogeneous exclusive CCA range" (HECR), in which systems in the heterogeneous environment can reliably sense the activities of each other. In the considered scenario, the HECR is the maximum distance that WLAN can sense 802.15.4b signals. Given the system parameters and assumptions, the HECR for IEEE WLAN and WPAN is 25m in AWGN channel. Peaceful and fair coexistence between them can be expected when they are located within the HECR. However, it becomes different when they are separated beyond the HECR. For WPAN systems, the CCA range of WLAN signals is more than twice as long as the communication range. And it is longer than the CCA range of its own signal type. That is, the WPAN is oversensitive to the WLAN signals. It can even sense a WLAN packet that is outside of the keep-out range of receiver in the worst case. 3 Although the oversensitive CCA avoids the 'hidden node' issue, it suffers from the 'exposed node' issue. This results in poor spatial reuse of frequency channels and low aggregation throughput since WPAN sometimes unnecessarily withdraw packet before transmission. As simulated in [11], the threshold optimized to maximize aggregate throughput is higher than the optimal threshold for a single hop. For WLAN systems, the CCA range of WPAN signals is about a quarter of the communication range. Packet collision may occur when WLAN traffic occurs immediately after the WPAN traffic.

Table 5. Minimum SNRs (dB) and corresponding distances (m) to achieve CCA (PFA <1%, PD>90%) with AWGN channel

	802.11b CCA		802.15.4b CCA	
	WPAN signals	WLAN signals	WPAN signals	WLAN signals
SNR (dB)	9.75	-4.5	-6	-9.25
Distance (m)	25	200	155	280

Although the HECR of 25 meters is not sufficient for outdoor applications, it seems to be good enough for most indoor applications. Typical bedside medical applications define by IEEE 1073 are within this range [24]. This is different from those of most coexistence studies in which it is usually assumed that WLAN cannot sense the activities of WPAN [6, 8, 9]. The HECR over fading channels is expected to be shorter than 25 meters depending on the fading parameters. But the asymmetric CCA issue still exists. Putting the oversensitive and insensitive CCAs together results in an unfair share of channel between WLAN and WPAN when they are separated beyond HECR. There is a preferential treatment of WLAN traffic. The WLAN is over-protected, while the WPAN is vulnerable.

4.2 Two-band clear channel assessment

The asymmetric CCA issue in heterogeneous medical networks environment must be solved. It is needed to recognize the signal source, WPAN signals or WLAN signals, when the medium is busy. When the channel is occupied by WLAN signals, an 802.15.4b device should increase its CCA threshold to lower the CCA sensitivity. On the other hands, when the channel is busy in WPAN signals, an 802.11b device should lower its CCA threshold to heighten the CCA sensitivity.

Figure 6 illustrates the mechanism of a two-band CCA. The 22 MHz WLAN channel depicted in dash-dotted line and the 2 MHz WPAN channel depicted in dotted line overlap each other. There are about 3 MHz space between adjacent WPAN channels, which are inside the WLAN channel. As shown in red-solid line in Fig. 7, we termed it auxiliary channel in this chapter. We added a new energy based CCA detector in the auxiliary channel to provide additional information. For example, the auxiliary CCA detector can be the same as the 802.15.4b CCA detector except that the working frequency is tuned to the auxiliary channel. For both WLAN systems and WPAN systems, there are two energy based CCA detectors tuned in its original channel and in the auxiliary channel, respectively. The two detectors have the same ability to conduct carrier sensing given the same configuration. Besides, there is a little increase in the complexity of device and the power consumption of CCA.

The two-band CCA in the WPAN/WLAN device conduct channel sensing simultaneously. When the channel is free, both CCA detectors indicate a free channel. Table VI lists the output states of the two-band CCA detector when the channel is busy. The channel state indications are the same in both systems. When the channel is occupied by WLAN signals, both CCA detectors indicate a busy channel. In contrast, when the channel is occupied by WPAN signals, the auxiliary CCA detector indicates a free channel. Therefore, the signal source can be easily distinguished.

In the two-band CCA, the performance of every energy detector can be analyzed as in Section III. The total performance can be expected as the AND of the two CCA detector.

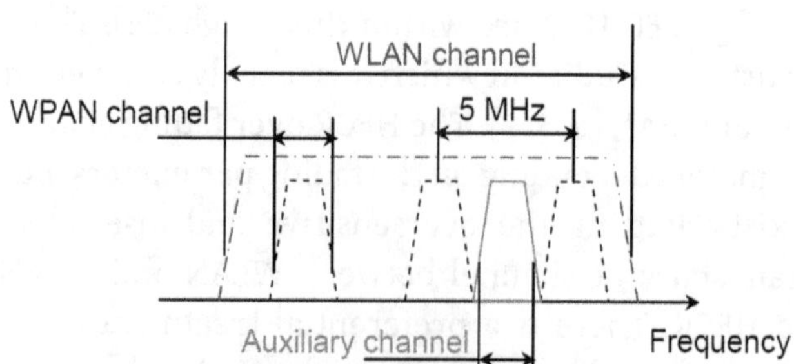

Fig. 6. Mechanism of two-band clear channel assessment

Table 6. Output states of the two-band CCA detector when the channel is busy

	802.11b		802.15.4b	
	CCAch_11b	CCAch_aux	CCAch_15.4 b	CCAch_aux
WPAN signals	√	×	√	×
WLAN signals	√	√	√	√

5. CONCISE SUMMARY

This chapter examines the coexistence issue within diverse medical networks for ubiquitous health care from the perspective of network access points. The energy-based CCA was selected because to the excessive congestion of the 2.4GHz ISM band, rendering feature-based CCA unsuitable for basic medical sensors.

Utilizing the central limit theorem, we have formulated closed-form formulas for energy-based canonical correlation analysis (CCA). We have demonstrated and validated the effect of noise uncertainty on CCA and asymmetric CCA in AWGN and fading channels. In the examined heterogeneous medical network environment for ubiquitous healthcare applications, WPAN is very sensitive to 802.11b signals, while WLAN exhibits insensitivity to 802.15.4b signals. When WPAN and WLAN are situated within the HERC, energy-based CCA can efficiently prevent potential packet collisions. The HERC is adequate for the majority of indoor medical applications. However, when they are distanced, WLAN loses its efficacy against 802.15.4b signals. The asymmetric CCA prioritizes WPAN traffic as secondary among heterogeneous networks. We have presented a two-band energy-based CCA, supplemented by an auxiliary channel CCA detector, to address the asymmetric CCA problem.

FOOTNOTES

1. Distance between the central frequencies of non-overlapped adjacent channel.
2. We assumed -174dBm/MHz thermal noise, 8dB implementation losses, and 8dB radio noise figure.
3. The keep-out range denotes to the minimum separation which WPAN and WLAN do not interfere each other.

REFERENCES

1. R. Istepanian, E. Jovano and Y Zhang, "Guest editorial introduction to the special section on M-Health: beyond seamless mobility and global wireless healthcare connectivity," IEEE Trans. Information Technology in Biomedicine, vol.8, no.4, p.405-414, 2004.
2. A. Soomro and D. Cavalcanti, "Opportunities and challenges in using WPAN and WLAN technologies in medical environments," IEEE Communication Magazine, vol.45, no.2, p.114-122, 2007.

3. D. Cypher, N. Chevrollier, N. Montavont, and N. Golmie, "Prevailing over wires in healthcare environments: benefits and challenges," IEEE Communication Magazine, vol. 44, no. 4, p. 56-63, 2006. http://www.wilho.net/

4. A. Lymberis "Smart wearable systems for personalized health management: current R&D and future challenges," Inter. Conf. of IEEE, vol.4, p.3716-3719, 2003.

5. N. Golmie, D. Cypher, and O. Rebala, "Performance analysis of low rate wireless technologies for medical application," Computer Communication, vol.28, no.10, p.1255-1275, 2005.

6. N. Golmie, N. Chevrollier, and O. Rebala, "Bluetooth and WLAN coexistence: challenges and solutions," IEEE Wireless Communication Magazine, vol.10, no.6, p.22-29, 2003.

7. I. Howitt and J.A. Gutierrez, "IEEE 802.15.4 low rate –wireless personal area network coexistence issues," IEEE Wireless Communication & Network Conf., vol.3, p.1481- 1486, 2003.

8. S. Pollin, M. Ergen, and A. Dejonghe, "Distributed cognitive coexistence of 802.15.4 with 802.11," Inter. Conf. on Cognitive Radio Oriented Wireless Networks and Communications, p.1-5, 2006.

9. Y. Xiao and N.H. Vaidya, "On physical carrier sensing in wireless ad hoc networks," IEEE Conf. on Computer Communications, vol.4, p.2525-2535, 2005.

10. H. Ma, H. Alazemi and S. Roy, "A stochastic model for optimizing physical carrier sensing and spatial reuse in wireless ad hoc networks," IEEE Conf. on Mobile adhoc and Sensor systems, 2005.

11. H. Zhai and Y. Fang, "Physical carrier sensing and spatial reuse in multirate and multihop ad hoc network," IEEE Conf. on Computer Communications, p.276-285, 2006.

12. J. Zhu, S. Roy, X. Guo, and W.S. Conner, "Leveraging spatial reuse in 802.11 mesh networks with enhanced physical carrier sensing," IEEE Conf. on Communications, vol.7, p. 4004-4011, 2004.

13. J. Zhu, B. Metzler, X. Guo, and Y. Liu, "Adaptive CSMA for scalable network capacity in high-density WLAN: a hardware prototyping approach," IEEE Conf. on Computer Communications, p.1-10, 2006.

14. Y. Zhu, Q. Zhang, Z. Niu and J. Zhu, "On optimal physical carrier sensing: theoretical analysis and protocol design," IEEE Conf. on Computer Communications, p.2351-2355, 2007.

15. K. Jamieson, B. Hull, A. Miu and H Balakrishnan, "Understanding the real-world performance of carrier sense," ACM SIGCOMM workshop on Experimental Approach to Wireless Network Design and Analysis, p. 52-57, 2005.

16. I. Ramachandran and S. Roy, "On the impact of clear channel assessment on MAC performance," IEEE Global Communications Conf, p. 1-5, 2006.
17. IEEE 802.15.4b standard, "Wireless medium access control and physical layer specification for low rate wireless personal area networks", 2006.
18. IEEE 802.11b standard, "Wireless medium access control and physical layer specification for low rate wireless local area networks", 2001.
19. V.I. Kostylev, "Energy detection of a signal with random amplitude," IEEE Conf. on Communications, vol.3, p. 1606-1610, 2004.
20. S.M. Kay, "Fundamentals of statistical signal processing: detection theory," Prentice-Hall PTR, New Jersey, 1998.
21. V. Erceg, et al., "An empirically based path loss model for wireless channels in suburban environments," IEEE J. on Selected Areas in Communications, vol. 17, no. 7, pp. 1205- 1211, 1999.
22. A. Sonneschein and P.M. Fishman, "Radiometric detection of spread-spectrum signal in noise of uncertain power," IEEE Trans. Aerospace Electronic Systems, vol.28, no.3, p.654-660, 1992.
23. IEEE P1073, "IEEE standard for medical device communications-overview and framework," 1996

26 Chapter MULTI-AGENT ARCHITECTURE FOR THE PHYSICAL LAYER OF A DISTRIBUTED BASE STATION NETWORK

1. INTRODUCTION:AN OVERVIEW

As wireless networks become more ubiquitous, effective resource allocation and management increasingly pose a significant issue. Two significant types of wireless network technology exist in the consumer market. Cellular mobile networks are characterized by a high degree of centralization and hierarchy. In contrast, wireless local area networks (WLANs) are implemented in an ad-hoc, unstructured fashion, hence eliminating the necessity for intricate and expensive planning. Nonetheless, WLANs, particularly those adhering to the very successful 802.11 standard, inadequately handle interference and are prone to failure under elevated traffic loads. Cellular networks and WLAN exemplify two fundamentally distinct methodologies in radio resource management, each possessing unique advantages and disadvantages.

This chapter aims to illustrate the viability of a connection-oriented self-organized wireless system that ensures efficient radio resource management while integrating the advantages of both cellular networks (reliable, connection-oriented functionality under high loads) and WLANs (ad-hoc deployment and distributed intelligence). This is accomplished through the multi-agent idea and localized synergistic micro-interactions among neighboring transceivers, resulting in the emergence of a global organization.

The concept of Multiple Agents (MA) pertains to the "ant" kind, in which diminutive minimalist agents perceive their surroundings and respond to them in a mutually dependant fashion. Social insects, primarily ants and bees, are the most frequently referenced biological examples. Such methodologies have been previously employed in the literature to address numerous combinatorial and optimization challenges (Beongku et al., 2003; Brueckner & Parunak, 2003; Muraleedharan & Osadciw, 2003).

This design philosophy contrasts with conventional methods that rely on establishing criteria using equations and models to frame the problem, hence deriving an optimal solution within a specified context. In the agent approach, an exact mathematical representation of the problem is neither necessary nor very beneficial. This method is appealing for addressing intricate multidimensional issues that would otherwise be unmanageable. Consequently, our objective is not to present an optimal architecture, but to exemplify how a Multi-Agent System (MAS) can be empirically constructed and refined to suit a particular application. Furthermore, it will be evident that this dynamically adaptive solution, despite its empirical basis, presents numerous advantages compared to a rigid analytically-derived alternative.

We will focus herein on Parunak's methodology (Parunak, 1997) because it offers an intuitive modeling framework, which is well suited to the empirical design approach.

This chapter presents a versatile distributed base station (DBS) framework for wireless networks that alleviates numerous constraints of existing networks to expand the solution space. A multitude of DBS can concurrently establish a network connection to the same mobile device, hence utilizing macrodiversity to enhance link quality and/or attain power efficiency. These DBS are engineered for automatic organization, enabling the network to structure itself independently. This is where MAS plays a role, providing the requisite distributed intelligence, adaptability, scalability, and auto-configuration attributes. However, the DBS architecture is challenging in at least three aspects:

1. It requires the continuously-updated solving of a large combinatorial problem, namely finding a good allocation of DBS resources to mobiles requiring service.
2. Interference must be handled in a transparent way so that mobiles can gain the best benefit of macrodiversity without being restrained by interfering mobiles.
3. Power control is an important aspect for both energy consumption and network capac- ity given that it is tightly-coupled with interference patterns.

The three aspects are interconnected, rendering optimal allocation a complicated combinatorial problem. It is NP-hard unless significant simplifying assumptions are imposed regarding geometry, propagation, or other factors. Furthermore, within the realm of mobility, a solution deemed ideal at a specific moment is not truly optimal if it lacks the capacity to readily adjust to fluctuating factors (such as the positions of mobiles, fading, etc.).

This intricate environment is really appropriate for a MAS design. Indeed, MA requires a dynamic environment to facilitate interaction. Each instance of power, channel, or connection allocation to mobile devices generated by a DBS impacts the linkages of other mobile devices. This establishes the necessary active environment in which agents can perceive parameters such as received power, interference, and connection quality, enabling local decision-making to produce new actions. The consequences of these activities are perceived by other agents. The subsequent section delineates the issues associated with the proposed DBS design. The MA design concepts employed in this study are delineated.. The fourth section details the proposed design of three categories of interacting agents respectively for :

1. macrodiversity connection management,
2. channel allocation, and
3. power level control.

The system has been successfully emulated. The results, encompassing simulations of intricate scenarios with randomly distributed DBS and mobile traffic, demonstrate firstly the quality of resource allocation achievable, and secondly the efficacy of MAS design regarding auto-configuration, scalability, and dynamic adaption capabilities.

A concluding succinct discussion will elaborate on Parunak's agent design principles to encapsulate the insights gained from developing multi-agent systems for the specific application.

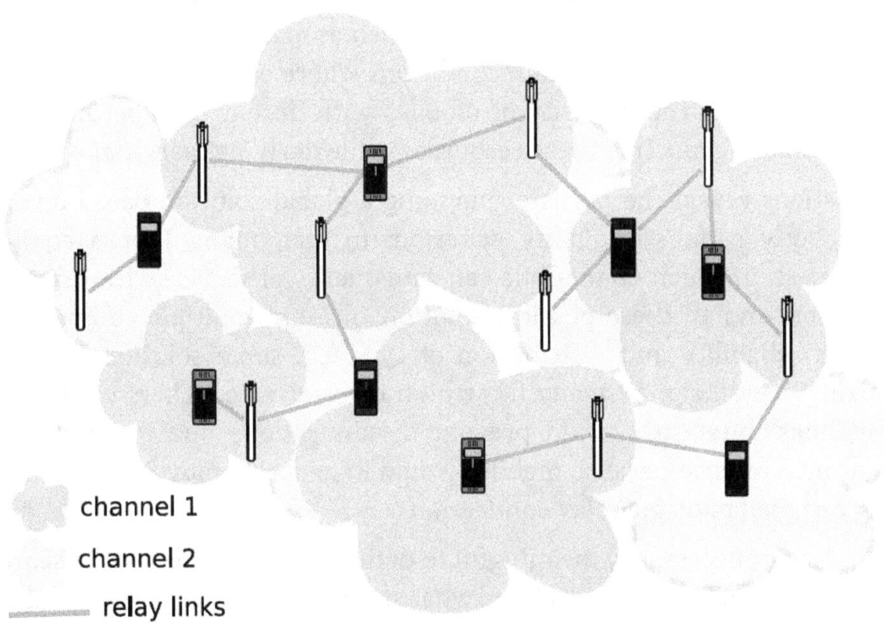

Fig. 1. Illustration of a DBS architecture exploiting 2 channels, and showing macrodiversity relay connections.

2. CHALLENGES OF THE DISTRIBUTED BASE STATION NETWORK

2.1 Macrodiversity Potential

In a perfectly geometrical network with homogeneous traffic and symmetric propagation con- ditions, each DBS needs only to connect to the closest mobiles to maximize the provided qual- ity of service. However, traffic is never homogeneous and varies across time and space in ac- cordance with the users' schedules and patterns of usage. Moreover, propagation conditions are highly dependent on location, with varying availability of lines of sight and saturation of the frequency band due to heavy traffic. In such a context, there is a need for a simple, scalable, dynamic system to allocate relay links to mobiles and to continuously adapt the al- location pattern to changing conditions.

DBS can choose to relay mobiles far away from themselves in order to provide them with more macrodiversity, and thus better balance resource allocation. However, this choice involves a trade off. The exponentially-decaying link quality with the mobile-DBS distance could lead a remote mobile to consume many valuable relay links while deriving only marginal benefits, whereas closer mobiles would obtain much higher macrodiversity benefits from those same resources. Also, macrodiversity links provide not only enhanced overall quality links, but also reliability against network disconnection when undergoing severe fading, and it facilitates handover for mobiles moving outside from the range of some DBS to others. Therefore, a single criterion such as maximizing the minimum QoS for all mobiles would fail in certain conditions where enough resources would be available to provide the majority of mobiles with decent QoS, because of a few mobiles consuming much of these resources while deriving marginal benefits.

Such situations reveal the perils of pursuing a global solution based on a single perhaps overly simplistic quality criterion. In fact, many Pareto equilibrium solutions exist, in which no mo- bile can gain quality of service without stranding another user. And all these possible solutions present multiple compromises on connection reliability and distribution of QoS. e.g. some solutions could favor maximizing overall signal strength for high transfer rate, others by distributing relaying links differently could prevent disconnections due to sudden strong fading or interference because mobiles would in general enjoy higher probability of being assigned multiple relay connections.

As such, it is not necessarily meaningful to define a priori goals for the search of a solution, as it is not known beforehand what are the benefits and drawbacks of each possible Pareto solution. This solution space is moreover hardly tractable due to the discrete nature of the problem, with a finite but large number of link resources to attribute. It is limited by physical conditions where some links may not be feasible due to the weakness of the considered signals. Also each link brings an increment of additional quality to the mobile's overall link quality, whose importance heavily depends on local propagation conditions that can vary continuously (with slow fading and changing mobile-DBS distances), or abruptly given the arrival of new connections in frequency allocation or strong fading situations. In this context, no analytically tractable mathematical framework exists leading to an optimum solution tak- ing into account all the dimensions of the problem. More specifically, one must consider that an optimal solution, at a given state of the network and a given frame in time, could be too heavily specialized to that particular situation, such that a sudden change (strong fading, new mobiles joining the network) would make it ineffective. By analogy, it is known in biology that a species too well adapted to its environment is heavily endangered due to its limited capacity to adapt to environmental changes. Hence, a good solution is not an optimal one, but a good enough one that provides margins for adaptation in time to face changes.

There is a strong need for distributed techniques which are flexible enough to be tuned to the desired compromises while being able to handle unexpected events.

2.2 Channel allocation

Channel allocation faces the same propagation issues as connection management. To under- stand the implications of channel management, we introduce the concept of channel footprint. In a given situation (mobiles and DBS positions and relative densities, available channels, power allocations, etc.), a mobile's channel footprint can be understood as the space it oc- cupies to maintain all its relaying links to DBS at a sufficient quality level. Hence, a second mobile, if emitting on the same channel inside this space, would affect some or all of the first mobile's connections.

In the cellular context, it is assumed that each mobile enjoys the same channel footprint which is controlled by the cell division of the space and an appropriate interference level threshold to allow or prevent the reuse of a channel across cells. In the 802.11 protocol, it is a handshake mechanism (the RTS/CTS exchange) which alerts neighboring transceivers that the channel will be in use, in order to control, to some extent, this channel footprint by preventing neigh- bors from reusing the channel in the vicinity, thus minimizing the hidden terminal effect (Ware et al., 2001).

In the DBS architecture, it would be appropriate that mobiles be offered varying channel foot- prints to adjust availability of channel resources and support the various needs of mobiles for macrodiversity. Indeed, mobiles needing more macrodiversity would require a larger foot- print. Moreover, mobiles close to all of their relaying DBS should allow other mobiles to reuse the same channel at a closer range, compared to mobiles far from all DBS. This holds since these mobiles can support higher interference power and still maintain a good signal to inter- ference plus noise ratio (SINR). This aspect of channel allocation was taken into consideration in the dynamic allocation scheme know as the umbrella cell system (Furukawa & Akaiwa, 1994). However, channel reuse should not necessarily always be maximized, since it could lead to locally unnecessarily compacted channel allocation, even in low traffic conditions. Hence, channel allocation should be able to adapt to always balance resources to sustain the high throughput rate of modern communication services.

Another aspect to consider is the irregular geometry of the DBS network. The DBS density will necessarily change across space given some maximum or mean local load. And also, local mobile traffic varies across time and space (e.g. from residential neighborhood to office centers). This leads to constantly changing disparities in local loads of the network to which it must adapt the channel allocation. In the cellular world, solutions exist in the form of Dynamic Channel Allocation schemes (DCA), such as the well-known segregation scheme by Akaiwa & Andoh (1993), allowing cells with higher loads to use more channels.

Finally, faster channel allocation adaptation is required with high mobility, as mobiles move in and out of DBS' ranges. In cellular systems, this aspect is only tackled via a handover mechanism. However, in the DBS concept, DBS share channels via the macrodiversity relaying links. Hence, mobiles need not change their channel simply because they change a relaying link. This additional complexity implies channel segregation algorithms are not as efficient in the DBS concept.

2.3 Power allocation

Power level management can strongly affect the previously described aspects of connections and channel management. It can also offer a powerful means to leverage the possibilities in terms of resource management. Indeed, in the context of DBS, a higher power level implies modifying the mobile's channel footprint, and hence allowing it to reach perhaps more DBS for more macrodiversity. Or, on the contrary, a lower power level will leverage the channel's reuse possibilities by generating less interference. Power control can therefore help to provide much higher resource availability, and can provide synergistic behavior with the channel and connection allocation to leverage the possibilities that macrodiversity can offer to balance the resources across mobiles, throughout the network.

However, there potentially exists a maximum power level dynamic range which limits the effectiveness of power control. Indeed, decentralized DCA implies sensing the availability of channels. For example, the 802.11 protocol implements CSMA (Carrier-Sense Multiple Access) to prevent improper reuse of channels. In the cellular world with DCA, a maximum sensed interference power level threshold is considered to decide if the channel is available. Therefore, the dynamic range of power-level adjustments cannot exceed a certain range such that mobiles with low emission power needs are not disrupted by the interference caused by a new connection from another mobile, perhaps much further away, but with a much higher power level. It is noteworthy that this power level range is dependent on the space distribution of mobiles (and channel allocation). The range itself may not be constant at all scales such that it could be high throughout the entire network when compared to smaller areas of the network. Indeed, the SINR is a relative quantity which depends on the spatial distribution of access points and traffic.

Power level allocation is also a contention process where each mobile strives to maximize its QoS. Considering the viewpoint of one mobile, in order to maximize its QoS, it wants to be within reach of a maximum number of DBS to maximize macrodiversity, and it also wants to maximize its SINR for each of its links. Therefore, it wants to maximize its power level. However, if all mobiles did so, none would get any benefit. And since no mobile can obtain any gains by reducing its power level, a non cooperative strategy is not a good choice for a game-theoretic approach to power level adaptation.

Necessarily, some mobiles will have to "accept" to reduce their power level in order to al- low other mobiles in need to enjoy better QoS by reducing interference and enabling them to reach more DBS for macrodiversity. Yet, and due to the non linearity of the propagation environment, there necessarily is a point of diminishing returns for mobiles to reduce their power level. While any reduction necessarily implies a reduction in interference, the potential gain for other mobiles does not necessarily offset or compensate (given a compromise choice at a global scale) the loss in QoS for this mobile. It is to be understood here that there exist trade-offs for an infinity of Pareto solutions. Therefore, and again, postulating one global uni-dimensional criteria (e.g. as is done in traditional algorithms (Grandhi et al., 1993)) to derive a power allocation method would not allow assessment of the potential benefits of different trade-offs. Indeed, the results of the proposed design will show how the traditional approach to power control (which consists in maximizing the minimum SINR for all mobiles) in spite of offering interesting capabilities in some situations, also prevents most mobiles from achieving their QoS potential.

2.4 Complexity, Dynamics and Scalability

2.4.1 Complexity

In existing types of networks, the complexity is constrained by simplifying the hypotheses. For example, in cellular networks, channel allocation is simplified by segregating channels given an interference power threshold in order to guarantee a minimum SINR for all mobiles in a cell. This assumption simplifies the evaluation of provided QoS, as it guarantees a mini- mum QoS for connected mobiles, and avoids the hidden terminal effect, such that there only remains to evaluate the probability of a connection being blocked (when all channels in a cell or sector are occupied).

In the considered architecture, such assumptions are not made a priori as the purpose of the DBS architecture is to maximize flexibility. And considering the number of possible combina- tions of connections, or channels or even power levels, it is obvious that an exhaustive search to find all Pareto solutions is pointless. Even considering an exhaustive search in the case of a very simple scenario with only a few mobiles is pointless, since in such cases, the non-linear effects and interactions of large networks would not apply and the obtained results would be too limited to draw meaningful conclusions.

Also, postulating a unidimensional criterion and over-simplifying the non-linear effects in- volved, in order to provide a tractable mathematical framework would limit the solution space and therefore restrict the possibilities of such an architecture.

MA offer interesting properties to cope with complexity. The approach involves segmenting the problem into mulitple subproblems where each is tackled by its own agent class. Heavy calculations for evaluating and selecting combinations are also avoided. Instead, specific com- binations are attempted and modified by agents' actions through local interactions.

2.4.2 Dynamics and Scalability

One particular aspect to consider is the fact that a given resource allocation solution must necessarily adapt to changes in a mobile wireless network. Such a solution must also adapt to unexpected events, such as the failure of a DBS. And finally it must scale, such that adding DBS locally will seamlessly, without any need for configuration, increase the capacity of the network in terms of either provided QoS or number of provided connections.

3. MULTI-AGENT DESIGN

To solve the resource allocation problem, with the previously described considerations, multiple agents or bio-inspired optimization seems appropriate, as such approaches provide the most important sought-after characteristics, namely

- scalability ;
- dynamic adaptation ;
- auto-configuration ;
- reliability facing unexpected events.

Following Parunak's (Parunak, 1997) design principles, three main characteristics need to be provided in a MA design: coupling, auto-catalysis, and function. Coupling implies that each MA process is coupled directly or not to the others and their environment (e.g indirectly using pheromones via an environment). Auto-catalysis implies that the agents' actions taken in the right direction1, by the nature of the agents' processes, favor similar actions leading the system to converge to a desirable state (positive feedback reinforcing the convergence towards the solution). And finally, the system must be such that a useful global function emerges out of the induced local interactions.

3.1 Coupling

To achieve coupling, Parunak explains that we first need an active environment. The radio propagation medium constitutes just such an environment, as each mobile emitting on a given channel influences the others due to interference. Hence, a mobile's movement changes the interference patterns for all others in its immediate vicinity. Additionally, mobiles are entities which strive to acquire connections and in so doing, they necessarily broadcast information to inform neighboring DBS of their presence and of their link quality. This forms an active environment in which information is exchanged to sustain coupled processes.

We emphasize the fact that DBS and mobiles do form appropriate entities to host agents that are small in size and scope. In particular, DBS, compared to central cellular base stations, are specifically meant to be small, and will necessarily have small scope as they can only relay a (smaller) limited number of mobiles in their vicinity.

As a final criterion related to coupling, agents should be mapped as entities, not functions since an agent does not implement a complete function. That is, the function optimizing resource allocation should be the result of the interaction of the agents and not be implemented as the output of one agent. Indeed, an ant (in ant colonies) does not find a shortest path alone.

In the proposed system, the agents are mapped to either mobiles or DBS. Their actions will then be to either allocate or deallocate a channel, or a connection, or modify a mobile's power level. Necessarily, all processes which modify resource allocation are all coupled since each agent's actions will not only influence the concerned mobile (changing channel, obtaining a new relay connection or changing its power level), but also influence the neighboring mobiles, modifying their own channel footprint, their QoS, hence influencing other agents, and coupling each agent's processes together indirectly.

3.2 Auto-catalysis

3.2.1 Flows

For agents to maintain their interactions, they must be designed to let the process evolve continuously. Therefore, agents should not be designed based on discrete state transitions, leading to pauses in the processes because of unverified conditions.

That is why we must favor flows instead of transitions. One way to achieve this is for agents to use volatile markers (i.e. permanent and non-obstructive source of information which dissipate in time as they become irrelevant –e.g. pheromones in ant colonies) to inform other agents on their particular state, so that the agents' processes continuously evolve rather than stop and wait for specific conditions.

It is a design choice that no explicit information exchange is performed concerning the positions of mobiles and DBS, available resources, etc. As mentioned, the available information stems from what DBS and mobiles can sense locally (mobiles' needs and QoS), which represents our volatile markers. These bits of information are by nature volatile, as they only stay in the environment as long as they are broadcasted by the mobiles, and hence are necessarily current.

Since agents should not wait for predefined conditions to take actions, it is a comparative basis that will trigger a corresponding action of:

1. allocating/deallocating a macrodiversity connection;
2. changing a mobile's channel (frequency hopping);
3. increasing/decreasing a mobile's power level to a certain amount.

3.2.2 Homeostasis

The notion stems directly from biology in which systems always strive to maintain an equi- librium or homeostasis point, e.g. the blood sugar concentration is maintained (mainly) by two different hormones which have opposite effects to balance the concentration.

This point of equilibrium must be sustained by an ongoing flow to ensure the system continu- ously explores the solution space and does not get stuck in a deadend. This flow is analogous to the variations of a stock market title whose value is influenced (at a macro level) by the traders' actions of selling and buying. In turn, at the micro level, the variations of the values influences the traders' decisions.

The corresponding aspect of our system is created by forcing DBS to continuously create and destroy connections, continuously change channels (via channel hopping), and continuously adjust power levels. Each of these actions — at the macro level of agents — influences the status of mobiles, and these changes are in turn sensed by surrounding mobiles and DBS.

In effect, the flow of actions makes the system converge to a homeostasis point. This point will be dependent on the the state of the network (traffic, available resources, etc.) due to the comparative basis that triggers actions. As long as there exists a bias observed by the agents that will trigger an action, the system will converge or oscillate to its homeostasis point. These variations are important, since without them, and if there is no other change in the system (e.g., induced by mobile motion), the sensed QoS of mobiles would never change, never trigger actions, and the system might simply stop short of an optimal state.

3.2.3 Amplification and limitation

Together, amplification and limitation constitute an other important aspect to generate the convergence to a homeostasis point. Amplification implies a positive feedback mechanism such that convergence (to a solution) is favored. In other words, the actions of an agent which lead the system in a desirable global direction should be favored and should also influence the surrounding agents to act in the same direction.

In effect, an MA system is comparable to a Genetic Algorithm (Goldberg, 1989) preserving "genes" that seem to provide the best fitness and hence are part of an optimal solution. The difference is that there are no external observing entities that measure via a metric the fitness of candidate solutions. Rather, it is the interactions between agents and their environment — the propagation medium — that must provide the natural selection function.

Limitation also implies preventing the whole system from focusing on one point (exacerbating the convergence of actions to a local minimum) and thus miss a better solution. Moreover, limitation can favor convergence by dampening the effect of amplification to prevent the system from going past a solution or oscillating around it without converging.

3.3 Function

Coupling may be trivial to obtain and auto-catalysis somewhat more involved, but if the process as a whole does not realize a useful function, then it is irrelevant. Function implies that the homeostasis point described previously is useful for the system, e.g. in biology the homeostasis point for the blood sugar concentration is such that enough sugar is available to fuel the cells, but not too much to avoid excessive sugar loss through the kidneys.

In our system, the sought-after function consists in

- maximizing the potential usage of the resources;
- and balancing them to offer a good compromise of quality across all mobiles, while not hindering the overall system performance.

Most often, function is obtained through a utility function which translates the flow of variations (of QoS) sensed into rational decisions. That is, it converts a multi-dimensional problem into a one-dimensional quantity upon which decisions for actions are based.

In spite of the fact that many frameworks attempt to provide mathematical support to de- rive such utility functions (such as game theory (Mackenzie & Wicker, 2001) or COIN theory (Tumer & Wolpert, 2004)), these frameworks mostly consider intelligent agents having the ability to learn (eventually using reinforcement learning techniques), which is not the nature of the proposed design. Ultimately, defining simple agent behavior to obtain an intended global behavior still relies on intuition and art such as in Conway's "game of life" (Elwyn R. Berlekamp et al., 1982), or with Wolfram's cellular automatons (Wolfram, 2002). Therefore, no systematic procedure is known which derives the locally-applicable utility function from the desired global behavior.

Function can also be sustained (especially if a utility function is not found) with

- behavior diversity and
- randomness.

Randomness can be helpful to introduce alternative solutions, that will or not be kept in time given how effective they are. Behavior diversity can be obtained by forcing neighboring agents to act differently so as to provide different reactions and experiments given identical stimulus. These properties support the function property by breaking the symmetry so as to prevent the system from entering any deterministic patterns which might hinder convergence. In the following section it is described how auto-catalysis and function are obtained for each class of agents.

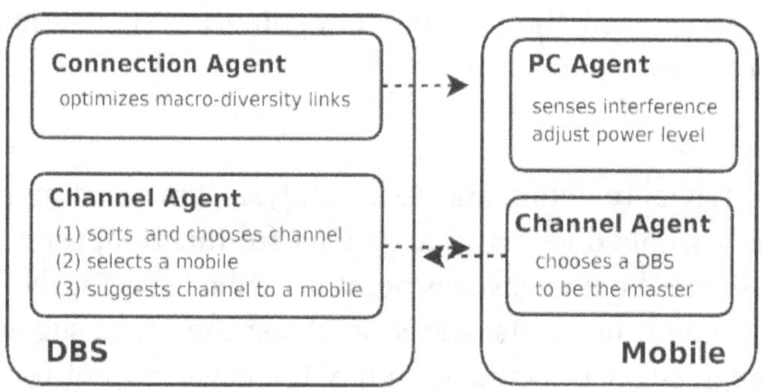

Fig. 2. Agents actions and mapping to entities.

4. AGENTS' DESIGN

4.1 Agents Sensing Abilities

A mobile broadcasts its actual QoS designated PT (m), so that DBS in its vicinity can sense its needs. This QoS corresponds to the total BER after macrodiversity combining the mobile's received signals. Moreover, a DBS senses the potential additional link quality it can provide (or already provides) to a mobile. Considering mobile m and DBS B, this additional link quality is named Pe (m, b), and represents the BER of the link from m to DBS b (Leroux et al., 2006). Also, to incorporate the notion of classes of QoS, the DBS knows that mobile m requires an overall quality of Pd (m), i.e. PT (m) < Pd (m).

For convenience, these values (Pe (m, b), Pd (m) and PT (m)) are expressed in a logarithmic scale of base 10 of the BER. It is shown in (Leroux et al., 2006) that the following holds in a Rice fading environment with different Rice fading parameters (SINR, K factor) values for each link:

$$\approx a + \sum_{b} P_e(m,b), \qquad (1)$$

where the relation (which implies that the combined BER is the sum in the logarithmic do- main of the individual link BERs) is exact for certain types of modulation (such as DPSK) and approximate for other types (such as coherent QPSK), and a is a constant related to the modulation.

By definition, if mobile m is not relayed by DBS b, we have

$$\text{Pe}\ (m, b) \triangleq 0. \qquad (2)$$

4.2 Connection Allocation

4.2.1 Coupling

Connection agents are mapped to DBS. Indeed, each DBS senses local information on mobiles' needs and can take decisions with regards to the allocation of connections. Mobiles can be relayed by many DBS offering more or less QoS. Therefore, a DBS decision (whether to relay or not a mobile) will influence what its neighboring DBS senses and therefore influence their actions. Hence, the whole network is interdependent and linked or coupled via macrodiversity links.

4.2.2 Flow of action

While attempting to maintain connectivity, DBS should continuously change their links to gradually converge to an optimal configuration which maximizes the benefits of macrodiversity. It is this flow of changes in connection allocation which sustains the properties of auto-catalysis and function.

In order to do so, two types of actions are defined : disconnection and reconnection. Each action is taken alternatively, given the number of active connections the DBS has. Suppose a DBS can provide at most N connections and has m active connections, it will perform

1. N - n disconnections, if it has m > N - n connections or,
2. N - m connections, if it has m ≤ N - m connections.,

where n is a system parameter (typically n = 1) under the designer's control. For large values of N, increasing n helps accelerate the convergence of the system, yet high values of n will suppress the iterative selection mechanism such that the system may not converge any longer. Hence two opposing "forces" must be designed to link the information sensed to the choice that must be taken : which mobiles should be connected or disconnected. Finally, the balance between these two forces should lead connections to a state that represents an homeostasis point.

4.2.3 Function

Randomness is incorporated by having the connection agents activate (to perform a connection or disconnection action) randomly, following a Poisson law considering a discrete model of time. This should also help to prevent any periodic pattern from taking hold.

A utility function is designed to link the information sensed to the choice of actions : links are rated according to a continuous function so the DBS can compare the links and decide which to connect or to disconnect.

Two metrics are designed, providing information on:

1. a measure of how well mobile m is served with respect to its requested QoS, i.e.

$$F_{\text{need}}(m) = \frac{P'_T(m)}{P_d(m)}, \tag{3}$$

2. and a measure of how much diversity DBS b is providing to m with respect to the mo- bile's overall link quality, i.e,

$$F_{\text{div}}(m,b) = \frac{P_e(m,b)}{P'_T(m)}. \tag{4}$$

PTt is understood in these definitions as the mobile's total link quality if DBS b is connected to the mobile (whether it is evaluating for connection or disconnection). These two simple functions provide sufficient information for the DBS to compare the mobiles' links and take a decision based on:

- how much a mobile needs more macrodiversity links;
- and to which extent this DBS is the one which will provide the mobile with an efficient macrodiversity link (relative to the other DBS currently serving the mobile).

These information bits still need to be combined, and this is where an appropriate trade-off is induced by using different combination functions.

To design the combination function, different characteristics must be considered:

1. If a mobile has no connection, it must be favored, since basic connectivity should take precedence.
2. If a mobile has only one connection, the DBS should not disconnect it.

Furthermore, there are two complementary compromises involved in the DBS' decision process:

1. either to remove a link because the mobile already enjoys sufficient QoS,
2. or to maintain it because it is the main DBS providing

it; and,

1. either to connect a mobile because it is in need,
2. versus not connecting it because the additional diversity brought to this mobile would be low (compared to other possible connections).

Finally, the function must provide a natural ordering to classify the compromises in order to take a decision.

The following function addresses all the characteristics discussed above:

$$C(m, b) = Fneed(m) \times \log (Fdiv(m, b)) . \qquad (5)$$

This function is necessarily positive or null. It is null if the mobile has no connection, since, if it were connected to the DBS, it would have PT (m) = Pe (m, b) which implies Fdiv = 1 giving a null value of the logarithm. Likewise, it is null if considered for disconnection and the mobile's only link is to the considered DBS. Hence, if this utility function is null, the agent will either privilege this mobile for connection or not disconnect it to keep the mobile's existing connection active.

The evaluation of the compromise is obtained by the multiplication of the two terms. Hence, the more the DBS provides diversity, or the higher is the current QoS enjoyed by the mobile, the higher is the function's value.

The choice of compromise itself comes derives from "shaping function" used prior to the multiplication of the two metrics. Simulation showed that the optimization happens most efficiently if the shaping function of the second term is concave (naturally, it should be strictly increasing), hence the use of the logarithm, which also provides the necessary null value for a mobile with a single link.

4.2.4 Limitation and amplification

Limitation and amplification is naturally obtained with the environment propagation proper- ties. Indeed, a poor signal quality will favor multiple connections (amplification), but distance (mobile to DBS) and the infrastructure link capacity of DBS will restrict excessive connection growth (limitation).

Also, this amplification (or attraction of macrodiversity links) and limitation sustains the homeostatic behavior where mobiles in need get more links up to an equilibrium point where additional links to these mobiles would overwhelmingly affect an otherwise well-served mobile.

4.3 Channel allocation

4.3.1 Flow

The flow of actions in the channel allocation agents naturally consists of the changes in channel allocation, or channel hopping which modifies mobiles' QoS and interference patterns which in turn should trigger other changes.

For this flow to be generated properly, appropriate actions are specified in the following.

4.3.2 Coupling

Following Parunak's principles, the sought-after function (optimizing the allocation) is di- vided into independent actions whose interactions should lead to the other two properties (auto-catalysis and function).

First, given the macrodiversity context, a mobile will choose one of its relaying DBS to be its "master" connection, which implies one type of action and one agent (to select the master) mapped at each mobile.

Second, DBS will choose mobiles (from their master links) and change their channels as is done in cellular systems. Except that here, the change, or channel hopping, will not be triggered by specified conditions (e.g. a mobile SINR falling below a threshold, or a mobile changing cell). Instead, the flow of channel hopping will be sustained by having DBS choose a mobile at each agent activation and change its channel. Channel allocation agents will activate in the same way that the connection agents do. Two types of actions must be defined:

1. choosing a mobile, and
2. choosing a channel.

Mapping these actions at the DBS level, rather than letting the mobile decide when to change channel makes sense in that DBS can gather information most effectively on the different channels in use, thus preventing mobiles from having to continuously scan channels.

4.3.2.1 Sensing

In addition to the mobile's sensed link quality, DBS can sense

1. the received power of surrounding mobiles pr (m, b);
2. and the interference level on various channels pI (b, c) (for channel c at DBS b).

4.3.3 Function

Maximizing the channel usage constitutes, in a sense, an effort against the second law of thermodynamics. Indeed, the channel allocation, if optimal at some point in time, will necessarily deteriorate with mobility as two mobiles transmitting on the same channel get closer to a point where the interference will degrade the offered QoS, such that resources are not balanced any- more. Considering this aspect, and rather than trying to solve an NP-complete problem, load balancing is obtained by always attempting to change the channels of mobiles in need such that they enjoy better SINR.

Three utility functions need to be designed taking as input what the agents can sense, and yielding a chosen parameter value as output.

a. Mobile m will choose a master DBS (among its relaying DBS) on activation (where its activation follows a Poisson law) based on the DBS from which it obtains the highest link quality:

$$b = \arg\max_{b}\{P_e(b,m)\}. \tag{6}$$

b. DBS b will choose a mobile (among mobiles connected as master to b), that is the most in need, i.e.

$$m = \arg\min_{m}\{F_{\text{need}}(m)\}. \tag{7}$$

c. Ideally, the DBS should try to use the channel with the lowest interference power level:

$$c = \arg\min_{c}\{p_I(b,c)\}. \tag{8}$$

However, it may be overwhelming for a DBS to systematically sense channels to maintain up- to-date information on interference lev vels on all channels, and this behavior (utility function c.) is therefore only used as a benchmark.

Akaiwa & Andoh (1993) suggested a selection mechanism which is used herein with some modifications. DBS b will scan channels in the order of a given priority list it maintains, and determine if a channel can be assigned according to

- whether the resulting SINR will be above an SINR threshold ;
- and (in addition to Akaiwa's method) whether it will also be above the actual SINR the mobile enjoys.

The SINR threshold represents a mean to control the hidden terminal effect. It is a studied pa- rameter in order to observe to which extend it prevents HTE while not limiting the flexibility of the system.

For Akaiwa's segregation algorithm, the priority list is obtained dynamically given the ratio for each channel of previous assignments versus previous assignment attempts.

Finally, a random priority list is proposed as a simple, yet effective (as we will see) alternative to the segregation algorithm approach.

4.3.4 Limitation

DBS will only test a limited number of channels given by the Chmax parameter, before giving up. Indeed, there is no guarantee that the DBS will find a channel that will suit the chosen mobile. Therefore, and instead of letting it scan all channels, it is forced to limit its search. Eventually, it will try again, or another DBS will, thus providing behavior diversity as well. In effect, the DBS are only trying to maintain channel assignments in a working state by "up- grading" the solution iteratively in an opportunistic fashion given the eventual availability of channels. It is the effect of a new channel allocation that will cause other DBS to also react and change channels for the mobiles that will see their QoS affected by the new neighboring interference. As this flow of action is sustained, the channel allocation remains functional and should adapt to changes.

4.3.5 Channel availability

An additional functionality is provided for channel availability. A few spare channels are reserved for the initial connection or reconnection of stranded mobiles (instead of using channels from the main pool). Then, a master DBS which has mobiles on these spare channels will attempt to change their channels as a priority instead of choosing another mobile. Such spare channels allow rapid network entry, providing higher availability as well as some time margin for the DBS to find free channels in the main pool. It therefore eases the process and the flow of channel hopping.

4.3.6 Alternatives

Some attempts were made in order to add additional functionality to better handle irregular topologies and classes of QoS. One such attempt was not only to change channels of mobiles in need to better ones, but to also change channels of over-served mobiles with worse ones. However, this approach proved fruitless. One reason is that it is not possible for DBS to differentiate between channels having high interference due to over-served mobiles or poorly served mobiles. And the change to a "worse" channel can have more cons (far too much degradation for other mobiles) than pros (compacting channels more efficiently to free resources). Indeed, the main challenge resides in the degradation of interference. And, in effect, better results are obtained by simple channel hopping with the poorly served mobiles until other mobiles are affected, react, and some balance is obtained.

The concept of classes of channels was also explored, where the threshold considered to assign a channel would be modulated given the class of the channel and the mobile's need, in order to generate classes of channels with less interference and some with more, for mobiles which can sustain it (which is also inspired from the umbrella-cell mechanism). No significant increase of performance has yet been obtained with this approach.

4.4 Power Allocation

4.4.1 Flow

Necessarily, the flow in power allocation is the result of changes in power level, which in turn changes interference, and the QoS of surrounding mobiles, which in turn should trigger other power level changes. This striving for amplified/ limited adjustments of power levels aims to converge to a point of equilibrium : an homeostasis point where the system actually exhibits its expected power control behavior.

4.4.2 Function

The previously defined Fneed(m) definition is considered. If it is above 1, the mobile is over served (it enjoys a BER better than requested) and should reduce its power level, or increase it if lower than 1. Yet, this in itself would be restrictive, as it would force all mobiles to the same mean quality Fneed value, without taking into account the non linearity of the problem due in part to the limited dynamic range of mobiles' power levels. Indeed, and as will be shown, the thermal noise at the receivers imposes a limit on the minimum power level a mobile can transmit without the resulting SINR being too low for the connection (however small the interference level is). And, of course, mobiles saturate at a maximal power level. Also, some mobiles might be able to obtain more quality while not restricting others to maximize their own, and if so, they should.

The Need variable is introduced to describe what could be the power level of the mobile given its Fneed(m) factor : it is the value to which the mobile's power level should converge to if nothing else changes (which is not the case as other mobiles will adjust their power level). When, for all mobiles, the current Needm value equals the current power level p(m), then the homeostasis point is reached. The variable is defined

$$\text{Needm}\,(\text{Fneed}(m)) = 2e(-\text{SFneed}\,(m)) \times (\text{SFneed}(m)+1) - 1, \qquad (9)$$

where the value S is a scaling parameter for Fneed(m) in order to allow mobiles to potentially obtain QoS higher than their requested Pd (m). Therefore, the Need function will not neces- sarily be smaller than the current power level if Fneed(m) > 1. And mobiles will not be forced to restrict their obtained QoS to a global mean value. In the current simulations, this QoS is maximized with S = 0.8, and this has been shown to hold in many different conditions of traffic, mobile speeds in (9) and available resources.

The exponential in (9) is a shaping function which also naturally affects the dynamics of the system. In effect, it affects mobiles' convergence speed differently given their needs, and this translates into behavior diversity as no mobile will react in a precisely proportional manner. The proposed function is of course not the only possible choice, but it has proved stable and effective. Again, for MAS, effectiveness does not lie in the mathematical exactness of the function, but in the interactions it will generate.

4.4.3 Homeostasis

Finally, this Need factor must be converted to a delta (step) value to adjust the power level. Homeostasis is obtained by comparing the Need value to the current power level the mobile uses to transmit. Hence, the delta value is in the form of Needm – pm. The mobile will then try to converge to a Needm value which depends on local interactions given itself and neighboring mobiles'Fneed values (given that these are indirectly linked via interference). Eventually, a non-linear concave function helps convergence so that with Needm and pm close, the gen- erated delta is kept small to slow down variations and help stabilize the convergence. We postulate

$$\Delta m = \beta \operatorname{sign}(Needm - pm)\ (|Needm -|)1.5 \qquad (10)$$

where the β factor is used to modify the dynamics of the system to attain the proper compro- mise between convergence speed and stability.

4.4.4 Limitation

Experience shows that this function is too unstable with high values of β. Still, it can be stabilized with additional scaling parameters, while maintaining fast adaptation in time with large values of β ≥ 5, which is important for mobility (β = 5 is used in the presented simulations). Therefore, it is proposed that Δ be scaled according to the current power level and also the desired power level (the Need value). That way, if these values are small, Δ is also kept small to prevent strong changes in the system that would otherwise suddenly generate exaggerated interference. Indeed, such changes would lead to complications such as breaking existing links or simply propagating exaggerated reactions throughout the system. Building upon (10), the following function is used :

$$\Delta m = pm \times |Needm| \times \beta \operatorname{sign}(Needm - pm)(|Needm - pm|)1.5 \qquad (11)$$

Finally, the delta value is constrained to not exceed the power level range:

$$\Delta_m < 0 \Rightarrow \Delta_m' = \max\{\Delta_m, \frac{-p_m}{2}\} \qquad (12)$$

$$\Delta_m > 0 \Rightarrow \Delta_m' = \min\{\Delta_m, \frac{1}{2}(1 - p_m)\}. \qquad (13)$$

As the mobile's PC agent activates, its power level is adjusted as follows:

$$p_m^{(\nu+1)} = p_m^{(\nu)} + \Delta'_m. \tag{14}$$

5. EVALUATION

5.1 Simulation platform

For the channel and power agents, simulations are based on the following platform. The results shown for the connection agents are based on a simpler scenario (detailed in the appropriate subsection), in order to isolate the effect of connection management and observe its convergence, while not confusing it with the effect of interference and power-level management.

Physical parameters

A square field of 25 square kilometers is considered, in which 1000 mobiles evolve and 100 DBS are scattered randomly. Hence, the traffic's and network resources' geometry are not uniform, thus generating good and bad coverage of different areas. A mobile moves in a random direction at a random speed taken (at the start of a scenario) out of a uniform distribution over [0, Vmax]. DBS can relay 25 mobiles each, such that the mean number of macrodiversity links per mobile is 2.5. A mobile's maximum transmit power is 1W at 1 meter of its antenna, and the propagation exponent is 4 (gij ~ 1/d-4). Rayleigh fading is considered, except near a DBS (closer than 100m) where a line of sight component is added with Rice factor K = 5 dB. Thermal noise at the receiver is considered for a bandwidth of 30kHz at a temperature of 20◦C, hence N0 = -129 dBW. The number of available channels is denoted Ch.

Agents' emulation

Simulations are run for 1000 seconds and repeated 10 times with different initializations of the geometry (DBS positions and mobiles' initial position, directions and speeds). Time is discretized with a time step of 1 second. At each time step, physical parameters are evaluated (mobile's position, propagation, interference, BER, connection outage). Agents activate randomly given a Poisson distribution to estimate the next activation time with parameter λ = 3 time steps. At each time step, the agents which activate evaluate their local state and take actions accordingly (adjust the power level, hop to a new channel, change connections of the concerned mobile, etc.).

Results

At each time step, the set of QoS indexes (total BER level given on a logarithmic scale PT (m) = log10 (BER(m))) for each mobile are sorted, thus providing a snapshot in time of the distribution of the network's resources across all mobiles. These sorted distributions are then averaged for all the time steps of the simulation. Given this information, it is then possible to compare how each algorithm distributes resources. The same is done for the power level allocation. Also, to verify the stability in time (considering the dynamic properties) of the algorithm, two factors are interesting to observe to understand how the system handles outage :

1. the mean number Nd of mobiles that loose all connections to the network per second, and
2. the mean time tr it takes for the network to reconnect a mobile after it has been disconnected.

The latter also provides insight on how well the system is able to provide resources to mobiles with high availability.

5.2 Connection agents

In order to show that the connection agents are indeed optimizing the connections to balance resources, a simple centralized algorithm based on heuristics is proposed.

Algorithm 1 Centralized connection allocation algorithm
Considering initially that all DBS provide connections to all mobiles, and as long as there exist DBS with more than N maximum connections :
A1 eliminate the connections with smallest Pe (m, b) as long as m has PT (m) < Pd (m) and provided that DBS b has more than N connections ;
A2 (compromise on QoS) remove the ones with smallest Pe (m, b) as long as m remains connected (another DBS is providing it a connection);
A3 (compromise on connectivity) finally remove connections with the smallest Pe (m, b) until b has N maximum connections.

This algorithm is optimum at maximizing the sum of QoS Σm PT (m), given it only removes the smallest values. However, and given its limited ability to make compromises, it will not be efficient at balancing resources for mobiles and preventing disconnections of some mobiles if the network is resources-constrained. Necessarily, it offers a different trade-off than the agent algorithm provides.

1. Three cases are observed:
2. there are not enough resources (Fig. 3(a)),
3. there are enough resources for connections, but not enough headroom / margin and the agent system is not able to achieve swarming and converge (Fig. 3(b)),

there are enough resources to connect all mobiles and provide sufficient QoS, i.e. the connection agent is efficient (Fig. 3(c)).

In practice, only the third case should be relevant provided that the network is appropriately scaled for the needs of the users.

For the results shown in Figs. 3 and 4, a trellis of 19 DBS is used with 200 mobiles. Channel management is not considered and each mobile has its own channel.

In the third case (Fig. 3(c)), three successive phases in time can be observed :

1. a connection stage, where connections are established to the closest mobiles;
2. a connection optimization stage, where connectivity is maximized, and
3. a connection rearrangement stage, where QoS is maximized.

Figure 4 depicts a sort of the QoS PT (m) of mobiles to provide insight on how well resources are balanced. In this simulation, two classes of QoS are created, each comprising 100 mobiles. Compared to the centralized algorithm, it is obvious that some load balancing is performed by the agent system.

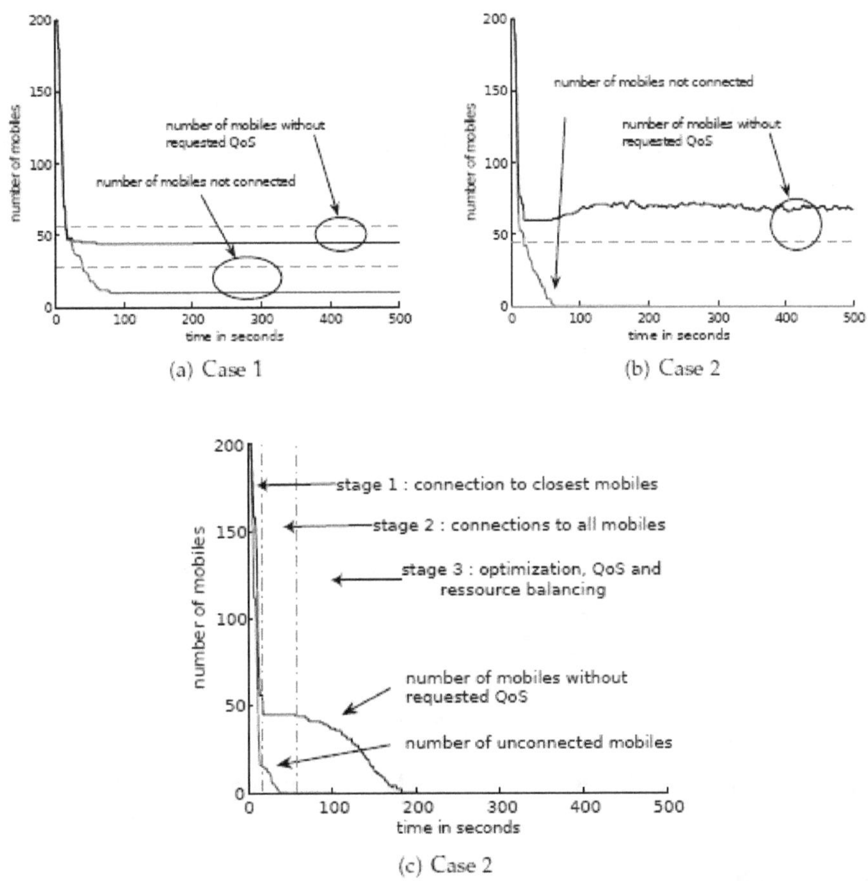

(a) Case 1 (b) Case 2 (c) Case 2

Fig. 3. Convergence of the connection management agents (horizontal dashed lines show results of the centralized heuristic algorithm).

Due to lack of space, figures for the dynamic behavior are not shown herein. However, it is important to note that, without requiring any information centralization or excessive signaling (which would generate delays), and based only on local interactions induced by connection and disconnection actions, the agent system is able to keep up (maintain the connection al- location in a relatively optimal state) fast enough to sustain mobiles moving at speeds of 50 km/h with connection agents activating in the mean only once every 3 seconds. Above that speed, performance in terms of QoS degrades smoothly as the agents are not able to converge fast enough to the optimal state. The system still provides much headroom as activation of agents could be much faster.

Given that the proposed design is bio-inspired, it is most interesting to observe "health parameters" (analogous to e.g. blood pressure in the human body) which give us insight on the capacity of the agents to achieve their function. For the connection agents, the mean number of connections should be close to the mean number of disconnections. This indicates that the agents have sufficient headroom (when faced with changes in the network) to actually swap connections for optimization. If there are more connections than disconnections, it means that the system is not able to keep up with changes so that some of the relay links are disconnected for physical reasons (e.g. loss of signal quality) instead of explicit decisions by the agents.

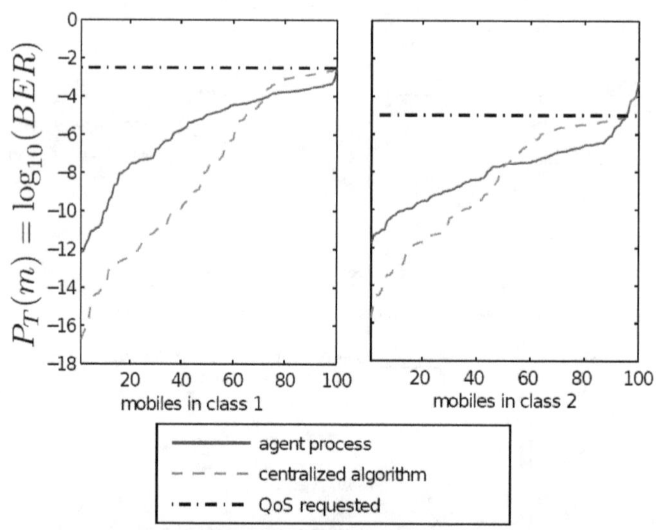

Fig. 4. Sorted profiles with 100 mobiles in class 1, 100 mobiles in class 2, and N = 25

5.3 Channel allocation

Channel management in the current context is hard to analyze and compare. Indeed, there ex- ist many parameters which are dependent and which render objective comparison of designs and algorithms rather difficult because of the many trade-offs involved.

For example, the hidden terminal effect (Nd) can be minimized at the expense of the capacity to reconnect quickly (tc). Also, QoS can be enhanced at the expense of connectivity. Indeed, the existence of a handful of unconnected mobiles implies more headroom (due to less inter- ference) for either QoS or faster reconnection.

The notion of block rate must, as it stands in a cellular context, be revisited, since in this distributed system, a mobile is not necessarily blocked because an attempt at connection fails. It might fail simply because the DBS suggesting the connection is not well positioned, and another DBS will try and succeed hopefully fast enough. However, the block rate (of blocked allocation attempts) still represents an interesting bit of information as it reveals how effective the agents are at trying to connect. It therefore translates the notion of fluidity. Yet, it is not directly comparable to the notion of block rate used in cellular networks.

In Figure 5(a), the effect of the SINR threshold is shown by comparing the number of lost connections per second (for 1000 mobiles) and the mean time it takes to reconnect them. There is an obvious ideal trade-off point. It is interesting to note that the best compromise, which also maximizes the mean number of connected mobiles (Fig. 5(b)) is just above 0dB. Indeed, such a threshold would be much higher in a cellular system. However, the DBS architecture allows much more flexibility and sustains lower SINR with macrodiversity.

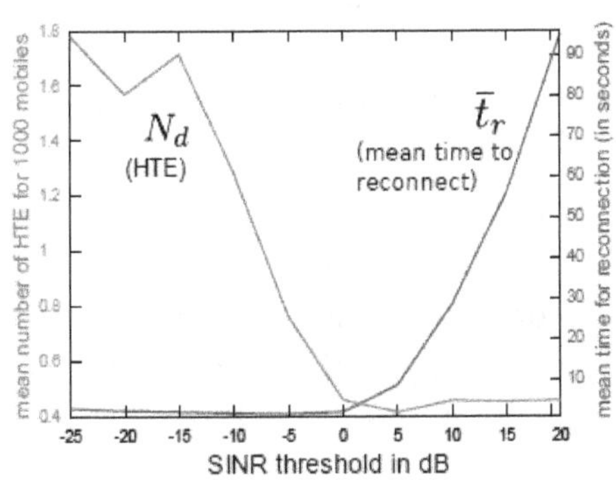

(a) Comparing the number of lost connections and the mean time before reconnection

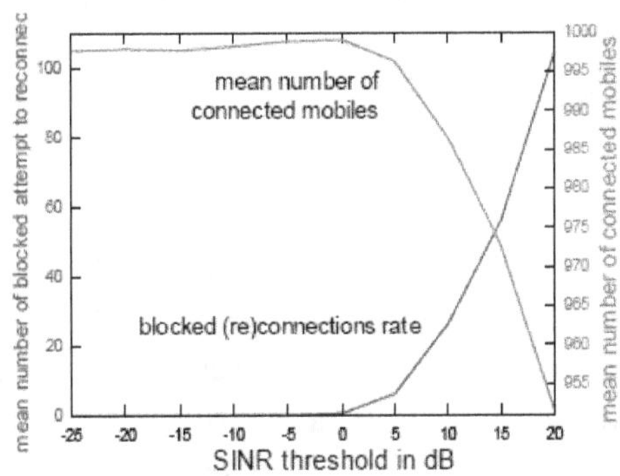

(b) Comparing the mean number of connected mobiles and the block rate

Fig. 5. Effect of the SINR threshold (Vmax = 5 m/s, Ch = 40, N = -129dBW).

Figure 6 shows the effect of using reserved channels for reconnection on a log-log scale. For this scenario, time has been discretized at one tenth of a second and agents activate in the mean once every second (or ten time units). In the mean, mobiles are reconnected up to ten times faster, without any loss in QoS. Numerically, slightly more mobiles get disconnected but a much larger number of mobiles are connected in the mean. Indeed, since more mobiles are in the mean connected, there is more interference to deal with, which makes it more difficult to prevent momentary disconnection. But the efficiency of reconnection is so much improved that in the mean, disconnection only occurs for less than 1 second (.8 seconds), and given the exponential distribution of reconnection time, 90% of the disconnections have smaller reconnection times. On the other hand, disconnection time is on the order of 5 seconds with no reserved channels.

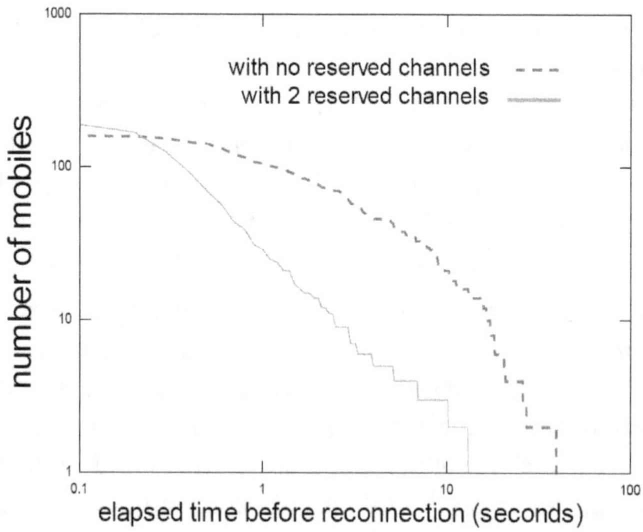

Fig. 6. Mean reconnection time with and without reserved channels. The Y axis represents the number of mobiles remaining unconnected since their disconnection (for 1000 mobiles during a 1000 seconds scenario length (Vmax = 5 m/s, Ch = 40, N = -129dBW).

Comparing the three different methods to select channels, little difference was observed in terms of the mean number of connected mobiles. Differences appear as trade-offs between mean number of disconnected mobiles and mean time of reconnection. The segregation method seems more efficient at minimizing disconnection, but takes more time to reconnect, compared to the random method. Differences appear most explicitly when looking at the provided QoS (Fig. 7). Choosing the channel with lowest interference power yields the best results, followed by the random choice and the segregation method. We notice an increased number of mobiles with their QoS demand met when the SINR threshold increases slightly. This is simply due to the fact that fewer mobiles are connected, generating less interference and higher QoS. However, this fact does not hold true for long, ince a further increase in the threshold leads to a rapid increase of the agents' block rate, showing that they are unable to keep up with changes, and are not finding free channels to adapt the allocation pattern. This leads to a fall in QoS (above 5-7 dB).

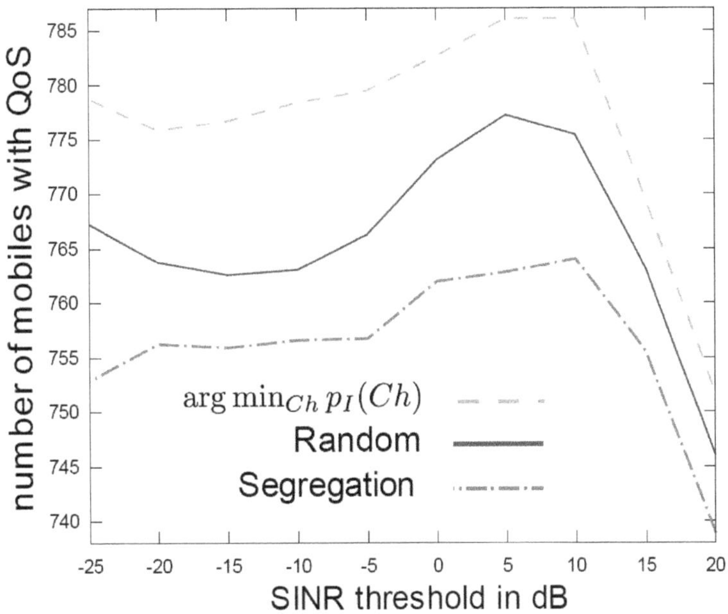

Fig. 7. Comparison of the performance of the three different methods for choosing channels (Vmax = 5 m/s, Ch = 40, N = -129dBW).

Finally, the maximum number of channel scans per allocation attempt Chmax, without power management, reveals an exponential gain which saturates at around 5-6 channels scanned per allocation attempt. However, combined with the effect of power management, no significant gain is observed. It appears that with power management, mobiles adjust their footprint thus offering more channel availability, such that only one channel test per allocation attempt is sufficient. And, optimization of the channel allocation occurs naturally through the many different attempts from all surrounding DBS in time. Therefore, complexity is kept to a minimum by having DBS only test and eventually allocate one channel per agent activation.

Connection management remains efficient as long as there are sufficient channel resources to provide a large enough channel footprint for the macrodiversity links. However, this mini- mum number of channels is low as macrodiversity links only require a small SINR to provide sufficient QoS after macrodiversity combination.

In the current simulated scenarios, 25 channels2 shared by a 100 DBS for 1000 mobiles, including 2 reserved channels (for (re)connection), are enough to provide sufficient flexibility to the connection agents for them to be able to swap links for optimization (this is with the synergistic effect of power level management). Below this threshold, there is too much interference for the connectivity potential of DBS to be fully exploited for macrodiversity, and those resources are left unused.

5.4 Power Control

This section begins with a description of two known PC algorithms adapted for the DBS con- text and used for benchmarking purpose. These are then compared through numerical experiments with the multi-agent-based power control (MAPC) method described in 4.4.

5.4.1 Centralized Power Control (CPC)

Grandhi's centralized power control (CPC) algorithm (Grandhi et al., 1993) is applied in the DBS architecture by considering the M master DBS for the M mobiles on a given channel with gij ($1 \leq I \leq M, 1 \leq j \leq M$) denoting the gain of the link from mobile i to DBS j, with DBS i being mobile i's master connection. Matrix A is defined as

$$Aij = gij / gii \text{ if } I \neq j, \tag{15}$$

$$Aii = 0. \tag{16}$$

And the SIR at the master DBS is defined as

$$\gamma_i = \frac{p_i}{\sum_{j=1}^{M} A_{ij} p_{ij}}. \tag{17}$$

The power level for each mobile is then given by the eigenvector associated with the largest positive eigenvalue of A.

Note that this algorithm is not trying to maximize each mobile's SIR. Rather, it finds a set of power levels which maximizes the lowest SIR, thus leading to each mobile's SIR being equal to the minimum (maximized) SIR. Also, the obtained power levels are proportional to at least the eigenvector and thus need to be scaled to fit inside the mobiles' power level range. This is where the instability of this algorithm becomes apparent, since under certain interference conditions, if a mobile is very close to its master DBS, its power level will be very low. Yet, since its SIR is forced to be equal to the other mobiles' SIR, proportionally, the noise at the receiver will have a much stronger impact leading to very poor SINR. Supposing a mobile faces 1W interference power and 0.1W noise power, and emits 10W to obtain a SIR of 10dB, it has an SINR of 9.6dB. In contrast, consider a mobile faced with .1W of interference; it emits 1W to obtain the same SIR of 10dB, but has an SINR of 7dB, hence an effective penalty of half. In order to minimize this effect, the minimum power level should be high enough so that noise remains as much as possible negligible. Hence, the power levels will be scaled such that the maximum power level evaluated is set to the maximum mobile's range.

On the other hand, a more complex evaluation of such effects would make it possible to lower the maximum power level, keeping it as low as possible, and hence, maximizing the efficiency of the link quality versus the power used per mobile.

5.4.2 SIR-balanced macro power control (SBMPC)

Yanikomeroglu's SIR-balanced macro power control (SBMPC) (Yanikomeroglu & Sousa, 1998) proposes an interesting algorithm for CDMA distributed antennas using macrodiversity. The algorithm aims to balance, over all mobiles, each mobile's aggregate (sum) SIR over all an- tennas. This is a valid approach in the context of Rayleigh fading. However, as mentioned in the introduction, in Rice fading, two similar average SIR values can lead to two different BER figures given each may not have the same K factor (i.e. fading impact is more or less severe). As such, balancing SIR does not balance BER with the relative importance of line of sight components varying depending on mobiles' locations.

As the SBMPC article suggests, it is straightforward to adapt the algorithm to a general cellular system. For all mobiles on one channel, we define the matrix B to describe the connections of mobile i (out of M mobiles) to DBS j (out of L DBS) such that

$$\text{Bij} = 1 \text{ if mobile i is relayed by DBS j,} \tag{18}$$

$$\text{Bii} = 0 \text{ otherwise.} \tag{19}$$

The global SIR for mobile i is then

$$\gamma_{i,SBMPC} = \sum_{j=1}^{L} B_{ij} \frac{g_{ij} p_i}{\left(\sum_{k=1}^{M} g_{kj} p_i k\right) - g_{ij} p_i}. \tag{20}$$

This equation is rearranged to obtain the power level of mobiles i = 2,. . ., M given the mobile i = 1 in an iterative manner:

$$\mathbf{P}^{(0)} = \{p_i^{(0)}\} = \left\{ \left(\sum_{j=1}^{L} B_{ij} g_{ij} \right)^{-1} \right\}, \ \forall i, \tag{21}$$

$$\gamma_1^{(v)} = \sum_{j=1}^{L} B_{1j} \frac{g_{1j} p_i 1^{(v)}}{\left(\sum_{k=1}^{M} g_{kj} p_i k^{(v)}\right) - g_{1j} p_i 1^{(v)}}. \tag{22}$$

$$p_i 1^{(v+1)} = p_i 1(v), \tag{23}$$

$$p_i^{(v+1)} = \frac{\gamma_1^{(v)}}{\sum_{j=1}^{L} \frac{B_{ij} g_{ij}}{\left(\sum_{k=1}^{M} g_{kj} p_i k^{(v)}\right) - g_{ij} p_i i^{(v)}}}, \ i \in \{2, \ldots, M\}. \tag{24}$$

Just like in the previous algorithm, the obtained power level vector needs to be scaled to minimize the noise effect.

Given that this is an iterative solution and the purpose is not to evaluate its convergence, the algorithm is run for 20 iterations at each simulation time step of a simulation. It has been verified that this is enough to ensure convergence.

5.4.3 Results

Figure 8(a) shows the base results, that is, with a static simulation scenario where fading is otherwise accounted for as if mobiles where moving, but mobility is not considered (to observe a nominal capacity without taking into account dynamic adaptation of the algorithms). Noise is also not considered in this case.

The plot reveals different aspects. First, with no PC, the QoS is clearly not balanced, but more importantly, not all mobiles can be connected as is seen from the right hand side of the graph. With the centralized algorithms, we can clearly see that QoS is balanced, and all mobiles are connected. On the other hand, MAPC is able to provide much more QoS to almost all mobiles, while only impeding (compared to SBMPC) very few mobiles.

What is most interesting in Table 1 is how the CPC handles outage extremely well. It takes only 1 second (1 iteration of the simulation) to reconnect a lost mobile, and the probability that a mobile is disconnected is extremely low. Even SBMPC is not as good, but remains excellent compared to no PC. MAPC is only doing slightly worse, but with a much enhanced QoS provided to all mobiles.

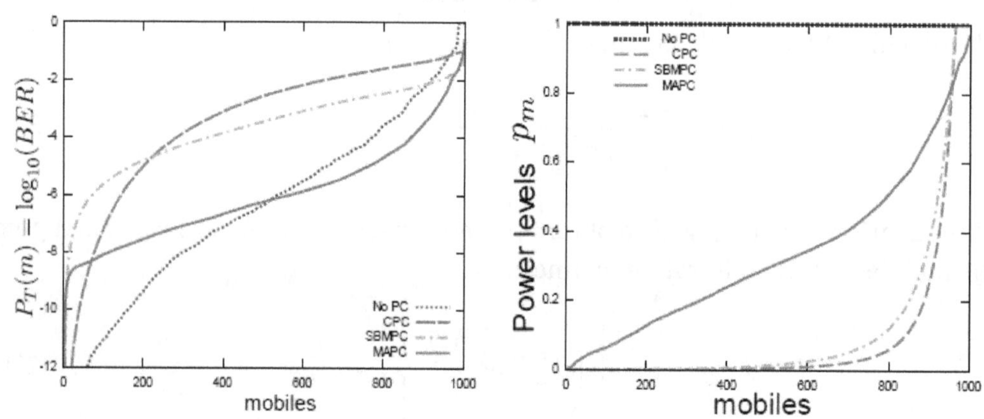

(a) Sorted BER profile averaged in time ($\text{mean}_t(\text{sort}_m(P_T(m)))$)

(b) Sorted power level ratio profile averaged in time ($\text{mean}_t(\text{sort}_i(p_i i))$)

Fig. 8. Ch = 40, N = 0, Vmax = 0.

Table 1. Outage behavior without mobility and noise with Ch = 40.

	No PC	CPC	SBMPC	MAPC
N¯d (10-6) x	570	8.9	130	190
t¯r (seconds)	24.2	1	2.0	2.65

Figure 8(b) reveals how both CPC and SBMPC offer similar distributions of the power levels. On the contrary, the MAPC power level allocation is radically different.

Faced with higher interference levels (Ch = 25), it can be seen that the centralized algorithms break down (Fig. 9(a)). Indeed, in high interference levels, maximizing the minimum SIR leads to very poor SIRs for all mobiles. In turn, this generates many disconnections. Figure 9(a) clearly shows that the traditional algorithms are here inefficient and even worse than without PC. Still the MAPC algorithm manages to provide acceptable levels of QoS, while still connecting more mobiles.

The situation deteriorates even more when noise is introduced. Figure 9(b) reveals how noise, as explained previously, renders the traditional algorithms unstable, generating lots of dis- connections. Indeed, the centralized algorithms, by maximizing the minimum SIR, force most mobile power levels to be extremely low (c.f. Fig.8(b)) supposing thermal noise is not an important factor. This may be valid for a regular hexagonal cell geometry with homogeneous traffic and high guaranteed SIR. However, it is not the case here, leading to very poor SINR, and also significantly exacerbating the HTE as such mobiles' presence on channels will not be sensed by other DBS, rendering the PC algorithm completely inefficient.

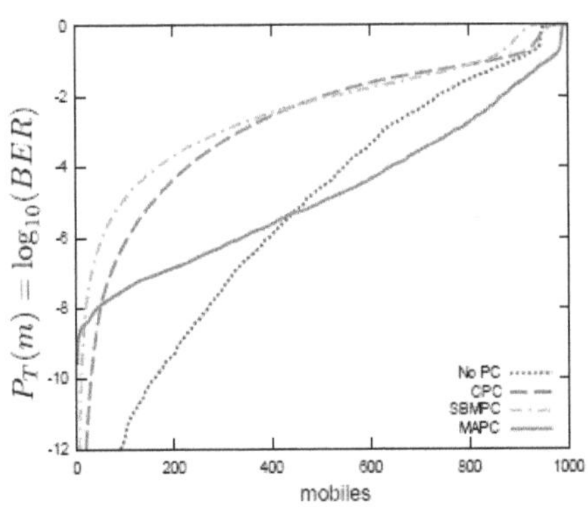

(a) Low channel resources, Ch = 25, $N = 0$, $V_{\max} = 0$.

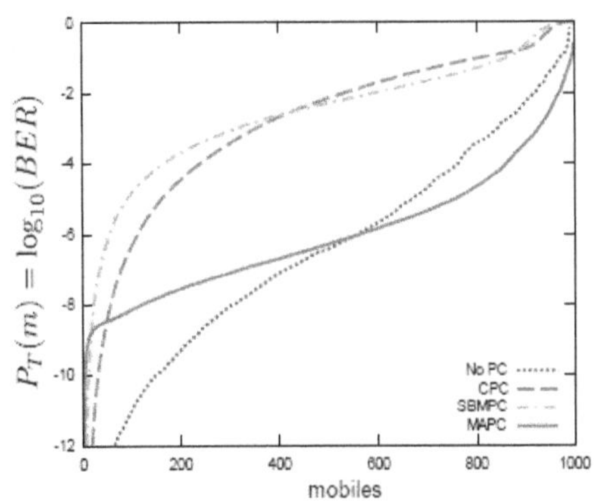

(b) Effect of thermal noise, Ch = 40, $N = -129$dBW, $V_{\max} = 0$.

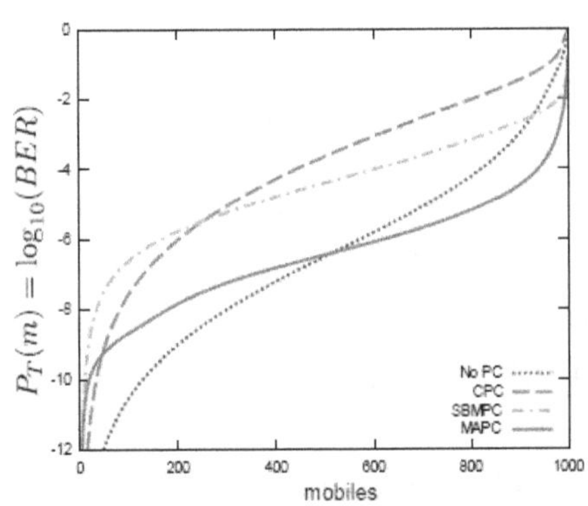

(c) Effect of high mobility, Ch = 50, $N = 0$, $V_{\max} = 5$m/s.

Fig. 9. Sorted BER profile averaged in time (meant (sortm (PT (m)))).

Also, facing important mobility (Figure 9(c)), the CPC algorithm loses its strength (of mini- mizing the outage probability) as Table 2 reveals. Indeed, with mobility, more interference is present because mobiles do not obtain an optimal reallocation of channels at each iteration. This implies far too many very low power levels with the CPC. This conflicts with the channel agents trying to reorganize the channel allocation as it generates important hidden terminal effects. This also shows that the CPC algorithm loses much of its capacity with even small changes of the efficiency of the channel allocation. In addition, we are not even considering the burden of calculating power levels at each iteration while first centralizing the data bits, which necessarily takes time and would prevent the algorithm from rapidly adapting to the changes in the system. SBMPC is doing much better, yet not as well as MAPC.

Table 2. Outage behavior with mobility (Vmax = 5 m/s) Ch = 50.

	No PC	CPC	SBMPC	MAPC
N¯d (10-4) X	9.8	19.1	3.8	1.8
t¯r (seconds)	5.13	2.4	2.2	1.38

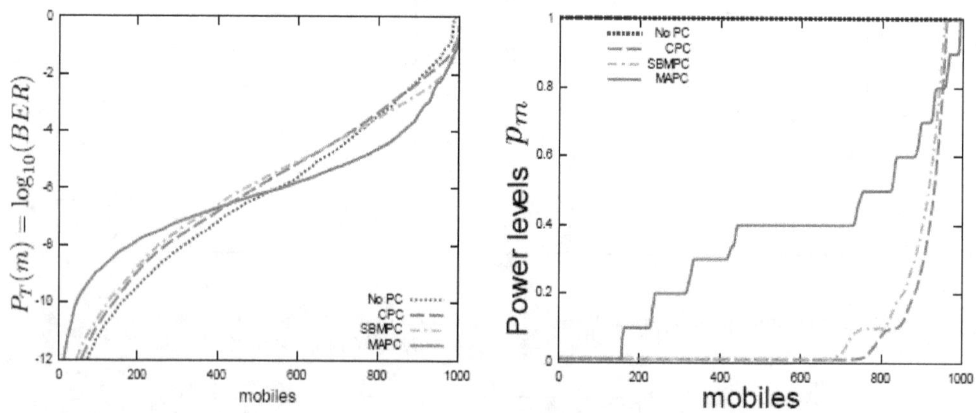

(a) Sorted BER profile averaged in time $(\text{mean}_t(\text{sort}_m(P_T(m))))$

(b) Sorted power level ratio profile averaged in time$(\text{mean}_t(\text{sort}_i(p_i i)))$

Fig. 10. Ch = 40, N = 0, Vmax = 0, discrete power level.

Figure 10(a) shows the behavior of the algorithms when power levels are restricted to a set of discrete values. The power level range is uniformly divided into 10 discrete levels (ratios of 0.1 to 1.0). While the MAPC is not as efficient as with continuous power range, it still remains the most efficient at uniformly balancing the QoS. The CPC and SBMPC algorithms loose their ability to balance QoS across all mobiles, since in order for them to work properly they need an important dynamic range of power levels (which is not the case here with only a 10x range). Therefore, these schemes only manage to obtain marginal benefit, minimizing disconnections (compared to no PC), and visually seem better than with no discretization as more mobiles obtain more QoS (compared to Fig. 8(a)). In a way, discretization helps the centralized schemes by preventing them from assigning excessively low power levels, yet also preventing them from achieving any proper resource balancing as the MAPC does.

Figure 10(b) shows the allocated power level over all mobiles in the discrete case. Considering dynamics, it was found that tuning the different parameters mentioned in the design (most specifically β and S) makes the agent system stable enough to prevent erratic changes of the power levels, while still allowing fast adaptation in the wake of abrupt (dis- crete) changes in interference levels.

It is also noteworthy that the power management proposed provides additional benefits to the channel agents (lowering connection loss rate, block rate and mean time for reconnection) and connection agents (offering them more headroom to swap links for optimization). Despite being designed independently, the various described agents remain stable working together in a synergistic way, such that one change induced by one type of agent (e.g. a connection change) is correctly compensated by the other types of agents (e.g. an adaptation of the power level) and not overcompensated, which would otherwise lead to erratic behaviors.

One of the great advantages of this approach is that each dimension of the problem can be tackled independently, by its own class of agents, without affecting the performance of the other classes. No explicit interaction mechanism between the agent classes needs to be de- signed, yet they synergetically cooperate to achieve desirable results with a surprisingly low implementation complexity.

6. CONCISE SUMMARY

The proposed proof-of-concept design outlined herein illustrates that minimalist multiagent systems possess all anticipated attributes: scalability, dynamic characteristics, efficiency, simplicity, adaptability, and auto-configuration. Furthermore, it constitutes an innovative and unexpectedly straightforward resolution to resource distribution. The power allocation system clearly yields significantly reduced spatial power distributions in contrast to conventional algorithms.

The heuristic-based multi-agent design approach seems to be effective. It necessitates comprehension of the fundamental mechanisms and trade-offs relevant to the issue, from which insights and intuition can be derived to inform the design of the agents.

Although the ultimate outcome to which the system will converge is uncertain a priori, it is also uncertain a priori what it should converge to. The present setting significantly differs from formal frameworks like information theory, which are often defined by a singular unidimensional criterion, such as channel capacity. In our multi-dimensional setting, information theory is currently unable to represent and comprehend the numerous options and trade-offs encountered by various mobiles and DBS with macrodiversity, where constrained resources result in interference. In this context, the suggested MA technique effectively illustrates through simulation that certain innovative allocation options, understood as compromises, can significantly enhance resource utilization efficiency, which inherently involves a notion of compromise.

The design is rather straightforward, but one must consider the ambiguity inherent in this method. Indeed, the proposed utility functions may have numerous alternatives. What is significant is not their precision, but that they furnish specific features that will support the interactions of agents. These features require further understanding and examination to elucidate the inner workings of the agent system. For example, the shaping function in the utility function of the connection agents uses a logarithm which could be replaced by a first degree approximation (x – 1) and still converge, but a concave function with similar properties (e.g. (x –1)2, null for x = 1 and strictly increasing for x > 1) would, despite providing some degree of convergence, fall short of a more balanced solution. The shaping function is therefore crucial to converge to certain Pareto solutions, and this remains to be studied in detail.

Concerning MA design, we considered more specifically the notion of homeostasis which is not explicitly mentioned in Parunak's methodology. The proposed design shows how the search for such an equilibrium helps in designing and tuning the properties of the agents' behavior to obtain the desired global function.

Considering future work, the proposed MA design and DBS architecture offers malleability and vast margins for tuning, enhancing, or providing additional functionality. It was studied in (Leroux et al., 2008) that the reuse of channels could be enhanced by pairing mobiles to cooperate in exploiting a single channel while multiplying their diversity gain. Interesting results have been found in this study. Yet, coupled with power-level control, the management of cooperation between mobiles revealed counter synergistic effects. To date, finding a way to have the cooperation and power-control agents interoperate in a synergetic manner remains an open problem.

Another additional functionality to be studied is beamforming. Channel allocation agents would need to be improved to account for dynamically-created directive beams and provide network-wide gains by minimizing interference .

Channelization also needs to be further studied, including a model to implement the IEEE 802.11 shared random access mechanism (CSMA/CA on conjunction with the so-called distributed coordination function) which is now globally deployed, rather then relying only on orthogonal channels (whether it be time/frequency/ or code division) as is the case in this study. Ultimately, practical solutions must be evaluated, as demonstrated in Leroux (2008), which indicated that macrodiversity might be achieved by minimally synchronized terminals at the packet level. Subsequently, the proposed MA strategies might be executed with consumer Wi-Fi terminals, potentially linking these terminals to a wired network to enhance synergy and so provide far more dependable and efficient connections.

The suggested system is hence not a mere undertaking for MA design. It signifies a significant foundation for a novel design paradigm in mobile wireless networking. It has significant opportunities for enhancements, innovative designs, and supplementary functionality.

FOOTNOTES

1. Since a priori goals are not explicitly defined, neither is the concept of a "right direction". Rather, a behavior is designed, tuned and retained because its auto-catalysis properties happen to converge to a solution which satisfies the needs of the system. Therefore, such a design allows wide exploration of the solution space rather then restricting to predefined goals by not including all the effects involved in the multidimensional problem. The design represents a certain creative process.
2. A cellular system with a channel reuse pattern of 7 hexagonal cells, would require 70 channels for 100 pico cells, without offering the flexibility the current architecture provides.

REFERENCES

1. Akaiwa, Y. & Andoh, H. (1993). Channel segregation-a self-organized dynamic channel al- location method: application to TDMA/FDMA microcellular system, IEEE J. Select. Areas Commun. 11(6): 949–954.
2. Beongku, A., Dohyeon, K. & Innho, J. (2003). A modeling framework for supporting QoS in mobile ad-hoc networks, Vehicular Technology Conference, 2003. VTC 2003-Spring. The 57th IEEE Semiannual 2: 935–939.
3. Brueckner, S. & Parunak, H. V. D. (2003). Self-organizing MANET management, in G. D. M. Serugendo, A. Karageorgos, O. F. Rana & F. Zambonelli (eds), Engineering Self- Organising Systems, Vol. 2977 of Lecture Notes in Computer Science, Springer, pp. 20–35.
4. Elwyn R. Berlekamp, John H. Conway & Richard K. Guy (1982). Winning Ways for your Math- ematical Plays, New York: Academic Press.
5. Furukawa, H. & Akaiwa, Y. (1994). A microcell overlaid with umbrella cell system, Vehicular Technology Conference, 1994 IEEE 44th, Stockholm, pp. 1455–1459.

6. Goldberg, D. E. (1989). Genetic Algorithms in Search, Optimization and Machine Learning, Kluwer Academic Publishers, Boston, MA.
7. Grandhi, S., Vijayan, R., Goodman, D. & Zander, J. (1993). Centralized power control in cellu- lar radio systems, Vehicular Technology, IEEE Transactions on 42(4): 466–468.
8. Leroux, P. (2008). Architecture d'un système de stations de base distribuées, PhD thesis, Université Laval.
9. Leroux, P., Roy, S. & Chouinard, J.-Y. (2006). The Performance of Soft Macrodiversity Based on Maximal-Ratio Combining in Uncorrelated Rician Fading, 17th annual IEEE inter- national symposium PIMRC'06, Helsinki, Finland.
10. Leroux, P., Roy, S. & Chouinard, J.-Y. (2008). Synergetic cooperation in a distributed base station system, Personal, Indoor and Mobile Radio Communications, 2008. PIMRC 2008. IEEE 19th International Symposium on, pp. 1–6.
11. Mackenzie, A. & Wicker, S. (2001). Game Theory and the Design of Self Configuring, Adaptive Wireless Networks, IEEE Commun. Mag. .
12. Muraleedharan, R. & Osadciw, L. A. (2003). Balancing the Performance of a Sensor Network Using an Ant System, 37th Annual Conference on Information Sciences and Systems (CISS 2003), Baltimore, MD. .
13. Parunak, H. V. D. (1997). "Go to the Ant" : Engineering Principles from Natural Agent Sys- tems, Annals of Operations Research .
14. Tumer, K. & Wolpert, D. (2004). Collectives and the Design of Complex Systems, Springer-Verlag, NY.

27 Chapter INTER-RAT HANDOVER BETWEEN WIMAX AND UMTS

1. INTRODUCTION: AN OVERVIEW

Different radio access technologies, including GSM/GPRS, UMTS, WiFi, and WiMAX, will comprise the future beyond third generation (B3G) or fourth generation (4G) systems. An extensive effort has been undertaken to identify the unresolved issues regarding future mobile systems. One critical issue is the future vertical transition management solution. There have been numerous mobility management solutions proposed, including SCTP (M. Afif, et al., 2006), MIPv6/FMIPv6 (D. Johnson, et al., 2004; R. Koodli, 2005), and inter-RAT (Radio Access Technologies) handover of 3GPP (3GPP TS 43.129; 3GPP TR 25.931). Among these solutions, the layer 2 inter-RAT handover solution of the 3GPP is a promising option due to its highly reliable handover procedure. Regrettably, the 3GPP inter-RAT solutions are limited to inter-RAT handover between cellular networks and do not support inter-RAT handover between WiMAX (Worldwide Interoperability for Microwave Access) and UMTS (Universal Mobile Telecommunication systems).

Another significant concern is the coupling scenario and interworking architecture that are employed to facilitate the efficient administration of inter-RAT handovers. There are various interworking architectures, including no coupling, lax coupling, tight coupling, and very tight coupling (integrated coupling), depending on the location of the coupling point (G. Lanpropoulos, et al., 2005). Mobile IP or a portion of Mobile IP is frequently employed as the handover management protocol in the loose coupling and tight coupling architectures. Therefore, these two types of coupling architectures necessitate fewer complex modifications to the current protocol stacks and are more adaptable than integrated coupling. Nevertheless, they frequently experience a prolonged handover latency, which can range from a few hundred milliseconds to several seconds. Generally, the incorporated coupling improves handover performance at the cost of introducing complex modifications to existing network protocol stacks.

In recent years, the IEEE and 3GPP organizations have each proposed their own interworking solutions for the convergence of heterogeneous networks. Specifically, the control plane is the sole focus of the ongoing 3GPP standard for interworking between UMTS and WiFi (3GPP TS 23.234), which establishes the interworking topologies, access gateways, AAA, charging, interfaces, and so forth.

It does not offer a solution to the handover issues in the user plane, such as packet loss and extended handover latency. However, IEEE 802.21 (IEEE 802.21, 2006) is an additional prospective vertical handover solution. This standard establishes a generic link layer to conceal the heterogeneities of a variety of RATs, as well as three types of services. Manufacturers continue to be responsible for resolving transfer issues. Due to these factors, this chapter will exclusively concentrate on the user plane, rather than the control plane, and will suggest an inter-RAT handover solution to address certain common handover issues. Additionally, our inter-RAT handover solution is applicable to a diverse array of interworking scenarios, in addition to the integrated and rigid coupling architectures. This solution is a unique approach to the interworking of UMTS and WiMAX, as it has not been previously documented in other standards or references.

2. 3GPP HANDOVER FEATURES

This section mainly describes procedures that are used by the MS to select a suitable cell to be connected to in the 3GPP cellular networks. For details, please refer to references (3GPP TS 25.331; 3GPP TS 43.129; 3GPP TS 44.060; 3GPP TR 25.931; J.P Romero, et al., 2005).

When a MS is switched on, it must first select a PLMN (Public Land Mobile Network) and a RAT (Radio Access Technology) automatically or manually. It searches for the most adequate cells so as to camp on a suitable cell. Then the MS will register its presence in the registration area of the chosen cell if necessary. As long as the MS remains in idle mode, it will continuously execute the cell reselection procedures in order to choose and camp on the most suitable cell of the selected PLMN. The events triggering the cell reselection may due to high path loss, downlink signaling failure and so on. If the new cell is in a different registration area, a Location Registration (LR) request is performed (3GPP TS 23.122).

When the MS is in the packet transfer or dedicated mode, the network use PS Handover to command a MS to move from its source cell to a new cell, and continue the ongoing PS service operation in the new cell. The handover trigger conditions could be serving cell resource limitation, measurement reports from a MS, and the cell change notification from a MS. This handover procedure between cells of the same RAT is also referred to as intra-RAT handover.

Depending on the PLMN availability and network configuration, it is possible that cell reselection and handover procedures involve a cell switch from one RAT to another RAT (e.g., from 2G GSM/GPRS/EDGE to 3G UMTS networks). The handover procedure between cells of different RATs is referred to as inter-RAT handover in 3GPP standards or vertical handover in IETF protocols.

In general, in contrast with the cell reselection, the intra-RAT handover and inter-RAT handover of 3GPP have the following distinct features:

- The network makes the handover decision depending on the measurement reports, network states and negotiation with target base station or cell.
- The network controls the whole handover procedure, including message transfer, handover timing, handover target, resource allocation, and context transfer.
- Only packet transfer mode or dedicated mode needs the handover procedure due to handover overheads.
- The handover can be considered as a kind of specific QoS-guaranteed cell reselection procedure.

It should be stressed that Mobile IPv6 and its extensions (D. Johnson, et. al., 2004; R.Koodli, 2005) support both network-initiated and terminal-initiated handover procedures. In this chapter, we only consider 3GPP inter-RAT handover procedures initiated by the network.

The conventional 3GPP inter-RAT handover procedure must involve the SGSN, whether for handover from GSM/GPRS to UMTS or from UMTS to GSM/GPRS. This is because the Link Control Sublayer (LLC) terminates at SGSN, which is in charge of making lossless packets forwarding during the MS mobility thanks to its retransmission mechanism. This is not a problem for GSM/GPRS or UMTS core network, because the SGSN is their common network entity. But for inter-RAT handover between 3GPP cellular network and IEEE wireless IP network like WiFi/WiMAX, it becomes a challenge for the packet lossless RAT switch procedure due to the lack of SGSN in IEEE wireless network. In the following sections, we utilize the 3GPP inter-RAT handover procedure, messages and signaling to resolve this problem for two typical coupling network architectures: integrated coupling and tight coupling.

3. INTER-RAT HANDOVER BETWEEN UMTS AND WIMAX IN INTEGRATED COUPLING ARCHITECTURE

In order to realize a seamless inter-RAT handover for future B3G or 4G mobile networks, a variety of interworking architectures and inter-RAT handover mobility managements have been proposed. Based on the integrated architecture, in this section, a novel common interworking sublayer (IW sublayer) is proposed at Layer 2 on RNC and MS to provide a seamless PS inter-RAT handover between UMTS and WiMAX systems. This IW sublayer scheme focuses on eliminating packet loss and reducing handover latency that are common problems for most inter-RAT handover scenarios. Compared with other context transfer schemes, the simulation results show the IW sublayer with ARQ mechanism can achieve a lossless and prompt handover procedure. In addition, this IW sublayer scheme can eliminate false fast retransmission of TCP traffics that is usually caused by packet losses or out-of-order packet arrivals. In what follows, the IW sublayers in integrated and tight coupling architectures are specified in this section and section 4 respectively.

3.1 Context Transfer

The problems during the inter-RAT handover period have been extensively studied in (G. Lanpropoulos, et al., 2005; S.L. Tsao, et al., 2002; N. Dailly, et al., 2006; J. Sachs, et al., 2006; H. Inaura, et al., 2003; H. Rutagemwa, et al., 2007), such as long handover latency, BDP (Bandwidth Delay Product) mismatch, delay spikes, packet losses, premature timeout, false fast retransmission. Among these problems, the packet losses and long handover latency are in particular not desirable for real-time and throughput-sensitive traffics. The most common solution is applying the context transfer mechanism (J. Sachs, et al., 2006; R. Koodli, 2005) or retransmission (3GPP TS 25.323; N. Dailly, et al., 2006) to accelerate the handover process or reduce the amount of lost packets. There exist the following typical context transfer and retransmission schemes: PDCP Synchronization, buffering-and-forwarding (B&F), SDU Reconstruction, R-LLC.

1. **PDCP Synchronization:** In 3GPP UMTS network (3GPP TS 25.323), the PDCP sublayer is applied to guarantee reliable data transmission service during Service Radio Network Subsystem (SRNS) relocation. For this purpose, PDCP maintains PDCP sequence numbers to avoid any data losses during SRNS relocation. After the successful relocation, the data transmission starts from the (first) unconfirmed SDU having a sequence number equal to the next expected sequence number by the PDCP entity. For instance, in the uplink, if some transmitted SDUs are still left unacknowledged, the data transmission is resumed by retransmission of the SDU with the "uplink send" sequence number equal to the uplink receive sequence number. Otherwise, the data transmission is resumed with the transmission of the first unsent SDU. Moreover, when the RLC entities mapped to a lossless PDCP entity are reset or reestablished for reasons other than SRNS relocation, then it is the PDCP's responsibility that the peer lossless PDCP entities do not go out of synchronization by the means of "PDCP sequence number synchronization procedure" (3GPP TS 25.323).

The retransmission mechanism of PDCP works well when a MS performs SRNS relocation during data transmission in the domain of UMTS. Unfortunately, in the scenario of inter- RAT handover, the PDCP will not take effect any more because:

- The other heterogeneous network system usually does not have the similar mechanism, especially IEEE 802 RATs such as WiMAX or WiFi.
- In addition, the WiMAX system has its own IP packet header compression mechanism rather than ROHC (3GPP TS 25.323) in UMTS. If the packets or frames stored in the source system with their particular headers and control

signaling parts are forwarded to the target systems directly, the target system may discard these unreadable packets, which will induce sequence number asynchronization and break down current communication connection.

In a word, the sequence number synchronization, header compression and retransmission mechanism of respective RAT complicate the inter-RAT handover procedure instead.

2. **Buffering-and-Forwarding:** R. Koodli (2005) propose to utilize buffering-and-forwarding mechanism (B&F) to forward unsent data packets from previous access router to new access router in FMIPv6 to eliminate packet losses during a handover period. In this IP solution the packets stored at link layer of one RAT usually cannot be retrieved to the IP layer. So, generally, there usually exist packet losses if an inter-RAT handover management protocol with B&F is realized only at IP layer or above.

SDU Reconstruction: J. Sachs (2006) proposes the SDU (Service Data Unit) reconstruction scheme. In order to make a lossless handover, the segments stored in the PDU (Packet Data Unit) buffer of source link are first reconstructed back to a SDU and then forwarded to the target link as well as the SDUs from the SDU buffer. When this proposal is applied to the inter-RAT handover from UMTS to WiMAX or from WiMAX to UMTS for TCP traffics, the handover performance may still degrade, for the following reasons:

- If a PDCP (Packet Data Convergence Protocol) PDU sequence number asynchronization takes place just before an inter-RAT handover from UMTS to WiMAX, the asynchronization problem cannot be resolved by WiMAX system. This leads to an unreliable handover procedure.
- A RLC (Radio Link Control) SDU whose corresponding RLC PDUs have not be successfully transmitted in total, cannot be reconstructed and will be discarded locally, because the successfully transmitted RLC PDUs have been already removed before.
- WiMAX and UMTS systems support different header compression algorithms. That means it needs a deliberate loop back setting in respective system.

From above discussion we can see that the PDCP sequence number synchronization mechanism, which is used to assure lossless handover in UMTS system, becomes an obstacle for inter-RAT handover when the context transfer mechanism is SDU reconstruction. We may suppose the PDCP sublayer is configured in transparent mode (i.e., not attach any PDCP header, no header compression and no sequence number synchronization) when the inter-RAT handover is based on this SDU reconstruction mechanism. But, what the point of using an UMTS network without PDCP sublayer?

3. **R-LLC:** N. Dailly (2006) introduce a novel sublayer called R-LLC (Link Layer Control) locating on the BTS for handover between GPRS and WiFi is proposed. This R-LLC sublayer takes the role of conventional LLC, and retransmits packets lost during inter-RAT handover when the retransmission timer expires. The simulation results in this reference (N. Dailly, et al., 2006) demonstrate zero packet loss for handover and cell reselection procedures. However, the packet loss is only indicated by retransmission timer expiration, which usually is set to 5 sec.. Obviously, such a long period is unfavorable to keep TCP congestion window from shrinking. In addition, the configuration of retransmission window is not specified.

Since these typical context transfer or retransmission schemes do not satisfy the inter-RAT handover requirements for interworking UMTS and WiMAX, in what follows, a novel context transfer scheme is proposed at a novel common sublayer – InterWorking (IW) sublayer.

3.2 InterWorking (IW) Sublayer

3.2.1 InterWorking (IW) Sublayer Description

In order to propose a feasible way to provide a seamless handover procedure, a promising solution is designed in terms of the following principles:

- Minimize altering the existing standards and protocol stacks as far as possible.
- Consider the UMTS as the center of the integrated system and preserve its signaling and control procedures as many as possible.
- In WiMAX access network, additional network components and new signaling and primitives could be added.
- The two integrated systems should guarantee seamless service continuity, and execute mobility management processes (e.g., connection establishment, handover) as fast as possible in order to maintain the required QoS.

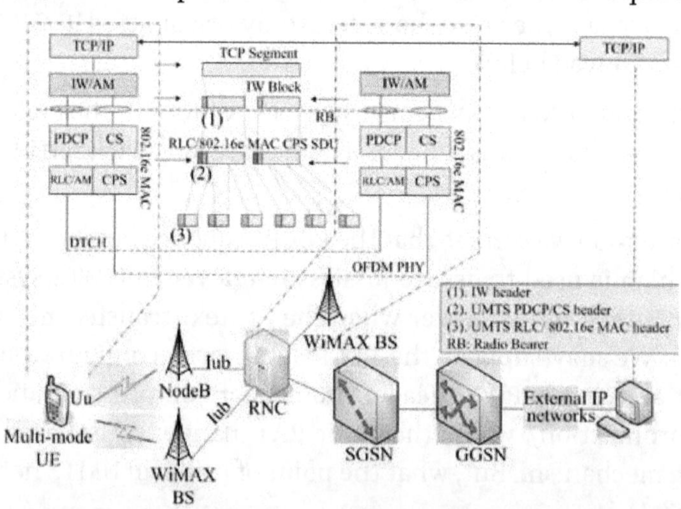

Fig. 1. IW sublayer working mechanism of integrated coupling

As stated above, our inter-RAT scheme is first based on the integrated coupling architecture. We assume UMTS to be the master home network with roaming privileges to WiMAX network. A novel common network entity named interworking sublayer (IW) is introduced on the top of PDCP (Packet Data Convergence Protocol) sublayer of UMTS and the Medium Access Control (MAC) CS sublayer of 802.16e on the RNC and MS, as shown in Fig.1. The WiMAX BS is integrated with the RNC (Radio Network Controller) through Iub interface. The IW takes the role of LLC sublayer of conventional cellular networks, such as retransmission mechanism and handover support. The main functions of IW sublayer are:

- Determination of a suitable target network.
- Primitive mapping between the IW and the UMTS network, or between the IW and the WiMAX network in case of inter-RAT handover.
- Support SR ARQ (Selective Repeat ARQ) mechanism, including packet segmentation and re-sequencing, retransmission, and retransmission window size adjustment.

In Fig. 2 and Fig. 3, the user and control planes of the proposed architectures are illustrated. It should be stressed that the SR ARQ retransmission mechanism is realized in the user plane. While in the control plane, IW sublayer shall translate handover related signaling between source and target networks. When an inter-RAT handover is made, the IW sublayer is activated according to the QoS requirements of a PDP (Packet Data Protocol). In the control plane, we prefer to reuse the RRC protocol functionality in the MS and RNC respectively, instead of building them from scratch. What is actually needed is to enhance RRC protocol entities in order to forward inter-RAT handover primitives to IW sublayer. In order to minimize the modifications to respective systems, IW sublayer also realizes some essential WiMAX-related primitives and makes RNC act as another WiMAX BS to the WiMAX network.

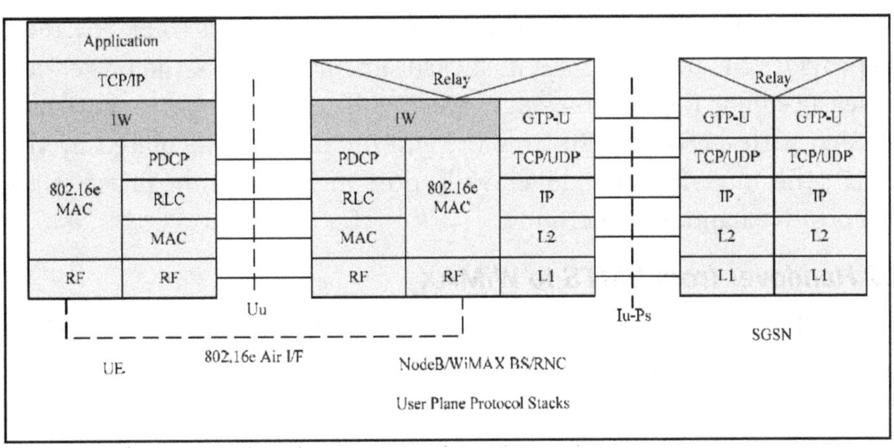

Fig. 2. User plane protocol stacks in integrated coupling architecture

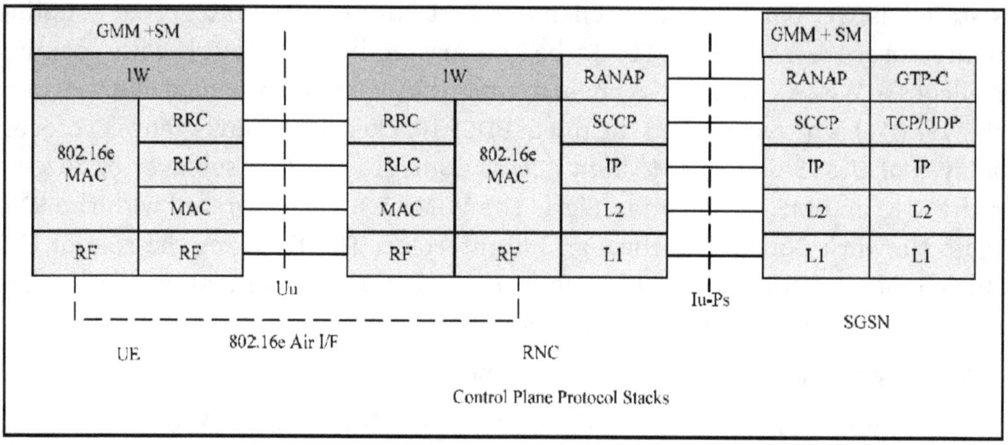

Fig. 3. Control plane protocol stacks in integrated coupling architecture

3.2.2 Signaling and Primitives

3.2.2.1 Overview

In order to have insight into IW sublayer working mechanism, this sub-clause describes the inter-RAT handover signaling procedures and primitives among IW, PDCP, RRC (Radio Resource Control) and WiMAX MAC. Some newly added cross-layer primitives are complemented to the conventional inter-RAT handover signaling procedures of 3GPP (3GPP TS 43.129; 3GPP TR 25.931). We suggest the future WiMAX and UMTS standards should support these primitives and parameters for the seamless and smooth inter-RAT handover.

Generally, the inter-RAT handover consists of handover preparation phase and handover execution phase. In the case of a handover from UMTS to WiMAX, when the inter-RAT handover conditions e.g. low RSSI or load increase, are met, the MS is instructed by the RNC to switch on its WiMAX transceiver. Then MS seeks and monitors the neighbor WiMAX BSs given in System Information Block (SIB) on BCCH of serving cell. After the WiMAX scanning intervals (IEEE 802.16e, 2005), the MS provides the network with its measurement results of the target networks using Measurement Reports message. Meanwhile, other important wireless link parameters, such as round trip time (RTT), BDP are also calculated by the RNC. After that, the inter-RAT handover will enter into execution phase if the RNC makes a positive handover decision.

3.2.2.2 Handover from UMTS to WiMAX

Fig. 4 describes the inter-RAT handover from UMTS to WiMAX and shows the exchanged messages and primitives.

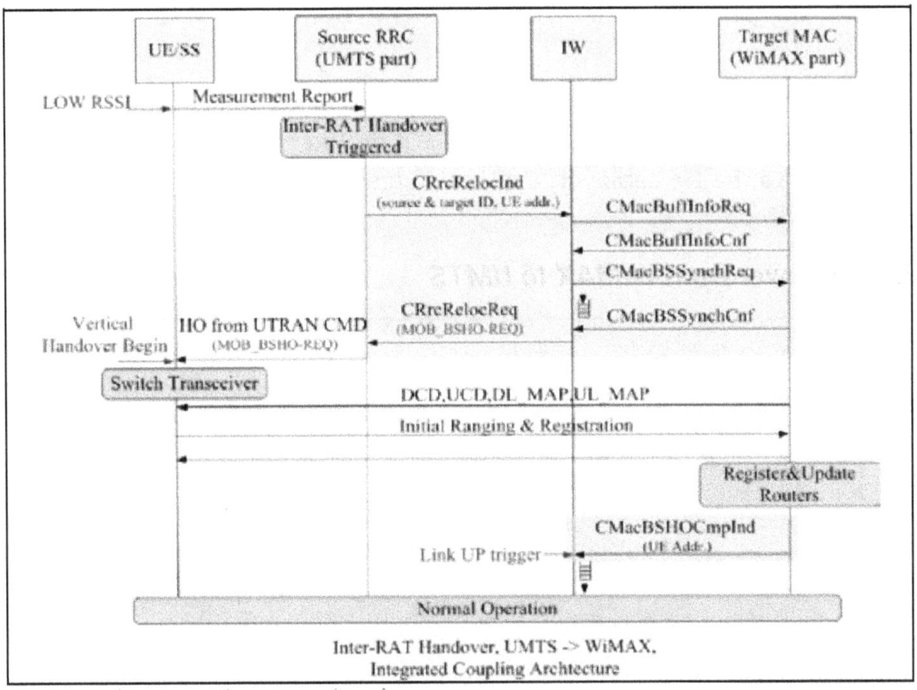

Fig. 4. Handover signaling procedure from UMTS to WiMAX

1. Based on measurement reports and knowledge of the RAN topology, the RNC, more precisely source RRC decides to initiate an inter-RAT PS handover.
2. The source RRC sends the CRrcRelocInd primitive (contains target WiMAX cell id) to the IW sublayer.
3. Then the IW sends the CMacBuffInfoReq primitive to the target WiMAX MAC to request the buffer characteristics. The WiMAX MAC shall return the CMacBuffInfoCnf primitive to inform the IW of the buffer size in its MAC sublayer. According to this information, the IW adjusts its retransmission window size. (Note that current WiMAX MAC does not support this interface, so the IW may adjust its retransmission window size to a default value).
4. At this stage, the IW sends the CMacBSSynchReq primitive to the WiMAX MAC to negotiate the location of the dedicated initial ranging transmission opportunity for the MS. This information is returned by primitive CMacBSSynchCnf.
5. After that, the IW begins to buffer data packets that require delivery order and sends a CRrcRelocReq primitive (including Transparent Container (MOB_BSHO-REQ)) to the source RRC.
6. The RRC sends the Handover from UTRAN Command message to the MS, which includes a MOB_BSHO-REQ.

7. The MS performs hard handover and normal WiMAX network entry procedure.
8. After the provisioned service flow is activated (IEEE 802.16e, 2005), the target WiMAX MAC sends CMacBSHOCmpInd primitive as a Link_Up (LU) trigger to the IW sublayer. On this trigger, the IW shall restart data packet forwarding.

3.2.2.3 Handover from WiMAX to UMTS

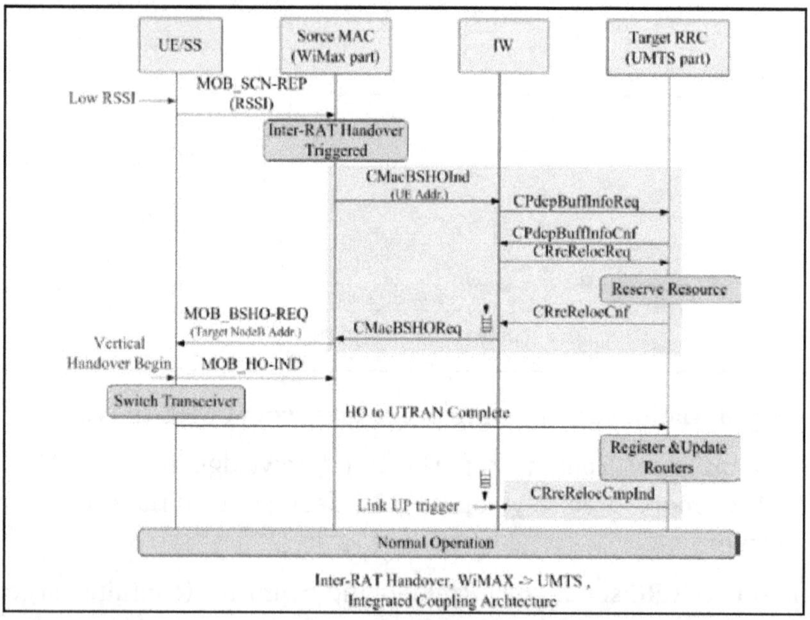

Fig. 5. Handover signalling procedure from WiMAX to UMTS

The inter-RAT handover from WiMAX to UMTS is described in Fig. 5.

1. After the scanning interval, the MS sends scanning report to WiMAX serving BS by message MON_SCN-REP that contains physical information such as mean RSSI.
2. The source WiMAX MAC sends CMacBSHOInd primitive to inform the IW sublayer of target cell id. The IW then sends CPdcpBuffInfoReq primitive to the target RRC of the UMTS network. The RRC shall return the CPdcpBuffInfoCnf primitive to inform the IW sublayer of buffer size and buffer occupation. According to this information, the IW adjusts its retransmission window size.
3. The IW sublayer sends a CRrcRelocReq primitive to the target RRC to apply for resource allocation. The result is returned in CRrcRelocCnf primitive by the target RRC.

4. Upon receipt of the CRrcRelocCnf, the IW suspends and buffers data packets that require delivery order.
5. IW sends CMacBSHOReq primitive to inform source MAC that the target network is ready.
6. The MS performs handover to one of BSs specified in MOB_BSHO-REQ and responds with a MOB_HO-IND message.
7. MS performs normal UMTS hard handover.
8. After the MS successfully finishes UMTS radio link setup, the target RRC shall send the CRrcRelocCmpInd primitive to the IW, and the IW restarts data packet forwarding.

Note that primitive CMacBSHOCmpInd and primitive CRrcRelocCmpInd are defined as the Link_Up (LU) triggers for handover from UMTS to WiMAX and for handover from WiMAX to UMTS respectively.

3.2.2.4 IW ARQ Mechanism

For the sake of achieving lossless inter-RAT handover, a modified Selective Repeat ARQ (SR ARQ) mechanism is applied to the IW sublayer during the handover period, which is renamed IW ARQ. The IW ARQ is an error control mechanism that involves error detection and retransmission of lost or corrupted packets. When a packet is accepted from upper layer, it is segmented into smaller IW blocks, each of which is assigned a sequence number (see Fig. 6). This new IW sub-header is used for block loss detection and block re-sequencing in the receiver to guarantee in-sequence delivery. Afterward, each IW block is transmitted through the UMTS or the WiMAX interface. These IW blocks are also queued in the retransmission buffer in order to be scheduled for retransmission. The IW ARQ transmitter maintains an adaptive window size that is set to target network buffer size. When an IW block is received by the receiver, a positive or negative acknowledgement (ACK/NACK) is sent back immediately for the purpose of reducing handover latency. In addition, in order to avoid dead lock due to IW ACK/NACK losses during a handover period, a status report timer is set when the receiver sends an ACK/NACK. When this timer expires, the receiver sends back a status report (ARQ feedback bitmap) providing the receipt status. This status report is map of the acknowledgement (ACK) or negative acknowledge (NACK) of each IW block within the window. Compared with conventional SR ARQ mechanism of RLC, the IW ARQ has the following features:

- **Receiver-Driven scheme:** the received status and ACK/NACK are sent back on receipt of an IW block initiatively without transmitter's polling message.
- **Support Link_Up (LU) trigger:** when a handover is finished, the target network will signal the IW sublayer with a Link_UP trigger. On receipt of

this trigger, the IW sublayer will retransmit blocks in retransmission buffer to avoid unnecessary waiting for an expiration of the status report timer.

- **Adaptive Window Size:** In order to avoid any buffer overflow in the target network when the packets are retransmitted by the IW sublayer after a handover, the IW ARQ window size is adaptively set to buffer size of the target network.

In Fig. 6, an example of the IW ARQ mechanism when the window size is 12 is depicted. The right parts are two retransmission mechanisms: IW ARQ and R-LLC. In this figure, the difference between them is in that the lost blocks are retransmitted when status report timer expires in R-LLC scheme, while IW ARQ retransmits unacknowledged blocks not only on the expiration of this timer but also on the Link_Up trigger.

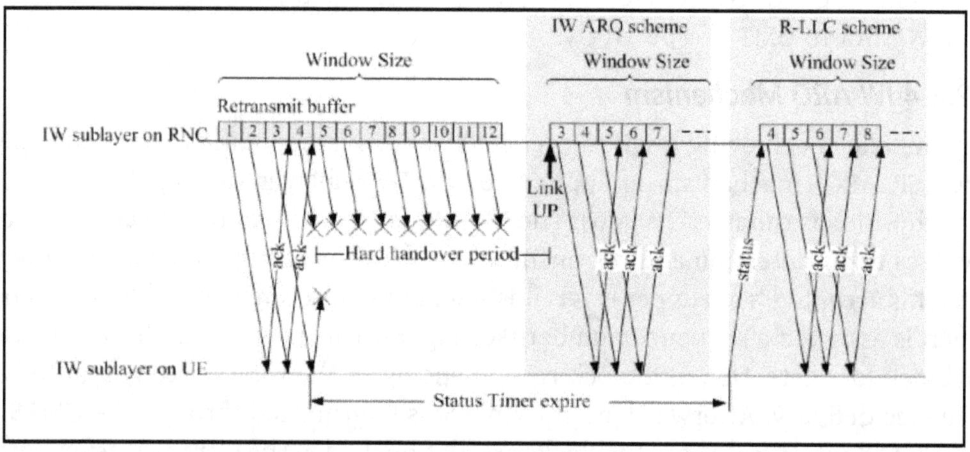

Fig. 6. IW ARQ and R-LLC protocol: an example of time evolution

3.3 Simulation Environment

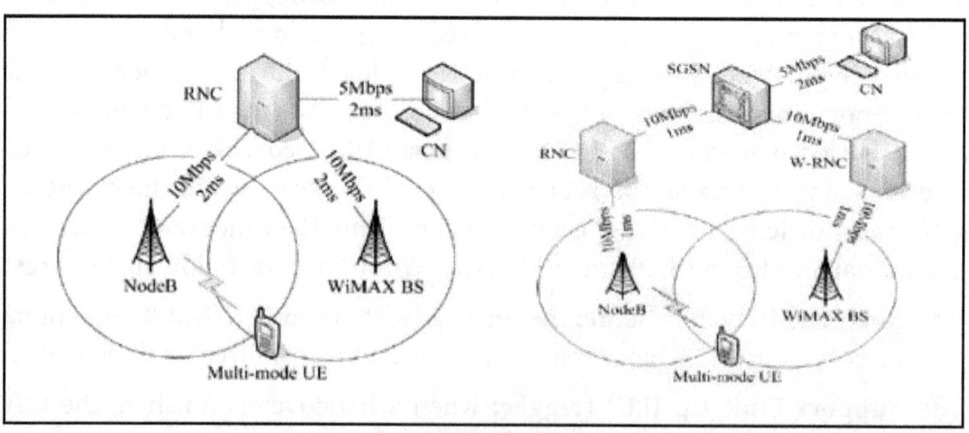

Fig. 7. Simulation topologies: integrated coupling (left) and tight coupling (right)

In order to analyze the performance of the IW sublayer during inter-RAT handover between UMTS and WiMAX, network-level simulations are carried out using NS2. Several extensions are made to this simulator, UMTS and WiMAX models, IW sublayer, multi- channel model, IW ARQ mechanism and new signaling and primitives. The simulation topologies for integrated and tight coupling scenarios are illustrated in Fig. 7. There is only one MS with two transceivers and no other background traffics in this "clean" scenario. The MS always has enough bandwidth to send packet whether it is in WiMAX region or in UMTS region. Note that in this topology, the transmission delay in the wired network is set very small deliberately to minimize its influence to handover procedure. An FTP session is examined, with the CN designated as the sender and the MS designated as the receiver. In UMTS module, a drop-tail policy is applied to radio network queues in PDCP and this queue length is set to 25 IW blocks. As to the WiMAX module, the queue length is set to 50 IW blocks, which considers the fact that generally the bandwidth of WiMAX is much higher. Other important simulation parameters are summarized in Table 1.

Table 1. Simulation Parameters

	Parameter	Value
IW	Fragment Switch	OFF
	Max retransmit count	10
	Default Windows size (block)	30
	Status Report Timer (s)	2.5
PDCP	TCP/IP Header compression,and Retransmission	no
	Allocated data rate	64kb/s
	Queue length	25
RLC	RLC Mode	AM
	Windows size (Blocks)	500
	Block size (Bytes)	20
	maxDAT	20
	Ack timerout period (ms)	50

	Parameter	Value
UMTS PHY	TTI (ms)	10
	Frame Duration(ms)	10
	BLER	1e-6
WiMAX MAC	Allocated data rate	unlimited
	Queue length	50
	Payload Header Suppression	no
	Frame duration (ms)	4
WiMAX PHY	Modulation	OFDM
	Interleaving interval (frames)	50
	FFT	256
	Number of subcarrier used	200
TCP/IP	Variant	Reno
	MSS (bytes)	512
	Default cwnd	32

3.4 Simulation Results in the Integrated Coupling Scenario

3.4.1 Handover form UMTS to WiMAX

For the simulation of inter-RAT handover from UMTS network to the WiMAX, an FTP session starts at 0.4 sec., and the MS starts to perform handover at about 4 sec. after it enters into the coverage region of WiMAX. The handover type is hard handover. At about 4.035 sec. the WiMAX network entry procedure is finished and the IW sublayer on the RNC receives a Link_Up trigger. Fig. 8 shows the packet flows of three kinds of context transfer schemes: R-LLC, SDU Reconstruction and IW ARQ.

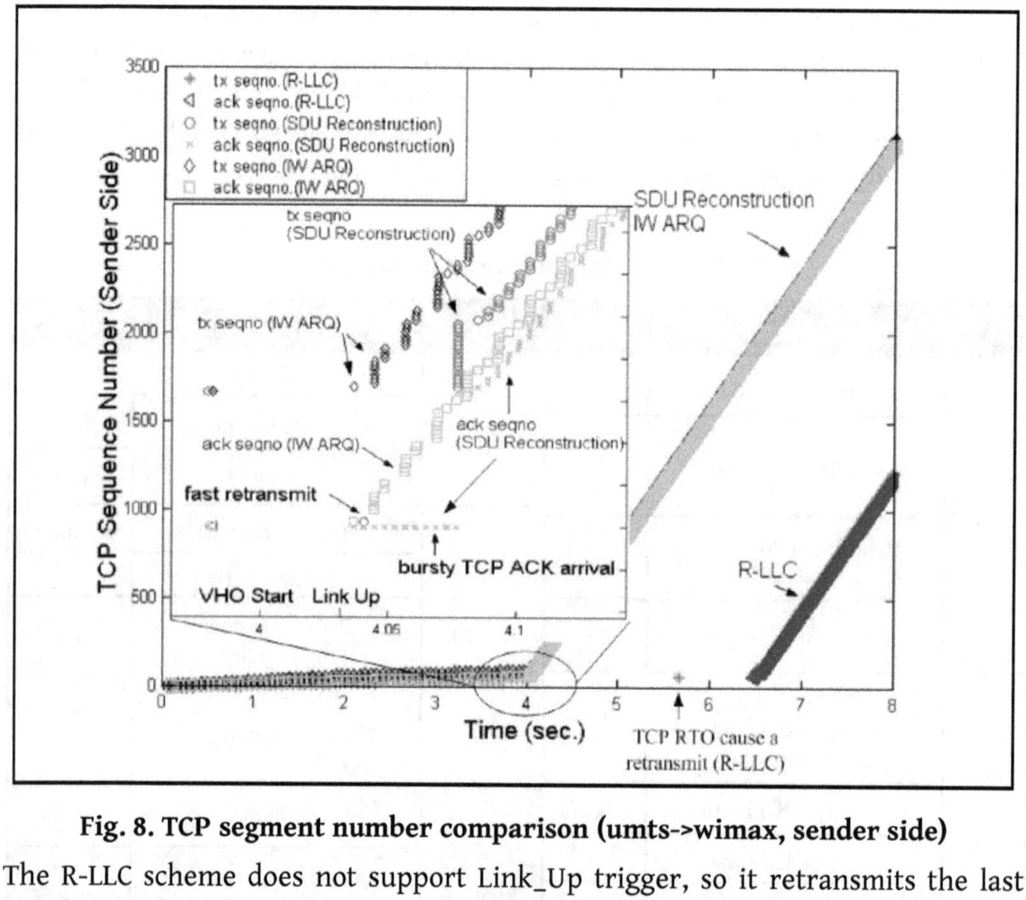

Fig. 8. TCP segment number comparison (umts->wimax, sender side)

The R-LLC scheme does not support Link_Up trigger, so it retransmits the last unacknowledged data packets on the expiration of status report timer. During this period, the TCP timer expires and the congestion window shrinks to one, as shown in Fig. 9. There is a retransmitted TCP segment at about 5.7 sec.

The SDU Reconstruction scheme reconstructs the RLC PDUs stored in the RLC retransmission buffer. However, if one PDU of a SDU is successfully transmitted, this PDU is deleted from retransmission buffer and the remaining PDUs of this SDU cannot be reconstructed and are discarded locally. The remaining RLC SDUs (TCP packets here) are forwarded to WiMAX network after handover on RNC. These arrivals of out-of-order packets generate several duplicate ACK and trigger TCP fast retransmission process. The TCP congestion window size shrinks to half of congestion window of steady state, and the average throughput is also reduced.

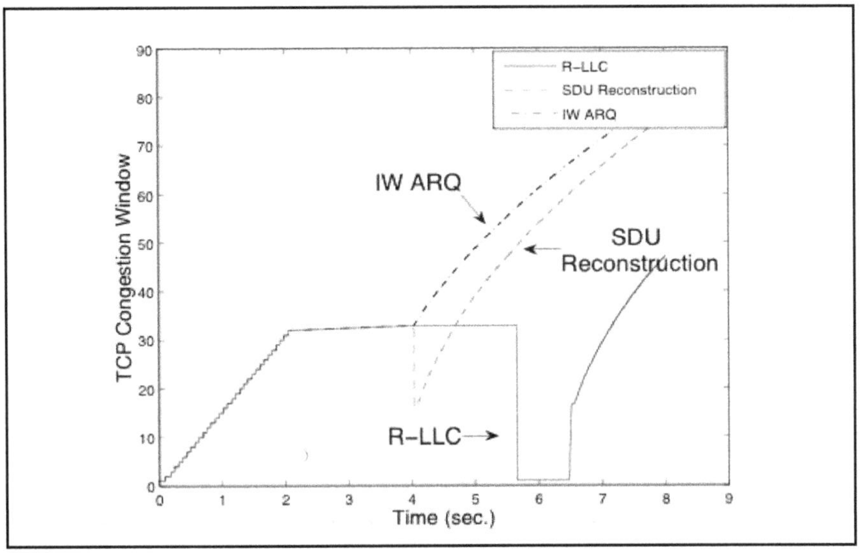

Fig. 9. TCP congestion window (umts->wimax)

The IW ARQ scheme adjusts its retransmission window according to the target network's queue size and forwards the IW blocks in its retransmission buffer on receipt of Link_Up trigger. After handover is over, there are no packet losses and the TCP ACK arrivals are not as bursty as those of SDU Reconstruction scheme thanks to the IW ARQ window mechanism (see Fig. 8 between 4 and 4.1 sec.).

3.4.2 Handover from WiMAX to UMTS

A typical problem during handover process from high bandwidth data network WiMAX to relative low bandwidth network UMTS is buffer overflow, which is caused by BDP mismatch between these two networks. The UMTS network is likely to undergo buffer overflow when a TCP congestion window for WiMAX is much larger than the buffer allocation per MS in UMTS RNC.

For SDU Reconstruction scheme, even though TCP congestion window is not larger than buffer size of UMTS, the buffered packet forwarded from WiMAX to UMTS still may have the probability to overflow the UMTS queue, because queue in WiMAX may buffer more packets than the queue size of UMTS due to inflated transmission time. For SDU Reconstruction scheme, in Fig.10, the buffer overflow in UMTS after handover leads to TCP retransmission starting at about 6.0 sec. The corresponding TCP window shrinks, as shown in Fig. 11.

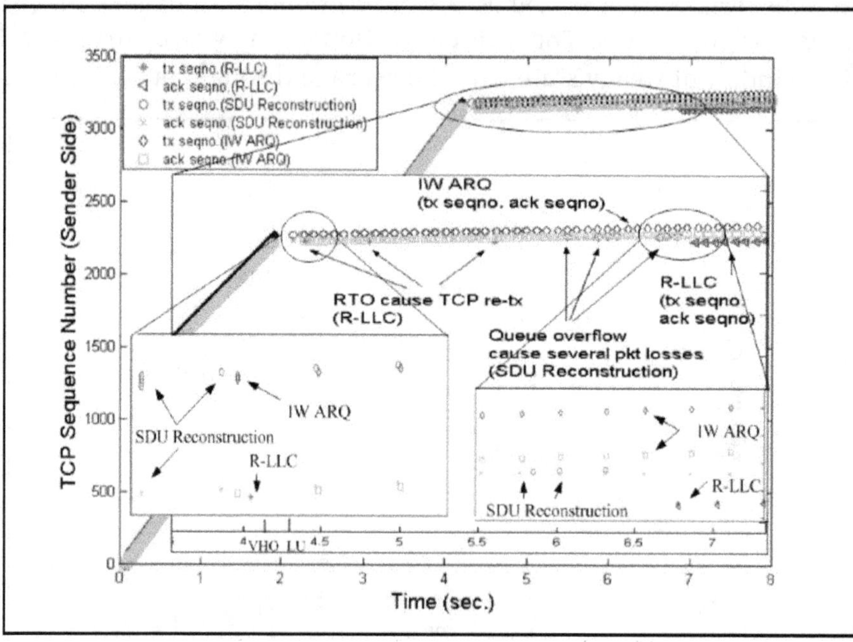

Fig. 10. TCP segment number comparison (wimax->umts, sender side)

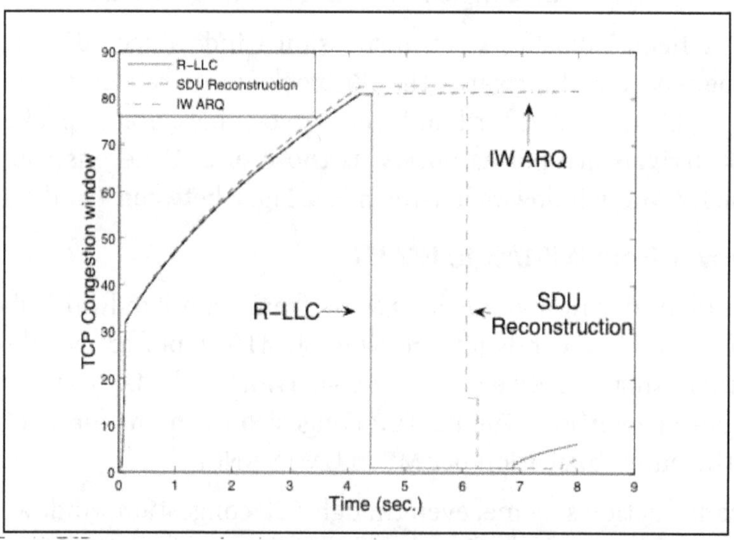

Fig. 11. TCP congestion window (wimax->umts)

For R-LLC scheme, the long status report period leads to TCP RTO and a segment is retransmitted by the TCP sender three times before a status report timer expires. The period of status report timer is set to 2.5 sec. in this scenario.

Whereas for IW ARQ scheme, the support of Link_Up trigger accelerates handover response time, and the adaptive IW ARQ window size effectively eliminates buffer overflow in the target UMTS network. It can be seen that the lossless handover of IW ARQ mechanism has a "side effect": eliminate the false fast retransmission caused by packet losses or out-of-order packet arrivals during a handover.

4. INTER-RAT HANDOVER BETWEEN UMTS AND WIMAX IN TIGHT COUPLING ARCHITECTURE

4.1 The IW Sublayer in the Tight Coupling Architecture

4.1.1 IW Sublayer Description

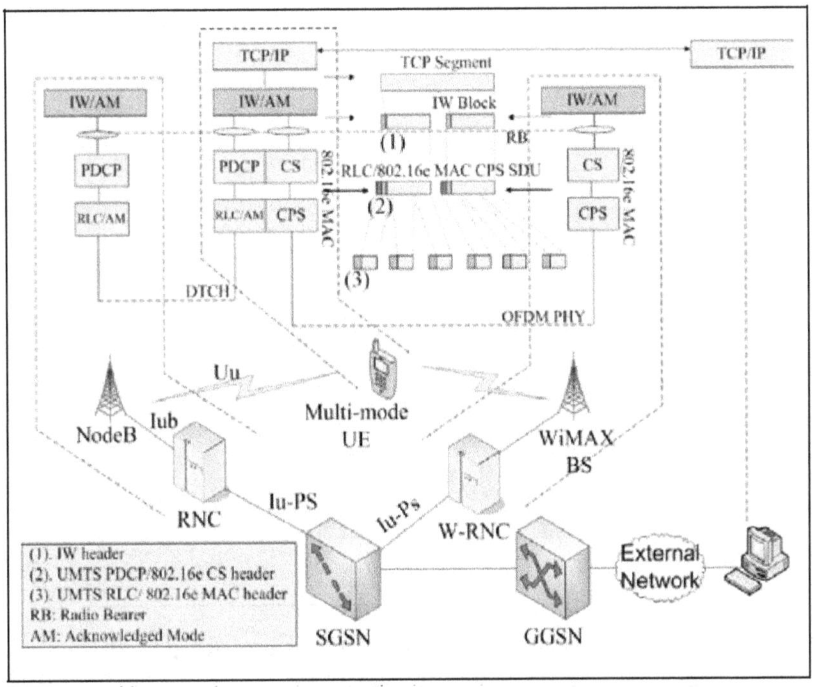

Fig. 12. IW sublayer working mechanism of tight coupling

In the tight coupling scenario, the WiMAX network may emulate a RNC (Radio Network Controller) or a SGSN (Serving GPRS Support Node). We only consider RNC emulation in this chapter. Thus, we introduce a new network component called RNC emulator for WiMAX (W-RNC) in the WiMAX access network, which connects with the UMTS CN (Core Network) at the Iu-PS interface, as shown in Fig. 12. Actually, the W-RNC is an enhanced WiMAX BS with a novel sublayer named IW sublayer, which lies on the top of WiMAX MAC (Medium Access Control) sublayer. The W-RNC with the IW sublayer has the following functions:

- Realize Iu-PS interface.
- Primitive mapping between the IW and the UTRAN network or between the IW and the WiMAX network in case of an inter-RAT handover.

- When an inter-RAT handover takes place, the IW sublayer functions as the LLC sublayer of conventional cellular networks by enabling the SR ARQ (Selective Repeat ARQ) mechanism that includes packet segmentation, re-sequencing, retransmission, and retransmission window size adjustment.
- When a handover takes place, the IW sublayer transfers context to target RNC or W- RNC where the counterpart sublayer locates. In order to provide a seamless inter-RAT handover between UMTS and WiMAX, a peer IW sublayer shall also be realized on the top of the PDCP sublayer on the conventional RNC. While on the MS, the IW sublayer is a common sublayer on the top of the PDCP sublayer of UMTS and the MAC sublayer of WiMAX.

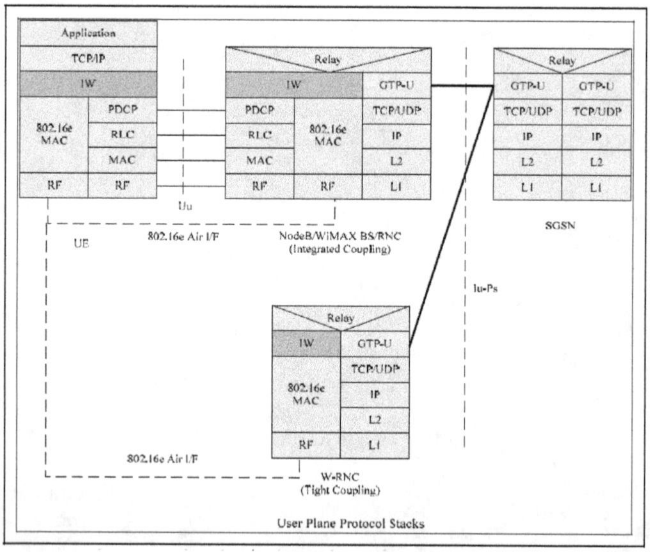

Fig. 13. User plane protocol stacks of tight coupling architecture

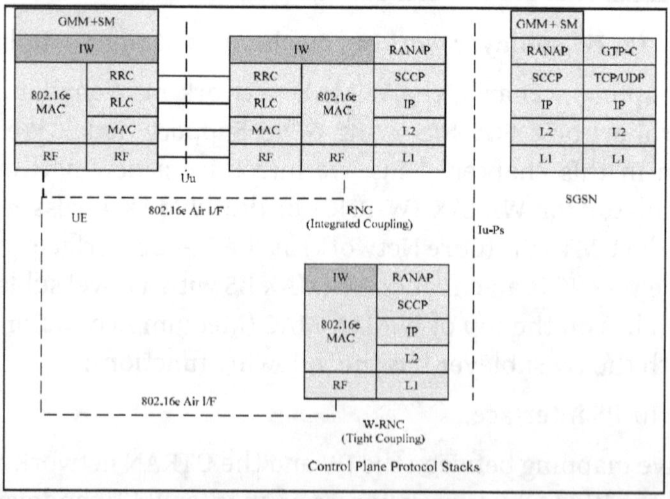

Fig. 14. Control plane protocol stacks of tight coupling architecture

In Fig. 13 and Fig. 14, the user and control planes of the proposed tight coupling architecture are illustrated. W-RNC is assumed to cover the same Routing Area (RA) like the RNC. The IW sublayer on the W-RNC communicates with its counterpart entity on the RNC in order to execute inter-RAT handover to/from its control area. The main contents of the communication between them are as follows:

- GTP-U sequence numbers as well as GTP packets that need to be forwarded by the W- RNC for PDP contexts requiring delivery order.
- IW ARQ parameters, such as windows size, queue length, retransmission timer period, and retransmission count.
- The IW blocks stored in local retransmission buffer.

There are two reasons why add IW ARQ mechanism to W-RNC in addition to SRNS (Serving RNS) context transfer of conventional RNC:

- When an inter-RAT handover takes place, there may exist packet sequence number asynchronization between the source RNC and the target WiMAX BS. It is necessarily that there exists a common context transfer mechanism for these two systems to assure a lossless handover.
- The second reason is that the WiMAX supports cell reselection initiated by MS for active traffics (like dedicated mode in UMTS), which is not the case in UMTS. Hence, the packets that are lost during the cell reselection from WiMAX to UMTS, cannot be retransmitted by the target network.

4.1.2 Signaling and Primitives

4.1.2.1 Handover from UMTS to WiMAX

This sub-clause describes the inter-RAT handover signaling procedures and primitives among IW, PDCP, RRC (Radio Resource Control) and WiMAX MAC in the tight coupling architecture. In the following figures, IW/RNC means the function combination of IW sublayer and RNC, so are the IW/W-RNC and MAC/W-RNC. Some newly added cross- layer primitives are augmented to the conventional inter-RAT handover signaling procedures of 3GPP (3GPP TS 43.129; 3GPP TR 25.931). We suggest the future WiMAX and UMTS standards should support these primitives and parameters for the smooth and seamless inter-RAT handover. The handover preparation period is similar to that of integrated coupling architecture and is omitted in this sub-clause.

Fig. 15 describes the inter-RAT handover from UMTS to WiMAX and shows the exchanged messages.

1. Based on measurement reports and knowledge of the RAN topology, the RNC, more precisely source RRC decides to initiate an inter-RAT PS handover.

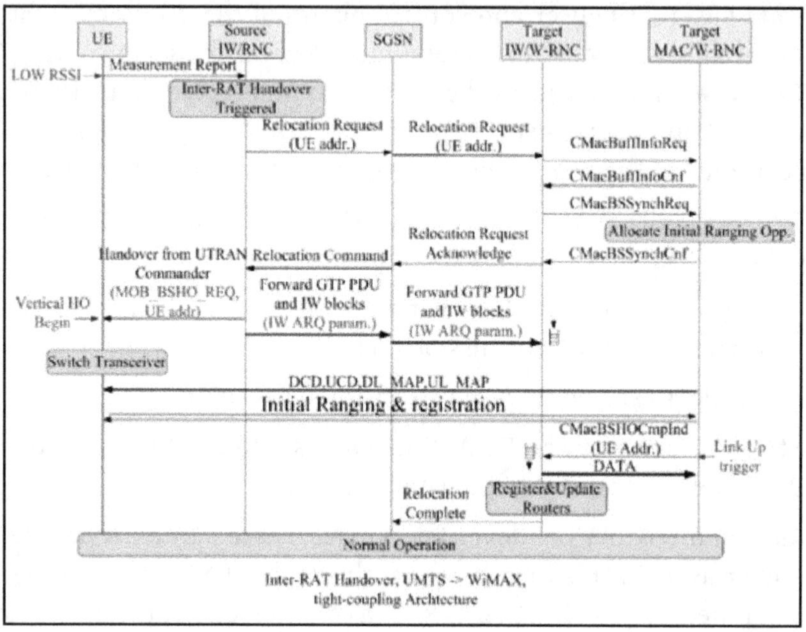

Fig. 15. Signaling procedure of the handover from UMTS to WiMAX

2. The source RNC sends a Relocation Request (contains target WiMAX cell id) message to the SGSN. The SGSN forwards Relocation Request message to target W-RNC.
3. Then the IW of target W-RNC sends the CMacBuffInfoReq primitive to the WiMAX MAC to request the buffer characteristics. The WiMAX MAC returns the CMacBuffInfoCnf primitive to inform the IW of the buffer size in its MAC sublayer. According to this information, the target IW adjusts its retransmission window size. It should be mentioned at this point that current WiMAX MAC does not support this interface, so the IW may adjust its retransmission window size to a default value.
4. At this stage, the target IW sends the CMacBSSynchReq primitive to the WiMAX MAC to negotiate the location of the dedicated initial ranging transmission opportunity for the MS. This information is returned by primitive CMacBSSynchCnf.
5. The target W-RNC sends the Relocation Request Acknowledge message to SGSN, and the SGSN continues the handover by sending a Relocation Command to source RNC (including Transparent Container (MOB_BSHO-REQ)).
6. Upon receipt of Relocation Command message, the IW of source RNC will forward IW context to target IW of W-RNC. The IW context consists of IW ARQ parameters, received IW ACK and remaining IW blocks that have not been transmitted successfully.

7. The RRC of the source RNC sends the Handover from UTRAN Command message to the MS.
8. The MS performs hard handover and normal network entry procedure.
9. After the provisioned service flow is activated, the target WiMAX MAC sends CMacBSHOCmpInd primitive as a Link_UP (LU) trigger to the IW sublayer. On this trigger, the IW starts data packet forwarding.

4.1.2.2 Handover from WiMAX to UMTS

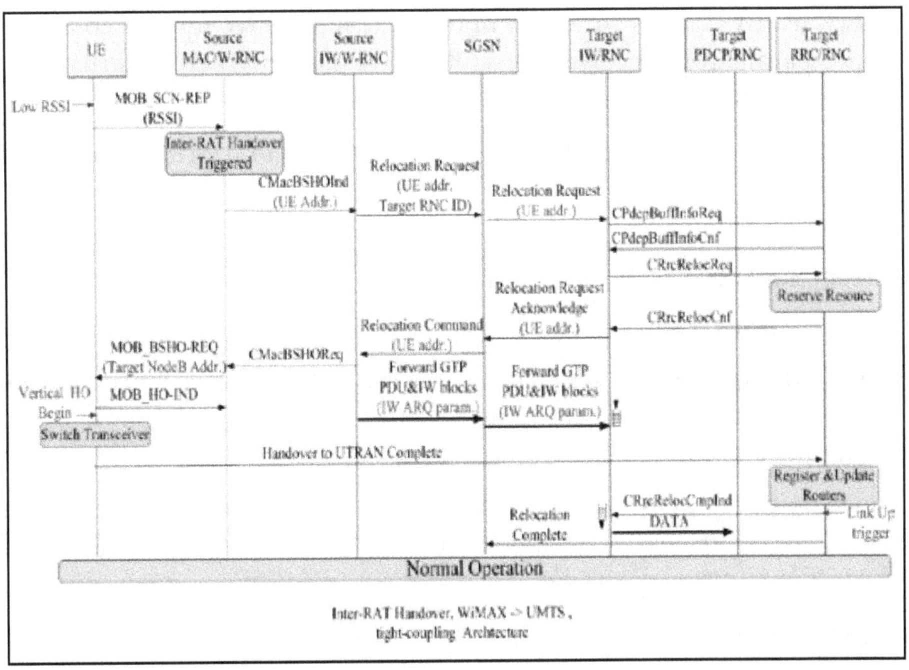

Fig. 16. Signaling procedure of the handover from WiMAX to UMTS

The inter-RAT handover from WiMAX to UMTS is described in Fig. 16.

1. After the scanning interval, the MS sends scanning report to WiMAX serving BS by message MON_SCN-REP that contains physical information such as mean RSSI.
2. The source WiMAX MAC sends CMacBSHOInd primitive to inform the IW sublayer of handover and target cell id. Then, the source W-RNC sends a Relocation Request (contains target cell id) message to the SGSN. The SGSN forwards Relocation Request message to target RNC.
3. The IW of target RNC sends CPdcpBuffInfoReq primitive to the RRC sublayer to request the buffer characteristics of the PDCP sublayer, and RRC returns the CPdcpBuffInfoCnf primitive to inform the IW of buffer size. According to this information, the IW adjusts its retransmission window size.

4. The target IW sends a CRrcRelocReq primitive to the target RRC to apply for resource allocation. The result is returned in CRrcRelocCnf primitive by the target RRC.
5. The target RNC sends the Relocation Request Acknowledge message (contains target RNC to source W-RNC transparent Container) to SGSN. The SGSN continues the handover by sending a Relocation Command to source W-RNC.
6. On receipt of Relocation Command message, the IW of source W-RNC will forward IW context to the IW of target RNC. The IW context consists of IW ARQ parameters, received IW ACK, and remaining IW blocks that have not been transmitted successfully.
7. The source IW sends CMacBSHOReq primitive to inform MAC that the target network is ready.
8. The MS performs handover to one of BSs specified in MOB_BSHO-REQ and responds with a MOB_HO-IND message.
9. MS performs normal UMTS hard handover.
10. After the MS successfully finishes UMTS radio link setup, the target RRC shall send the CRrcRelocCmpInd primitive to the IW, and the IW starts data packet forwarding.

Note that primitive CMacBSHOCmpInd and primitive CRrcRelocCmpInd are defined as the Link_Up (LU) triggers for handover from UMTS to WiMAX, and for handover from WiMAX to UMTS respectively.

4.1.3 Buffering-and-Forwarding (B&F) in Tight Coupling Architecture

We have mentioned that: in FMIPv6 protocol (R. Koodli, 2005), in order to make a handover lossless, previous access router (PAR) will forward buffered packets destined for the MS during the handover period to the new access router (NAR) through an established tunnel, after receiving the new care-of-address (NCoA) of the MS from the NAR. One essence of this IP layer handover solution is the utilization of buffering-and-forwarding (B&F) context transfer scheme. In our IW sublayer solution, the B&F scheme is also applied to forward GTP-U packets, IW blocks and so on from source IW sublayer to target IW sublayer. It becomes meaningful and interesting to compare IW sublayer handover solution with FMIPv6 in tight coupling architecture. For fairly comparing the inter-RAT handover performance of IW sublayer solution with that of FMIPv6, we also only realize the B&F scheme in the IW sublayer in our inter-RAT handover scenario, where the RNC or W-RNC takes the responsibility of buffering and forwarding. This kind of Layer 2 realization considers the fact that: the conventional IP sublayer terminates on the GGSN in the UMTS network, which suffers from longer transmission delay between the MS and the GGSN at IP layer. It must be stressed that this Layer 2 realization of B&F has better performance than IP layer realization like FMIPv6 thanks to the ability to directly operate Layer 2 data packets stored in one RAT. In the simulation subclause, we will inspect these two kinds of context transfer schemes- IW ARQ and B&F in the tight coupling architecture. If the handover performance of IW ARQ is better than that of B&F at Layer 2, we can say that the IW sublayer solution is more suitable for inter-RAT handover than FMIPv6.

4.2 Simulation Results in the Tight Coupling Scenario

4.2.1 Handover from UMTS to WiMAX

For the simulation of inter-RAT handover from UMTS network to the WiMAX, an FTP session starts at 0.4 sec., and the MS starts to perform handover at about 4 sec. after it enters into the coverage region of WiMAX. The handover type is hard handover. At about 4.035 sec, the WiMAX network entry procedure is finished and the IW sublayer on the RNC receives a Link_Up trigger. Fig. 17 shows the packet flows of two kinds of context transfer schemes: buffering-and-forwarding (B&F) and IW ARQ.

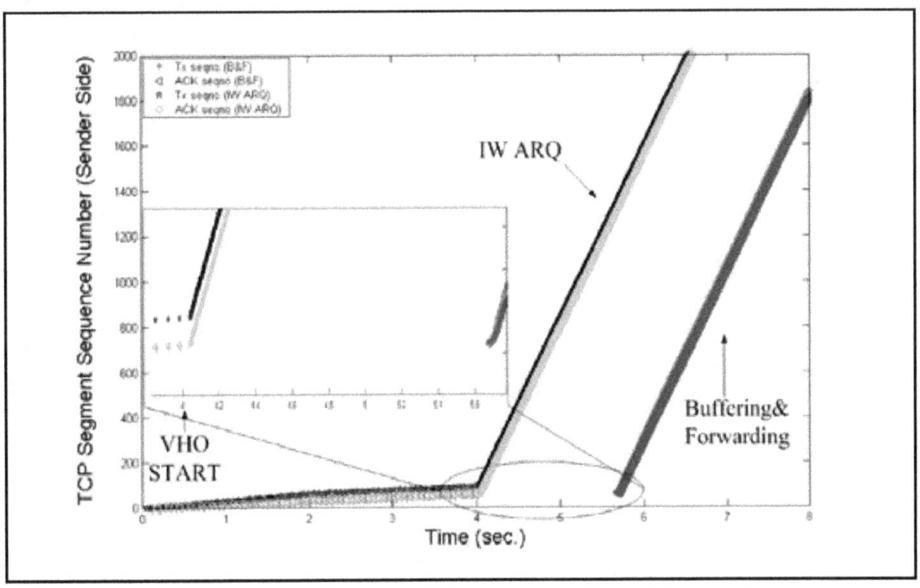

Fig. 17. TCP segment number comparison (umts->wimax, sender side)

During the handover period, there are no new TCP segment arrivals and consequently no segments are forwarded through the tunnel between RNC and W-RNC for both context transfer schemes (see Fig.18). One can see from Fig. 18 that, in B&F scheme, the TCP sender retransmits the last unacknowledged segments on the timeout of TCP retransmission timer (RTO) at about 5.7 sec. During this period, the congestion window shrinks to one, and throughput reduces significantly.

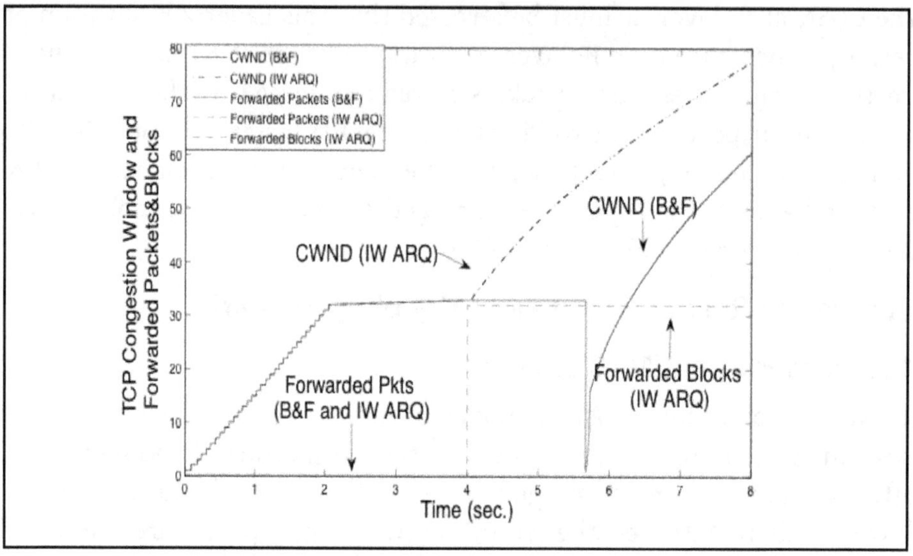

Fig. 18. TCP congestion window (umts->wimax)

The IW ARQ scheme adjusts its retransmission window according to the target network's queue size, and sends the IW blocks that are forwarded from the source IW on receipt of Link_Up trigger. After the handover, there will be no packet losses and TCP congestion window does not shrink thanks to the retransmission mechanism.

4.2.2 Handover from WiMAX to UMTS

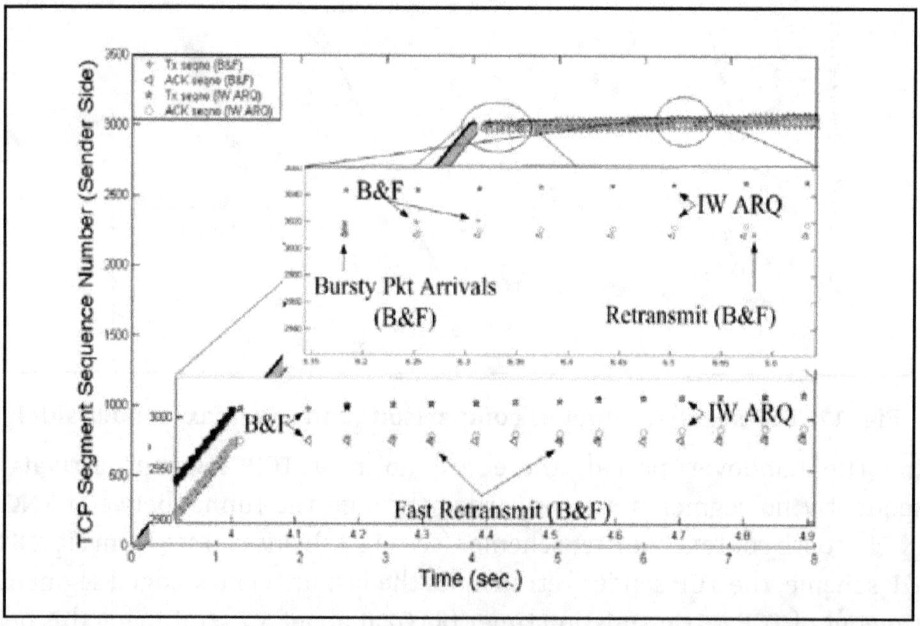

Fig. 19. TCP segment number comparison (wimax->umts, sender side)

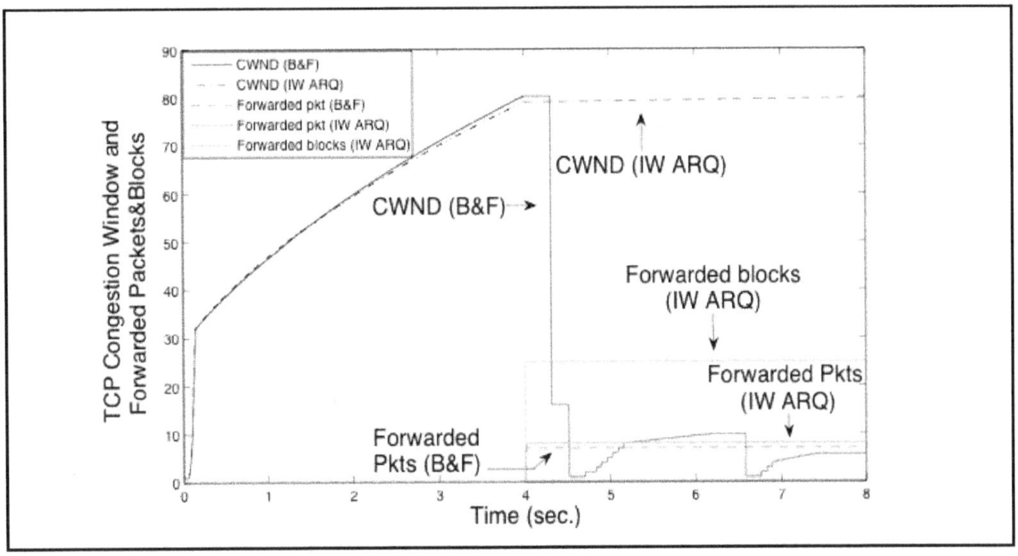

Fig. 20. TCP congestion window (wimax->umts)

When a handover from WiMAX to UMTS happens, there exist some TCP segments and IW blocks, which are forwarded from W-RNC to RNC through the tunnel for two schemes, as shown in Fig.20. For B&F scheme, the arrivals of tunneled segments (about 8 segments) trigger the fast retransmissions twice at time 4.31 sec. and 4.51 sec. for the lost segments during the handover (see Fig. 19), and then congestion window size reduces significantly. From then on, the TCP sender retransmits the segments numbering from the first lost segment to the tunneled segments. The receiver will acknowledge again those segments that have been tunneled before at about 6.18 sec, which herein trigger the bursty segment arrivals. Furthermore, those retransmitted segments that have been tunneled during handover procedure delay the ACK feedback of new segments, and in consequence lead to a retransmission caused by RTO at 6.58 sec.. We can see that, the B&F scheme degrades the handover performance instead of improving it for TCP traffics due to the lack of a mechanism that recovers the lost packets.

For IW ARQ scheme, there is no packet loss during the handover. The support of Link_Up trigger accelerates handover response time, and the adaptive IW ARQ window size effectively eliminates buffer overflow in the target UMTS network. The only price for this lossless handover procedure is that the IW sender may retransmit a couple of IW blocks that possibly have been received by IW receiver but the corresponding ACKs are lost in the air during the handover period.

5. CONCISE SUMMARY

The introduction of the proposed inter-RAT handover solution for interworking UMTS with WiMAX is the primary focus of this chapter. Initially, the initial portion delineates the mechanism for reselection and handover of 3GPP cells. This section provides the primary framework for the development of a novel mechanism that addresses the common challenges associated with inter-RAT handover between UMTS and WiMAX. Subsequently, a novel Layer 2 inter-RAT handover scheme is developed on the basis of the integrated coupling and tight coupling architectures to facilitate seamless mobility between UMTS and WiMAX networks. For example, in an integrated coupling architecture, a new common sublayer, the IW sublayer, is erected on top of the PDCP (UMTS) and MAC (WiMAX) sublayers. This sublayer is located on the RNC and MS. Additionally, a novel retransmission scheme known as IW ARQ is proposed at this sublayer to expedite the handover process and eradicate packet losses during the handover process. In contrast to other context transfer mechanisms, such as R-LLC, SDU Reconstruction, and buffering-and-forwarding, IW ARQ is capable of achieving a lossless and fast handover procedure for TCP traffic as a result of the introduction of the SR ARQ mechanism. The simulation results obtained on the NS2 emulator serve as confirmation of the superior transition performance. Furthermore, this innovative IW sublayer scheme can also eradicate the false fast retransmission that occurs as a result of packet loss or out-of-order packet arrivals during a handover period. It also offers a suitable framework for resolving the TCP issue of BDP mismatch, premature RTO, and other related issues.

REFERENCES

1. 3GPP TS 04.18. Technical Specification Group GSM/EDGE Radio Access Network; mobile radio interface layer 3 specification; radio resource control protocol
2. 3GPP TS 05.08. Technical Specification Group GSM/EDGE Radio Access Network; Radio subsystem link control (release 99)
3. 3GPP TS 23.060. Technical Specification Group Services and System Aspects; General Packet Radio Service (GPRS); Service description, stage 2 (Release 7), v7.4.0
4. 3GPP TS 23.122, "Technical Specification Group Core Network and Terminals; Non-Access- Stratum (NAS) functions related to Mobile Station (MS) in idle mode", (Release 7), V7.2.0
5. 3GPP TS 23.234. 3GPP system to Wireless Local Area Network (WLAN), interworking; System description (Release 6), V6.5.0
6. 3GPP TS 25.304. User Equipment (UE) procedures in Idle Mode and Procedures for Cell Reselection in Connected Mode
7. 3GPP TS 25.323. Technical Specification Group Radio Access Network; Packet Data Convergence Protocol (PDCP) specification, (Release 7), V7.5.0

8. 3GPP TS 25.331. Technical Specification Group Radio Access Network; Radio Resource Control (RRC); Protocol Specification (Release 7), v7.5
9. 3GPP TR 25.922. Technical Specification Group Radio Access Network; Radio resource management strategies (Release 7), V7.10
10. 3GPP TR 25.931. Technical Specification Group RAN; UTRAN functions, examples on signaling procedures, (Realease 7), V7.4.0
11. 3GPP TS 43.022, "Technical Specification Group GSM/EDGE; Radio Access Network; Functions related to Mobile Station (MS) in idle mode and group receive mode", (Release 7), V7.2.0
12. 3GPP TS 43.129. Technical Specification Group GSM/EDGE" Radio Access Network; Packet-switched handover for GERAN A/Gb mode; Stage 2 (Release 7), V7.2.0
13. 3GPP TS 44.060. Technical Specification Group GSM/EDGE Radio Access Network; General Packet Radio Service (GPRS), Radio Link Control/Medium Access Control (RLC/MAC) protocol (Release 7), V7.9.0
14. 3GPP TS 45.008. Technical Specification Group GSM/EDGE; Radio Access Network; Radio subsystem link control (Release 7), V7.8.0
15. Johnson, R. Cuny & N. Wimolpitayarat. (2005). Inter-System Handover for Packet Switched Services", 2005 6th IEE International Conference on 3G and Beyond, pp: 1-5, 7-9 Nov. 2005
16. Johnson, C. Perkins, & J. Arkko. (2004). IP Mobility Support in IPv6, http://www.ietf.org/rfc/rfc3775.txt, IETF, June 2004
17. Seurre, P. Savelli & P.J. Pietri. (2003). GPRS for Mobile Internet, Artech House Ltd, 2003
18. G. Lanpropoulos, N. Passas, L. Merakos & A. Kaloxylos. (2005). Handover Management Architectures in Integrated WLAN/Cellular Networks. IEEE Communication Survey & Tutorials. Vol.7, No.4, pp: 30-44, Fourth Quarter 2005
19. H. Inaura, G. Montenegro, R. Ludwig, A. Gurtov & F. Khafizov. (2003). TCP over Second (2.5) and Third (3G) Generation Wireless Networks, IETF, RFC 3481
20. H. Rutagemwa, S. Park, X.M. Shen & J.W. Mark. (2007). Robust Cross-layer Design of Wireless Profiled TCP Mobile Receiver for Vertical Handover, IEEE Tans. On Vehicular Technology, Vol.56, No. 6, pp: 3899-3911, Nov. 2007
21. Http://www.isi.edu/nsnam/ns
22. IEEE 802.16e (2005). IEEE Standard for Local and metropolitan area networks Part 16: Air Interface for Fixed and Mobile Broadband Wireless Access Systems

Amendment 2: Physical and Medium Access Control Layers for Combined Fixed and Mobile Operation in Licensed Bands, 2005

23. IEEE 802.21 (2006). Standard and Metropolitan Area Networks: Media Independent Handover Services, Draft P802.21/D00.05, January 2006
24. J.P Romero, O. Sallent, R. Agusti & A.D.G. Miguel. (2005). Radio Resource Management Strategies in UMTS, John Wiley & Sons, Ltd, 2005
25. J. Sachs, B. S. Khurana & P. Mahonen. (2006). Evaluation of Handover Performance for TCP Traffic Based on Generic Link Layer Context Transfer, IEEE International Symposium on Personal, Indoor and Mobile Radio Communications, 2006 (PIMRC'06), pp: 1-5, Sept. 2006
26. M. Afif, P. Martins, S. Tabbane & P. Godlewski. (2006). SCTP Extension for EGPRS/WLAN Handover Data, 31st IEEE Conference on Local Computer Networks, pp: 746-750, Nov. 2006
27. N. Dailly, P. Martins & P. Godlewski. (2006). Performance evaluation of L2 handover Mechanisms for Inter-Radio Access Networks, IEEE Vehicular Technology Conference, 2006 (VTC2006-Spring), pp: 491-495, May 7-10, 2006
28. N. Vulic, I. Niemegeers & S.H de Groot. (2004). Architectural Options for the WLAN Integration at the UMTS Radio Access level, IEEE Vehicular Technology Conference, 2004 (VTC 2004-Spring), pp: 3009-3013, May 17-19, 2004
29. R. Koodli. (2005). Fast Handovers for Mobile IPv6, http://www.ietf.org/rfc/rfc4068.txt, IETF, July 2005
30. S.L. Tsao & C.C. Lin. (2002). Design and Evaluation of UMTS/WLAN interworking Strategies, IEEE Vehicular Technology Conference, 2002 (VTC2002-Fall), pp: 777-781, 2002

28
Chapter

MHD-CAR: A DISTRIBUTED CROSS-LAYER SOLUTION FOR ENHANCING SEAMLESS MOBILITY MANAGEMENT PROTOCOLS

1. INTRODUCTION: AN OVERVIEW

The architecture of the Next Generation Network (NGN) is transforming into a highly heterogeneous infrastructure that is comprised of a diverse array of Wireless Access Technologies (WAT). One of the primary obstacles in a technologically diverse network is the provision of ubiquitous communication services to mobile entities, which may have varying mobility patterns and speeds, regardless of their location and/or the underlying WAT. This necessitates the development of effective mobility management solutions that would offer mobile entities location management and handover management services. The handover management service allows the mobile entity to modify its point of connection to the Internet, while the location management service is responsible for monitoring the location of the mobile entities. The primary objective of any effective mobility management solution is to facilitate the seamless inter-WAT transition and provide effective and rapid location monitoring and updating services. The concept of seamless handover refers to handovers that occur with minimal latency and packet losses.

Providing a seamless transference is a significant challenge due to the fact that the location update occurs subsequent to the successful completion of the handover. The handover procedure is conducted at the data link layer (L2) and the network layer (L3) in accordance with the established protocols at each layer. The L2 handover procedure allows the mobile node (MN) to transition its link connectivity from its serving access point (AP) or base station to the new one. The MN will be required to complete the L3 handover procedure to ensure that the MN IP is capable of functioning on the new link after the link connectivity has been successfully established. The MN is virtually disconnected from the network until the transition is finalized, which results in data loss. The sum of the delay incurred by the handover procedure prescribed at L2 and L3 is the handover latency, which in turn determines the quantity of data lost. This suggests that the latency of the L3 handover process is directly influenced by the latency of the L2 handover process and the scheduling of the provisioning of L2 triggers that will initiate the L3 handover process.

Therefore, it is crucial to consider the impact of the L2 handover process on the L3 specified handover operations in order to create a seamless handover methodology. This necessitates the development of a cross-layer mobility management solution that will facilitate the exchange of critical information between L2 and L3, thereby improving the overall performance of the transfer process.

In this chapter, we provide a comprehensive overview of a cross-layer solution known as Multi-Hop Discovery of Candidate Access Router (MHD-CAR). This solution not only enhances the operational efficiency of seamless mobility management protocols in general, but also optimizes the standard Candidate Access Router Discovery (CARD) protocol (Liebsch et al., 2005). Additionally, it possesses inherent cross-layer capabilities that have the potential to contribute to low latency handovers.

2. TECHNICAL BACKGROUND

To provide mobility management to MNs, IETF has specified Mobile IPv6 (MIPv6) protocol at L3 (Perkins et al., 2004). However, it is an established fact that the handover performance of MIPv6 is not seamless, in that it incurs a high handover latency and packet delay. This is because the MIPv6 operation is based on a break-before-make operation in which the MN will initiate the MIPv6 protocol after it has disconnected from its serving AP as it moves out of its coverage range. After the disconnection, the MN will search and connect to the appropriate new in-range wireless AP. After establishing link connectivity (or performing L2 handover), the MIPv6 handover process will be initiated which is based on a sequential execution of a series of sub-processes; namely Care-of-Address configuration, Duplicate Address Detection (DAD) test, Home Registration, Return Routability Test and Correspondent Registration. Each of the sub-process will incur a finite amount of delay (DAD test alone incurs a delay of 1 sec) contributing thereby to the total handover latency. During the execution of the MIPv6 protocol, the MN remains disconnected from the Internet and is unable to transmit or receive packets resulting in data losses. Hence, the MIPv6 handover latency, which is in excess of 1.5 seconds (Yousaf et al., 2008(c)), is unsuitable for delay sensitive and throughput sensitive applications.

To provide seamless handover services, IETF has specified Fast Mobile IPv6 (FMIPv6) protocol in RFC 5268 (Koodli, 2008) which extends the standard MIPv6 protocol. The main operational concept of FMIPv6 is based on the ability of the MN to detect and negotiate a handover with the New Access Router (NAR) in advance while the MN is still connected to its Present Access Router (PAR). During handover negotiation with NAR, a bi-directional tunnel is established between the PAR and NAR so that packets arriving at the PAR (and destined towards the MN) are tunnelled towards NAR where they will get buffered. These buffered packets will get forwarded to the MN soon after it establishes link connectivity with the AP associated with the NAR and becomes IP capable on the NAR's link. In other words, FMIPv6 is based on a make-before-break concept which not only reduces handover latency but also the packet loss by virtue of the tunnelling and buffering of packets.

However, the key to the success for the FMIPv6 handover operation is the ability of the MN to detect and identify the presence of in-range Candidate Access Routers (CARs) and then select an appropriate NAR from amongst the identified CARs. The FMIPv6 protocol specification only specifies the handover operation by assuming that the MN has already identified and selected a suitable NAR and hence does not provide any specific mechanism to this end. The method of discovering CARs and selecting NAR is left to the discretion of the user.

Candidate Access Router Discovery (CARD) is one such standard solution (Liebsch et al., 2005) the protocol facilities of which can be utilised by FMIPv6 to enable a MN to discover CARs and hence select NAR.

The summary of the CARD protocol and its interaction with the protocol operation of FMIPv6 is given in the following sub-section.

2.1 CARD Protocol

The CARD protocol is a standard IETF solution the operational details of which are specified in RFC 4066. The protocol provides a generic mechanism that allows a MN to acquire the necessary and relevant information about the ARs that are potential candidates for the MN's next handover. It is based on the exchange of a series of request and reply messages between the MN and its serving AR and also amongst ARs as well. The messages exchanged between the MN and its serving AR (i.e., PAR) is designated as MN-AR CARD Request and MN-AR CARD Reply message, whereas those exchanged between the ARs are termed as AR-AR CARD Request and AR-AR CARD Reply message. These messages are transported as options inside the ICMPv6 message. The format of the CARD Request and CARD Reply message is illustrated in Figure 1 and 2 respectively.

```
 0                   1                   2                   3
 0 1 2 3 4 5 6 7 8 9 0 1 2 3 4 5 6 7 8 9 0 1 2 3 4 5 6 7 8 9 0 1
|-|-|-|-|-|-|-|-|-|-|-|-|-|-|-|-|-|-|-|-|-|-|-|-|-|-|-|-|-|-|-|-|
|     Type = 0    |     Code = 0    |            Checksum           |
|-|-|-|-|-|-|-|-|-|-|-|-|-|-|-|-|-|-|-|-|-|-|-|-|-|-|-|-|-|-|-|-|
|   Subtype - 0   |                  Reserved                     |
|-|-|-|-|-|-|-|-|-|-|-|-|-|-|-|-|-|-|-|-|-|-|-|-|-|-|-|-|-|-|-|-|
|   Type - 138    |     Length      |Vers.|P|C|A|T|   Reserved    |
+-+-+-+-+-+-+-+-+-+-+-+-+-+-+-+-+-+-+-+-+-+-+-+-+-+-+-+-+-+-+-+-+
|                        Sequence Number                        |
+-+-+-+-+-+-+-+-+-+-+-+-+-+-+-+-+-+-+-+-+-+-+-+-+-+-+-+-+-+-+-+-+
|  Sub-Options
|-|-|-|-|-|-|-|-|-|-|-|-|-|-|-|-|-|-   -   -   -   -   -   -   -
```

Fig. 1. Format of the CARD Request Message Carried as an Option in ICMPv6 Message

```
 0                   1                   2                   3
 0 1 2 3 4 5 6 7 8 9 0 1 2 3 4 5 6 7 8 9 0 1 2 3 4 5 6 7 8 9 0 1
+-+-+-+-+-+-+-+-+-+-+-+-+-+-+-+-+-+-+-+-+-+-+-+-+-+-+-+-+-+-+-+-+
|     Type = 0    |     Code = 0    |            Checksum           |
+-+-+-+-+-+-+-+-+-+-+-+-+-+-+-+-+-+-+-+-+-+-+-+-+-+-+-+-+-+-+-+-+
|   Subtype - 0   |                  Reserved                     |
+-+-+-+-+-+-+-+-+-+-+-+-+-+-+-+-+-+-+-+-+-+-+-+-+-+-+-+-+-+-+-+-+
|   Type - 139    |     Length      |Vers.|P|U|L|   Reserved      |
|-|-|-|-|-|-|-|-|-|-|-|-|-|-|-|-|-|-|-|-|-|-|-|-|-|-|-|-|-|-|-|-|
|                        Sequence Number                        |
|-|-|-|-|-|-|-|-|-|-|-|-|-|-|-|-|-|-|-|-|-|-|-|-|-|-|-|-|-|-|-|-|
|  Sub-Options
|-|-|-|-|-|-|-|-|-|-|-|-|-|-|-|-|-|-   -   -   -   -   -   -   -
```

Fig. 2. Format of the CARD Reply Message Carried as an Option in ICMPv6 Message

The CARD protocol is designed to perform the following two functions namely;

1. Reverse Address Translation (RAT)
2. Discovery of CAR Capabilities (DCC)

The ***RAT function*** enables a MN to map the L2 identifiers (L2-IDs) (e.g., a MAC address for 802.11 networks) of one or more in-range APs to the IP address (L3-IDs) of the associated CAR connected to it. The L2-IDs are typically discovered during the scan operation initiated by the MN as a reaction to the link condition going below a certain specified threshold value of SNR or RSSI.

The ***DCC function*** on the other hand, allows the MN to acquire the capability's information of the discovered CARs. The notion of capabilities implies of the various QoS aspects offered by a CAR that would then be used as input to the MN's target AR (TAR) selection algorithm to make optimal handover decisions. The DCC function will prevent the MN to make inaccurate network selections and hence connections to the wrong one in case of many available CARs.

Central to the CARD operation is a L2-L3 address mapping Table called a CAR Table, which is managed and maintained inside each AR. The information content of the CAR Table is used to resolve the L2-IDs of a Candidate AP (CAP) to the IP address and capabilities of the associated CAR.

RFC 4066 suggests the use of a central entity called a CARD Server as one of the strategy to populate the CAR Table. During boot up time all ARs within the administrative domain of the CARD Server will register their IP addresses and the L2-IDs of the associated CAPs with the CARD Server. The CARD Server will then be queried during the RAT process.

The functionality of the CARD protocol extends many benefits which are outlined in (Trossen et al., 2002). For example, the information that the MN acquires due to the CARD operation will enable it to select and connect to an appropriate network that would provide the necessary service to the MN based on its application requirements. This can be beneficial to multi-homed MNs as it may also enable the MN to select the least-cost network and enable inter-WAT handoff. It can also be used to perform load balancing by enabling the MN to switch its connection from a heavily loaded AR to a comparatively lightly loaded one.

2.1.1 Operational Summary

The CARD protocol operation, depicted in Figure 3, is typically initiated upon receiving appropriate L2-Triggers or when the MN discovers L2-ID(s) of in-range CAP(s) as part of a scan operation. The MN will be able to discover the L2-ID(s) when it is in the overlapping coverage region of two or more neighbouring AP(s). The MN will then request its current AR to resolve the identity (RAT function) and discover the capabilities (DCC function) of the CAR(s) associated with the CAP(s) whose L2 ID(s) is carried in the MN-AR CARD Request message. The current AR will check in its local CAR Table for a corresponding entry against the L2 ID(s). If the current AR fails to resolve the identity of the associated CAR(s), it will send an AR-AR CARD Request message (depicted as AR-Server Req in Figure 3) to a central CARD Server, to which all the ARs would have registered their identity information (IP address, address prefix or prefix length) during boot up time. The CARD Server will return the IP(v6) address(es) of the CAR(s) via an AR-AR CARD Reply message (depicted as AR- Server Rep in Figure 3), and the current AR will update its local CAR Table with the resolved CAR information. The initial idea of performing RAT function using a centralised server was first presented in (Funato et al., 2002) which has been adopted by RFC 4066 as one of the probable method.

The current AR, depending on the status of the C-flag (capabilities request flag) in the MN- AR CARD Request message, will then directly contact the resolved CAR(s) and perform capabilities discovery via AR-AR CARD Request/Reply message pair and then send the resolved identities and capabilities of the CAR(s) to the MN via a

MN-AR CARD Reply message. It may be mentioned that the identity and capabilities information are carried in specified message sub-options and containers the details and format of which is given in (Liebsch et al., 2005). Based on the capabilities information and preset criteria, the MN will select an appropriate TAR to which it will perform a handover with. This process will ensue every time the handover is imminent.

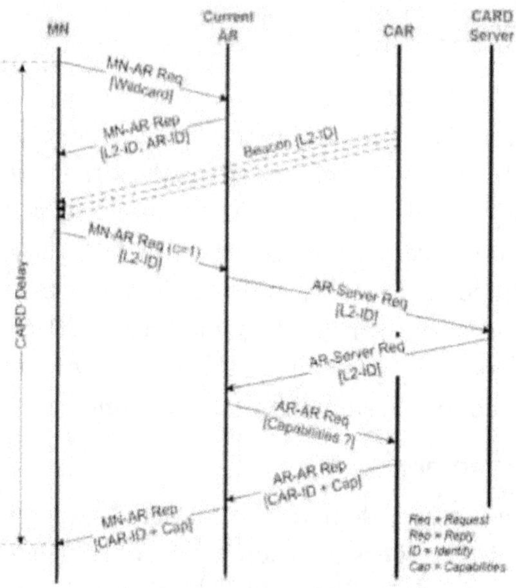

Fig. 3. The CARD Protocol Operation

Upon connecting to the target AR the MN will send a wildcard MN-AR CARD Request to obtain the information of its CAR Table in order to improve the prospects of the next CAR discovery. It is observed that the maintenance and management of local CAR Tables is critical to the effectiveness of CARD protocol in terms of assisting seamless and fast handover by way of quick address resolution and capabilities discovery.

2.2 FMIPv6 Operation with CARD Protocol

Figure 4 illustrates the FMIPv6 protocol operation in conjunction with the CARD protocol. The only difference is that the MN-AR CARD Request and MN-AR CARD Reply message are piggybacked on the FMIPv6 protocol specified Router Solicitation for Proxy (RtSolPr) and Proxy Router Advertisement (PrRtAdv) messages respectively (Liebsch et al., 2005). The RtSolPr and PrRtrAdv are ICMPv6 type messages the format of which is specified in (Koodli, 2008).

The MN will start scanning for in-range APs in response to deteriorating link conditions. The MN will then send the L2-ID(s) of the scanned AP(s) to the upper layer (i.e., L3) in the form of L2 trigger which will initiate the CARD operation as described in Section 2.1.1. The PAR after acquiring the identities and capabilities of the available CAR(s) against the L2-ID(s) provided by the MN in the RtSolPr message will send this information as [L2-ID, AR-Info]1 tuple appended to the PrRtAdv message. The MN will then select a suitable NAR from amongst the discovered CAR(s) based on some TAR selection criteria which is beyond the scope of this chapter.

Based on the identity information of NAR, the MN will auto-configure (Thomson et al., 2007) a prospective New Care of Address (pNCoA) and will send this in a Fast Binding Update Message (FBU) message to the PAR indicating the NAR to which the MN wishes to handover its connection. The PAR will then notify the NAR of the pCoA and request for a handover by sending a Handover Initiate (HI) message. The NAR in response will acknowledge the handover request by transmitting a Handover Acknowledge (HAck) message towards the PAR. The PAR upon receiving the HAck will immediately set up a forwarding tunnel with the NAR (referred to as PAR-NAR tunnel) and will start tunnelling subsequent packets destined for the MN towards NAR where they will get buffered. In the meantime the PAR, upon processing the HAck, will inform the MN of the NAR's decision via a Fast Binding Acknowledgement (FBAck) message. It should be noted that all this operation is executed while the MN is still connected to the PAR.

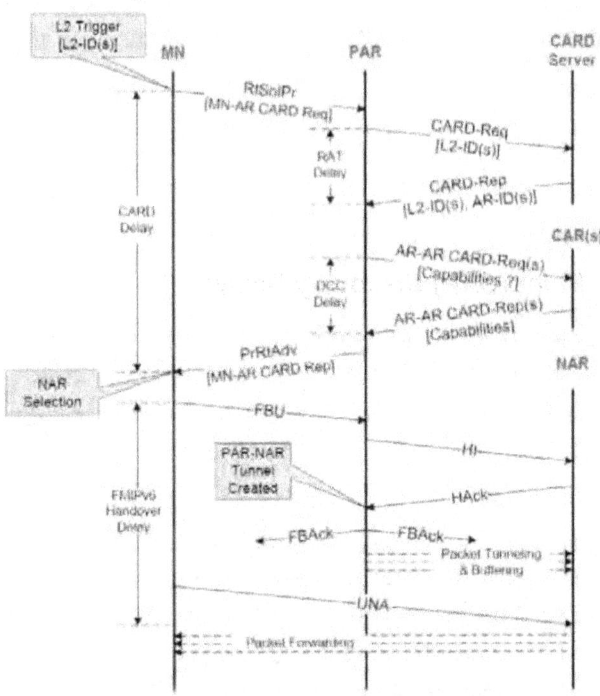

Fig. 4. The FMIPv6 Predictive Handover Operation Utilizing the CARD Protocol for NAR Discovery

After the MN moves out of the communication range of PAR, it will establish link connectivity with the New Access Point (NAP) and will announce its presence to the NAR by sending an Unsolicited Neighbour Advertisement (UNA) message (Narten et al., 2007) to the NAR. The NAR will immediately forward all the buffered packets, and the subsequent packets arriving via the PAR-NAR tunnel, towards the MN. The MN will then inform the HA and the CN(s) of its new location as per the MIPv6 protocol rules (Perkins et al., 2004), after the completion of which the handover is said to be complete.

It should be noted that the FMIPv6 protocol specifies two handover modes namely Predictive Handover Mode and Reactive Handover Mode, depending on whether the MN receives the FBAck on the PAR's link or not. Of the two modes, the Predictive Handover Mode is more seamless and hence is the preferred and default mode.

Besides FMIPv6, the CARD protocol functionality can also be used by the MIPv6 protocol to facilitate the MN's decision to select the appropriate AR for handover that would best serve its QoS requirements. For further details see (Liebsch et al., 2005).

3. PROBLEM STATEMENT

As described previously, central to the success of the FMIPv6 protocol is the ability of the MN to discover and select NAR using the CARD protocol facilities. However the process to discover and select NAR depends on two discovery processes namely:

1. CAP discovery, and
2. CAR discovery.

Both of these processes will influence the overall discovery process in consideration of the inherent process limitations described below.

Candidate Access Point (CAP) Discovery Delay:

The CAP discovery process is undertaken by the technique specified for the underlying WAT, whereas the CAR discovery process is carried out by the CARD protocol after the L2 provides it with the identities of the discovered CAP(s) using specific L2 constructs such as triggers, events, hints etc.

Since the CARD protocol, and hence the FMIPv6 protocol, rely on the timely and accurate provisioning of these L2 constructs, therefore the performance inadequacies of the L2 specified operations will have adverse consequences on the performance of the CARD and thus the FMIPv6 protocol. For example, in reference to the IEEE 802.11 WLAN, the MN is required to perform scan operations (active or passive) to determine the presence of in- range CAP(s). However, as pointed out in (Mishra et al., 2003), the scan operation accounts for almost 90% of the L2 handover delay and can be approximately up to 400 ms. It should also be noted that during the scan operation, the MN is unable to transmit or receive packets resulting in data loss. Besides packet loss, the CAP discovery delay will translate into the delayed provisioning of L2 triggers which in turn will delay the initiation of the CARD protocol.

Thus in order to reduce the packet loss and ensure the timely initiation of the CARD protocol, the duration of the scan operation must be reduced.

Candidate Access Router (CAR) Discovery Delay:

The CAR discovery process is undertaken by the L3 specified CARD protocol after receiving L2 triggers. As described, the CARD protocol performs RAT and DCC function by the exchange of CARD Request/ Reply messages. This incurs a high signalling cost especially over the error prone radio links. Besides signalling cost, each function incurs a finite amount of delay which is also influenced by the location of the CARD Server and its topological distance from the PAR. Besides influencing the delay, the CARD Server is a central network entity that must be managed and maintained thereby increasing the cost of network management. The CARD Server also introduces a potential single-point-of-failure, the failure of which will result in a failed handover.

In consideration of the above performance issues, a unified solution approach is desired that must incorporate the following recommendations;

1. Minimize the duration of the L2 scan operation, and hence the CAP discovery delay.
2. Ensure the timely delivery of L2 triggers to initiate the CARD process.
3. Remove the dependence of the CARD protocol on a central CARD Server.
4. Reduce the signalling load of the CARD protocol, especially over the error prone wireless link.

This implies a tightly coupled liaison between L2 and L3 operations and calls for a cross-layer management solution that must incorporate the above recommendations to enable a MN to discover NAR in the shortest possible time with low signalling latency and high probability of success.

4. RELATED WORK

Two approaches for discovering CARs worth mentioning is Push-Mode-Multicast based Candidate Access Router Discovery (PMM CARD) (Dario et al., 2006(a)) and Access Router Information Protocol (ARIP) (Kwon et al., 2005). PMM CARD introduces added complexity of maintaining and managing multicast groups and addresses and its performance is restricted within a single operator's domain, whereas ARIP does not scale to complex network architectures and is not dynamic. Beside introducing additional signalling messages, ARIP requires the ARs to maintain identity information of the adjacent AR's but , similar to (Ono et al., 2003), suggests manual set up by the network administrator or by the automatic learning of the AR's from the handover information offered by the MNs. This makes ARIP unscalable to complex network architectures. Also both the above proposals do not provide any cross-layer management capabilities and have not been designed keeping in view the requirements and dynamics of a fast moving MN in the context of NGN.

In this chapter we present an enhanced and scalable mechanism for discovering CARs that can enable a fast moving MN to discover the identity and capabilities of the CARs which may not be geographically adjacent and/or directly linked to the PAR. We term this new approach as Multi-hop Discovery of Candidate Access Routers (MHD-CAR), which is a simple approach that does away with the complexity and limitations of both PMM CARD and ARIP. The MHD-CAR provides an inherent scalable cross-layer mobility management solution that eliminates the performance issues discussed earlier by incorporating the solution recommendations.

The protocol details of the MHD-CAR protocol is submitted to the IETF as an Internet Draft (Yousaf, Wietfeld, 2008(a)) and the proof of concept presented in (Yousaf et al., 2008(b)).

5. MHD-CAR OPERATION SUMMARY

MHD-CAR is a distributed mechanism proposed to enhance the operational reliability and robustness of seamless and fast handover protocols without introducing any additional message(s) and/or relying on any central server.

In MHD-CAR ARs dynamically update their local CAR Table with the identity information of not only the neighbouring ARs but also of CARs located multiple wireless-hops away through an iterative exchange of unsolicited AR-AR CARD Reply message and without relying on a CARD Server.

The CAR Table information of the current AR is then transferred to a MN on the fly where it updates/refreshes a local cache called New Access Network (NAN) Cache allowing the MN to resolve the CAR(s) locally with minimum exchange of Request/ Reply messages over the error prone radio link.

The MHD-CAR protocol operation is depicted in Figure 5 and the functional details are discussed in the subsequent sub-sections.

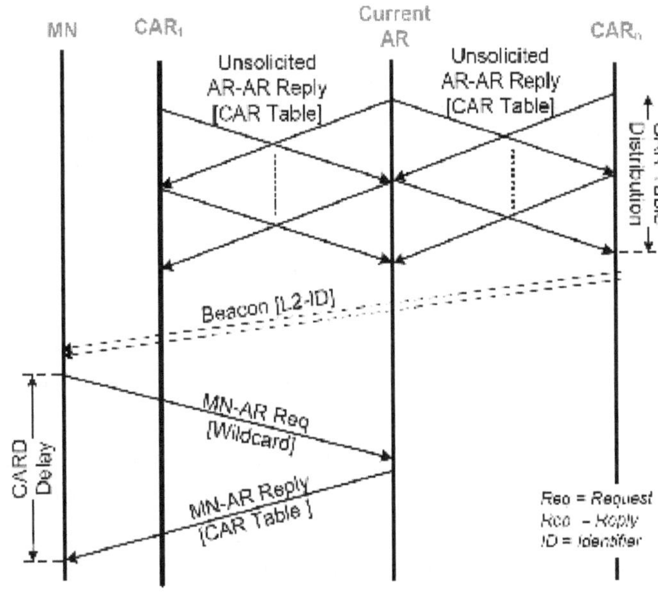

Fig. 5. MHD-CAR Protocol Message Sequence Diagram

5.1 CAR Table Initialization

The composition of the CAR Table in the context of MHD-CAR is different from the one proposed in (Liebsch et al., 2005) in that it offers more detailed information content. Table 1 shows the conceptual design of CAR Table in the context of MHD-CAR that contains not only the identities of the CAP/CAR but also information regarding the type of wireless access technology and the channel number in use by a CAP. It also informs about the capabilities of the CAP in terms of supported bit-rate and SSID (in case of 802.11), and most importantly the 'Distance' parameter, which is a measure of the distance of a CAR, in terms of the number of wireless-hops, with reference to the local AR maintaining the CAR Table.

At initialization, each AR will populate its CAR Table with its own (and associated AP(s)) identity and capabilities information and set the 'Distance' parameter to zero, indicating local AR information.

For the MHD-CAR operation, it is imperative that each AR should be aware of the identity of the neighbouring AR and the associated AP(s) and store this information in its local CAR Table with a Distance value set to 1. The neighbour association can be established dynamically using the handover information of a bootstrapping MN as an input to establish a neighbour relationship. The first handover between any two neighbouring ARs will serve as a bootstrapping handover that would invoke the discovery process between the two ARs. This idea was first presented in (Shim, Gitlin, 2000), (Trossen et al., 2003) and also endorsed by the official CARD protocol standard (Liebsch et al., 2005) , which is adopted by the MHD-CAR operation for CAR Table initialisation and described as follows.

Table 1. Conceptual Design of the CAR Table

CAR Table		
AP Information	**AR Information**	**Capabilities**
macaddr MAC Address	*ipaddr* IP Address	*double* Bitrate AP
int L2 Type	*prefix* Network Prefix	*string* SSID
int Channel Number	*int* Prefix Length	*int* Distance avpair User Defined QoS AV Pair

When some MN performs an inter-AR handover, it will inform its current AR about the identity of the previous AR using a Router Identity message option appended to the MN-AR CARD Request message (Liebsch et al., 2005). The serving AR will acknowledge this with a MN-AR CARD Reply message and will store the identity of the MN's previous AR in its CAR Table and indicate it as its immediate neighbour. The serving AR will then send an unsolicited AR-AR CARD Reply message to the previous AR informing it of its own identity and identifying itself as its neighbour. The previous AR will thus store the identity information of the MN's current AR in its local CAR Table as an immediate neighbour indicated by the Distance value of 1. In this way, all the ARs along the motion path of the MN will bootstrap their local CAR Tables with the identity of the neighbouring ARs. Besides the identity information, the two ARs must also exchange the capabilities information with each other. This process will also eliminate the reliance on maintaining a CARD Server. It may be noted that the identity information contains both the IP address of the AR and the L2-Id(s) of the associated AP(s).

5.2 CAR Table Distribution

After the ARs are bootstrapped with the identity and capabilities of the neighbouring ARs, each AR will exchange its local CAR Table information with the neighbouring AR(s) through the iterative exchange of unsolicited AR-AR CARD Reply Message, where the number of iterations is equal to the specified maximum distance, in wireless-hops, corresponding to the maximum entries an AR will maintain in its CAR Table.

In the first iteration, the ARs will exchange their local CAR Table information (see Table 1) with their neighbouring ARs, which will add this new information to their local CAR Tables and increment the Distance value by 1. Now each AR will have information about the AR(s) two wireless-hops away and this will be indicated by the Distance value of 2. It should be noted that the ARs do not forward the received inter-AR messages in order to prevent network flooding.

During the second iteration, the above process will be repeated and the receiving ARs will compare the new information with their present CAR Table entries and if no match is found, it will add the new CAR information to its local CAR Table by incrementing the distance parameter by 1.

Distribution Iteration	CAR Table Contents in ARs [Access Network Identifier (*ID*) – *Distance (D)*]																							
	AR_A		AR_B		AR_C		AR_D		AR_E		AR_F		AR_G		AR_H		AR_I		AR_J		AR_K		AR_L	
	Id	D	Id	D	Id	D	Id	D	Id	D	Id	D	Id	D	Id	D	Id	D	Id	D	Id	D	Id	D
0	A B	0 1	B A C	0 1 1	C B D	0 1 1	D C E	0 1 1	E D F	0 1 1	F E G	0 1 1	G F H	0 1 1	H I G	0 1 1	I H J	0 1 1	J I K	0 1 1	K J L	0 1 1	L K	0 1
1	A B C	0 1 2	B A C D	0 1 1 2	C B D A E	0 1 1 2 2	D C E B F	0 1 1 2 2	E D F C G	0 1 1 2 2	F E G D H	0 1 1 2 2	G F H E I	0 1 1 2 2	H I G F J	0 1 1 2 2	I H J G K	0 1 1 2 2	J I K H L	0 1 1 2 2	K J L I	0 1 1 2	L K J	0 1 2
2	A B C D	0 1 2 3	B A C D E	0 1 1 2 3	C B D A E F	0 1 1 2 2 3	D C E B F A G	0 1 1 2 2 3 3	E D F C G B H	0 1 1 2 2 3 3	F E G D H C I	0 1 1 2 2 3 3	G F H E I D J	0 1 1 2 2 3 3	H I G F J E K	0 1 1 2 2 3 3	I H J G K F L	0 1 1 2 2 3 3	J I K H L G	0 1 1 2 2 3	K J L I H	0 1 1 2 3	L K J I	0 1 2 3
3	A B C D E	0 1 2 3 4	B A C D E F	0 1 1 2 3 4	C B D A E F G	0 1 1 2 2 3 4	D C E B F A G H	0 1 1 2 2 3 3 4	E D F C G B H A I	0 1 1 2 2 3 3 4 4	F E G D H C I B J	0 1 1 2 2 3 3 4 4	G F H E I D J C K	0 1 1 2 2 3 3 4 4	H I G F J E K D L	0 1 1 2 2 3 3 4 4	I H J G K F L E	0 1 1 2 2 3 3 4	J I K H L G F	0 1 1 2 2 3 4	K J L I H G	0 1 1 2 3 4	L K J I H	0 1 2 3 4

Fig. 6. Conceptual Representation of the Iterative CAR Table Distribution Process in MHD- CAR

This new entry will thus be marked with the Distance value of 3, indicating that the corresponding CAR is at distance of three wireless-hops.

The above inter-exchange of unsolicited inter-AR Reply messages will continue until each AR has the information about CAR, which is at the specified maximum distance from the current AR, after which the CAR Tables are said to have converged. The maximum distance for which an AR is supposed to maintain CAR information is a constant that depends on the network topology and can be specified by the administrator. The ARs will then periodically exchange their local CAR Table information with their neighbouring AR(s) after every 60 seconds, or when there is some change in the contents of it (for example, change in capabilities information). During CAR Table initialisation and distribution process, the ARs will transmit the unsolicited inter-AR messages at a uniformly distributed random time between 0 and 100 msec.

The iterative CAR Table distribution process is illustrated in Figure 6, which shows the contents of the CAR Table of an AR for each iteration of the distribution process. The distribution takes place for a Distance value of 4, i.e., the iterative distribution process will continue till each AR has information about ARs which are up to 4 wireless hops away. Figure 6 illustrates the process for the reference topology shown in Figure 7 composed of 12 Access Networks (AN) (from A to L), where the domain of each AN is defined by an AR and an associated AP. For the sake of demonstration and simplicity only the AN Identity and Distance parameters of a CAR Table are considered in Figure 6. The identity (Id) is characterised by the [L3-ID, L2-ID] pair and is denoted by the AN identifier, whereas the Distance (D) signifies the topological distance of a CAR/CAP from the local AR in terms of wireless hops. The entries indicated in red signify the new entries that get stored in the CAR Table during the particular distribution iteration. Iteration # 0 signifies the contents of the CAR Table during the initialisation process as explained above.

Figure 7 clearly shows how the ARs (e.g., F) acquire the information of CARs (for instance B & J) that are not immediate neighbours through the iterative distribution of the CAR Tables.

Table 2. Conceptual Design of New Access Network (NAN) Cache

NAN Cache	
CAP Information	**CAR Information**
bool Reachability *macaddr* MAC Address *int* L2 Type *int* Channel Number *double* Bitrate *double* Last Received Beacon time *double* RSSI *string* SSID	*ipaddr* IP Address prefix Network Prefix int *Prefix* Length *int* Distance

5.3 Mobile Node Operation

The CARD protocol specification (Liebsch et al., 2005) suggests a MN to maintain address and capability information of CAR(s) discovered during previous CARD operation in a local cache to avoid requesting the same information repeatedly and to select an appropriate TAR as quickly as possible when a handover is imminent, but it does not specify the conceptual design of such a cache. Besides, this proposal will only improve the CAR selection if the MN is revisiting some previously visited CAR domain, a situation not very much likely in case of high speed MNs.

MHD-CAR proposes a MN to maintain a local cache called New Access Network (NAN) cache (see Table 2) that maintains the identity and capabilities information of not only the neighbouring CAR(s) and associated CAP(s) but those located multiple wireless-hops away. This will allow the MN to perform RAT and DCC functions locally without the exchange of any MN-AR CARD Request/Reply message pair with its current AR, or without involving a CARD server, every time handover is imminent.

The information content of the NAN cache, that is expected to enhance the MN's TAR selection process and handover related decision tasks, is derived mostly from the CAR Table that is usually pulled by the MN on the fly from its current AR (via a wildcard MN-AR CARD Request Message) when the MN senses that it is moving away from its current AR. The MN will then add and/or refresh the relevant entries of its cache. The NAN cache also derives some of the AP related information from the periodic beacon signals received from the in-range wireless APs.

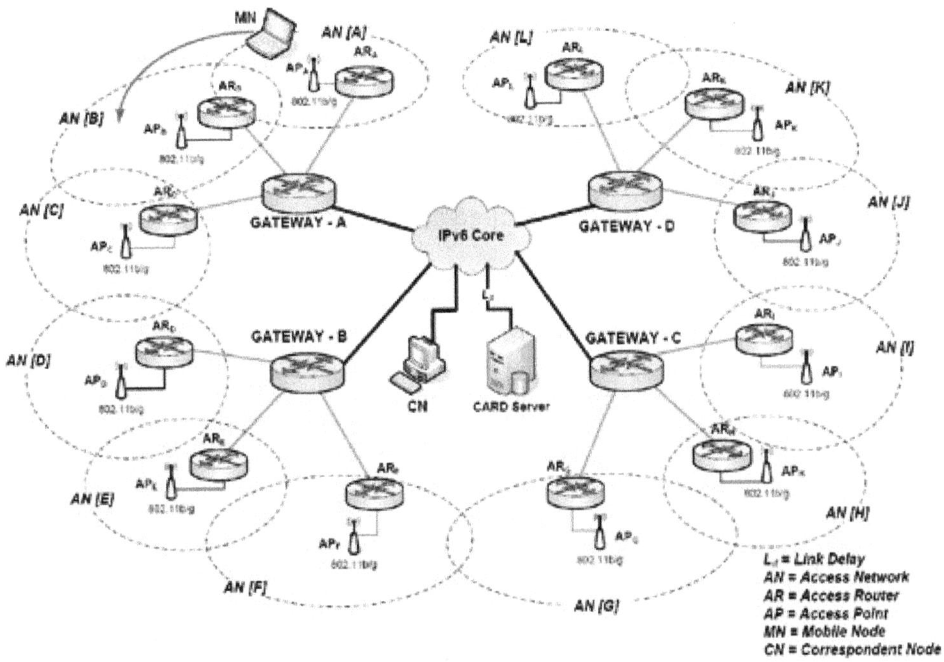

Fig. 7. Simulation Topology

6. PERFORMANCE ANALYSIS

In this Section we present the results of the simulation experiments comparing and analyzing the performance of the proposed MHD-CAR mechanism to that of the IETF's CARD protocol using the CARD server. Both the protocols are modeled in our mobility management framework (Yousaf et al., 2008(c)) developed in OMNeT++ (OMNeT++) and using realistic message structures and timer implementations.

The simulation experiments and its analysis is similar to the one presented by us in (Yousaf et al., 2008(b)) with the difference that in this chapter we have extended our simulation model to realise a more realistic hierarchical network topology instead of a flat network topology in which all the ARs were directly connected to their immediate neighbours via Ethernet links. In a flat network topology, the ARs will be able to derive the identity of their neighbouring ARs by simply sending relevant messages directly and hence populate their local CAR Tables. In contrast, to realise the MHD-CAR protocols in the hierarchical network topology, we have extended our simulation framework with the bootstrapping mechanism (see Section 4.1) that would enable the ARs to discover the IP address of the neighbouring ARs. With this major difference, the same experiments were repeated and found the results to match those presented previously in (Yousaf et al., 2008(b)).

The simulation network topology is shown in Figure 7 and the experiments are carried in a homogeneous 802.11b wireless environment using a free space propagation model at 2.4 GHz for a radio channel over a total coverage area of 800m x 800m. To initialise the CAR Tables, in ARs a bootstrapping MN is moved across the reference network at the beginning of the simulation enabling each AR to become aware of the IP address of the previous neighbouring AR. The results expressed in this Section will also apply equally to a heterogeneous environment because the MHD-CAR operation is defined at the network layer.

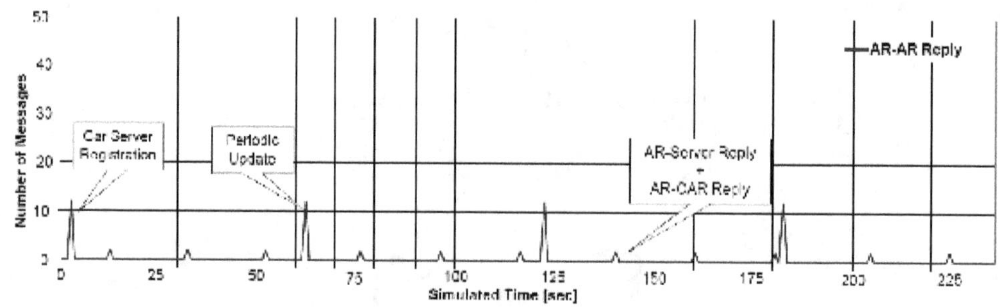

(a) AR-AR Message Throughput in CARD

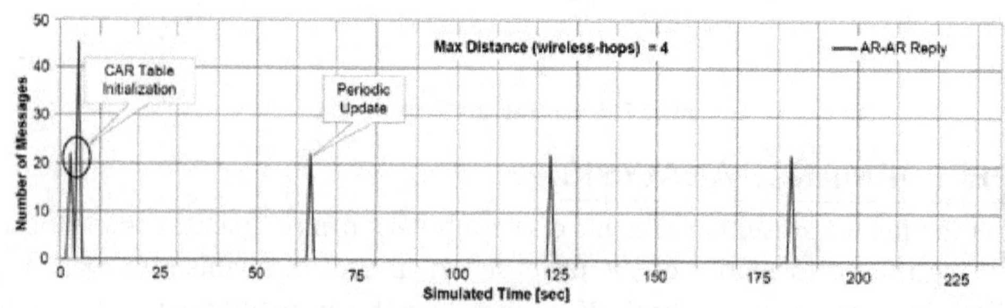

(b) AR-AR Message Throughput in MHD-CAR

Fig. 8. Inter AR Message Throughput in (a) CARD, and (b) MHD-CAR

A single simulation run consists of a MN moving across 12 ARs, starting from ARA and undergoing 11 handover instances, discovering and resolving the next CAP(s)/CAR(s) while it is still connected to its current AR. The experiments are repeated 100 times for each of the 25 seed values generated using the OMNeT++'s sedtool thereby constituting a total of 2500 runs each for simulating CARD and MHD-CAR protocol. The results are then expressed as average sum of the measured parameters.

6.1 Impact of MHD-CAR on Signaling Load

The average signalling load over the wireless link (MN-AR Messages) and the wired links (AR-AR Messages) for both the CARD and MHD-CAR is compared in

Figure 10 and the results tabulated in Table 3. The ARs in both CARD and MHD-CAR periodically update their CAR Tables after 60 seconds and in our simulation this update takes place three times.

6.1.1 Signaling load over the Inter-AR links

In CARD each AR, during boot-up time, register its identity information with the CARD server and keeps the CARD server updated by sending unsolicited AR-Server Reply Messages periodically after every 60 seconds. The number of unsolicited AR-Server Reply Messages transmitted during boot-up time and during periodic updates remains equal and corresponds to the number of ARs. In between the periodic updates, the current AR will exchange AR-AR CARD Request/Reply message pair with the CARD Server for performing RAT function (upon MN's request) and AR-AR CARD Request/Reply message pair with the resolved CAR(s) for performing the DCC function. This is seen in Figure 8(a) where we show the occurrence of the average inter-AR (Server & CAR) reply message throughput.

In MHD-CAR however, since the MN is able to locally resolve the identity and capabilities of CAR(s) based on the information in NAN Cache (see Section 4.2), the AR does not need to exchange any request/reply message pair with some server or neighbouring AR(s) thereby resulting in 100% reduction of inter-AR signalling load related to discovering CAR(s). This is depicted in Figure 8(b) where the ARs only exchange unsolicited AR-AR Reply messages with their neighbouring ARs as part of the periodic update of the local CAR Table after every 60 seconds.

Table 3. MN-AR & AR-AR Message Load Comparison

	Messages			
	MN-AR		AR-AR 2	
	Requests	Replies	Requests	Replies 3
CARD	23	23	22	58
MHD-CAR	12	12	0	66
Message Load (%)	-47.8 %	-47.8 %	-100 %	+13.8%
Total Load Reduction (%)	47.8%		17.5%	

Since there is no central server, the inter AR update message throughput in MHD-CAR is 83.33% higher than CARD but overall recording a 17.5% reduction in the post boot-up exchange of inter-AR message (see Table 3).

During boot-up MHD-CAR records a much higher throughput than CARD due to the iterative inter-AR exchange of local CAR Tables (see Section 4.1 & 4.2) till the Table entries have converged to the maximum specified distance, which is four in our scenario. Evidently the value of maximum distance will have a direct impact on the number of inter-AR messages, but this is of no serious consequence as it happens only once and that too during initialisation via bootstrapping, afterwards which the CAR Tables converge very quickly. Figure 8(b) shows a sharp surge of inter-AR messages during CAR Table initialisation and distribution period but it is seen that the ARs converge within the first 3-4 seconds. Table 3 lists and compares the average number of inter-AR messages exchanged for both the protocols and depicts the percentage reduction in the overall inter-AR messages induced by MHD-CAR.

6.1.2 Signalling load over wireless link

As depicted in Figure 9, a MN in a CARD protocol will exchange MN-AR CARD Request/Reply message pair with its current AR twice, once in the beginning (soon after connecting to it) to request a list of CAR(s) information maintained in its CAR Table; and the second time when handover is imminent and the MN will need to resolve the L2-ID(s) (received in the beacon messages from in-range AP(s)) that may not have been present in the current AR's CAR Table, and/or to find out the capabilities of the CAP(s)/CAR(s), so that the MN may select a suitable target AR based on some selection criteria (Dario et al., 2006(b)). This approach is suitable for a slow moving MN with a long dwell time in a single cell but not suitable for a fast moving MN.

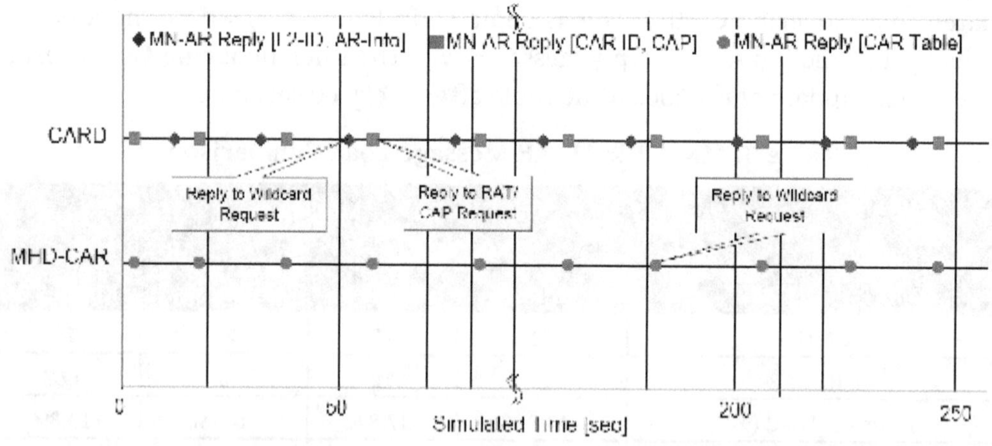

Fig. 9. MN-AR Reply Message Timestamps for CARD and MHD-CAR over the Wireless Link

In contrast, MHD-CAR requires only a single exchange of MN-AR CARD Request/ Reply Message pair, in which the MN sends a wildcard request and the current AR will send the contents of its CAR Table (see Table 1) in the corresponding reply message and the MN will cache the information in its NAN Cache (see Table 2). This will contribute towards the reduction of the signalling load over the wireless link by almost 48%, as seen from the comparison of the message timestamps of MN-AR Reply messages transmitted by the CARD and MHD-CAR depicted in Figure 9 and hence the throughput reduction achieved by MHD-CAR over the wireless link is clearly evident. Table 3 lists and compares the average number of MN-AR messages exchanged over the wireless link for both the protocols and depicts the percentage reduction of message load induced by MHD-CAR with reference to the scenario depicted in Figure 7.

6.2 Impact of MHD-CAR on Scanning Delay

It is a known fact that the L2 handover delay is a major delay component adding to the overall handover latency for MIPv6 (Yousaf et al., 2008(c)) and thus a major impediment to the performance of higher layer mobility management schemes. The main contributing factor to the L2 handover latency is the delay incurred by the channel scan operation as part of the CAP discovery process (see Section 3). Typically a MN after losing its connectivity with its current AP will perform the 802.11 all-channel scan (active/passive) on, in our case, 13 frequency channels. This scan-delay is certainly not suitable for attaining seamless handover performance for fast moving MNs and various methods have been proposed in this respect. One of the consensus solutions to reduce the L2 handover delay is to perform scanning on selective channels (Park et al., 2004) or perform a pro-active scan, i.e., before a MN loses its connection with its current AP (Haito et al., 2007).

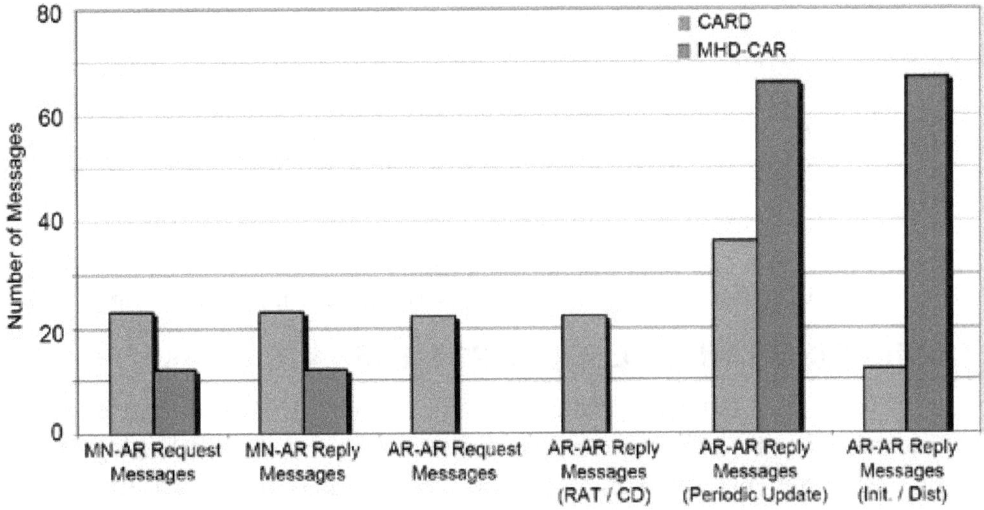

Fig. 10. Signalling Load Comparison of CARD and MHD-CAR

The MHD-CAR based on the information available in the NAN Cache proposes to reduce the scan delay by enabling a MN to perform target scanning on selective frequency channels. The MN, instead of waiting to disconnect from the current AP, will start to scan for only those channels that correspond to the nearest CAP(s) as specified by the Distance parameter in the NAN Cache, and if the CAP(s) are not located (or are out of range) will proceed to select and scan the next set of frequency channels corresponding to next farther CAP(s). The MN will typically start the scan process when the RSSI from the current AP falls below a certain threshold. Figure 11 compares the performance of MHD-CAR's target scanning with the 802.11 all-channel scan.

From the Figure 11 it is evident that the performance of MHD-CAR's target scanning incurs less delay than the full channel scan, however the delay performance is a function of the size of the NAN Cache and location of the MN. For example it is observed that when the Distance value is 4 and MN is undergoing the 7th handover, target scanning incurs more delay. This increase in delay, however still less than the full-channel scan, is due to the fact that the MN is at ARG and the CAR Table in the ARG will have a total of 8 CAR entries and thus the MN has to scan all the 8 channels.

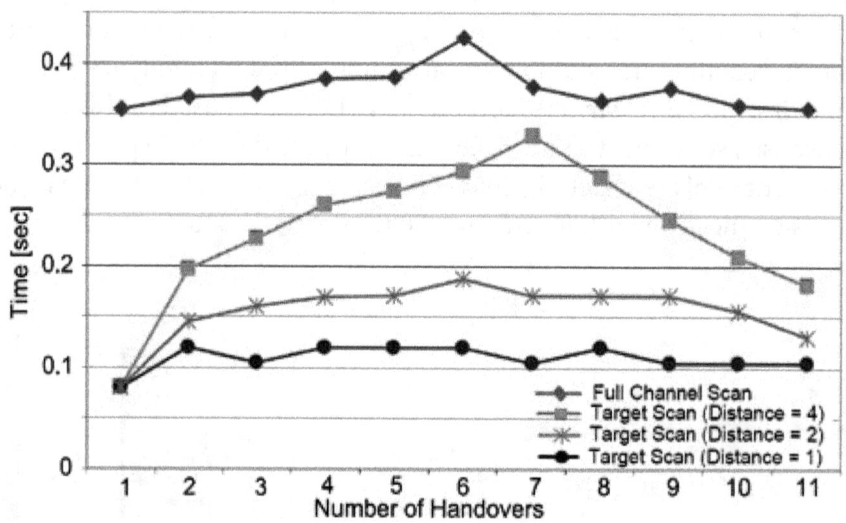

Fig. 11. Performance of MHD-CAR's Target Channel Scanning

7. COMPARISON WITH IEEE 802.21 MIHS

The IEEE 802.21 is an emerging standard (IEEE Std 802.21) that aims at imparting seamless mobility to MNs traversing diverse radio access technologies in a heterogeneous network environment. The motivation is to facilitate inter-WAT handover between IEEE 802 and non-IEEE 802 access networks in such a way that the process negotiation is independent from the specific features of the underlying access network technology. In other words, IEEE 802.21 is being designed to provide Media Independent Handover (MIH) service that is tasked with the handover initiation and handover preparation whereas leaving the task of handover execution to other protocols like FMIPv6. The prerequisite to preparing a MN for a handover is the discovery of new links in the vicinity and this, according to (George et al., 2008), may involve maintaining a remote information server (similar to a

CARD Server) that can be queried to get information about the available networks in the area of a specific MN and/or relying on the MN's scanning operation to select the network of its choice.

The MIH services are being realised by defining Media Independent Handover Function (MIHF), which is implemented as a separate protocol stack located between the Network Layer and the Data Link layer as shown in Figure 12. The MIH operation is dictated by the MIHF exchanging events, commands and information messages with the adjacent layers. It should be noted that the MIHF is supposed to be located within the protocol stack of both the MN and the Network Node mandating major revision of the present network infrastructure and nodes. This would also mean major enhancements and modifications to the individual media specific technologies (802.11, 802.16, CDMA, UMTS, GSM, GPRS, etc) in the form of defining and developing new SAPs and primitives that would interface with the generic SAP and primitives defined for the IEEE 802.21 before a MN can take advantage of the MIH services (Eastwood & Migaldi, 2008). This would entail a major re-engineering effort involving the upgrade of the whole network infrastructure and protocol standards. Besides, the IEEE 802.21 model diverges from the standard ISO/OSI reference protocol model by introducing an intermediate layer between L2 and L3.

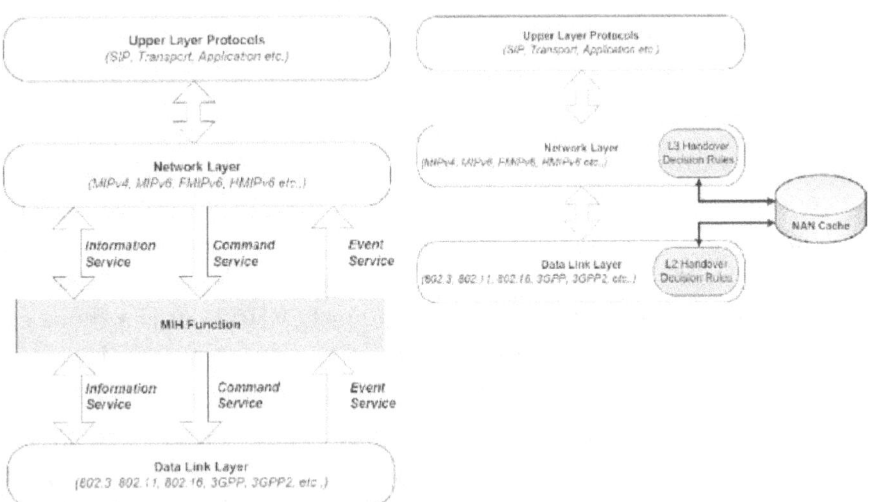

(a) (b)

Fig. 12. Conceptual Models of (a) The IEEE 802.21 MIH Service Model, and (b) The MHD- CAR Protocol

Similar to IEEE 802.21, the operational scope of MHD-CAR is to provide a mechanism to enable a multi-homed MN to undergo inter-RAT handover by providing the requisite information content that would enable a MN to choose the best network that would suit its application service requirements. However, in sharp contrast to IEEE 802.21 service model depicted in Figure 12(a) which is implemented as a protocol stack, the MHD-CAR is based on managing and maintaining a NAN Cache inside the MN that can be accessed by the mobility functions defined at the network layer and the data link layer. This translates into defining simpler interfaces at L2 and L3 for interaction with the NAN cache rather than demanding major revisions from the access technologies as in the case of IEEE 802.21 highlighted above. The NAN Cache thus provides cross-layer capabilities.

In contrast to IEEE 802.21, the MHD-CAR protocol is simply an optimised version of the existing CARD protocol without introducing any new messages, interfaces and/or network entities, or deviating from the reference ISO/OSI reference model making it scalable and deployable and without any burden on the network itself.

8. CONCISE SUMMARY

In this chapter, we have presented the operational and functional details of a proposed protocol, MHD-CAR, which has been developed in response to the rigorous performance requirements of fast-moving MNs in terms of seamless and rapid handovers in a heterogeneous wireless network environment. The standard CARD protocol is optimized by MHD-CAR, which allows an MN to discover the identity and capabilities of CARs that are not only neighboring but also located multiple hops away on the move. This is accomplished with minimal reliance on the network. This is anticipated to improve the performance of seamless handover protocols such as FMIPv6 by guaranteeing the precise selection of NAR with minimal discovery latency.

The MHD-CAR is a distributed mechanism that enables ARs to communicate their identities and capabilities to neighboring ARs and ARs that are located multiple wireless hops distant without the need to maintain and manage a central CARD server. This information is stored in the local CAR Tables of each AR, and it is subsequently transmitted to the MN upon request. MHD-CAR is a more efficient, reliable, survivable, and scalable protocol than the CARD protocol as a result of the distributed mechanism. The MHD-CAR is readily integrable into the current deployment infrastructure, as it does not introduce any new protocol messages.

It significantly outperforms the IETF's CARD protocol in terms of the significant reduction of signaling burden over both the inter-AR links (by 17.5%) and the error-prone wireless link (by 48%), while utilizing the CARD protocol messages. This reduction in signaling load is accomplished by the MN's ability to execute RAT and DCC functions locally, utilizing the information content of the NAN cache, without relying on the network.

The MHD-CAR scheme is also significant in that it facilitates cross-layer liaison between the L2 and L3 mobility functions. This is accomplished by incorporating a

NAN cache into the MN, which offers the MN a topological snapshot of the identity and capabilities of access networks that may be located at a distance of multiple hops from its current point of attachment. This allows an MN to conduct target scanning on specific channels, thereby significantly reducing the CAP discovery latency and improving the accuracy of the TAR selection process. This will have a direct effect on the overall handover latency, and fast-moving MNs will significantly benefit from it.

The MHD-CAR is a lightweight and significantly simplified alternative solution that offers the primary functional services of the 802.21 MIHS, in contrast to the IEEE 802.21 standard as observed. While MHD-CAR was not intended to serve as a substitute for 802.21, it does possess the same operational, functional, and motivational capabilities. The IEEE 802.21 WG was established to establish a unified global mechanism by defining a common MIH layer that is situated between the Network Layer and the Data Link Layer. The WG also defined common triggers that would be generated independently of the underlying access technology. The objective was to facilitate the MN's precise network selection and to establish mechanisms that would facilitate IP mobility protocols such as FMIPv6. Nevertheless, this is being implemented at the expense of complexity and deviates from the stratified approach outlined in the base ISO/OSI standard by incorporating a new layer between L2 and L3. Additionally, it would require modifications to the current access technologies to align with the MIHS signaling scheme. For instance, distinct SAPs must be established for each access technology. It would also entail the exchange of signaling messages between the network and the MN, even over the air interface.

Consequently, MHD-CAR offers the same conceptual functionalities as MIHS, but it does so in a much more straightforward and scalable manner, without violating the functional boundaries of the standard OSI/ISO protocol reference model.

FOOTNOTES

1. The AR-Info corresponds to the identity and capabilities of an AR.
2. The inter-AR messages are inclusive of the AR-Server messages for the CARD operation
3. The AR-AR Reply messages take into account only the replies messages exchanged after the initialization and distribution process.

REFERENCES

1. Dario, D.; Femminella, M.; Piacentini, L. & Reali, G. (2006(a)). Performance Evaluation of the Push-Mode-Multicast based Candidate Access Router Discovery (PMM CARD), Computer Networks, Volume 50, No. 3, (February 2006) page numbers (367-397), ISSN 1389-1286.

2. Dario, D.; Femminella, M.; Piacentini, L. & Reali, G. (2006(b)). Target Access Router Selection in Advanced Mobility Scenarios. Computer Communications, Volume 29, No. 3, (February 2006), page numbers (337-357), ISSN 0140-3664.
3. Eastwood, L. & Migaldi, S. (2008). Mobility Using IEEE 802.21 in a Heterogeneous IEEE 802.16/802.11 –Based, IMT-Advanced (4G) Network, IEEE Wireless Communications, Vol. 15, No. 2, (April 2008) pp. 26-34, ISSN: 1536-1284.
4. Funato, D.; He, X.; Williams, C.; Takeshita, A.; Ali, M. & Nakfour, J. (2002). Geographically Adjacent Access Router Discovery Protocol. draft-funato-seamoby-gaard-01.txt, Internet Draft (IETF), June 2002. Work in Progress.
5. George, L.; Salkintzis, A. & Passas, N. (2008). Media-Independent Handover for Seamless Service Provision in Heterogeneous Networks. IEEE Communication Magazine, Vol. 46, No. 1, (January 2008) pp. 64-71, ISSN 0163-6804.
6. Haito, W.; Tan, K.; Zhang, Y. & Zhang, Q. (2007). Proactive Scan: Fast Handoff with Smart Triggers for 802.11 Wireless LAN, Proceedings of 26th IEEE International Conference on Computer Communications (INFOCOM), pp. 749-757, ISBN 1-4244-1047-9, Alaska (USA), May 2007, IEEE, USA.
7. IEEE Std 802.21. Draft D9.0, IEEE Standard for Local & Metropolitan Area Networks: Media Independent Handover Services.
8. Koodli, R. (2008). Mobile IPv6 Fast Handovers, Request for Comments (Proposed Standard) 5268, Internet Engineering Task Force, June 2008.
9. Kwon, D.; Kim, Y.; Bae, K. & Suh, Y. (2005). Access Router Information Protocol with FMIPv6 for Efficient Handovers and their Implementations. Proceedings of Global Telecommunications Conference (GlobeCom), pp. 3814-3819, ISBN 0-7803-9414-3, St. Louis (Missouri), IEEE, December 2005, USA.
10. Liebsch, M.; Singh A.; Chaskar, H.; Finato, D. & Shim, E. (2005). Candidate Access Router Discovery Protocol (CARD), Request for Comments (Proposed Standard) 4066, Internet Engineering Task Force, July 2005.
11. Mishra, A.; Shin, M. & Arbaugh, W (2003). An Empirical Analysis of the IEEE 802.11 MAC Layer Handoff Process, Proceedings of ACM SIGCOMM Computer Communication Review, Volume 33, No. 2, pp. 93-102, ISSN 0146-4833, April 2003.
12. Narten, T.; Nordmark, E., Simpson, W. & H. Soliman, (2007). Neighbor Discovery for IP Version 6 (IPv6)", Request for Comments (Draft Standard) 4861, September 2007.
13. OMNeT++. Community Site, http://www.omnetpp.org, July 2009.
14. Ono, N.; Kimura, T. & Fujii, T. (2003). A Study on Autonomous Neighbour Access Router Discovery for Mobile IP. Proceedings of 57th IEEE Vehicular

Technology Conference (VTC), pp. 2241-2245, ISBN 0-7803-7757-5, Jeju, April 2003, Korea.

15. Perkins, C.; Johnson, D. & J. Arkko, (2004). Mobility Support in IPv6, Request for Comments (Proposed Standard) 3775, Internet Engineering Task Force, June 2004.
16. Park, S; Kim, H.; Park, C.; Kim, J. & Ko, S. (2004). Selective Channel Scanning for Fast Handoff in Wireless LAN using Neighbour Graph, In: Personal Wireless Communications, Lecture Notes in Computer Science, page numbers (194-203), Springer, ISBN 978-3-540-23162-2, Berlin / Heidelberg, September 2004.
17. Shim, E. & Gitlin, R. (2000). Fast Handoff Using Neighbor Graph Information. draft-shim- mobileip-neighbor-00.txt, November 2000. Work In Progress.
18. Thomson, S.; Narten, T. & Jinmei, T. (2007). IPv6 Stateless Address Autoconfiguration, Request for Comments (Draft Standard) 4862, Internet Engineering Task Force, September 2007.
19. Trossen, D.; Krishnamurthi, G.; Chaskar, H. & Kempf, J. (2002). Issues in Candidate Access Router Discovery for Seamless IP-Level Handoffs. draft-IETF-seamoby-cardiscovery- issues-04.txt, Internet Draft (IETF), October 2002. Work In Progress.
20. Trossen, D. ; Krishnamurthi, G.; Chaskar, H.; Chalmers, R. & Shim, E. (2003). A Dynamic Protocol for Candidate Access Router Discovery. draft-trossen-seamoby-dycard-01.txt, Internet Draft (IETF), March 2003. Work In Progress.
21. Yousaf, F. Z. & Wietfeld, C. (2008, a). Multi-Hop Discovery of Candidate Access Routers (MHD-CAR), draft-yousaf-ietf-network-mhdcar-00.txt, Internet Draft (IETF), April 2008. Work in Progress.
22. Yousaf, F. Z.; Müller, C. & Wietfeld, C. (2008, b). Multi-Hop Discovery of Candidate Access Routers (MHD-CAR) for Fast Moving Mobile Nodes, Proceedings of 19th IEEE International Symposium on Personal, Indoor and Mobile Radio Communications (PIMRC), pp. 1-5, ISBN 978-1-4244-2643-0, Cannes, September 2008, France.
23. Yousaf, F. Z.; Bauer, C. & Wietfeld, C. (2008, c). An Accurate and Extensible Mobile IPv6 (xMIPv6) Simulation Model for OMNeT++", 1st ACM/ICST International OMNeT++ Workshop on the SIMUTools Conference, Marseille, March 2008.

29 Chapter

MOBILITY IN IP NETWORKS: PROTOCOLS AND ARCHITECTURES FROM THE LINK LAYER TO THE APPLICATION LAYER

1. INTRODUCTION: AN OVERVIEW

The concept of portability gained popularity as the Internet and mobile devices, such as notebooks and PDAs (Personal Digital Assistants), became more prevalent. This refers to the ability of the user to establish a new connection to the Internet by taking their device with them.

A node in the Internet is identified by an IP (Internet Protocol) address that uniquely designates its point of attachment to the Internet. Packets are routed to the node based on this address. Consequently, in order to receive datagrams, a node must be situated on the network denoted by its IP address (Akyildiz et al, 2004). Nevertheless, the IP protocol does not permit the present IP address to be valid in the visiting network when the device transitions to a new network. Consequently, the device must request a new IP address upon entering the new network (Figure 1). Consequently, it was imperative to establish a system that would enable nodes to remain accessible and maintain continuous connections while transitioning from their initial (home) network to a visiting (new point of attachment) network in a seamless manner.

Mobile IP Protocol (MIP), also known as MIP, was one of the initial solutions proposed to address this issue in IP networks (Perkins, 1997). The MIP protocol is designed to address the issue of node mobility by redirecting packets to the mobile node (MN) at its present location. The MIP scheme was well-suited for interdomain mobility, enabling MN to navigate between networks from various domains.

However, the protocols that have been proposed for interdomain mobility are not suitable for intrasubnet mobility. This is due to the fact that the processing capacity of the MNs is insufficient to support the new protocols, which renders these solutions unsuitable for deployment in the majority of mobile devices. The problems are related to the complexity of the proposed solutions which make their implementation on small mobile devices such as cell phones and handhelds unfeasible. In fact, manufactures of such devices never considered supporting the present solutions (Zagari et al, 2008).

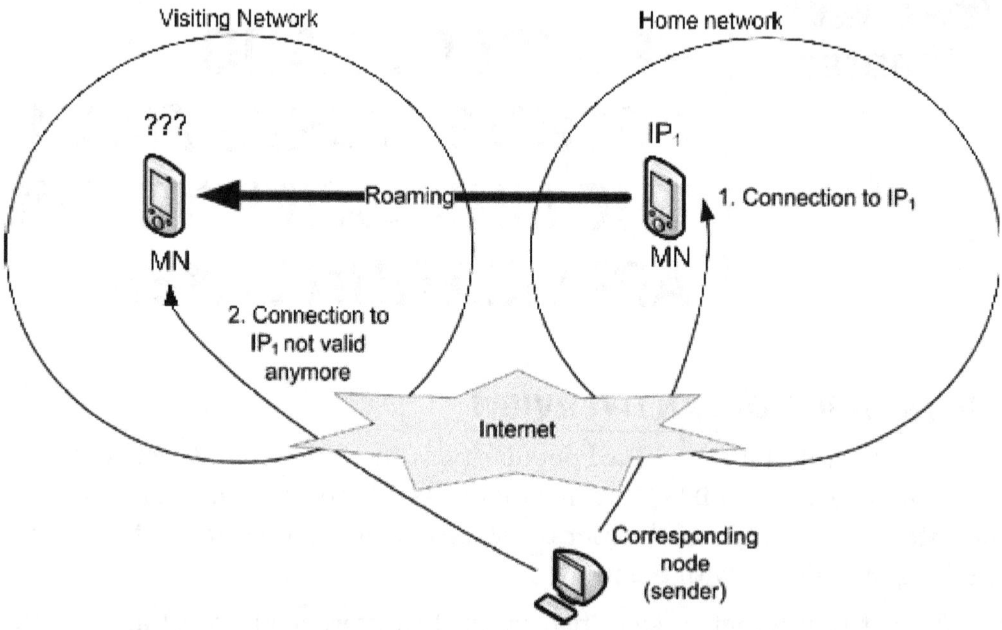

Fig. 1. Current IP address not valid in a visiting network

New protocols for mobility between networks within the same domain were proposed following MIP. The objective of micromobility protocols is to enhance localized mobility by minimizing handover overheads. Mobility provided by transport and session layer schemes are also alternative methods for enabling continuous mobility.

The purpose of this chapter is to offer a comprehensive examination of mobility protocols and architectures. The protocols and architectures will be categorized based on the mobility range (intra and inter domain), the layer in which they operate (from the link layer to the application layer), and the support required from the mobile node. We will emphasize "network-centered" solutions, which are those in which the network manages mobility wholly without the necessity of installing mobility protocols on the mobile nodes. The protocols and architectures examined in this chapter are being proposed by standardization bodies, such as the Internet Engineering Task Force (IETF), industry-driven forums, such as the 3GPP, the academy, and the industry..

2. MOBILITY ISSUES

The mobility process starts with the mobile node's attachment to a local wireless network. The node attachment process happens when a MN enters in the coverage of a wireless access point. In this point a L2 (Layer 2) attachment process is performed. After that, the MN must acquire its IP address from the network. After obtaining its new address, the network is able to route packets to/from the mobile node (Johnson et al, 2008).

When the MN moves away from the current access point, it may detect another wireless access point. Handover is "the process by which an active MN changes its point of attachment to the network, or when such a change is attempted. The access network may provide features to minimize the interruption to sessions in progress" (Manner & Cojo, 2004) by preserving the transport (or higher layers) connections such a way the packets are forwarded to the MN via the new access point.

Mobility management is the key to enable this seamless mobility. It enables wireless or mobile networks to search and locate mobile devices for network communications and to maintain network/applications connections as the MN moves into a new service area. The mobility management is composed of mainly two services: location management and handover management.

Location management consists of two operations: registration or location update and paging, to enable a network to discover the current point of attachment of an MN for information delivery (Saha et al, 2004). Location update is used in support of idle users, and paging is used in support of active communications (Campbell et al, 2002).

Location update procedures need the MN to periodically inform the system to update relevant location databases with its up-to-date location information (Akyildiz et al, 2004). Paging is the ability to track idle mobile hosts. For protocols using this kind of tracking, idle MNs do not have to register if they move within the same paging area, but only if they change paging area (Campbell & Gomez-Castellanos, 2000).

Handover management enables the network to maintain a MN's connection as it continues to move and change its access point to the network (Saha et al, 2004). There are many types of handover, among which are:

- horizontal and vertical: horizontal handover occurs between wireless cells of the same technology; vertical handover occurs between two different networks of different technologies. This chapter is dedicated to study horizontal handover only.
- mobile and network initiated: in MN initiated handovers the MN is responsible for initiating handover requests, while in network initiated handover the network is responsible for indicating that a handover must occur.

- MN and network controlled: in MN controlled handover, the MN must participate in the handover process, while in the network controlled handover the network handles the entire process.
- fast: fast handover tries to reduce the latency during a handover.
- seamless: change the MN's point of attachment to an IP-based network, without losing ongoing connections and without disruptions in the communication.

The basic terminology for mobility is (Perkins, 2002; Manner & Kojo, 2004):

- home network: a network having a network prefix matching that of a mobile node's permanent address;
- home address: the IP address acquired when registering in its home network; a stable address that belongs to the mobile node and is used by correspondent nodes to reach mobile nodes;
- home agent (HA): A router located on the home network that acts on behalf of the mobile node while away from the home network;
- correspondent node (CN): Any node that communicates with the mobile node;
- foreign network: Any network (other than the home network) visited by a mobile node;
- foreign agent (FA): A router located on the foreign network that acts on behalf of the MN in this network;
- care-of-address (CoA): An address that is assigned to the mobile node when located in a foreign link.

2.1 Classification parameters

Existing proposals for mobility can be broadly classified into different types, based on many parameters. We will employ a taxonomy based on 4 axis: Mobility Range, Mobility Routing, Mobility Signaling and Mobility Layer. In this section we will briefly introduce each one of them.

2.1.1 Mobility Range

In this work we adopted the definitions by Manner & Kojo (2004) for the mobility scope.

Micromobility

Also called intradomain mobility or local mobility (Kempf, 2007), is the process of mobility over a small area. Usually this means mobility within an IP domain with an emphasis on support for active mode using handover, although it may include idle mode procedures also. Micromobility protocols exploit the locality of movement by confining movement related changes and signaling to the access network.

Macromobility

Also called interdomain mobility or global mobility (Kempf, 2007), is the process of mobility over a large area. This includes mobility support and associated address registration procedures that are needed when a MN moves between IP domains. Interdomain handovers typically involve macromobility protocols. MIP can be seen as a means to provide macro mobility.

2.1.2 Mobility Routing

Defines how the MNs' location information database is created and maintained.

Routing based

Routing based schemes aim to exploit the robustness of conventional IP forwarding. A distributed mobile host location database is created and maintained within the network domain. The database consists of individual flat mobile-specific address lookup tables and is maintained by all the mobility agents within the domain (Chiussi et al, 2002).

Tunnel based

In tunnel based schemes, the location database is maintained in distributed form by a set of foreign agents in the access network. Each foreign agent reads the incoming packet's original destination address and searches its visitor list for a corresponding entry. If the entry exists then it contains the address of next lower level foreign agent.

The sequence of visitor list entries corresponding to a particular mobile host constitutes the host's location information and determines the route taken by its downlink packets. Entries are created and maintained by registration messages transmitted by mobile hosts (Campbell & Gomez-Castellanos, 2000). Tunnels may be IP-IP (IP over IP) or MPLS (Multi-protocol Label Switching).

2.1.3 Mobility Signaling

Defines if the mobility signaling is carried out by the network alone or also needs the mobile node participation in the signaling process.

Mobile Node Centric

In this approach, the MN must execute an instance of the mobility protocol, thus participating actively in the mobility management process. But the requirement for modification of MNs software may increase their complexity; considering these nodes have less computational capacity, it may lead to performance degradation on the MN.

Network Centric

In network-based mobility management approach, the serving network handles the mobility management on behalf of the MN; thus, the MN is not required to participate in any mobility-related signaling. Contrary to the latter approach, the MN's performance is not degraded by processing signaling and mobility protocol management.

2.1.4 Mobility Layer

Defines the responsibility of each layer in the mobility management process.

Link Layer

This class includes mobility protocols that use link layer information, when the point of attachment changes, to provide mobility management while the node preserves its network- layer (L3) address. This can fulfill some of the attributes of a micromobility protocol.

Layer 2½

This class uses MPLS to provide mobility management and signaling. MPLS (Rosen et al, 2001) is a technology that substitutes conventional packet forwarding within a network, or part of a network, with a fast operation of label lookup and switching. Each MPLS packet has a label. Label swapping is done by associating labels with routes and using the label value in the packet forwarding process.

In an MPLS cloud, switches are called Label Switching Routers (LSRs) and a connection or tunnel between two endpoints is formed by the union of several LSRs along a route. It is called a Label Switch Path (LSP). When a packet enters into an MPLS cloud, the egress LSR classifies the packet accordingly to the rules defined in its Forwarding Equivalence Class (FEC) and each FEC has an association with a particular LSP.

Through this mapping (FEC - LSP), a label is assigned to the package, which only identifies the LSP to the downstream LSR in the LSP, so that they can continue this procedure until reach the egress (edge) LSR. In core LSRs, the procedure is simpler, since the packet reclassification is no longer required, but just forwarding it to the downstream LSR. Note that the label has only local significance. Before a packet leaves an MPLS domain, its MPLS label is removed (Ren et al, 2001).

Network Layer

All mobility management and signaling is carried out by L3 protocols, based or not in the Mobile IP protocol.

Transport Layer

Mobility on transport layer intends to maintain TCP (Transmission Control Protocol)'s end- to-end reliability and correctness semantics while allowing redirecting the endpoints of an existing transport session (e.g., a TCP connection or a series of UDP – User Datagram Protocol- packets) to arbitrary addresses (Maltz & Bhagwat, 1998).

Application Layer

Mobility provided by application layer protocols intends to allow communication end systems to support mobility, heterogeneity, and multihoming. Terminal mobility also allows a device to move between IP subnets, while continuing to be reachable for incoming requests and maintaining sessions across subnet changes (Schulzrinne & Wedlud, 2000).

Session mobility also allows a user to maintain a media session even while changing terminals. For example, a user may want to continue a session initiated on a MN on the desktop PC when entering his/her office. IPv4 or IPv6 mobility does not directly support such session mobility (Nasir & Mah-Rukh, 2006).

3. MOBILE IP

The Mobile IP (MIP) (Perkins, 1997; Johnson et al, 2004) uses a stable IP address assigned to mobile nodes. This home address is used to allow the MN to be reachable by having a stable entry in the DNS service, and to hide the IP layer mobility from upper layers. A consequence of keeping a stable address independently of the mobile node's location is that all correspondent nodes try to reach the MN at that address, without knowing the actual location of the mobile node. Therefore, if there are packets forwarded to the home address, and the MN is not at its home network, its home agent is responsible for tunneling packets to the MN's new location.

MIPv4 (Mobile IP for IPv4 networks) solves the mobility problem by allowing the MN to use a second IP address: the CoA. This address changes at each new point of attachment and it indicates the network prefix, identifying the MN's point of attachment with respect to the network topology. The CoA is composed of a valid prefix in a foreign network. Thus, the MN will have a home address and one or more CoAs when moving between networks. MIPv4 works by the cooperation of three separable mechanisms (Perkins, 1998): discovering the CoA, registering the CoA and tunneling to the CoA. The operation of Mobile IP protocol can be briefly described by the following steps (Figure 2):

1. The mobility agents (HA and FA) announces their presence through messages called Agent Advertisement (optionally, these messages can be requested by mobile agents through messages called Agent Solicitation);
2. A MN receives these messages and determines whether it is on its home network or on a foreign network;
3. When a MN detects it moved to a foreign network, it obtains a CoA in that network. The CoA can be allocated by the foreign agent or some

other address configuration mechanism, such as DHCP (Dynamic Host Configuration Protocol);

4. When the MN is operating in the new network, it needs to register its CoA with its HA, through the exchange of Registration Request and Registration Reply messages;
5. Datagrams sent to the MN's home address by a CN are intercepted by the local HA and tunneled to the MN's CoA. The datagram is received at the exit of the tunnel, and finally delivered to the mobile node in the new network;
6. Datagrams sent by the MN are generally delivered to the destination using standard routing mechanisms, not necessarily through the HA.

The cooperation between MN, HA and CN is called triangular routing, as we can see in Figure 2, which summarizes the MIPv4 operation.

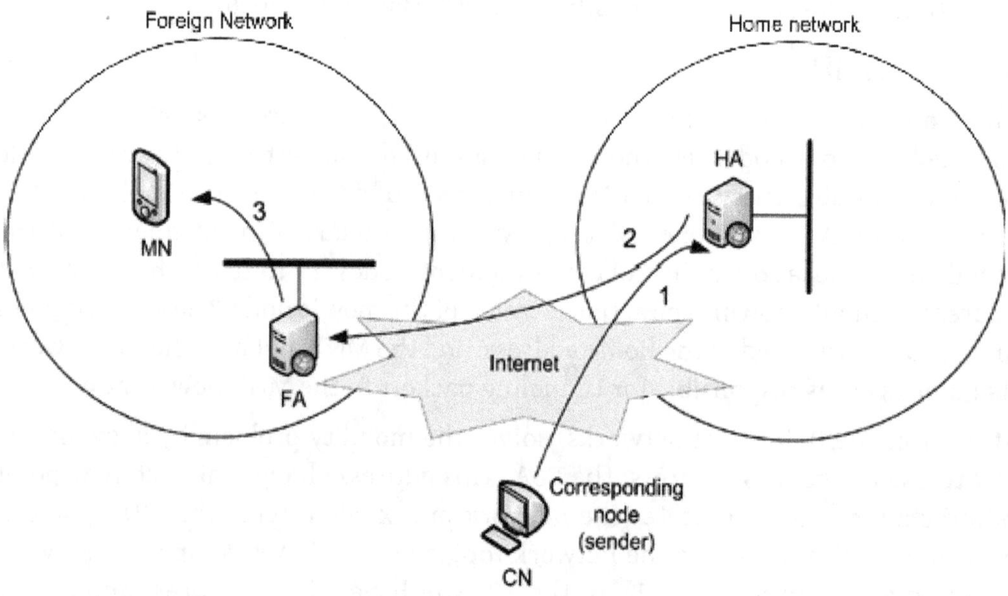

Fig. 2. MIPv4 Operation

The triangular routing generates a processing overhead on HA, in addition to this being a single point of failure in the network. The MIPv6 solves this problem by optimizing the route.

Mobile IPv6 (Johnson, 2004) is intended to provide mobility support in IPv6 networks. In order to know where the MN is found, an association between home address and care-of address should be performed (binding). This combination of CoA is made by the MN and the HA. This association is achieved by a binding registration where the MN sends messages called Binding Updates (BU) to HA, which responds with a message Binding Acknowledgment (BA) (Figure 3).

The correspondent nodes may carry out route optimization, or they can store bindings between MN's home address and CoA. Thus, a MN can supply information about its location to the corresponding nodes, through the Correspondent Binding Procedure, which is a mechanism for authorizing the establishment of binding, called the return routability procedure.

Using the Route Optimization process, the CN must support MIPv6 and the MN must register with the CN. In this case, the CN, before sending a package, looks for a cached association between MN's HA and CoA. If there is an association, the package will be routed to the CoA of mobile node directly. This eliminates congestion at the home link and the HA.

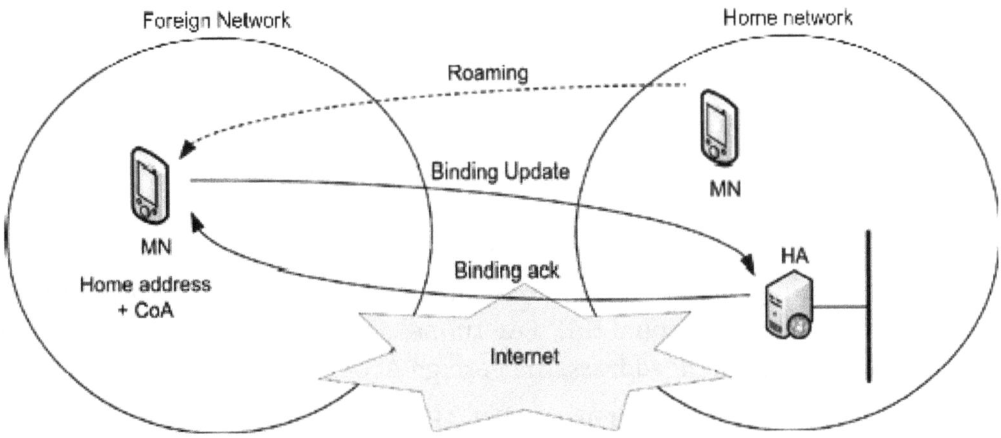

Fig. 3. MIPv6 Operation

MIPv4 and MIPv6 only define means of managing macromobility but do not address micromobility separately. Indeed, it uses the same mechanism in both cases. So, this protocol is not suited for micro mobility management, because of its high signaling load and long handover delay (Habaebi, 2006), namely movement detection, new CoA configuration, and Binding Update, is often unacceptable to real-time traffic such as Voice over IP (Koodli, 2008).

4. LINK LAYER RELATED MICRO-MOBILITY

FMIP - The Mobile IPv6 Fast Handovers (FMIPv6) protocol (Koodli, 2008) aims to reduce MN movement detection latency and new MN's CoA (Care-of Address) configuration latency by providing information to the MN when it is still connected to its current subnet. After discovering available access points, the MN requests subnet information from these APs: prefix, IP address, and L2 address of their associated routers. If the MN eventually attaches to one of the APs, the movement detection delay is reduced because the MN doesn't need to perform router discovery.

The MN formulates a new CoA (NCoA) based on the prefix of the new subnet and sends a message to its current access router, Previous Access Router (PAR), which communicates with the New Access Router (NAR) to determine whether the NCoA is unique. The PAR also establishes a tunnel to redirect packets arriving for PCoA (Previous CoA) to NCoA. After performing a handover the MN announces its attachment immediately with an Unsolicited Neighbor Advertisement message (Narten et al, 2007) to circumvent the delay associated to neighbor's address resolution. FMIPv6 also defines a different behavior when the MN doesn't receive acknowledge message prior to its handover. There is also an adaptation of FMIPv6 to IPv4 networks (Koodli & Perkins, 2007).

IP-IAPP – The IP-IAPP proposal (Samprakou et al, 2004) extends 802.11f IAPP (IEEE, 2003) to support inter-network handover via L2 specific methods. IP-IAPP defines the Home Access Point (HAP) that is the AP to which the MN was last associated inside its home network, similar to the Home Agent in MIP.

When the MN moves to a different network, it sends a modified IEEE 802.11 Reassociation.Request (IEEE, 1997) to an AP, the Foreign Access Point (FAP), informing IP addresses of HAP, MN, and Previous FAP (PAP) and this message triggers the mobility management procedure. The FAP communicates with the HAP to establish a bi-directional HAP-FAP tunnel and the HAP starts mapping the MN IP address to the FAP IP address, the Foreign Agent Care of Address (FACOA).

When the MN reassociates with a new FAP (NAP), the same procedure is performed with the addition of a communication between the PAP e NAP to establish a temporary unidirectional tunnel between them. The proposal has also been improved with the provision of more advanced services: secure inter-AP IP-IAPP communications, zero patching on the clients software, and support of clients which use a dynamic IP address (Samprakou et al, 2007).

The IEEE 802 Executive Committee approved IAPP withdrawal in 2006, because "the trial use period of 802.11F has expired, there has been no significant deployment of 802.11F implementations and, the functionality provided by 802.11F is being addressed in other standards fora"(IEEE P802.11, 2005).

5. MOBILITY WITH MPLS

All of the architectures discussed in this section consider that the MPLS cloud is surrounded by the Internet cloud and that micromobility is to be applied in MPLS cloud while MIP is to be applied in Internet cloud.

Mobile MPLS – The Mobile MPLS is a macro mobility protocol that borrows the mechanisms defined in the MIP standard and applies it to MPLS networks, so that the IP-in- IP tunnels are substituted by MPLS tunnels. The main objective in this migration is to improve the delay time in the tunneling packets from the HA to the

FA. Another objective is to facilitate the use of QoS services that are native to MPLS networks (Ren et al, 2001).

In order to track the MN location, an entry in the LIB (Label Information Base) table at the HA is created for each MN that is registered with it. When the MN arrives at a foreign network, it registers itself with this FA and obtains a CoA from it. The FA sends this information to the MN's HA and it establishes a new LSP for that FA.

After the completion of the LSP connection, the HA changes the LIB entry for that MN to reflect the out label and port interface gathered from the previously created LSP. In doing that, whatever packet that is sent to the MN's home network will be tunneled to this LSP, arriving at the FA in which the MN is actually connected. A lack of an entry about out label and port interface for the MN at the LIB table at the MN's HA means that the MN returned to its home network.

Three scenarios were discussed. The first one considered was that both FAs and HAs were inside the same administrative MPLS domain. The second one considered was that HAs and FAs were inside different administrative MPLS domains. In order to establish a tunnel between them, Mobile MPLS suggests the use of a border protocol such as BGP (Border Gateway Protocol) (Rekhter & Rosen, 2001). The third scenario considered was that HA and FA were inside a different network tunneling technology, such as MPLS and IP clouds. LER is responsible for de-tunneling packets from the MPLS cloud and re-tunneling it inside the IP cloud.

H-MPLS - Hierarchical Mobile MPLS (Yang & Makrakis, 2001) extends Mobile MPLS, which is a macro mobility protocol, in order to introduce into it micro mobility features. The main objective is to reduce the signaling overhead in creating a LSP from HA to FA, due to MN frequent handover in a small-size cells wireless environment.

To do that, H-MPLS introduces a new element, called FDA (Foreign Domain Agent) whose function is between that defined for HA and FA, as described in the MIP standards. The role of FDA is to track MN local mobility inside a MPLS domain. There is only one FDA per MPLS domain and many FA per subnetworks inside this domain.

The dynamics of the protocol is as follows: whenever a MN enters a foreign MPLS domain and it is its first registration, it acquires a CoA from its FA LSR and registers with it. This FA sends a Registration Request to its FDA, which has an equivalent function of a FA, but its scope is for a domain. This FDA will send back a Label Request message to FA and put as its FEC, the MN's CoA. At meanwhile, FDA will send a Registration Request message to HA, in the same way that was described in Mobile MPLS, but putting its IP address as a FEC for this LSP. So, at this point, there will be two LSPs, one from HA to FDA and another one from FDA to FA.

Now, if a MN does a handover, but stays in the same domain as the previous FDA, only the LSP from the new FA to FDA needs to be established. To avoid FDA sending packets to MN via the old FA, due to an out-of-date entry cache, the new FA sends a Binding Update message to old FA instructing it to create a LSP to the new FA in order to tunnel packets arriving at the MN's old location.

LEMA - Label Edge Mobility Agent (Chiussi et al, 2002) is a tunnel-based micro mobility architecture that uses MPLS as a network transport technology. This network is composed of an overlay network whose nodes are called LEMA, an LER that has its function augmented with LEMA features. This overlay network tracks MN location by building a set of LEMAs nodes from the highest to the lowest LEMAs that compound a path.

Highest LEMAs are the ingress node which registers its address in the HA database, and acts as FA in the MIP protocol; while the lowest LEMA is the access router, which remove the MPLS tunnel and delivers messages to the AP which the MN is connected to. This kind of scheme makes a hierarchical network, where only the LEMAs that compose a path to track the MN need to be aware of it.

Others features that can be attributed to it are fast handover capability, scalable design, QoS capability and gradual deployment. It is the MN's role to define the set of LEMAs that compose its path inside a LEMA network. This path is chosen based on a set of parameters, such as: available bandwidth, mobility patterns, and so on. The algorithm employed to choose a particular set is an open issue, and could be of high complexity. Finally, all LEMAs are connected to themselves by pre-established LSPs.

MM-MPLS - Micro Mobile MPLS (Langar et al, 2004) extends mobile MPLS with the principles employed by MIP-RR (L3 protocol) to support micro mobility on MPLS networks. It introduces a new component, called Label Edge Router/Gateway (LER/GW) that resides between HA and FA agents, as defined in the MIP protocol. It acts as a foreign domain agent to HA and it is this address that the MN must register at HA database when it first gets into the domain at which LER/GW is administrating.

So, there is a tunnel/LSP from HA to LER/GW, and an LSP from LER/GW to FA, with MN CoA's address as a FEC. FA here is an AR (Access Router) that remove the MPLS tunnel and delivers the packet to MN that is registered on it. Whenever MN moves to another FA, which is under the same LER/GW, only a regional registration is required that will create a new LSP from LER/GW to the new FA, using the new MN CoA's address as FEC. MM- MPLS uses LDP (Label Distribution Protocol) as signaling protocol in MPLS cloud.

I-LIB - Intermediate Label Information Base (Fowler & Zeadally, 2006) maintains the same idea of MM-MPLS architecture in general, where a FDA is placed between HA and FA. FDA has the same role as described early, i.e., its CoA address is registered at HA database and a tunnel connect HA to FDA. On the other side, FDA keeps track of MN by establishing a LSP to FA that is directly connected to it. Whenever a MN does a handover and establishes a new connection to a new FA, this new FA will try to establish a LSP to FDA, sending a Registration Request.

Here is where this proposal differs from the previous ones. Instead of establishing a new LSP from scratch, linking the new FA to the FDA, any segments that are common between the new path and the old path will be preserved. As such, any LSR that already has an entry in its LIB could preserve it and just update it to show the new configuration (the new segment that connects the MN). In order to do that, a new LIB is proposed which augmented the old ones with new fields to contemplate mobility issues. Among the fields that are required, the previous and new MN's CoAs must be accounted for. It is necessary to modify the packet since the FDA and HA know the MN by its old CoA, while the FA knows the MN by its new CoA.

6. NETWORK LAYER

Cellular IP - The CIP (Valko, 1999) architecture is composed of different wireless access networks (CIP access networks) connected to the Internet through a gateway. MIP manages mobility between these CIP access networks, while Cellular IP handles mobility within one domain. The IP address of the gateway is used as the MIP CoA. Thus, packets are first routed to the host‘s HA and then tunneled to the gateway, which "detunnels" packets and forwards them toward base stations, using host-specific routing path.

Base station (BS) components serve as wireless access points and also route IP packets, but IP routing is replaced by Cellular IP routing and location management. Base stations cache the path taken by uplink packets from MN to gateway for a period of time and use the reverse path to route downlink packets. In order to route packets to idle MNs, Cellular IP employs paging.

HAWAII - HAWAII divides the network into a hierarchy of domains. All issues related to mobility management within one domain are handled by a gateway called a domain root router, which uses a specialized path setup scheme which installs host-based forwarding entries in specific routers to support intra-domain micromobility (Ramjee et al, 1999). While moving inside its home domain, the MN maintains its stable IP address.

MIP mechanisms are used when the MN moves into a foreign domain. However, if the foreign domain is also based on HAWAII, then the MN is assigned a co-located CoA from its foreign domain to which packets for the MN are tunneled. The domain root router routes the packets to the MN using the host-based routing entries. When the MN moves between different subnets of the same domain, only the route from the domain root router to the BS serving the MN is modified, and the remaining path remains the same, and connectivity is maintained using dynamically established paths.

The protocol contains three different messages for establishing, updating and refreshing host specific routes for the MN in the domain root router and any intermediate routers on the path towards the mobile host. The protocol also has four different path setup schemes, aiming to reduce disruption to the user traffic during a handoff, classified into two types based on the way packets are delivered to MNs. In the first type, packets are forwarded from the old base station to the new and, in the second type, they are diverted at the crossover router.

MIP-RR - MIP-Regional Registration (Fogelstroem et al, 2007) is an optional extension to the Mobile IPv4 protocol, and proposes a mean for mobile nodes to register locally within a visited domain. By registering locally, the number of signaling messages to the home network is kept to a minimum, and the signaling delay is reduced. This protocol introduces a new network node called the Gateway Foreign Agent (GFA). Besides the regular MIP Registration messages, a new pair of registration messages, Regional Registration Requests/Replies, is used between MNs/FAs/GFAs.

There are two models of how the MN uses Regional Registration. In the first model, the FAs in a visited domain advertise the address of the GFA, and, when a mobile node first arrives at this visited domain, it performs a home registration. At this registration, the mobile node registers the address of the GFA as its CoA with its HA. When moving between different foreign agents within the same visited domain, the mobile node only needs to make a regional registration to the GFA. In the second model, the FA can indicate that dynamic assignment of GFA is to be used, if being the FA's responsibility to choose the GFA after receiving a Registration Request from the MN.

PMIP - The Proxy MIP (Gundavelli et al, 2008) is a network-centric micromobility approach that relies on tunnels inside a domain to direct traffic to mobile nodes. PMIPv6 reuses many concepts of MIPv6, like the HA functionality, and defines two new entities, the Mobile Access Gateway (MAG) and the Local Mobility Anchor (LMA).

A MAG typically runs on the Access Router. It is responsible for detecting the mobile node attachments, and, if security policies are fulfilled, establishes tunnels to the LMA for directing traffic to the mobile nodes reached via this MAG. A MAG also emulates (via Router Advertisements messages) the mobile node's home network in such a way that the mobile node may change the default router in a handover, but preserves the remaining L3 parameters. As the mobile node moves inside the domain, tunnels between MAG and LMA and routes on the LMA are updated.

LMA maintains a binding cache entry for each currently registered MN, providing reachability to the MN's address. When the LMA receives a packet targeted to the mobile node it forwards the packet via the tunnel ending on the MAG to where the node is attached. PMIPv6 employs local binding update messages between MAG and LMA for signaling purposes and only a single hierarchy of tunnels. Indeed, Proxy MIP considers IPv4 support, but this requires an extension to the original protocol, since it uses some IPv6 features such as auto-configuration and extension headers.

HMIPv6 - To support local mobility, Hierarchical Mobile IPv6 (HMIPv6) extends Mobile IPv6 and IPv6 Neighbor Discovery (Narten et al, 2007) and introduces Mobility Anchor Point (MAP), a new Mobile IPv6 node. A mobile node entering an HMIP domain receives Router Advertisements containing information about one or more local MAPs and configures two CoAs: an on-link CoA (LCoA) and a Regional Care-of Address (RCoA).

The LCoA is configured on a mobile node's interface based on the prefix advertised by its default router. It is a standard Mobile IP CoA and has a different name just to be distinguished from RCoA. The RCoA is configured on the MAP's link and is obtained by the MN from the MAP employing the address mechanisms described by RFC 4877 (Devarapalli & Dupon, 2007).

After configuration, the MN sends two binding update (BU) messages. The first is a local BU to the MAP to bind the MN's RCoA to its LCoA and to establish a bi-directional tunnel between them. The second is a BU to the home agent to bind the MN's home address to its RCoA. The MAP receives all packets on behalf of the mobile node it is serving and encapsulates and forwards them directly to the mobile node's LCoA.

When the mobile node moves within the same MAP domain, it only needs to register its new LCoA with its MAP, limiting the amount of Mobile IPv6 signaling outside the local domain. The RCoA remains unchanged and the home agent (HA) or the correspondent nodes (CNs) are not aware of the change in LCoA.

DMA - The Dynamic Mobility Agent (Misra et al, 2001) architecture uses the Intra-Domain Mobility Management Protocol (IDMP) (Das et al, 2002) to manage intradomain mobility. The architecture defines two entities to achieve mobility support: Mobility Agent (MA) that acts as a domain-wide point for packet redirection, and the Subnet Agent (SA) that provides subnet-specific mobility services. Two CoAs are associated with a MN: Global CoA (GCoA) and Local CoA (LCoA).

The GCoA is the address used by macromobility protocols to redirect packets and remains unchanged as long as the MN stays in the current domain. The LCoA is an address from the subnet the MN is attached to. IDMP is used in the communication between the MN and the SA, and between the MN and the MA.

When the MN first arrives at the domain, it obtains an LCoA and the SA assigns the MN a MA. The MN registers its LCoA with the MA and obtains a GCoA. After the macromobility updates process is performed by the MN, the packets from remote hosts, tunneled or directly transmitted to the GCoA, are intercepted by the MA and tunneled to the MN's LCoA. When the MN moves to new subnet it obtains a new LCoA and informs its MA of the new LCoA, updating the GCoA-LCoA mapping.

7. TRANSPORT LAYER MOBILITY

MSOCKS is a split-connection proxy-based architecture that uses TCP Splice technique to achieve the same end-to-end semantics as normal TCP connections (Maltz & Bhagwat,1998). A special host, called a proxy, is placed in the communication path between a mobile node and a correspondent node. An end-to-end TCP connection between a mobile node and a correspondent node are split into two separated connections: one connection between the mobile node and proxy and another between the proxy and the correspondent node. The MSOCKS protocol extends the SOCKS protocol (Leech et al, 1996) to redirect TCP streams to a mobile node's changing location.

When the mobile node changes the address of its network interface it opens a new connection to the proxy and sends an MSOCK message specifying the connection identifier of the original connection. The proxy unsplices the old mobile-node-to-proxy connection from the proxy-to-correspondent-node connection, and splices in the new mobile-node-to- proxy connection. Only the proxy is aware of the mobile node migration and the communication between the proxy and the correspondent node remains unchanged. This technique also allows the mobile node to change the network interface used to communicate with the proxy.

TCP Migrate – This mobility architecture (Snoeren & Balakrishnan, 2000) (Snoeren et al, 2002) allows an application running on mobile hosts to support transparent connectivity across network address changes. As MNs change their network attachment point, new addresses can be assigned through DHCP, manually or using an auto-configuration protocol. To locate mobile hosts in the new network, Domain Name System (DNS) is used and its ability to support secure dynamic updates.

Because most Internet applications resolve hostnames to an IP address at the beginning of a transaction or connection, this approach is viable for initiating new sessions with mobile hosts. When a host changes its network attachment point (IP address), it sends a secure DNS update to one of the name servers in its home domain updating its current location. The name-to-address mappings for these hosts are un-cacheable by other domains, so stale bindings are eliminated.

Nevertheless, when a MN moves during a previously established connection, it may suspend the open connection and reactivate it from the new address, sending a special packet (Migrate SYN) to the correspondent node, which carries a token that identifies the previous connection. This SYN packet signals the correspondent node to re-synchronize the connection with the MN at the new point of attachment (new address). Thus, it is possible to provide mobility support as an end-to-end service, according to the application's specific requirements, without changes in the network layer.

8. APPLICATION LAYER MOBILITY

Mobility using SIP - The SIP (Session Initiation Protocol) is a signaling protocol, widely used for setting up and tearing down multimedia communication sessions over the Internet. It can be used in any application where session initiation is necessary.

The SIP registration mechanism is considered the application-layer equivalent of the MIP registration mechanism. However, while mobile IP binds a permanent IP address identifying a host to a temporary CoA, SIP binds a user-level identifier to a temporary IP address or host name (Schulzrinne & Wedlund, 2000). An INVITE message is sent by a MN to its CN to set up a communication session. The mechanism to provide MN mobility during an active session foresees that the MN needs to send another INVITE message to the CN to communicate the information about the new parameters of the communication session after the handover, using the same call identifier as the original call setup.

This solution has some drawbacks (Salsano et al, 2008). The second INVITE is sent end-to- end, and this could lead to high delays. Moreover, the handover procedure relies on the capability of the CN to handle this procedure, thus increasing MN processing needs. An auxiliary mechanism is necessary if the MN and CN move at the same time.

9. MOBILITY PLANE ARCHITECTURE

The Mobility Plane Architecture (MPA) (Zagari et al, 2008) is an instance of a reference architecture for micromobility support in IP networks (Prado et al, 2008). The goal of MPA is to speed up the handover process in order to minimize communication disruptions when the mobile node changes its network point of attachment. One of the requirements of this architecture is to place the burden demanded by micromobility on the network, not on the mobile nodes. Another requirement is to use, ideally, only well established network protocols. The key point of MPA is to employ an overlay network built above a transport network for directing traffic to the mobile nodes. This overlay network is composed of network elements called Mobility Aware Router (MAR), which are routers enhanced with MPA's functionalities. MPA employs point-to-multipoint (P2MP) tunnels in order to encapsulate traffic directed to the mobile nodes and allows a gradual deployment once the architecture elements are installed only at the MARs.

MPA addresses the following issues related to mobility in IP networks: tunnel management (tunnel establishment, shutdown, and topology updating); secure mobile node attachment and handover; tracking of mobile node actual point of attachment (location); routing on the overlay network (decoupled from routing on the transport network); and quality and class of service (QoS/CoS) offered to the mobile nodes.

9.1 Functional Description

The architecture defines the following basic elements:

- Transport network - an IP network from which the network operator wishes to offer mobility services.
- Point-to-multipoint (P2MP) tunnel - a tunnel with a topology forming a tree. Nodes in the tree are MARs and arcs are tunnel segments connecting MARs. The tunnel has a single ingress (root) MAR, branch MARs (nodes with branching level greater than one), and egress MARs (leaves of the tree). A packet being forwarded through the tunnel may or may not be replicated at a branch MARs according to the policies enforced by these MARs.
- Access router - a router (usually an egress MAR) connected to a wireless access point.
- Access network - an IP subnetwork formed by the access routers and access points.
- Overlay mobile network - logical network built with one or more P2MP tunnels established through the transport network.

Figure 4 illustrates these basic elements. In addition to the basic elements, four functional blocks (FB) are defined:

- Tunnel Management (TM) Functional Block: TM is the entity responsible for P2MP tunnel establishment, shutdown, and re-routing. It must provide interfaces to the network management system and to the human operator. Tunnel management is a function carried out by MARs.
- Mobile Routing (MR) Functional Block: MR is the entity responsible for tracking the mobile nodes actual point of attachment and for interacting with the MARs forwarding engine in order to route traffic to the mobile nodes correct location. Mobile routing is a function carried out by MARs.
- Address Configuration (AC) Functional Block: AC is the entity responsible for supplying L3 addresses to the mobile nodes when they connects or reconnects to the access network. Address configuration is a function carried out cooperatively by MARs and mobile nodes.

- Handover Helper (HH) Functional Block: HH is the entity responsible for facilitating the handover process with functions including L2 notification (triggering), L2 re-association, secure node attachment, and handover-related signaling. This function can be spread among MARs, network equipments (e.g., wireless switches), and mobile nodes.

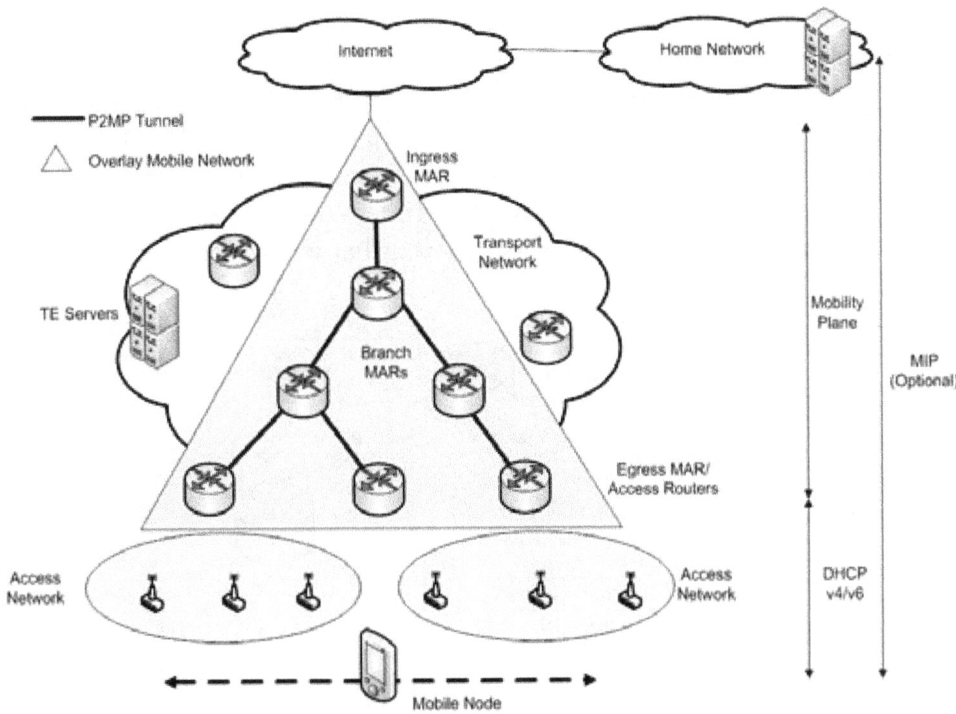

Fig. 4. MPA overview

9.2 Operations Basics

When a packet targeted to a mobile node reaches an ingress MAR, it is tunneled until it reaches an egress MAR able to route the packet to the mobile node. When the mobile node performs a handover, the AC FB presented on the mobile node and on the network interact in order to provide the mobile node with a new L3 address. If the address is identical to the previous one the transport connections are not broken due the handover. The handover also triggers a mobile node location update on the MR FB. The location updating process updates the mobility routing tables on the MARs in such a way that when a packet is targeted to the mobile node the packet is routed to the egress MAR serving the link the mobile node is attached to.

Let us consider the mobile routing and the location update processes. Figure 5 shows a mobile node attached via access router M4. When the mobile node moves to a link served by M5, the entry related to this node on the mobile routing table at M2 must be updated with a different tunnel segment (in this case from segment

C to D). If the mobile node roams to a link served by M7, the mobile routing table at M1 and M3 must be updated. Table updates are performed as soon as the mobile routing protocol messages indicating the new point of attachment are processed by the branch MARs.

The entries on the mobile routing table are soft state, meaning that the entries are dropped if location update messages confirming them cease. Soft state is a clear way to drop routes to mobile nodes when they no longer are reached through these routes. This scheme demands that a mobile node perform network attachments periodically in order to generate location update messages that will refresh the routes to it. A way to force the mobile nodes to perform periodic attachments is to provide them L3 address with a short lease time. When the lease time is close to expire, a mobile node performs address renewal that will trigger address location update messages in its behalf.

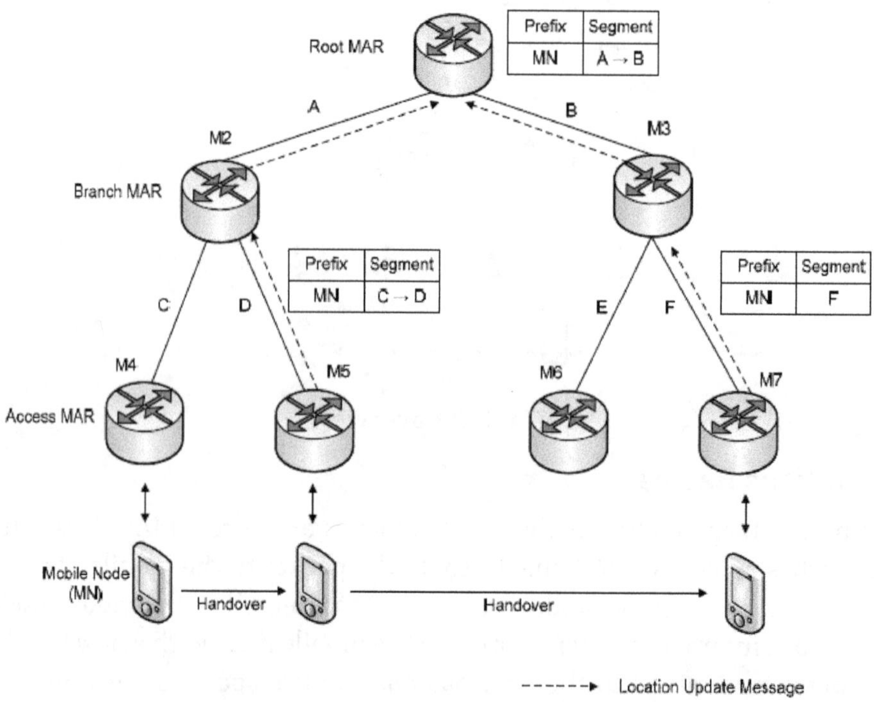

Fig. 5. MN Routing in MPA

9.3 MPA advantages

The MPA architecture presents the following advantages:

1. The solution is not limited to IPv6, being deployable on both IPv4 and IPv6 networks. Since it relies on tunneling, mixed deployments with IPv4 on the access network and IPv6 on the transport network, and vice-versa are possible.

2. The solution is not affected by middle boxes such as firewall and NAT boxes placed anywhere on the access, transport, or backbone networks.
3. The solution demands no complex protocols such as MIPv6 on the mobile nodes. Since it relies only on the standard IP protocol stack, the solution supports all the commercially available mobile nodes based on, for instance, Windows Mobile, Symbian, and PalmOne operating systems. The architecture does not forbid enhancements deployed on the mobile nodes in order to improve handover speed and security, for instance. Such enhancements can be installed in user space or in the operating system kernel (e.g., as device drivers).
4. The solution preserves the L3 address of the mobile nodes when they roam inside the access network, causing no disruption of transport connections maintained by the mobile nodes.
5. The solution does not restrict the mobile node to employ macromobility protocols such as MIPv6.
6. The solution complies with security mechanisms related to L2 (e.g. WPA), L3 (e.g. IPSec), and L4+ (e.g., SSL, HTTPS).
7. The solution combines P2MP tunneling management, QoS/CoS management, and mobile node location tracking into the same protocol (RSVP-TE), reducing implementation and operating costs.
8. The solution does not interfere on services already deployed on the transport network such as VPN and VoIP.
9. Only well standardized protocols are employed by the architecture. When extensions to protocols are necessary they are introduced as opaque objects already foreseen by these protocols.

For more details on MPA description, implementation (using IPv4 and IPv6) and performance analysis, see Prado (2008), Zagari (2008), Johnson (2008), and Zagari (2009). Badan et al (2009) details the MPA implementation using MPLS.

10. GENERAL ANALYSIS AND RESEARCH DIRECTIONS

Table 1 summarizes all the protocols and solutions seen in this chapter.

Table 1. General Classification

Protocol	Mobility Range	Mobility Routing	Mobility Signaling	Mobility Layer
CIP	Micro	Routing	MN-centric	L3
DMA	Micro	Tunnel	MN-centric	L3
FMIP	Micro	Tunnel	MN-centric	L2
Hawaii	Micro	Routing/Tunnel	MN-centric	L3

HMIP	Micro	Tunnel	MN-centric	L3
H-MPLS	Micro	Tunnel	MN-centric	L2½
I-LIB	Micro	Tunnel	MN-centric	L2½
IP-IAPP	Macro/micro	Tunnel	MN-centric	L2
LEMA	Micro	Tunnel	MN-centric	L2½
MPA	Micro	Tunnel	Network-centric	L3
MIP	Macro	Routing/Tunnel	MN-centric	L3
MIP-RR	Micro	Tunnel	MN-centric	L3
MM-MPLS	Micro	Tunnel	MN-centric	L2½
Mobile MPLS	Macro	Tunnel	MN-centric	L2½
MSOCKS	Micro	Routing	MN-centric	L4
PMIP	Micro	Tunnel	Network-centric	L3
SIP	Macro	Routing	MN-centric	L5
TCP Migrate	Macro	Routing	MN-centric	L4

As this work is a non-exhaustive selection of mobility solutions, our comments are limited to these protocols revised in this chapter.

There are a majority of MN-centric solutions, since the beginning of mobility management research, with the Mobile IP. Newer solutions, such as MPA and PMIP, work as network- centric solutions, and it is our belief that this class of mobility signaling will have more research focus and implementations, because of its advantages to the final user: they do not need protocol installation of configuration on the MN, no overheads on devices to handle mobility, and no intervention from the final user to adopt a particular mobility solution.

Another interesting issue is the network layer protocol. About 10 years ago nobody believed in IPv4 for mobility, which is why both MIPv6 and its extensions appeared at that time. Since then, however, the IPv6 protocol has not been massively adopted, so there is reawakened interest in IPv4 (PMIP and MIPv4 raised again, for example). Now, 4G researchers and professionals say IPv6 is inevitable because each cell phone and mobile devices must have a fixed (stable) IP address. Solutions compatible only to IPv4 must foresee this IPv6 adoption and implement a compatible version of their protocol, if intended to be used in the next future.

Not mentioned in this chapter, solutions for mobility must adopt security mechanisms for authentication, authorization and general security procedures. For example, for the MPA architecture, the access points can be configured to authenticate mobile nodes based on WPA2 employing Pre-Shared Keys (PSK) or RADIUS. PSK is easy to configure but is not as secure as RADIUS-based authentication. RADIUS authentication can be strengthened by using certificates installed on the mobile nodes. As RADIUS transactions take long time (500ms in our testbed network), RADIUS-based authentication increases considerably the handover overhead.

In order to speed up RADIUS-based authentication, a cache mechanism can be employed such as PMK (Pairwise Master Key) caching (also called proactive key caching). In this mechanism, once a mobile node completes successfully a RADIUS transaction, the access point stores the PMK supplied by the RADIUS server in the cache. When the mobile node connects to a new access point, the access point queries the cache (using the mobile node's MAC address as a search key) in order to recover the PMK assigned to the node. If an entry is found, the access point accepts the mobile node without the need of a RADIUS transaction. In this case, the PMK found on cache is used to secure the communication between the mobile node and the access point.

As suggestions for future research directions in mobility management, we can point out the development of architectures able to:

- integrate macro and micro mobility into a single mobility solution;
- support both vertical and horizontal handover (e.g., between WiFi and 4G networks);
- support clean slate solution, by designing the network from the mobility requirements (and not to incorporate mobility extensions over the existing networks).
- These solutions decouple host identity from network address as suggested by HIP (Host Identity Protocol) and other related solutions;
- restrict handover within the L2, employing, for instance, tunneling over Ethernet (instead of over IP or MPLS), flat routing (based on MAC – Media Access Control - address), etc.

11. CONCISE SUMMARY

The objective of this chapter was to provide a comprehensive examination of mobility architectures and protocols. Numerous solutions were demonstrated, including those related to the link layer and those at the application layer, which encompassed network, transport, and intermediary layer protocols. Additionally, we introduced MPA, our mobility management solution, which employs a network-centric paradigm.

Some of the solutions that were reviewed were abandoned, while others are still being investigated. However, further research is required to enable the widespread deployment and utilization of mobility management solutions. While the new mobility architectures and protocols are constantly being investigated, all new solutions are limited by the following factors: the ability to be deployed over existing IPv4 (and future IPv6) fixed networks, the ability to operate without upgrading with the mobile nodes already in the market, the ability to comply with current network operation practices, the ability to be scalable without compromising the quality of service, and the ability to introduce new services with stringent communication requirements, such as media streaming (e.g., IP TV), location, and entertainment services. The obstacle in mobility for IP networks is the necessity of adhering to these factors, which are regrettably not limited to the technical issues that are frequently addressed by network architects.

FOOTNOTES

1. Seamless mobility: capability to change the mobile node's point of attachment to an IP-based network, without losing ongoing connections and without disruptions in the communication.

REFERENCES

1. Akyildiz, I., Xie, J., & Mohanty, S. (2004). A Survey of Mobility Management in Next- Generation All-IP-Based Wireless Systems. *IEEE Wireless Communications, 11* (4), 16–28.
2. Badan, T., Zagari, E., Prado, R., Cardozo, E., Magalhaes, M., Carrilho, J., Pinto, R., Berenguel, A., Moraes, D., Johnson, T., & Westberg, L. (2009). A Network Architecture for Providing Micro-Mobility in MPLS/GMPLS Networks. *Proceedings of IEEE Wireless Communications and Networking Conference* (pp. 1-6).
3. Campbell, A. T., & Gomez-Castellanos, J. (2000). IP Micro-Mobility Protocols. *ACM SIGMOBILE Mobile Computing and Communications Review, 4* (4), 45 – 53.
4. Campbell, A. T., Gomez, J., Kim, S., Wan, C.-Y., Turany, Z. R., & Valko, A. G. (2002). Comparison of IP Micromobility Protocols. *IEEE Wireless Communications, 9* (1), 2– 12.
5. Chiussi, F. M., Khotimsky, D. A., & Krishnan, S. (2002). A Network Architecture for MPLS- Based Micro-Mobility, *Proceedings of the IEEE Wireless Communications and Networking Conference*, vol. 2, pp. 549-555.
6. Chiussi, F., Khotimsky, D., & Krishnan, S. (2002). Mobility Management in Third- Generation All-IP Networks. *IEEE Communications Magazine, 40* (9), 124–135.
7. Das, S., Mcauley, A., Dutta, A., Misra, A., Chakraborty, K., & Das, S.K. (2002). IDMP: an intradomain mobility management protocol for next-generation wireless networks. *IEEE Wireless Communications, 9* (3), 1536-1284.

8. Devarapalli, V., & Dupon, F. (2007). Mobile IPv6 Operation with IKEv2 and the Revised IPsec Architecture. *Request For Comment (RFC) 4877*, Available at: www.faqs.org/rfcs/rfc4877.html.

9. Fogelstroem, E., Jonsson, A., & Perkins, C. (2007). Mobile IPv4 Regional Registration. *Request For Comments (RFC) 4857*, Available at: www.ietf.org/rfc/rfc4857.txt.

10. Fowler, S., & Zeadally, S. (2006). Fast Handover over Micro-MPLS-based Wireless Networks, *Proceedings of the 11th Symposium on Computers and Communications* (pp. 181-186).

11. Gundavelli, S., Leung, K., Devarapalli, V., Chowdhury, K., & Patil, B. (2008). Proxy Mobile IPv6. *Request For Comment (RFC) 5213,* Available at: http://tools.ietf.org/html/rfc5213.

12. Habaebi, M. H. (2006). Macro/Micro-Mobility Fast Handover in Hierarchical Mobile IPv6. *Computer Communications, 29* (51), 611– 617.

13. IEEE Document P802.11/D6.1.97/5 Wireless LAN, MAC and Physical Specifications, June 1997.

14. IEEE Recommended Practice for Multi-Vendor Access Point Interoperability via an Inter- Access Point Protocol Across Distribution Systems Supporting IEEE 802.11TM Operation. Mar, 2003.

15. IEEE P802.11 Working Group. (2005). Approved Minutes of the IEEE P802.11 Full Working Group. Available at: https://mentor.ieee.org/802.11/dcn/05/11-05-1136-00-0000- minutes-working-group-nov-2005.doc.

16. Johnson, D., Perkins, C., & Arkko, J. (2004). Mobility Support in IPv6. *Request For Comments (RFC)* 3775, Available at: www.ietf.org/rfc/rfc3775.txt.

17. Johnson, T., Zagari, E., Prado, R., Badan, T., Cardozo, E., & Westberg, L. (2008). Performance Analysis of a New Architecture for Mobility Support in IP Networks, *Proceedings of the International Wireless Communications and Mobile Computing Conference* (pp. 706- 711).

18. Kempf, E. (2007). Problem Statement for Network-Based Localized Mobility Management. *Request For Comments (RFC)* 4830, Available at http://www.ietf.org/rfc/rfc4830.txt.

19. Koodli, R., & Perkins, C. (2007). Mobile IPv4 Fast Handovers. *Request For Comment (RFC) 4988*, Available at: www.faqs.org/rfcs/rfc4988.html.

20. Koodli, R. (2008). Mobile IPv6 Fast Handovers. *Request For Comment (RFC) 5268*, Available at: www.faqs.org/rfcs/rfc5268.html.

21. Langar, R., Le Grand, G., & Tohme, S. (2004). Micro Mobile MPLS Protocol in Next Generation Wireless Access Networks, *Proceedings of the IEEE Symposium on Computer and Communication* (pp. 14-17).

22. Leech, M., Ganis, M., Lee, Y., Kuris, R., Koblas, D., & Jones, L. (1996). SOCKS Protocol Version 5. *Request For Comment (RFC) 1928*, Available at: ww.faqs.org/rfcs/rfc1928.html.

23. Maltz, D.A., & Bhagwat, P. (1998). Msocks: an Architecture for Transport Layer Mobility, *Proceedings of the Seventeenth Annual Joint Conference of the IEEE Computer and Communications Societies,* vol.3, pp. 1037-1045.

24. Manner, J., & Kojo, M. (2004). Mobility Related Terminology. *Request For Comment (RFC) 3753*, Available at: www.faqs.org/rfcs/rfc3753.html.

25. Misra, A., Das, S., McAuley, A. & Das, S.K. (2001). Autoconfiguration, Registration and Mobility Management for Pervasive Computing. *IEEE Personal Communications Magazine, 8* (4), 24-31.

26. Narten, T., Nordmark, E., Simpson, W., & Soliman, H. (2007). Neighbor Discovery for IP version 6 (IPv6). *Request For Comment (RFC) 4861,* Available at: www.faqs.org/rfcs/rfc4861.html.

27. Nasir, A., & Mah-Rukh. (2006). Internet Mobility using SIP and MIP. In *Proceedings of the Third International Conference on Information Technology: New Generations* (pp 334 - 339).

28. Perkins, C. (1997). Mobile IP. *IEEE Communications Magazine*, *35* (5), 84-99.

29. Perkins, C. (1998). Mobile Networking through Mobile IP. *IEEE Internet Computing, 2* (1), 58- 69.

30. Perkins, C. (2002). IP Mobility Support for IPv4. *Request for Comments (RFC) 3344*, Available at: www.ietf.org/rfc/rfc3344.txt.

31. Prado, R., Zagari, E., Cardozo, E., Magalhaes, M., Badan, T., Carrilho, J., Pinto, R., Berenguel, A., Barboza, D., Moraes, D., Johnson, T., & Westberg, L. (2008). A Reference Architecture for Micro-Mobility Support in IP Networks, *Proceedings of the Thirteenth IEEE Symposium on Computers and Communications* (pp. 624 – 630).

32. Rekhter, Y., & Rosen, E. (2001). Carrying Label Information in BGP-4. *Request for Comment (RFC 3107)*, Available at: http://www.ietf.org/rfc/rfc3107.txt.

33. Ramjee, R., Porta, T. L., Thuel, S., Varadhan, K., & Wang S. (1999). Hawaii: A Domain- Based Approach for Supporting Mobility in Wide-Area Wireless Network, *Proceedings of the IEEE International Conference on Network Protocols* (pp. 283-292).

34. Ren, Z., Tham, C.-K., Foo, C.-C., & Ko, C.-C. (2001). Integration of Mobile IP and Multi- Protocol Label Switching. *Proceedings of the IEEE International Conference on Communications* (pp. 2123–2127).

35. Rosen, E.,Viswanathan, A., & Callon, R. (2001). Multiprotocol Label Switching Architecture. *Request For Comments (RFC) 3031*, Available at: http://www.ietf.org/rfc/rfc3031.txt

36. Saha, D., Mukherjee, A., Misra, I., Chakraborty, M., & Subhash, N. (2004). Mobility Support in IP: a Survey of Related Protocols. *IEEE Network*, *18* (6), 34–40.

37. Salsano, S., Polidoro, A., Mingardi, C., Niccolini, S., & Veltri, L. (2008). Sip-based Mobility Management in Next Generation Networks. *IEEE Wireless Communications*, *15*(2), 92–99.

38. Samprakou, I., Bouras, C., & Karoubalis, T. (2004). Fast and Efficient IP Handover in IEEE 802.11 Wireless LANs. *Proceedings of the International Conference on Wireless Networks* (pp. 249-255).

39. Samprakou, I., Bouras, C., & Karoubalis, T. (2007). Improvements on IP IAPP: A Fast IP Handover Protocol for IEEE 802.11 Wireless and Mobile Clients. *Wireless Network*, *13* (4), 497–510.

40. Schulzrinne, H., & Wedlund, E. (2000). Application-layer Mobility Using SIP. *SIGMOBILE Mobile Computing and Communications Review*, *4* (3), 47–57.

41. Snoeren, A. C., & Balakrishnan, H. (2000). An End-to-end Approach to Host Mobility, *Proceedings of the 6th ACM/IEEE International Conference on Mobile Computing and Networking* (pp. 155-166).

42. Snoeren, A. C., Balakrishnan, H., & Kaashoek, M. F. (2002). The Migrate Approach to Internet Mobility, *Proceedings of the Student Oxygen Workshop* (pp. 14-17).

43. Valko, A. G. (1999). Cellular IP: A New Approach to Internet Host Mobility. *SIGCOMM Computer Communication Review*, *29* (1), 50-65.

44. Yang, T., & Makrakis, D. (2001). Hierarchical Mobile MPLS: Supporting Delay Sensitive Applications Over Wireless Internet. *Proceedings of the International Conferences on Info-tech and Info-net* (vol. 2, pp. 453-458).

45. Zagari, E., Prado, R., Cardozo, E., Magalhaes, M., Badan, T., Carrilho, J., Pinto, R., Berenguel, A., Barboza, D., Moraes, D., Johnson, T., & Westberg, L. (2008). MPA: a Network-Centric Proposal for Micro-Mobility Support in IP Networks, *Proceedings of The 6th Annual Communication Networks and Services Research Conference* (pp. 609- 616).

46. Zagari, E., Prado, R., Badan, T., Cardozo, E., Magalhaes, M., Carrilho, J., Berenguel, A., Moraes, D., Dolphine, T., Johnson, T., & Westberg, L. (2009). Design and Implementation of a Network-Centric Micro-Mobility Architecture. *IEEE Wireless Communications and Networking Conference* (pp. 1-6).

30 Chapter | POSITIONING INSIDE INDOOR MOBILE SYSTEMS

1. INTRODUCTION: AN OVERVIEW

Currently, individuals traverse significantly longer distances on a daily basis than our relatively recent predecessors did during their careers. The technological revolution has exhilarated humanity and propelled us towards globalization. However, globalization encompasses more than merely enhanced transportation methods or individuals traversing greater distances. A vast quantity of information, omnipresent and readily available, encapsulates the core of this process. As a result, the channels of information dissemination are becoming overly saturated for unrestricted use; for instance, the frequency spectrum has emerged as a crucial natural resource with a cost associated with its leasing. Nonetheless, the cost of lacking the information is typically significantly greater. We are utilizing diverse wireless technologies to optimize the frequency spectrum's efficiency. These new technologies have fostered the intrinsic tendency of people to exchange information irrespective of their location. The heightened uncertainty over the user's position has resulted in an increase in the information encompassed within that position. Consequently, services leveraging the location awareness functionalities of mobile devices and/or networks, commonly known as Location Based Services (LBS or Location Services - LCS), have been developed. Examples of services utilizing mobile location include emergency call localization, mobile yellow pages, tracking and monitoring, location-sensitive charging, and targeted advertisements. As these services evolve, greater efforts are directed towards maximizing location-dependent information derived from wireless technology. The bigger the volume of available information, the more precise the position[1] estimate becomes.

Whereas in outdoor environment the satellite-based positioning techniques, such as the Global Positioning System (GPS), have considerable advantages in terms of accuracy, the problem of position determination in an indoor environment is much farther from having a unique solution. Cellular-based, Computer vision, IrDA (Infrared Data Association), ultrasound, satellite-based (Indoor GPS) and RF (Radio Frequency) systems can be used to obtain the user's position indoors. Positioning technologies, specific for indoor environment, such as computer vision, IrDA and ultrasound require deployment of additional infrastructural elements. Conversely, the efficacy of satellite- and cellular-based positioning technology is frequently inadequate for standard location-based services in indoor settings. The growth of IEEE 802.11 clients and infrastructure networks, along with the ability to integrate a wide range of location-based services into existing WLAN networks without additional equipment, renders WLAN positioning approaches pertinent and subjects of rigorous research.

2. PERFORMANCE PARAMETERS AND APPROACHES TO POSITIONING

The determination of user's location can be seen as a simple mechanism consisting in calculating the whereabouts of the user. Those whereabouts could be descriptively expressed or in terms of geographic or some other coordinates. Nonetheless, it is practically impossible to obtain the exact location of a user, in 100% of the cases, regardless of the user and its environment (Collomb, 2002). Therefore, it is only an estimate of the user's location that can be obtained and, it is very important to know how proximate the actual location and location estimate are. To achieve that, it is necessary to characterise this location estimate. On the other hand, it is also significant to describe the positioning technique itself in terms of its practicality and viability. All this is generally done through a set of performance parameters: Accuracy (Distance Error, Uncertainty, Confidence, and Distance error's Cumulative Distribution Function), Coverage and Availability, Latency, Direction and Velocity, Scalability, Complexity and Cost effectiveness.

The first group of performance parameters is used to characterise the quality of a location estimate.

Accuracy – This is undoubtedly the most important performance parameter as it illustrates the essential characteristic of a positioning technique. This parameter enables to determine whether the calculated position is close to the exact position. This parameter is composite and consists of three different values that must be taken into account:

- Distance Error,
- Uncertainty, and
- Confidence.

The Distance Error corresponds to the difference between the exact location of the user (i.e. of his/her terminal) and the calculated position, obtained through a position determination method. It is also referred to as Location Error or Quadratic Error in terms of two- dimensional positioning. Distance Error is generally expressed in units of length, such as meters.

Determining the Distance Error can be very useful in depicting the particular position determination cases. However, in order to express the positioning capabilities of a technique it is usually much more suitable to exploit the Distance Error statistics via Uncertainty and Confidence parameters.

Bearing in mind that the calculated user's location is not the exact location but is biased by the Distance Error, it can be seen that the calculated position does not enable resolving the single point at which the user is located, rather an area. Depending on the positioning techniques used, this area may have different shapes (e.g. a circle, an ellipse, an annuli, etc). For that reason, the Uncertainty value represents the distance from the "centre" of this area to the edge of the furthest boundary of this area. In other words, the Uncertainty value can be seen as the maximum potential Distance Error. The value of uncertainty is expressed with the same unit as for the Distance Error.

However, the Uncertainty value is not sufficient to describe the Accuracy of a positioning technique. The determination of the Uncertainty value goes through a statistical process and does not enable to guarantee that 100% of the calculated positions have a Distance Error lower than the Uncertainty value. That is the reason why the Uncertainty value is usually associated with a Confidence value, which expresses the degree of confidence that one can have into the position estimate. This degree of confidence is generally expressed in percentage or as a value of probability.

As a consequence, it is the combination of Uncertainty and Confidence that validly describe the accuracy of a positioning technique.

The other way of expressing the Accuracy, i.e. the performance or requirements associated to location determination, is through the Distance error's Cumulative Distribution Function (CDF). This approach is more comprehensive and inclusive due to the fact that a particular Uncertainty, Confidence pair can always be read of the graph for each and every Confidence or Uncertainty value. When assessing the technique's suitability for LBSs, expressing the Accuracy of a positioning technique through an Uncertainty, Confidence pair might be descriptive enough for a certain LBS. On the other hand, stating a positioning technique's CDF is more general and depicts the technique's accuracy for all potential LBSs.

Coverage and Availability – Accuracy is not the only parameter to be considered in order to characterise a location estimate. Coverage and Availability must be considered too. These two parameters are linked together:

- The Coverage area for a positioning method corresponds to the area in which the location service is potentially available, and
- The Availability expresses the percentage of time during which the location service is available in the coverage area and provides the required level of performance.

Latency – Location information makes sense only if it is obtained within a timeframe which remains acceptable for the provision of the LBSs. Latency represents the period of time between the position request and the provision of the location estimate and it is generally expressed in seconds.

Direction and Velocity – Although the herein presented work is restrained to the initial position determination algorithms, there are additional tracking algorithms that rely on multiple sequential position determinations in order to estimate the speed vector of the user. In such cases, two additional parameters have to be calculated: the Direction followed by the user and his/hers Velocity. These parameters are generally expressed in degrees and meters per second, respectively.

Scalability – The scalability is a desired and welcomed characteristic of a positioning system. It represents the positioning system's ability to readily respond to any augmentation. The augmentation can be in terms of Coverage area, Availability, frequency and total number of positioning requests, etc.

Complexity – There are many definitions for complexity depending on the domain of application. Nevertheless, in terms of positioning systems, complexity is most often referred to as the property that describes the difficulty of setting up the positioning system.

Cost effectiveness – This abstract characteristic of a positioning system is not entirely independent of its other performance parameters (e.g. Complexity and Scalability).

For example, the greater the Complexity of the system, the lower the Cost effectiveness. One of the ways of describing it is as a ratio between the benefits it provides (how broad range of LBSs it enables) and the costs it induces for the user.

As can be seen from the aforementioned, the latter three parameters don't have standardized units and are usually of descriptive nature.

The approaches and metrics used in order to obtain the user's position are also worth discussing. There are a few fundamental methods of acquiring the user's location:

1. Based on the identification of "base station" to which the user is associated (Cell-ID or Cell of Origin – COO) – This simple approach assumes that the estimated location of a user is equal to the location of a "base station" to which the user is associated. In other words, the user is estimated to be in a location of the "nearest" node of the network. This method is used both in indoor and outdoor environments (GSM, UMTS). Its popularity, despite inferior performances, is due to the simplicity of implementation. Obviously, the accuracy is proportional to the density of the network nods.

2. Based on the time of signal arrival (Time of Arrival – TOA) – Being that the waves (electromagnetic, light and sound) are propagating through the free space at constant speed, it is possible to asses the distance between the transmitter and a receiver based on the time that the wave propagates in-between those two points. This approach assumes that the receiver is informed of the exact time of signal's departure. Being that this is not always easily accomplished, the alternative approach takes into account the time needed for signal to propagate in both directions (Round Trip Time – RTT). This way, one station is transmitting the predefined sequence. The other station, upon receiving the sequence, after a strictly defined time interval (used for allowing the stations of different processing power to process the received information), resends the sequence. The station that initially sent the sequence can now, by subtracting the known interval of time that the signal was delayed at second station from the measured time interval, asses the time that signal propagated to the other station and back and, consequently, the distance between the stations. This approach is less dificoult to implement than TOA, since it does not require the stations to be synchronised.
3. The distance between the stations can be measured based on the differences in times of signal arrival (Time Difference of Arrival – TDOA) – With this approach, the problem of precisely synchronised time in transmitter and receiver is resolved by using several receivers that are synchronised whereas the transceiver, whose location is being determined, does not have to be synchronised with the receivers. Upon receipt of the transmitted signal, a network node computes the differences in times of the signal's arrival at different receivers. Based on that calculation, the user's location is determined as a cross section of two or more hyperboles. Owing to that, these techniques are often referred to as hyperbolic techniques.
4. Based on the signal's angle of arrival (Angle of Arrival – AOA or Direction of Arrival – DOA) – The idea, with this approach, is to have directional antennas which can detect the angle of arrival of the signal with the maximal strength or coherent phase. This procedure grants the spatial angle to a point where the signal originated (and whose location is determined). Vice versa, the mobile terminal can determine the angle of arrival of the signal from the known reference transmitters. Being that this approach is often implemented through the use of antenna arrays, the latter approach can have significant impact on the mobile terminal and is, therefore, less commonly exercised.

5. Based on the received signal strength (Received Signal Strength Indication – RSSI) – The free space signal propagation is characterised with predictable attenuation dependent on the distance from the source. Moreover, in real conditions, the attenuation also largely depends on the obstacles and the configuration of the propagation path. That is why there are various mathematical models which describe the wave propagation for diverse surroundings and, ultimately, estimate the signal attenuation for the observed environment. This approach grants the distance of the entity whose position is being determined, to one or more transmitters.
6. Based on the fingerprint of the location (Database Correlation or Location Fingerprinting) – With this approach, the certain, location dependant, information is acquired in as many Reference Points (RPs) across the coverage area of the technique. This data is stored into so called Location Fingerprints Database. Afterwards, when the actual position determination process takes place, the information gathered at the unknown location is compared with the pre-stored data and the entity's position is estimated at a location of a pre-stored fingerprint from the database whose data are "closest" to the measured data.

Most often, the estimated position with TOA and RSSI approaches is determined by lateration. The process of lateration consists of determining the position of the entity when the distance between the entity and one or more points with identified positions (i.e. refernce points) is known. To uniquely laterate the position in N-dimensional space, the distances to N+1 reference points ought to be known. With TDOA approach, the estimated position is obtained as a cross-section of two or more hyperbolas in two-dimensional space, or three or more hyperbolic surfaces in case of three-dimensional space. The process of angulation is employed with AOA and DOA approaches. This process estimates the location of a user as a cross-section of at least two rays (half-lines) originating at known locations. The lateration and angulation processes are depicted in Fig. 1. As for the Location Fingerprinting approach, the estimated location is obtained by utilizing the correlation algorithm of some sort. This algorithm determines, following a certain metric, the "closeness" of the gathered data to the pre-stored samples from the location fingerprinting database.

Apart from these, basic, approaches, there are a number of other choices and hybrid techniques that combine the aforementioned approaches when determining the estimated position of the user.

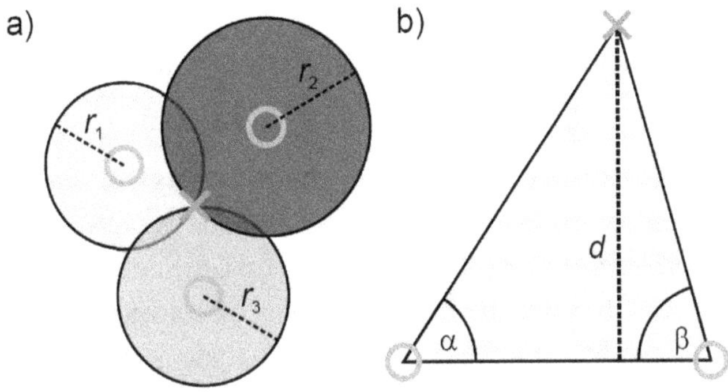

Fig. 1. The processes of estimating a user location: a) Lateration and b) Angulation (Green circles represent the known positions and the red cross stands for the estimated location)

3. CLASSIFICATIONS OF POSITIONING SYSTEMS

There are more than a few classifications of positioning systems. While some of them are very strict, others can be very arbitrary and overlapping. Without the need to judge or justify any of them, the most common ones are given herein.

Regarding the type of provided information, positioning techniques can be split into two main categories: Absolute and Relative positioning.

Absolute positioning methods consist in determining user location from scratch, generally by using a receiver and a terrestrial or satellite infrastructure. A well-known example of systems based on "absolute positioning" is the American GPS.

Relative positioning methods consist in determining user location by calculating the movements made from an initial position which is known. These methods do not rely on an external infrastructure, but require additional sensors (e.g. accelerometers, gyroscopes, odometers, etc). Inertial Navigation Systems used in commercial and military aircrafts are a good example of systems based on relative positioning.

LBSs currently offered by wireless telecommunication operators or by service providers are all based on absolute positioning methods and not on relative positioning methods, since these services are offered to users whose initial position is generally not known.

Within the "absolute positioning" family, the measurements and processing required for determining user's location can be performed in many different ways and rely on different means. Thus, many different absolute positioning methods can be used for determining user's location. These methods can be clustered into different groups, depending on the infrastructure used. Hence, the positioning techniques can be divided into:

- Satellite-based,
- PLMN-based (Public Land Mobile Network based), and
- Other (such as: WLAN, Bluetooth, RFID, UWB, etc).

The first group, which is known by the largest audience, is the "Satellite positioning" group. This group relates to the positioning methods which are based on the use of orbiting satellites, such as the GPS, Glonass or Galileo. Many applications and services based on satellite positioning have been developed during the past years (e.g. in-vehicle navigation, fleet management, tracking and tracing applications, etc). They generally require the use of dedicated receivers. Today, more and more devices such as PDAs or mobile phones include a satellite positioning capability, and this trend should persist in the future.

The second group, the "PLMN positioning" group, corresponds to the location techniques which have been developed for public land mobile networks. Initially deployed in the US under the pressure of the FCC mandate which forces US carriers to locate users placing calls to the 911 emergency number, location technologies are now being implemented in most of European wireless telecommunication networks for commercial purposes. Most of cellular positioning methods are incorporated in mobile telecommunication standards (2G/2.5G/3G/3.5G), but some solutions remain based on proprietary techniques.

The third and last group, the "Other positioning" group, corresponds to those technologies which have not been developed specifically for positioning purposes, but that can be used, in addition to their primary function, for determining user's location. These technologies encompass WLAN and Bluetooth for instance.

Another distinction can be made, depending on the "place" where the position calculation is made. In some cases, the main processing is performed at the terminal level. In other cases, the main processing is performed in the network. Therefore, the positioning techniques can be classified into:

- Network-based (also referred to as mobile-assisted), and
- Terminal- or Mobile-based (also referred to as network-assisted).

Satellite technologies, as a rule, fit in the Terminal-based positioning techniques. As for the positioning techniques from the PLMN and other groups, they can not be apriori associated to either of the Terminal- or Network-based groups.

Finally, the positioning techniques can be classified according to the environment of their coverage. Hence, the positioning techniques can be divided into:

- Outdoor, and
- Indoor.

Although there are intense research efforts to adopt the Satellite-based positioning techniques for Indoor environment, thay are still considered to fit into Outdoor groop. PLMN-based positioning can be implemented in both Indoor and Outdoor envornments, whereas techniques from "Other" group usually fit Indoor environments.

Positioning techniques designed for a particular Indoor environment in most cases fit into Relative positioning group.

Bearing in mind the ongoing convergence process of telecommunication systems and numerous, newly developed, hybrid positioning techniques, the indoor/ outdoor categorization as well as other aforementioned classifications ought to be regarded more as guidelines than as strict lines that divide techniques into disjoint sets.

4. NON-RADIO INDOOR POSITIONING SYSTEMS

This section contains a brief overview of the non-radio positioning systems most commonly used in indoor environment.

4.1 IrDA Positioning Systems

IrDA technologies are based on devices with infrared light transceivers. This light occupies the part of spectrum between the visible light and the radio-waves. Upon encountering an obstacle, such as wall, the major part of the IR light's energy is being absorbed. Therefore, in order to communicate properly, two IR devices must have unobstructed Line of Sight (LoS) path between them. This poses a limitation for employing this technology in positioning purposes.

The most popular application of this technology for positioning use is the "Active Badge" technique (Want et al., 1992). The person or entity, whose position is being determined, possesses a device, badge alike, which periodically emits its ID code via IR transmitter. The IR sensors must be deployed in the coverage area (building). The position of the user is then determined based on the Cell-ID principle. With respect to the attributes of the IR light, the sensors must be deployed in every room in which the positioning feature is needed. Consequently, the accuracy of this technique is on a room level.

Other techniques based on this technology offer various accuracy and applications. The systems with greater number of IR receivers and transmitters on each device are proposed (Krohn et al., 2005). These systems are able to accurately estimate the position of a mobile communication device (e.g. PDA, laptop, digital camera, etc.) in order to allow them to automatically synchronise or perform other location dependent tasks. These activities are supposed to be performed on a flat, table alike surface. The obtained distance error is less than 20cm in more than

90% of the cases. On the other hand, there are systems that augment the "Active Badge" technique by using more IR sensors, micro VGA display and, optionally, video cameras. These systems provide so called Argumented Reality (Maeda et al., 2003). The typical application of an Argumented Reality system would be for the museum environment, where the visitor would be, via micro display (in eyeglasses, for example), fed with the information related to the exhibit he is currently experiencing.

4.2 Ultrasound Positioning Systems

The term ultrasound is related to the high frequency sound waves, above the part of spectrum perceivable to the human ear (20kHz). Although the ultrasound is most frequently used in medicine, there are other areas of application such as: biomedicine, industry (e.g. flow-meters), chemistry, military applications (sonic weapon), etc. As for the positioning purposes, the greatest benefit of using the ultrasound positioning is the product of a fact that ultrasound propagates through the air at limited speed, which is by far smaller than the speed of light. Therefore, the implementation of techniques based on time of flight (i.e. TOA, TDOA) of signal is very much facilitated. Moreover, the mechanic nature of sound waves grants ultrasound positioning techniques immunity to electromagnetic interference which could also be considered as an advantage. It ought to be pointed out that ultrasound waves do not penetrate, but rather reflect of walls. Therefore, the ultrasound receiver, in order to detect the signal, must be in the same room as transmitter but LoS is not necessary.

Ultrasound positioning systems can be classified according to the number of ultrasound "base stations" (transmitters and/or receivers) in each room (Dijk, 2004). The basic ultrasound positioning technique comprises one receiver in each room, and a ultrasound emitting tag which is worn by the entity that needs to be positioned. In this case, the accuracy is on the level of the room. These systems are commercially available for some time now.

More sophisticated ultrasound positioning systems invoke the use of a greater number of transmitters in each room as well as the use of RF (seldom IR) signals for precise determining the time delay (Fraser, 2006). In this case, the controlling unit, which is connected to all the ultrasound emitters in one room as well as with RF transmitter, determines the exact time when each of the transmitters is about to send its chirps. Commonly, the RF signal is emitted first and then the chirps from all ultrasound transmitters are emitted separated by known time intervals. The receiver, knowing the separating time intervals and the propagation speed of RF and ultrasound waves, can now calculate, based on the time it received each of the chirps, the distance to each of the ultrasound emitters. The position is then determined by lateration. Consequently, for three- dimensional positioning at least four transmitters per room are required. The accuracy is in range of 10cm in 90% of the cases.

Furthermore, the system that eliminates the need for RF transmitter has been developed (McCarthy & Muller, 2003). With this system, the processing power of the receiver can be reduced, and the whole system is less complex. The transmitters are cyclically emitting chirps in constant time intervals whereas the receiver is employing an extended Kalman filter for resolving the chirp transmission and receipt times.

5. INDOOR RADIO POSITIONING SYSTEMS

The RF positioning techniques employ different parts of the frequency spectrum. Some are implemented on existent short-range radio interfaces and serve as added services, while others are especially developed for positioning. The most common RF technologies which, through the use of these techniques, enable positioning are: RFID, UWB, Bluetooth and WLAN.

5.1 RFID (Radio-Frequency IDentification) Positioning Systems

The beginnings of this technology go far back to the time of the Second World War Over the recent years, due to the cheaper RFID components, the expansion of this technology is occurring.

RFID system consists of tags, reader with antenna and accompanying software. The tags are usually placed on entities whose position needs to be determined. The Line of Sight between the tag and a reader is usually not necessary. The tags can contain additional information apart from its ID code which broadens the usage this technology.

There are three types of RFID tags:

- Passive tags do not have their own power supply. In order to operate, they use the energy, induced on their antenna, from the incoming radio wave from the reader. Using that energy, the passive tag replays by emitting its ID code and, optionally, additional information. Passive tags have very limited range (from a few cm up to a couple of meters). Their advantage is within the scope of cheap construction, compact size and cheap production.
- Active tags are encompassed with power supply witch enables them unrestrictive signal emission. This kind of tags is more reliable and immune to highly polluted RF environments. Their range can go up to a few hundreds of meters.
- Semi-active tags are equipped with battery power supply. Recent constructions enable a battery life span of more than 10 years.

RFID devices can operate in different frequency bands: 100 – 500 kHz, 10 - 15 MHz, 850 – 900 MHz, and 2.4 – 5.8 GHz (Don Chon et al., 2004).

RFID positioning techniques are based on knowing the position of the reader. When the tagged object enters the range of the reader, its position is assumed to be equal to the position of the reader (similar to Cell-ID). Correspondingly, it is possible to deploy tags across the coverage area. In that case the reader is mounted on the entity whose position is being determined. The accuracy depends on the density of deployed objects (tags/readers) across the coverage area. With active tags, the positioning accuracy can be upgraded with the RSSI information.

Most common application areas of RFID technology are in replacing the barcode readers, product tracking and management, personal documents identification, identification implants for humans and animals, etc. It is interesting to mention that the latter aforementioned application raises numerous ethical issues and there are organized groups worldwide opposing the implementation of this technology.

5.2 Bluetooth Positioning Systems

Bluetooth is a short-range, low-consumption radio interface for data and voice communication (Muller, 2001). Initially conceived in the mid 90s by the Ericsson Mobile Communication as a technology that ought to replace the cable in personal communications, Bluetooth shortly gained significant popularity. Ericsson was joined by IBM, Microsoft, Nokia and Toshiba. They formed Bluetooth Special Interest Group (SIG) with an aim to standardize Bluetooth specifications. Independent group, called Local Positioning Working Group, had a goal of developing the Bluetooth profile which would define the position calculation algorithm as well as the type and format of the messages that would enable Bluetooth devices to exchange position information.

The basic Bluetooth specification does not support positioning services per se (Bluetooth Special Interest Group Specification Volume 1 and 2, 2001). In absence of such support, various research efforts have produced diverse solutions. Bahl and Padmanabhan used the RSSI information for in-building locating and tracking (Bahl & Padmanabhan, 2000). Patil introduced the concept of reference tags and readers (Patil, 2002). He also investigated separately cases when Bluetooth supports and does not give support to RSSI parameter. On the other hand, the research by Hallberg, Nilsson and Synnes goes to saying that RSSI parameter is unreliable for positioning purposes and that its employment ought to be avoided with Bluetooth positioning systems (Thapa & Case, 2003).

In addition, there are ideas of exploiting other parameters than RSSI for positioning purposes. Link Quality and Bit Error Rate (BER) are most commonly referred in this context. However, it should be stated that these solutions are still under development, and that Link Quality is not uniquely defined and is therefore dependent on the equipment manufacturer. Also, BER parameter is not defined in the basic Bluetooth specifications and must be extrapolated from the message received as a response to echo command supported at L2CAP layer. All in all, these parameters undoubtedly contain location dependent information, but the extraction of that information is still subject to research.

The accuracy of Bluetooth positioning systems is decreasing with the increase in the maximal range of the system (Hallberget al., 2003). That is, with the range increase, the positioning system uncertainty is increased as well, therefore the accuracy is worsened. The improvement of accuracy can be achieved through communicating with more than one Bluetooth nodes and possibly utilizing some of the aforementioned parameters (RSSI, Link Quality, BER). Finally, the major application of Bluetooth technology is expected in ad-hoc networks and the positioning techniques and LBS should be conceived and designed accordingly.

5.3 UWB (Ultra-WideBand) Positioning Systems

Ultra-wideband is a short-range high data throughput technology. The ultra-wideband signal is defined (Harmer, 2004) as a radio-signal that occupies at least either 500MHz of frequency spectrum or 20% of the central frequency of the band. There are many ways in which the UWB signal can be generated. Two, most important from the positioning point of view, are:

1. Impulse UWB – By generating very short impulses, with sub nanosecond duration, that are mutually separated several tenths of nanoseconds. Clearly, this signal inherently possesses very wide band.
2. Frequency Hopped UWB – By generating the typical DSSS (Direct-Sequence Spread Spectrum) with the signal spectrum ranging from 10 to 20MHz which is then hopped around 1GHz frequency, applying between 10 and 100 thousands of hops per second. Unlike conventional radio-signals, the impulse UWB signals are practically immune to multipath propagation problems. With conventional signals, the reflected component of the signal is, in its large part, overlapped with the component that is travelling the direct path. Hence, the direct and reflected component interfere at the receiver causing fading. Contrary to that, with impulse UWB technology, due to the very short pulse duration, the reflected component is most often arriving at the receiver after the direct component has been completely received. With respect to this feature, the UWB positioning techniques utilising high resolution TOA approach come as the logical choice. Typically, the position accuracy of 1m in more than 95% of the cases is achievable.

Employing the mobile nods of the UWB network for accuracy improvement is also under research. Computer simulation (Eltaher & Kaiser, 2005) shows that the positioning error could be further reduced by employing a larger number of antennas with the beamforming capabilities.

Bearing in mind the amount of research in this area, the wider scale commercialisation of indoor UWB positioning systems can be expected in proximate future.

5.4 WLAN Positioning Systems

Positioning techniques in WLAN networks are growing in popularity. The reason for this can be looked in-between the widespread of 802.11 networks and the fact that a broad scope of LBSs can be brought into an existing network without the need for any additional infrastructure. There are a number of approaches to the positioning problem in WLAN networks. Unquestionably, the most popular ones are based on the Received Signal Strength Information (RSSI). Nevertheless, there are other approaches that depend on timing measurements or require additional hardware but offer superior accuracy and/or faster implementation in return (Llombart et al., 2008; King et al., 2006; Sayrafian-Pour & Kaspar, 2005).

Positioning with the use of RSSI parameter can be, in its essence, regarded as the path loss estimation problem. The nature of the path loss prediction in an indoor environment is extremely complex and dependent on a wide variety of assumptions (e.g. type of the building, construction, materials, doors, windows, etc.)(Nešković et al, 2000). Even if these basic parameters are known, precise estimation of the path loss remains a fairly complex task.

Depending on the side on which the position calculation process takes place, positioning in WLAN networks with the use of RSSI parameter can be either network-based or client- based. Whereas the client-based solutions gather the RSSI vector from the radio-visible APs, the network-based solutions have a central positioning engine which collects the client's signal strength vector from the APs and produces the position estimate. The network-based solutions do not require clients to have a specific software installed which is of great essence for security purposes. Moreover, the client does not need to be associated with the network the positioning can be done solely based on the probe requests the client sends (in case of active scanning). Network-based solutions could also have an important advantage over the client-based ones when used in WLAN networks employing the Automatic Radio Management (ARM). This centralized mechanism is used to obtain the optimal radio coverage by changing the channel assignment and adjusting the output power and/or radiation pattern of the APs. Contrary to the client-based solutions, the network-based positioning engine could take into account the changes made by ARM mechanism while the ARM mechanism would present a setback for the client-based solutions. On the other hand, client's Network Interface Cards do not have to be consistent regarding the radiated power which may, depending on the positioning algorithm used, present an analogue problem for network-based solutions. In this work, for explanatory purposes, usually the client-based solution will be presented. However, the reader should keep an open mind towards the analogue network-based option.

Regarding the approach used to determine the user's position, WLAN positioning techniques can be categorised as: propagation model based, fingerprinting based or hybrid. Propagation model based techniques rely on statistically derived mathematical expressions that relate the distance of an AP with the client's received signal strength. The estimated position of the user is then obtained by lateration. Therefore, if there are less than three radio-visible APs (for two-dimensional positioning) the estimated user's position is ambiguous. Also, the model derived for one specific indoor environment is usually not applicable to other indoor environments.

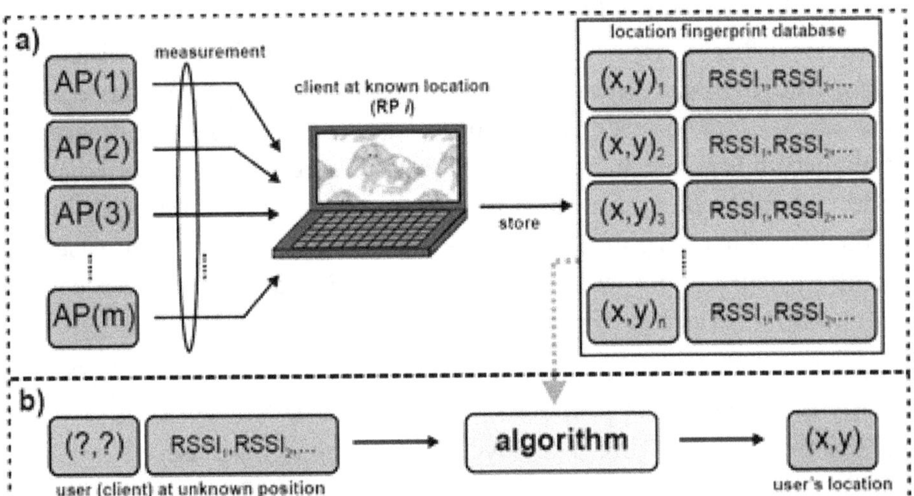

Fig. 2. Two phases of positioning: a) training phase – mobile client is recording RSSI vectors across RPs and stores them in fingerprint database, and b) positioning phase – based on the measured RSSI vector and database access, the algorithm estimates the user's location

Fingerprinting techniques are most commonly used for WLAN positioning. They are conducted in two phases: the off-line or training phase, and the on-line or positioning phase. The off-line phase comprises collecting the RSSI vectors from various APs and storing them, along with the position of the measurement, into a fingerprinting database. In the on-line phase, the estimate of the user's position is determined by "comparing the likeliness" of the RSSI vector measured during the on-line phase with the previously stored vectors in the database. The fingerprinting process is shown in Fig. 2. These techniques have yielded better performance than other positioning techniques, but are believed to have a longer set-up time.

Hybrid techniques combine features from both propagation modelling and fingerprinting approaches, opting for better performances than propagation model techniques and shorter set-up time than fingerprinting techniques (Wang & Jia, 2007).

The prospects of using RSSI parameter for indoor positioning were first systematically analysed in "RADAR" (Bahl & Padmanabhan, 2000). According to this research, it is better to use RSSI than SNR (Signal to Noise Ratio) for positioning purposes since the RSSI parameter is much more dependent on the client's position than SNR. Two algorithms to establish the user's location were proposed. The first one is the Nearest Neighbour (NN) algorithm which compares the RSSI vector of a mobile client against the RSSI vectors previously stored in the fingerprinting base. An extension to the proposed algorithm was also considered: the estimated location is not identified as only one RP whose RSSI vector is closest to the observed RSSI vector, but calculated as a "middle" point of k closest RPs (kNN algorithm). This analysis has shown that algorithm performance improved for k = 2 and k = 3. For larger k, the performance had started to decrease. The second algorithm is based on a simple propagation model with Rician distribution assumed. It ought to be emphasized that both approaches require a minimum of three radio visible access points (APs). The measuring campaign comprised 70 RPs. At each RP measurements were made for four orientations of the receiver, and each measurement was averaged from 20 samples.

To produce the maximum amount of information from the received RSSI vectors, the Bayesian approach was proposed (Li et al., 2006). This concept yields better results than the NN algorithm. The Bayes rule can be written as:

$$p\left(l_t \mid o_t\right) = p\left(o_t \mid l_t\right) p\left(l_t\right) N \quad (1)$$

where lt is location at time t, ot is the observed RSSI vector at time t, while N is a normalizing factor that enables the sum of all probabilities to be equal to 1. In other words, at a given time t, the probability that a client is at location lt, if the received RSSI vector is ot, is equal to the product of the probability to observe RSSI vector ot at location lt and the probability that the client can be found at location lt. The process of estimating client's location is based on calculating the conditional probability p (lt |ot) for each RP. The estimated client's location is equal to the RP with the greatest conditional probability. To accomplish this task, two terms on the right hand side of Eq. (1) ought to be calculated. The first term, also referred to as the likelihood function, can be calculated based on the RSSI map (for all RP) using any approach that will yield probability density function of observation ot for all RPs. As for the a priori probability p (lt) , it ought to be calculated according to the client's habits. However, for most cases the assumption of uniform distribution across all RPs is valid. The measurements were made at 70 RPs. As with the previously discussed techniques, the measurements were made for four orientations of a receiver, and each measurement was averaged from 20 samples.

Another project, named Horus (Youssef & Agrawala, 2005; Eckert, 2005), had the goal of providing high positioning accuracy with low computational demands. This is also a probabilistic approach in which time series of the received signal strength are modelled using Gaussian distributions. Due to the time dependence of the signal strength from an observed AP, the authors of this project have shown that the time autocorrelation between the time adjacent samples of signal strength can be as high as 0.9. To describe and benefit from such behaviour, they have suggested the following autoregressive model:

$$s_t = \alpha s_{t-1} + (1-\alpha)\upsilon_t, \quad 0 \le \alpha \le 1 \tag{2}$$

where υt is the noise process and st is a stationary array of samples from the observed AP.

Throughout the off-line phase, the value of parameter a is assessed at each RP and stored into the database along with Gaussian distribution parameters m and s . In the on-line phase, Gaussian distribution is modified according to the corresponding values of a retrieved from the fingerprinting database. Alike to the kNN algorithm, the Horus system estimates the client's location as a weight centre of k RPs with the highest probabilities. The principal difference to the kNN algorithm is that, in case of Horus system, the k most likely RP are multiplied with their corresponding probabilities. For verification purposes, the authors made measurements at 612 RPs, and each measurement was averaged from 110 samples.

More relevant information about the statistical modelling approach towards location estimation can be found in (Roos et al., 2002) and in the references found therein.

Battiti et al. (2002) were the first to consider using Artificial Neural Networks (ANNs) for positioning in WLAN networks. This approach does not insist upon a detailed knowledge of the indoor structure, propagation characteristics, or the position of APs. A multilayer feedforward network with two layers and one-step secant training function was used. The number of units in the hidden layer was varied. No degradation in performance was observed when the number of units grew above the optimal number. For verification purposes, measurements were made at 56 RPs, and each measurement was averaged from 100 samples.

In most studies, WLAN positioning techniques are compared on the subject of their accuracy while other attributes of a positioning technique such as latency, scalability, and complexity are neglected. Another aspect that is seldom analyzed is size of the environment in which the technique is implemented.

It also ought to be pointed out that averaging the RSSI vectors in the on-line phase has an immense impact on the technique's latency, so the scope of location based services that could be utilized with such techniques is significantly narrowed. Moreover, bearing in mind that all presented approaches require at least three radio-visible APs in each RP (which is seldom the case in most WLAN installations), feasibility of sound frequency planning is uncertain. Consequently, the degradation of packet data services is inevitable with respect to positioning in larger indoor areas (i.e. large number of APs is required). Enabling the radio-visibility of three APs across the indoor environment is usually constructively irrational and economically unjustified. Hence, the presented techniques cannot be applied to the majority of existing WLAN networks optimized for packet data services.

Finally, there are other studies that accompany the research for sophisticated positioning in WLAN networks. Other relevant research efforts comprise the impact of Network Interface Card on the RSSI parameter, compensation of small-scale variations of RSSI, clustering of locations to reduce the computational cost of positioning, use of spatial and frequency diversity, methods for generating a larger location fingerprinting database by interpolation, and unequal fusing of RSSI from different APs (Kaemarungsi, 2006; Youssef & Agrawala, 2003; Ramachandran & Jagannathan, 2007; Li et al., 2005; Zhang et al.,2008).

6. CASCADE-CONNECTED ANN STRUCTURES FOR WLAN POSITIONING

The ANNs are an optimisation technique known to yield good results with noise polluted processes (Hasoun, 1995). They are generally classified as a fingerprinting technique. In the off-line phase, the set of collected RSSI fingerprints is used to train the network and set its inner coefficients to perform the positioning function. In the on-line phase, the trained network replaces trilateration and position determination processes.

Two basic concepts, a single ANN and a set of cascade-connected ANNs structures with space partitioning, have been presented herein. These models were implemented in Matlab and verified on a 147m x 67m test bed with eight APs. For training purposes, the traingda – gradient descent training function with adaptive learning rate was selected. All neural units had the hyperbolic tangent sigmoid transfer function. Being that the input probability distribution function of RSSI values is near Gaussian, the Mean Square Error (MSE) was selected as a criterion function (Hanson, 1988).

Regarding the purpose that ANN is intended for and, moreover, the nature of the problem, it has been concluded that multilayer feedforward neural networks with error backpropagation have substantial advantages in comparison to other structures (Nešković, 2000). The outer interfaces of the ANN must match the number of the APs on the input side (i.e. eight inputs), and the number of coordinates as outputs (i.e. two outputs).

Multilayer feedforward networks can have one or more hidden layers with perceptron units. The hidden layers with corresponding perceptron units form the inner structure of the ANN. There is no exact analytical method for determining the optimal inner structure of the network. However, there are algorithms that, starting with an intentionally oversized network, reduce the number of units and converge to the optimal network structure. Also, there are other algorithms such as the cascade correlation learning architecture (Fahlman & Lebiere, 1990) that build the network towards the optimal structure during the training process. However, being aware of the fact that these procedures can be complex and that determining the most optimal structure was not the central scope of this research, we intentionally slightly oversized our network's inner structure knowing that an oversized network will not yield degradation in performance. We also adopted that the first hidden layer ought to have more perceptrons than the input layer so that the input information is quantified and fragmented into smaller pieces (Shang & Wah, 1996). The number of perceptrons in the following hidden layers ought to decrease, converging to the number of perceptrons in the output layer. Bearing that in mind, the chosen structure for single ANN (type 1) approach consisted of the input layer, three hidden layers and the output layer. The number of perceptrons per layer was (from input to output) 8-15-9-5-2.

When utilizing space partitioning, the positioning process is split into two stages where each stage could be implemented with the most suitable model. In this case, the two-step space partitioning is implemented utilizing cascade-connected ANNs. The block scheme of this system is shown in Fig. 2.

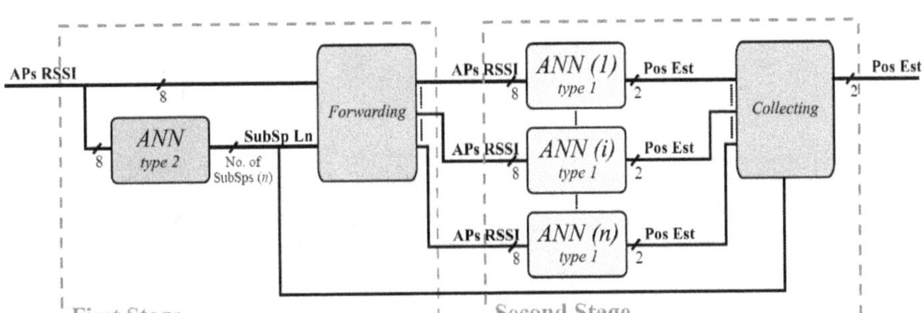

Fig. 2. Cascade-connected ANNs system structure (the input is the observed RSSI signal vector, APs RSSI, and the position estimate vector, Pos Est, is the output)

In the first stage, an ANN (type 2) is used to determine the likeliness of a measured RSSI vector belonging to one of the subspaces. This ANN (type 2) has 8 inputs and the number of outputs is equal to the number of subspaces the environment is partitioned to. Each output corresponds to the likeliness that a received RSSI vector originates from a particular subspace. The outputs of the type 2 ANN, SubSp Ln, are connected to the Forwarding block which, depending on the inputs, employs only one of the second stage networks by forwarding the APs RSSI vector.

The inner structure of ANN (type 2) is designed using the same guidelines as with the single ANN model. Therefore, it also has three hidden layers and the number of perceptron units in those layers is varied to fit the different number of subspaces. The second stage ANNs are type 1 networks with structure identical to the previously described ANN used with the single ANN approach.

In the off-line phase, type 2 ANN is trained with the fingerprinting database that originates from the whole environment. The targeted output vector has only one non-zero element (equal to 1). The index of that element corresponds to the number of the subspace from which the RSSI vector originates. Type 1 networks are trained following the training methodology from the single ANN approach with the only difference being that each type 1 ANN is trained with only the part of the fingerprinting database which originates from a particular subspace.

In the on-line phase, the first stage ANN estimates the likeliness that the received RSSI vector originates from a particular subspace. The Forwarding block then determines the most likely subspace by searching for the maximum value in the output vector from the ANN (type 2) and forwards the APs RSSI vector only to the second stage ANN that correspond to that subspace. The appropriate second stage ANN then determines the estimated position of the user and, finally, the collecting block forwards that estimate to the structure output.

Several space separation patterns were chosen yielding a different number of subspaces ranging from 4 to 44. The space partitioning patterns that have been employed are shown in Fig. 3.

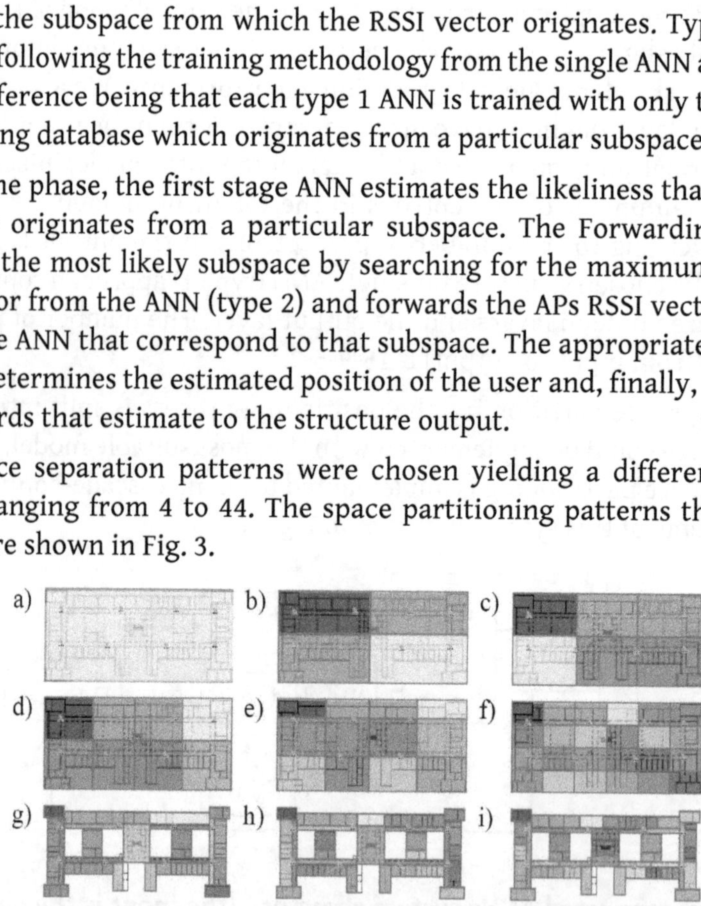

Fig. 3. Space partitioning patterns: a) no space partitioning (1x1), b) 2x2, c) 2x3, d) 2x4, e) 3x4, f) 4x6, g) x24, h) x32, and i) x44

The partitions with a smaller number of subspaces were made on geometrical bases. However, with the increase in the number of subspaces, the subspace size decreased until it came to a room size level. It was then worth to consider partitioning space in an other manner. Starting with 24 subspaces (which was also portioned on geometrical bases), the partitions were made on "logical" bases (i.e. x24, x32 and x44). This logical separation opted for subspaces to be as homogeneous in the propagation manner as possible (e.g. partitioning was made trough walls wherever possible). Note, the single ANN model is herein referred to as 1x1 partitioning.

For the purpose of determining the optimal training parameters, as well as the optimal training duration, the complete set of measurements was split into two subsets. The larger subset was used to train the ANNs, while the smaller, containing measurements from a 100 randomly chosen RPs, was used to validate the obtained models.

The results obtained for different space partition patterns, for optimally trained ANNs, are presented in Table 1.

From Table 1, it can be seen that, with geometrical partitioning, the overall median and average distance errors decrease with the increase in number of subspaces. This behaviour is even more emphasized with the distance errors in the correctly chosen subspace which confirms the influence of environment size on positioning accuracy. When concerning the logical partitioning, slightly better results are obtained for 24 subspaces (4x6 vs. x24) but, with the further increase in the number of subspaces, the average distance error is starting to rise again. Also, with the increase in the number of subspaces the probability of correct subspace being chosen declines as expected while the probability of correct room estimation rises from 26% for a 1x1 positioning to as much as 66% for a x24 configuration, after which it starts declining a little.

Table 1. Performance overview for different partitioning patterns

Pattern	1x1	2x2	2x3	2x4	3x4	4x6	x24	x32	x44
Overall Average DEa [m]	9.26	9.00	8.97	8.91	8.54	8.28	8.14	8.58	9.11
Overall Median DEa [m]	7.75	7.49	6.87	5.86	5.59	5.10	4.57	4.70	4.44
Average DEa in ISb [m]	-	21.3	22.7	21.2	19.0	18.0	18.4	19.5	19.2
Median DEa in ISb [m]	-	15.4	17.4	15.3	16.3	14.7	17.5	15.8	16.1
Average DEa in CSc [m]	9.26	8.35	6.99	6.96	5.76	4.20	4.07	3.78	3.72
Median DEa in CSc [m]	7.75	7.33	6.13	5.52	4.40	3.87	3.56	3.39	3.32
Probability of CSEd	1.00	0.95	0.87	0.86	0.79	0.71	0.72	0.69	0.65
Probability of CREe	0.26	0.42	0.48	0.52	0.58	0.62	0.66	0.62	0.61

a Distance Error, b Incorrect Subspace, c Correct Subspace , d Correct Subspace Estimation, e Correct Room Estimation

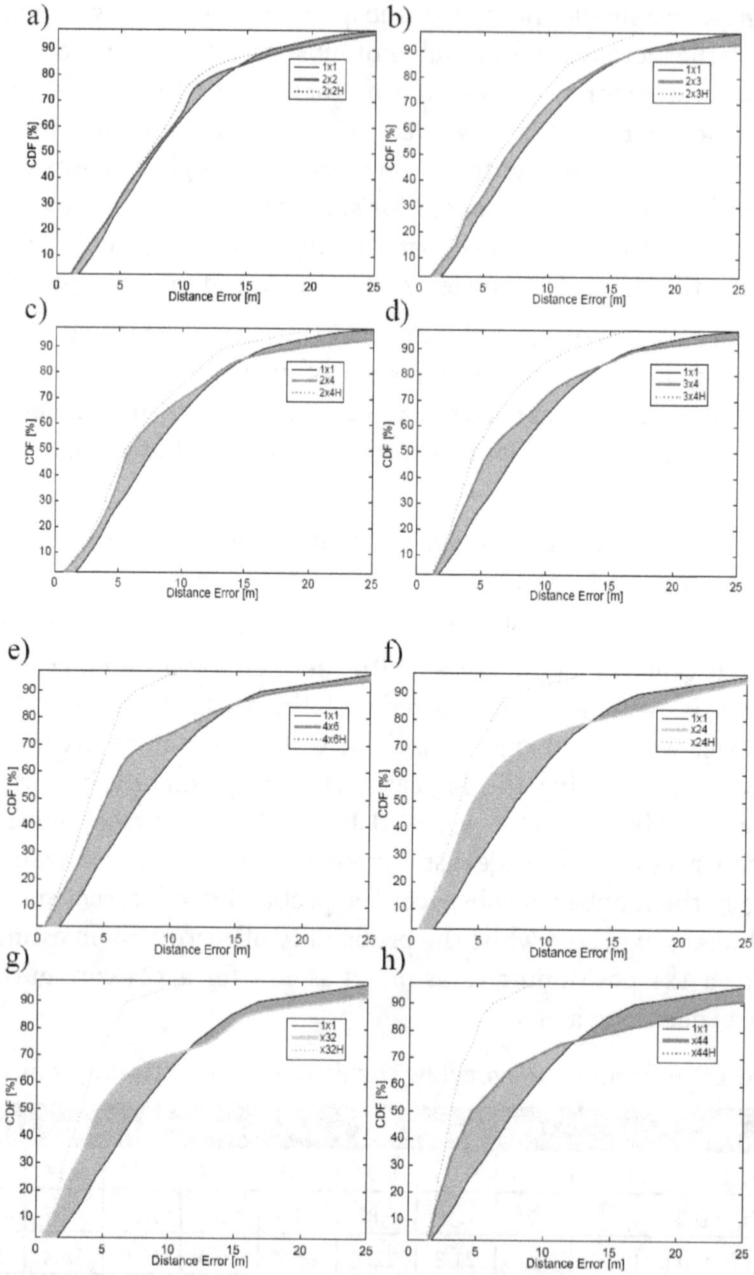

Fig. 4. Cumulative Distribution Function of distance error: a) 1x1and 2x2 partitioning and correct subspace estimation – 2x2 H; b) 1x1and 2x3 partitioning and correct subspace estimation – 2x3 H; c) 1x1and 2x4 partitioning and correct subspace estimation – 2x4 H; d) 1x1and 3x4 partitioning and correct subspace estimation – 3x4 H; e) 1x1and 4x6 partitioning and correct subspace estimation – 4x6 H; f) 1x1and x24 partitioning and correct subspace estimation – x24 H; g) 1x1and x32 partitioning and correct subspace estimation – x32 H; h) 1x1and x44 partitioning and correct subspace estimation – x44 H

To better understand and discuss the performances of cascade-connected ANNs with space partitioning, we observed and compared the distance error's Cumulative Distribution Function (CDF) of a single ANN approach with the cascade-connected ANNs. Fig. 4. shows the obtained CDFs for representative space partitioning patterns.

The green shaded regions in Fig. 4 can be regarded as a partitioning gain relative to 1x1 positioning, whereas the red shaded regions may be viewed as a partitioning loss. It is evident that, through geometrical partitioning, as illustrated in Fig. 4. a) – e), the gain regions expand with the augmentation of subspaces. In relation to logical space partitioning, as illustrated in Fig. 4 f) – h), it is evident that optimal performance is achieved with the x24 pattern, yielding an average distance error of 8.14m and a median error of 4.57m. As the number of subspaces continues to rise, the advantage of reducing the median error has diminished, despite the ongoing decrease in median error within the correct subspace. Conversely, the average distance error is beginning to increase again due to the heightened likelihood of selecting an incorrect subspace. Consequently, when the number of subspaces continues to increase, the partitioning win surfaces expand, but the partitioning loss surfaces also elevate. Moreover, it is noteworthy that as the number of subspaces increases, the cumulative distribution function begins to exhibit a knee approximately at the 60th percentile. This results in two effects: the green surfaces are expanding as previously said, and the intersection angle between the space partitioning model and 1x1 positioning is increasing, while the intersection point is being shifted towards lower percentiles. The latter effect adversely affects positioning performance.

Ultimately, when the Average DE in the correct subspace, as presented in Table 1, is juxtaposed with the average subspace area (total area size divided by the number of subspaces), it becomes evident that as the size of the subspaces increases, the rise in average error approaches saturation. Therefore, with the same density of RPs and APs, any further enlargement of the test bed should result in just a negligible increase in the DE. The selected verification environment was sufficiently expansive to thoroughly examine the impact of test bed size on positioning accuracy..

FOOTNOTES

1. Sometimes, in literature, the words position and location have different meaning. Most often, position translates to the set of numerical values (such as geographical coordinates) which describe the user's placement, whereas the location usually refers to the descriptive information depicting the user's whereabouts (such as Picadilly Circus, London, UK). Nevertheless, this work treats both words interchangeably.

REFERENCES

1. Bahl, P. & Padmanabhan, V. (2000). „Radar: An in-building RF_based user location and tracking system", Proceedings of the IEEE Infocom 2000, Tel-Aviv, Israel, vol. 2, Mar. 2000, pp. 775-784.
2. Battiti, R., Nhat, T. L., Villani, A. (2002). Location-aware Computing: A Neural Network Model For Determining Location in Wireless LANs. Technical Report # DIT-02- 0083 (Feb. 2002)
3. Bluetooth Special Interest Group (2001). Specification Volume 1, Specification of the Bluetooth System, Core. Version 1.1, February 22, 2001.
4. Bluetooth Special Interest Group (2001). Specification Volume 2, Specification of the Bluetooth System, Profiles. Version 1.1, February 22, 2001.
5. Hae Don Chon, Sibum Jun, Heejae Jung, Sang Won An, (2004). „Using RFID for Accurate Positioning",Journal of Global Positioning Systems, 2004, Vol. 3, No. 1-2: 32-39
6. Collomb Frédéric, (2002). Location Service Study Report (Loc_Serv_Study_Rep_PU.doc), Mobile and Vehicles Enhanced Services, 2002.
7. Eckert, K. (2005). Overview of Wireless LAN based Indoor Positioning Systems, Mobile Bussines Seminar, University of Mannheim, Germany, (2005)
8. Eltaher A., Kaiser T., (2005). „A Novel Approach based on UWB Beamforming for Indoor Positioning in None-Line-of-Sight Environments", RadioTeCc, October 26-27, 2005, Berlin, Germany.
9. Esko O. Dijk, (2004). „Indoor ultrasonic position estimation using a single base station", Technische Universiteit Eindhoven, 2004. October 6, 2004, p44-45
10. Fahlman, S., Lebiere, C. (1990). The cascade-correlation learning architecture. Advances in Neural Information Processing Systems 2, pp. 524–532 (1990)
11. Fraser M., (2006). „Mobile and Ubiquitous Computing: Sensing Location Indoors.", COMSM0106, 2006.
12. Hallberg, Nilsson, Synnes, (2003). „Positioning with Bluetooth", Telecommunications, 2003. ICT 2003. 10th International Conference on, Volume 2, Issue , 23 Feb.-1 March 2003 Page(s): 954 - 958 vol.2
13. Harmer D., (2004).„Ultra Wide-Band (UWB) Indoor Positioning", Thales Research and Technology UK Ltd. ARTES 4 Project. ESTEC December 2004.
14. Hasoun H. M. (1995). Fundamentals of Artificial Neural Networks. Massachusetts Institute of Technology (1995)
15. Hanson, S. J., Burr, D. J. (1988). Minkowski-r Backpropagation: Learning in Connectionist Models with non-Euclidean Error Signals, Neural Information

Processing Systems (Denver, 1987), (editor Anderson D. Z.), pp. 348-357, American Institute of Physics, New York (1988)

16. Kaemarungsi, K. (2006). Distribution of WLAN received signal strength indication for indoor location determination. 1st International Symposium on Wireless Pervasive Computing, 2006. pp.6 (Jan. 2006)
17. King, T., Kopf, S., Haenselmann, T., Lubberger, C., Effelsberg, W. (2006). COMPASS: A Probabilistic Indoor Positioning System Based on 802.11 and Digital Compasses. University of Mannheim, D-68159 Mannheim, Germany, TR-2006-012
18. Krohn, A. Beigl, M. Hazas, M. Gellersen, H.-W, (2005). „Using fine-grained infrared positioning to support the surface-based activities of mobile users", Distributed Computing Systems Workshops, 2005. 25th IEEE International Conference on, Telecooperation Office, Karlsruhe Univ., Germany.
19. Li, B., Salter, J., Dempster, A., Rizos, C. (2006). Indoor Positioning Techniques Based on Wireless LAN. AusWireless '06, Sydney (March 2006)
20. Li, B., Wang, Y., Lee, H.K., Dempster, A., Rizos, C. (2005). Method for yielding a database of location fingerprints in WLAN. Communications, IEE Proceedings-Volume 152, Issue 5, pp.580 - 586 (Oct. 2005)
21. Llombart, M., Ciurana, M., Barcelo-Arroyo, F. (2008). On the scalability of a novel WLAN positioning system based on time of arrival measurements. 5th Workshop on Positioning, Navigation and Communication, 2008. WPNC 2008, pp. 15 – 21 (March 2008)
22. Masaki Maeda, Takefumi Ogawa, Takashi Machida, Kiyoshi Kiyokawa, Haruo Takemura, (2003). „Indoor Localization and Navigation using IR Markers for Augmented Reality", HCI International 2003 Interactive demo
23. Michael R. McCarthy, Henk L. Muller, (2003). „RF Free Ultrasonic Positioning", University of Bristol, 7th International Symposium on Wearable Computers, October 2003.
24. Muller N. (2001). „Bluetooth Demystified", McGraw-Hill, New York, 2001.
25. Nešković A., Nešković N., Paunović Dj., (2000). „Indoor Electric Field Level Prediction Model Based on the Artificial Neural Networks", IEEE Communications Letters, vol. 4, No. 6, June 2000
26. Patil, A. (2002). „Performance Of Bluetooth Technologies And Their Applications To Location Sensing", Michigan State University, 2002.
27. Ramachandran, A., Jagannathan, S. (2007). Spatial Diversity in Signal Strength based WLAN Location Determination Systems. 32nd IEEE Conference on Local Computer Networks, 2007. pp. 10 - 17 (Oct. 2007)

28. Ramachandran, A., Jagannathan, S. (2007). Use of Frequency Diversity in Signal Strength based WLAN Location Determination Systems 32nd IEEE Conference on Local Computer Networks, 2007. pp.117 - 124 (Oct. 2007)

29. Roos, T., Myllymaki, P., Tirri, H. (2002). A statistical modeling approach to location estimation. Mobile Computing, IEEE Transactions on, Volume 1, Issue 1, pp.59 – 69, (First Quarter 2002)

30. Roy Want, Andy Hopper, Veronica Falcao, and Jon Gibbons, (1992). „The Active Badge location system", ACM Transactions on Information Systems, 10(1):91–102, January 1992.

31. Sayrafian-Pour, K., Kaspar, D. (2005). Indoor positioning using spatial power spectrum. IEEE PIMRC 2005. Volume: 4, pp. 2722- 2726 (Sept. 2005)

32. Shang Y., Wah W. B. (1996). Global Optimization for Neural Network Training, IEEE Computer Society, pp. 45-56 (March 1996)

33. Thapa K., Case S., (2003). „An indoor positioning service for Bluetooth Ad Hoc networks", in: MICS 2003, Duluth, MN, USA.

34. Wang, H., Jia, F. (2007). A Hybrid Modeling for WLAN Positioning System. International Conference on Wireless Communications, Networking and Mobile Computing, 2007. pp.2152 - 2155 (Sept. 2007)

35. Youssef, M., Agrawala, A. (2005). The Horus WLAN Location Determination System. Int. Conf. on Mobile Systems, Applications And Services, pp.205–218 (2005)

36. Youssef, M., Agrawala, A. (2003). Small-scale compensation for WLAN location determination systems. Wireless Communications and Networking, 2003. Volume 3, 20-20 pp.1974 – 1978 (March 2003)

37. Youssef, M.A., Agrawala, A., Shankar, A. U. (2003). WLAN location determination via clustering and probability distributions. Proceedings of the First IEEE International Conference on Pervasive Computing and Communications. pp.143 – 150 (March 2003)

38. Zhang, M., Zhang, S., Cao, J. (2008). Fusing Received Signal Strength from Multiple Access Points for WLAN User Location Estimation. International Conference on Internet Computing in Science and Engineering, 2008. pp.173 - 180 (Jan. 2008)

31 Chapter POSITIONING IN AD HOC NETWORKS

1. INTRODUCTION: AN OVERVIEW

An ad hoc network is characterized as a decentralized wireless network established spontaneously for a particular objective. These networks were conceived years ago for military applications, aimed for facilitating communication among devices in a very confined environment. In such a network, devices dynamically join and exit, making the existence of any network infrastructure untenable. This aspiration for decentralized, on-the-fly networks has since broadened to encompass several domains beyond the military. Currently, numerous mobile services necessitate the self-organizing capabilities provided by ad hoc networks. Examples encompass packet tracking, internet gaming, and measurement systems, among others. Ad hoc networks offer distinct advantages for mobile services; nevertheless, they also present challenges that conventional network protocols cannot address, such as optimal routing, network fragmentation, diminished computational capability, and energy-constrained devices.

In ad hoc networks, placement plays a crucial role, mostly due to the dynamic nature of the environment. Indeed, numerous services necessitate that nodes ascertain the location of users to execute their functions effectively. Wireless sensor networks primarily focus on services that require placement to fulfill their functions. These networks represent a subclass of ad hoc networks characterized by dense topologies functioning in an ad hoc manner, comprising small terminals with limited energy and computational capabilities. In ad hoc networks, particularly in wireless sensor networks, nodes are distributed across a specific area without accurate awareness of the topology. This topology is, in fact, changeable. Consequently, various uncertainties (e.g., node density and coverage, the network's energy distribution, the existence of darkened areas, and the positioning of nodes within the coverage region) are likely to impede the efficacy of ad hoc services. Awareness of the terminals' positions can significantly enhance service performance.

Positioning is essential not only for service supply but also for the construction of ad hoc protocol stacks. Ad hoc protocols must confront many challenges absent in conventional cellular networks due to alterations in topology and insufficient communication equipment.. Routing is one of the best examples of the dependence of ad hoc networks on positioning. Studies such as (Stojmenovic, 2002) demonstrate that only position-based routing protocols are scalable, i.e., able to cope with a higher density of nodes in the network. The same seems to apply to other management and operation tasks in ad hoc networks.

1.1 The Location problem in ad hoc networks

Nodes in an ad hoc network can be grouped into three categories according to the positioning capabilities: beacon nodes, settled nodes, and unknown nodes. *Beacon nodes*, also known as *anchors* or *landmarks*, are those able to compute their position on their own, i.e., without using an ad hoc location algorithm. Accordingly, they implement at least one location technique (e.g., GPS, map matching), which can be used as standalone. Beacon nodes usually constitute the reference frame necessary to set up a location algorithm. *Unknown nodes* are those nodes that do not know their position yet. When an ad hoc network is set up, all nodes except the beacon nodes are unknown. *Settled nodes* are unknown nodes that are able to compute their position from the information that they exchange with beacon nodes and/or other settled nodes. The purpose of the ad hoc location system is thus to position as many nodes as possible, turning them from unknown to settled nodes (Bourkerche et al., 2007).

Location systems in ad hoc networks function in two steps: local positioning and positioning algorithm. The former is responsible for computing the position of an unknown node from the metrics gathered. The second step consists of the positioning algorithm, which indicates how the position information is managed in order to maximise the number of nodes being settled.

1.2 Measuring the performance of location solutions

Performance of location solutions in ad hoc networks can be computed according to several parameters. The main ones are presented below.

1.2.1 Accuracy

Ad hoc positioning requires good accuracy since most of the networks in ad hoc mode are deployed in constrained scenarios, often indoors. In such environments, accuracy is especially relevant, since a few meters of error in the position may cause the node to be identified in another room, floor, or even building. Furthermore, nodes are expected to be very close (e.g., in medical applications), and inaccurate positions could hinder operation and maintenance tasks or even prevent location-based applications from performing their duty. Thus, location algorithms for ad hoc networks must produce positions for settled nodes of the highest possible accuracy.

1.2.2 Latency

The location solutions must be able to converge, i.e., to produce as many settled nodes as possible in the shortest time. Ideally, the location solutions for ad hoc networks should turn all the unknown nodes into settled nodes in a defined time. However, optimality in terms of accuracy (and many other factors) may collide with latency, which means that the convergence (and hence the latency) of the location solution depends on the accuracy requested, among many other factors. Latency is also modulated by the mobility of the nodes in the network. The faster the nodes move, the shorter the convergence period needs to be. It must be noted that, in the case that convergence is not achieved, estimated positions would not involve the actual location of nodes, and this lack of accuracy would be spread by the network according to the location algorithm used. Hence, it would degrade the accuracy of the location solution.

1.2.3 Form factor of terminals

Ad hoc devices tend to be small, especially in the case of wireless sensor networks. The requirement of small form constrains the capabilities of these devices, which prevents sophisticated (and usually more complex) algorithms from being used. This, in turn, prevents the best QoS from being reached.

1.2.4 Energy-efficient design

Due to restrictions on their size, ad hoc devices tend to include very-limited batteries. Accordingly, location solutions must avoid using complex algorithms or sensing multiple metrics in order to compute the position, since these would limit the lifetime of nodes and hence of the entire network.

1.2.5 Self-organising design

Ad hoc devices are likely to move. Algorithms developed for positioning in such networks should account for the overhead generated by the changes in the topology of the ad hoc network. Changes in the topology are produced by nodes moving around the network area or being added to and removed from the ad hoc network.

1.2.6 Random nature of the ad hoc network

Ad hoc devices can be added and removed from the network during its life cycle. Depending on the scenario, these changes in the topology of the network can be noticeably intense. Location solutions in ad hoc networks should be insensitive to the structure of the network.

1.2.7 Scalability

The algorithm should minimise the impact of adding a new terminal to the network. This means that the amount of resources consumed by the network due to the addition of the new node should be as low as possible. Scalability does not necessarily involve the use of simple algorithms. However, it should allow as many ad hoc devices as possible to be positioned with the same amount of resources.

1.2.8 Node density

In actual deployments of ad hoc networks, devices are not likely to be homogeneously distributed along the layout. The density of terminals is variable in space and time, and hence location algorithms should not assume isotropic conditions.

1.2.9 Beacon percentage

Beacons tend to be fixed nodes often plugged to wired power sources, which make them more durable. Beacons are set up by the network operator, and, consequently, they collide with the ad hoc philosophy. Moreover, it is difficult to ensure that the percentage of beacons visible for an unknown node remains uniform. Accordingly, location algorithms should be as insensitive to beacon percentage and beacon placement as possible.

2. LOCATION METRICS

There are several metrics than can be used as input for location techniques. Those metrics are usually known as observables, since they refer to what can be observed and subsequently measured. Timestamps, angles, and signal strength are metrics commonly used by location techniques to compute the position of the nodes. The former usually involves timestamps for the sending and receiving moments associated with one or several signals. Precision of timestamps directly depends on the clock present in the ad hoc devices. These clocks are usually low-profiled, mainly due to the small form-factor and the cost of devices. Consequently, this impacts the accuracy of the time-based observables and ultimately the positions fixed by the location solution. Furthermore, accessing the hardware clock is rather difficult in most of the current devices and technologies. The same does not apply to signal strength, which is usually available in most of the ad hoc technologies. Consequently, there are several location techniques that use this metric for positioning. Furthermore, this metric provides accurate observables, even though it does not mean that positions computed from these observables achieve the same degree of accuracy.

Finally, angular information is proposed for positioning in several solutions. This metric consists of measuring the angle or direction of arrival (AoA / DoA) of signals coming from several nodes to the target one, or vice versa. Fig. 1 illustrates this metric, where the red- coloured angles (i.e., ε_1 and ε_2) stand for the error produced in the angle-of-arrival estimate.

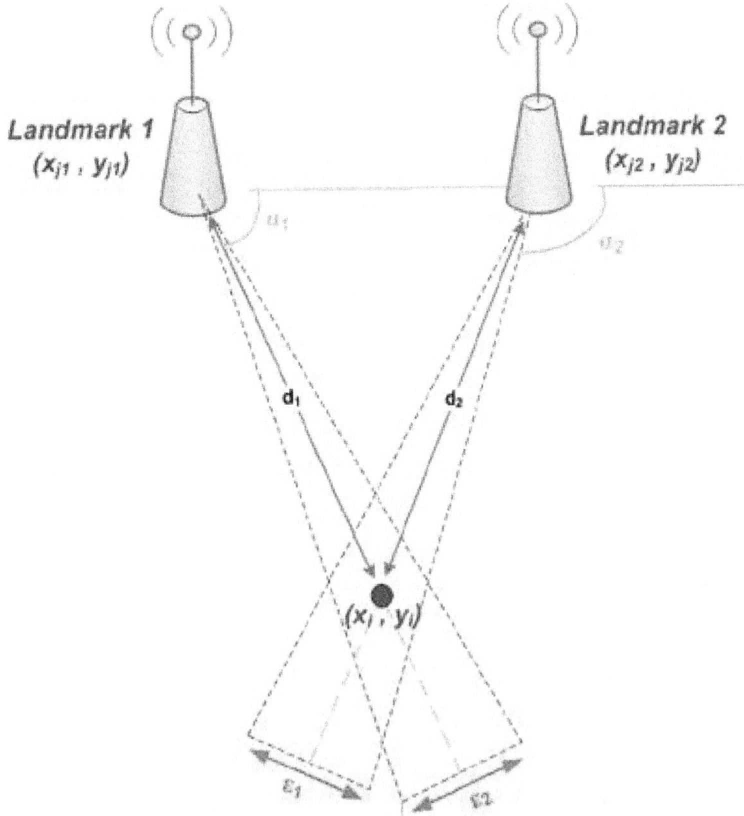

Fig. 1. Positioning according to the angle/direction of arrival

According to Fig. 1, the angles of arrival can be computed as

$$\alpha_k = -\tan^{-1}\left(\frac{y_i - y_{jk}}{x_i - x_{jk}}\right), \tag{1}$$

where (x_i, y_i) is the position (in two dimensions) of the node to be positioned and (x_{jk}, y_{jk}) is the position (in two dimensions) of the landmark k.

The use of this metric involves using arrays of antennas in order to capture the angle in which the signal is being received. Furthermore, the positioning error derived from the angle-estimation error depends on the distance between the pair of entities involved in the angle estimation. Consequently, this metric is rarely used; the hardware is costly, the error is range-dependent, and this metric often involves the customisation of network equipment.

3. LOCATION TECHNIQUES

Ad hoc networks use a subset of the location techniques proposed for other cellular technologies (e.g., UMTS, IEEE 802.11, etc.). These techniques can be classified into two main groups: ranging-based and angle-based. The following sections describe the techniques in detail.

3.1 Ranging based on signal strength

Ranging-based techniques are based on computing the distance between two nodes (i.e., ranging) and then computing the position of the unknown node by using a multilateration algorithm. Range estimations can be computed from several metrics, but two are preferably used: signal strength and timestamp. Techniques based on the former estimate the range between two nodes according to the received and transmitted power. Radio path models depend on the distance according to a certain power, known as path-loss slope. This means that distance can be computed from transmitted and received signal strength, which is information easily accessible in the network. According to general knowledge on radio propagation, received power can be expressed as

$$P_{rx} = P_{tx} - P_{1m} - 10\alpha \log(d), \quad (2)$$

where P_{rx} and P_{tx} are, respectively, the received and transmitted power in dB(m), P_{1m} stands for the losses at 1 meter from the transmitter location, d is the distance in meters between the transmitter and receiver placements (i.e., the ranging), and α is the path-loss gradient (or slope).

Modelling the radio path losses, such as those in Equation (2), is a difficult task. Obstacles in the propagation path affect the signal in several ways, namely, reflection, diffraction, and absorption. The consequence is that signals reach the receiver following more than a single path (a phenomenon known as multipath), and, consequently, the received signal strength suffers random variations. Accordingly, different radio path models are proposed depending on the scenario in which the network is going to be deployed. However, the propagation conditions are likely to change (even dramatically) with time as new obstacles appear. Hence, such models would need to be recalibrated periodically (constantly in the worst case). Indoors is one of the most constrained scenarios, and, consequently, most of the location solutions based on signal strength ranging are proposed for such an environment. An example of a radio propagation model used in location is proposed in (Seidel & Rapport, 1992), where the free space model was adapted to indoor environments by adding several parameters, such as the number of floors in the path or the number of walls. However, it is demonstrated not to be a satisfactory approach since the number of obstacles is not known a priori. Other approaches tried to improve radio signal propagation models for indoors (Wang et al., 2003; Lassabe et al., 2005), but accurate distance estimates are not yet available. Despite all these issues, several proposals are available for signal ranging. One of the first approaches was presented in (Bahl & Padmanabhan, 2000), where several models specifically addressed to ranging-based location solutions were proposed and tested experimentally. Due to the randomness of the received signal, poor results were obtained with all models, if compared with other location techniques based on signal fingerprinting. Better results are reported in (Kotanen et al., 2003), where the authors propose processing the signal- strength observables prior to position computation. This previous stage aims to reduce the noise of the measurements so that more accurate positions can be fixed. Furthermore, an extended Kalman filter is used to compute the position, which minimises the variance of the distance estimation. This solution provides accuracy figures of less than three metres, even though worse results are expected under arbitrary propagation conditions.

3.2 Ranging based on time measurements

Considering the number of solutions currently proposed, time-based ranging seems to be a more appealing technology than solutions based on signal strength. This is because, compared to signal strength, time measurements tend to be more stable and less sensitive to environmental conditions. Time-based ranging solutions can be classified into two groups according to the number of signals/paths under consideration: time of arrival and time- difference of arrival. The former is based on estimating the distance between two nodes. It is achieved by marking transmission (t_{tx}) and reception (t_{rx}) times and then applying to compute the distance, where *c* stands for the propagation time (usually the speed of light). Equation (3) can only be applied if timestamps are taken under the same time line, i.e., when all nodes in the network are time-synchronised. However, this is not the normal case. Thus, the 2-way time-of-arrival approach was proposed to overcome this issue. This approach computes the propagation time under a round-trip-time approach, i.e., measuring the time spent by the signal in travelling the forward (*Node 1* to *Node 2*) and backward (*Node 2* to *Node 1*) paths. Fig. 2 illustrates this procedure, which is explained in detail in (Ciurana et al., 2007). Since all timestamps are taken using the same clock (in *Node 1*), propagation time (*Tprop*) can be computed as half the time measured for both paths (RTT), as long as processing time (*Tproc*) is negligible (or calibrated). The position of the target node (i.e., the one to be located) can be computed by multilateration once enough measurements are achieved (e.g., 3 or more for 2D positioning). The accuracy of time of arrival directly depends on the precision of the time estimations. Accordingly, there are several works addressing improvements in the accuracy of time of arrival observables.

$$d = c \cdot (t_{rx} - t_{tx}) \tag{3}$$

Some examples can be found in (Ibraheem & Schoebel, 2007) and (Reddy & Chandra, 2007), which present approaches improving the traditional correlation-based methods.

Time-difference of arrival consists of observing ranging differences, rather than just observing distances. Therefore, the node that is going to be positioned measures the ranging difference between its position and the position of a pair of landmarks (or even settled nodes). Time difference of arrival is also known as hyperbolic multilateration, since it superposes several hyperbolas in order to fix the node's position. It provides better accuracy than time of arrival and hence is preferred in cellular networks (3GPP, 2002; 3GPP, 2004). However, time-difference solutions present the same issue as time of arrival: nodes have to be time-synchronised. Furthermore, the 2-way approach cannot easily be applied to the time-difference of arrival technique, and hence synchronisation error has to be estimated (by means of specific measurement devices) or removed (taking the location measurements with a common clock).

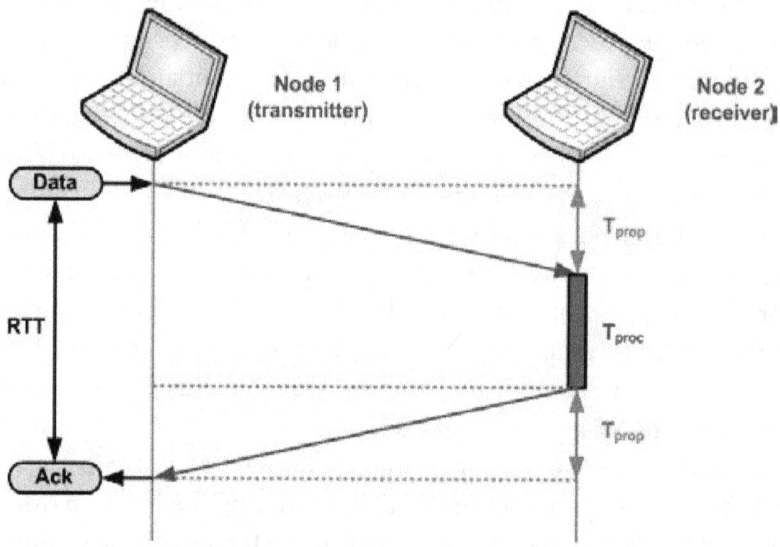

Fig. 2. RTT estimation through 2-way time of arrival approach

3.3 Triangulation based on angular measurements

This location method uses the direction or angles of arrival of several signals as the metric to compute the position. Therefore, the location techniques based on angulation are also known as Angle of Arrival (AoA) or Direction or Arrival (DoA). The position of the user can be computed according to several approaches. One of the simplest consist of intersecting the lines computed as

$$y_i = y_{jk} - (x_i - x_{jk})\tan\alpha_k, \quad (4)$$

where α_k is computed according to Equation (1). There are several (and more complex) proposals based on numerical approach and closed forms to carry out positioning with angulation, as presented in (Pages-Zamora et al., 2002).

4. LOCATION ALGORITHMS

Local positioning has been widely addressed for cellular networks, and the main methods and procedures remain valid for ad hoc networks. Hence, positioning algorithms draw the greatest amount of interest from the research community for location in ad hoc networks.

4.1 Taxonomy of location algorithms in ad hoc networks

4.1.1 Centralised vs. Distributed

Centralised algorithms rely on a network entity (e.g., location server) that gathers the location information from all the unknown nodes and then computes their position. The main advantage is that global optimisation can be performed, as the information of all nodes is available in the location server. Centralised systems are often used in cellular networks such as public land mobile networks (PLMNs), but they collide with the random nature of ad hoc networks. The location server has to be significantly more powerful than regular nodes. Moreover, the data gathered by the server must be synchronised: all measurements must be performed at specific times. If synchronisation is not assured, optimality cannot be reached, and the system may be degraded. Additionally, topology in such systems can be displayed as a tree, with the root at the location server. Therefore, nodes near the server quickly run out their batteries, since they concentrate most of the location traffic coming from unknown nodes; this reduces the ad hoc network lifetime.

In *distributed* location algorithms, some or all nodes are able to compute their position (and the position of other nodes depending on the specific algorithm). Thus, distributed location is more robust to node failures. Distributed algorithms also converge faster than centric solutions after topology changes and are usually insensitive to data synchronisation requirements, since only local or regional data are accounted for. There are several degrees of distributed algorithms. The most common are the localised or pure distributed algorithms, where all unknown nodes are able to compute their position once the necessary local metrics are available.

4.1.2 Incremental vs. concurrent

Incremental positioning algorithms start with only a few beacon nodes. Then, in each step, the position of a reduced amount of unknown nodes is computed using the information provided by settled and beacon nodes. The positions of such nodes are used in subsequent iterations to compute the location of other unknown nodes. The advantage of iterative algorithms is their simplicity. However, they tend to propagate their positioning error, since they use metrics obtained from settled nodes for subsequent local positioning. Furthermore, the convergence of incremental location algorithms is not always guaranteed. In *concurrent* algorithms, all nodes are able to compute their position normally using local information. Accordingly, they are more complex than iterative algorithms, but they can avoid error propagation and hence achieve better accuracy results.

4.1.3 One hop vs. multi-hop

Location involves exchanging information to measure the metrics used to compute the node's position. *One hop* algorithms use only information (i.e., metrics) local to the unknown nodes (e.g., ranging to the node's neighbours). On the other hand, *multi-hop* algorithms use information of all nodes that can be reached from the node in a certain number of hops, usually two. Muti-hop techniques allow more accurate positions to be computed and fewer beacon nodes to be deployed in the system (Savvides et al., 2001). The main drawbacks are the overhead generated by the multi-hop estimation and the subsequent use of additional resources in the nodes to store such data.

4.1.4 Beacon-Based, Mobile Beacon-Based and Beacon-Less

Ad hoc location algorithms can be classified according to the presence of beacon nodes in three categories: localisation with beacons, localisation with moving beacons, and localisation without beacons (Sun et al., 2005). *Localisation-with-beacons* algorithms are those in which a percentage of nodes are fixed beacons, i.e., beacons that do not change their location. The major challenge of algorithms that rely on beacons is to maximise the accuracy and coverage while at the same time minimising the number of landmarks in the network. Localisation with *moving beacons* algorithms are similar to algorithms based on beacons, but here the beacons are no longer fixed and move through the network. A moving beacon is perceived by unknown nodes as different beacons (i.e., one per message exchanged, from different positions of the mobile beacon). Fewer landmarks are necessary, and more accurate positions can be achieved since beacon density is perceived as higher than it actually is. The main drawback with mobile beacon algorithms is that mobile beacons have to cover the entire ad hoc network and ensure that unknown nodes see the mobile beacons with a suitable frequency, which is often difficult to achieve. The last category, known as *beacon-free* location, involves those algorithms in which no node is aware of its position (i.e., all nodes are unknown). Thus, all nodes work together to compute their position using only their local information. This kind of algorithm usually works with a local coordinate system, which may require translation of the achieved positions into a global coordinate system so that they can be used by a location-based service or protocol.

4.1.5 Range-free vs. range-based

In *range-based* algorithms, the local position is computed according to ranging measurements (i.e., distance or angle estimates). Accordingly, they involve multilateration techniques, which are usually hardware-demanding and therefore energy-consuming. Accordingly, range-based algorithms are suitable for ad hoc networks with powerful terminals (e.g., in technologies such as IEEE 802.11). On the other hand, technologies with more constrained terminals, such as those present in wireless sensor networks, favour the use of range-free algorithms for positioning. *Range-free* algorithms do not rely on ranging to compute the position of unknown nodes; rather, they consist of simpler approaches based on proximity.

4.3 State of the art

The first location solutions proposed for ad hoc networks used centralised algorithms similar to techniques proposed for mobile networks. In (Doherty et al., 2001), the authors propose to manage the location as a convex-optimisation problem: a mobile server is defined to gather all the location data (e.g., distances, angles of arrival, etc.) from unknown nodes in order to compute their positions. The advantage is the simplicity and optimality of the positions computed. However, it involves delivering a significant amount of data to a location server that must be powerful enough to handle complex data structures. Moreover, the cost of the algorithm proposed for this technique is cubic in the number of connections, which seriously constrains the scalability of the approach.

In order to overcome those drawbacks, distributed algorithms are present in many solutions. The *centroid* algorithm (Bulusu et al., 2000) is a one-hop pure-distributed positioning algorithm in which few beacons are spread in the ad hoc network forming a grid. Unknown nodes compute their position by estimating their range to the three closest beacons and a trilateration algorithm. The main benefit is that it is insensitive to the node density and does not add significant overhead in the network. The main drawback of this method is a larger error in the positioning. Another interesting example of a one-hop algorithm is proposed in the *Lighthouse* project (Römer, 2003), in which a single base station sees all sensors in the network. This full coverage is achieved by means of a beam that rotates at known speed. Stations are able to compute their position knowing the rotation speed, the width of the beam, and the signal time-of-flight. Although the accuracy might not be suitable for many applications in ad hoc networks (it provides a bias up to 14 metres), it represents an improvement in scalability.

Recent proposals emphasise distributed behaviour. The *Ad hoc Localisation System (AhLOS)* presented in (Savvides et al., 2001) is an example of this trend. AhLOS is a one-hop pure- distributed algorithm that uses three trilateration algorithms: atomic, iterative, and collaborative. Atomic trilateration involves a one-hop scenario, where the nodes have three or more beacons in sight so that they can compute their positions directly. The main drawback of this approach is that it relies on a high density of beacons. Iterative trilateration relaxes this assumption, considering all the nodes that compute their position by means of atomic trilateration (i.e., settled nodes) as new beacons. It allows fewer beacons at the cost of less accuracy. Despite covering most of the situations, these two trilateration approaches are not sufficient to position all the nodes in the ad hoc network, since unknown nodes with only one neighbour cannot be positioned. The authors of AhLOS followed a collaborative multilateration approach to overcome this situation, consisting of identifying those unknown nodes that cannot be handled by atomic and iterative algorithms and creating groups that collaborate in order to compute the position of those nodes. This may involve solving large nonlinear systems depending on the size of the groups created.

The *Ad hoc Positioning System (APS)* presented in (Niculescu & Nath, 2003) combines two concepts: beacon-based positioning and ad hoc propagation (i.e., multi-hop). The algorithm proposed in APS consists of four stages. Firstly, some beacon nodes are spread by the network. Secondly, nodes with some landmarks in sight measure their distance to the beacon nodes in terms of some metric, such as propagation time, number of hops, etc. Then, the information gathered by nodes in the neighbourhood of landmarks is propagated (and updated) using a proper algorithm. Finally, once a node has the ranging information of three or more beacons, it computes its position using a multilateration approach. The algorithms for propagating the ranging information in the ad hoc network are the main contribution of (Niculescu & Nath, 2003): *DV-Hop, DV-distance, Euclidean,* and *DV-Coordinate*. In the first, all nodes build ranging tables containing the position coordinates and the distance in hops to the landmarks. These data are flooded in the network in a controlled way, so that all nodes know how far they are from landmarks. On the other hand, landmarks use such data to compute the average distance of one hop, according to the hops and the distance between them. This is achieved by:

$$c_i = \frac{\sum_{\forall j \neq i} \sqrt{(x_i - x_j)^2 + (y_i - y_j)^2}}{\sum_{\forall j \neq i} h_j}, \tag{5}$$

where c_i indicates the hop distance calculated by the landmark *i*, *(x,y,z)* are the coordinates of a landmark and h_j stands for the amount of hops from landmark *i* to *j*.

This average (i.e., c_i) is then flooded in the network using a singleton approach: once a node receives an announcement packet from a landmark containing the average value computed by such a landmark, it discards any other further announcement packet. The average distance is then stored in the nodes, which then use it to turn distances in hops into real ranges. Finally, nodes compute their position using a multilateration approach. The advantage of this approach is that it is insensitive to the ranging error, since ranging is based on hop counting. However, it introduces more overhead than other algorithms. Moreover, accuracy is degraded in non-dense networks.

The *DV-distance* approach is similar to DV-Hop but exchanges real distances instead of distances in hops. Multi-hop distances are computed as the sum of the distances between nodes involved in the path. Thus, this approach becomes more sensitive to ranging error. Normally, the denser the ad hoc network is, the better the accuracy. On the other hand, it improves the consistency of the DV-Hop approach, working similarly in isotropic and non- isotropic networks.

The *Euclidean* approach involves a multi-hop algorithm, which gathers ranging information up to 2 hops. Thus, the algorithm generates quadrilaterals involving one unknown node, two neighbours, and a landmark, and it infers the distance from the node to the landmark using trigonometric formulation. The advantage of this approach is that the ranging error can be estimated, stored, and subsequently flooded together with the distance; this allows distance-weighted approaches to be used and hence more accurate positions to be achieved. The main drawback is that a 2-hop approach involves additional traffic in the network (even more than in DV-Hop and DV-Distance algorithms) as well as more resources needed in the node to store the additional information, resulting in more quickly depleting node batteries running.

The last approach presented in (Niculescu & Nath, 2003) is the so-called *DV-Coordinate*, which is similar to the solution proposed in (Capkun et al., 2001). DV-Coordinate is based on each node computing the position of its neighbourhood according to a local coordinate- system. Then in a second step, called the registration stage, nodes exchange information to build the transformation matrices, which allow coordinates of local systems to be transformed from one local system to another. A global transformation matrix is necessary to achieve global coherence. DV-Coordinate performs almost the same as Euclidean. However, this approach impacts the scalability of the location system, since it depends on the square of the nodes in the network and involves sending two pieces of data instead of just a distance. In (Niculescu & Nath, 2003/2), the authors extend DV-Coordinate and presented the *Local Positioning System (LPS)*, which uses ranging and angle of arrival information to compute the position of unknown nodes, in a fashion similar to the DV- Coordinate. However, the LPS reduces the overhead of the DV-Coordinate systems, thus improving the scalability and updating only a reduced number of nodes each time, not the whole network.

The *Amorphous Localisation* algorithm (Nagpal et al., 2003) is similar to APS. It consists of computing the distance from nodes to beacons in terms of hops. However, the hop-distance is calculated offline according to the node density expected in the network. Then, a multilateration approach is followed to compute the position. The main drawback of this algorithm is the offline stage, which seriously constrains the scalability of the algorithm in dynamic ad hoc networks.

A one-hop range-based concurrent pure-distributed algorithm is proposed in (Fu et al., 2006) for networks based on DSSS, such as those based on IEEE 802.11. This algorithm is based on propagating the clock from node to node so that the nodes involved in the positioning work in a synchronised fashion. Then the ranging to neighbour nodes is estimated, and a multilateration algorithm is applied. The synchronisation is achieved by means of the pseudo-noise code used in the DSSS, and, consequently, the time-resolution achieved matches with the code duration. Accordingly, the algorithm only works if times- of-flight are much longer than the code duration, which is expected to be the usual case.

The *Approximation of the Point-In-Triangulation Test (APIT)* is presented in (He et al., 2003) as another example of a one-hop range-based location algorithm. It is based on generating as many triangles as possible involving three beacons. Then, the APIT algorithm evaluates whether the unknown node is inside each triangle. Finally, it overlaps all the triangles, reducing the final positioning error. The authors evaluate the algorithm through simulation and conclude that this approach outperforms the *centroid* algorithm. Furthermore, this approach achieves accuracy figures similar to those obtained in the *APS* and *Amorphous Localisation* algorithms but requiring a lower node density and introducing less overhead. On the other hand, it requires beacons with a radio range longer than that of regular nodes. All these approaches to the ad hoc location rely on active multilateration; i.e., positioning an unknown node involves a certain amount of location traffic in order to estimate the distances to landmarks. Active location constrains the scalability of location algorithms in ad hoc networks, in which topology and mobility are inherent to the network definition. The next sections introduce a passive algorithm for location in collaborative networks (e.g., ad hoc, wireless sensor networks, etc.), which aims to boost the scalability on positioning systems.

5. PASSIVE POSITIONING

Recent advances in indoor positioning have led to proposals that time-of-arrival (TOA) techniques for locating users are preferable to other techniques, such as fingerprinting. Time-of-arrival solutions achieve accuracy figures that are similar to those obtained by other techniques, but they do not require additional assistance for setup and maintenance. Conversely, time-of-arrival techniques need to calculate a client's range from at least three receivers at known positions in order to obtain a 2D position. In addition, all the signal transmitters involved in the TOA positioning system must be synchronised. Two-way TOA techniques, such as those presented in (Ciurana et al., 2007) and (Yang et al., 2008), cope with this issue by computing the range from the client (i.e., unknown node) to the base station (i.e., landmark) using a round-trip-time (RTT) procedure. Since only the client's clock is used to calculate the range, synchronisation between base stations is no longer necessary. The drawback is that more traffic is generated on the network, thus reducing the available throughput.

A recent proposal on ad hoc location presented in (Martin-Escalona & Barcelo-Arroyo, 2008) extends the capabilities of time-of-arrival location techniques, allowing unknown nodes in a network to position themselves in a passive fashion, i.e., without injecting traffic into the network. The following sections explain this technique, named *passive TDOA*, in detail.

5.1 Description of assisted passive-TDOA algorithm

The passive-TDOA algorithm listens to the access medium for messages that can be used to compute time-difference of arrival (TDOA) figures. The only assumption of the algorithm is that the nodes operate in a collaborative network. Note that this is the case for most of the wireless local area networks, especially those based on ad hoc protocols. In this text, one more assumption is taken only for explanatory purposes: the messages used to compute TDOAs are generated by unknown nodes running a 2-way TOA technique.

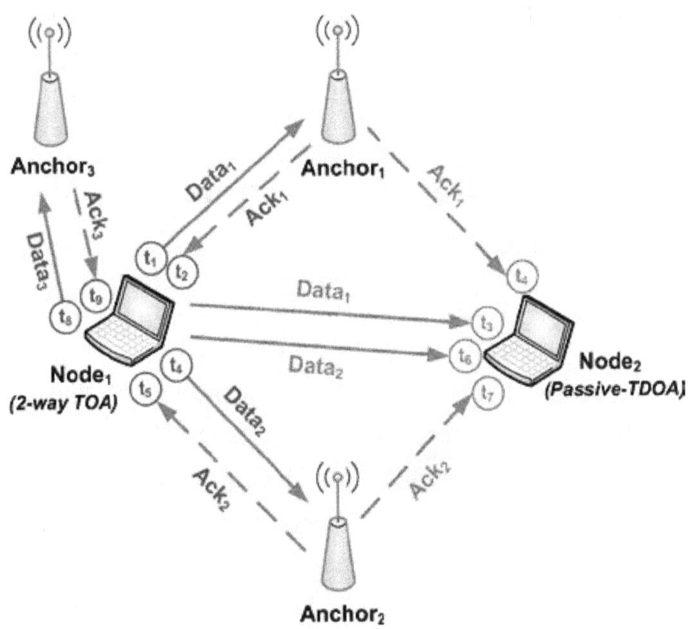

Fig. 3. Operation of the passive-TDOA algorithm

The performance of the positioning algorithm is described in Fig. 3, which shows a network with three anchors or landmarks (i.e., $Anchor_1$ to $Anchor_3$) and two regular nodes with positioning capabilities (i.e., $Node_1$ and $Node_2$). At a given time, $Node_1$ begins a TOA positioning process to locate itself. Thus, $Node_1$ sends data message ($Data_1$) to $Anchor_1$ at t_1, which replies with an acknowledgement (Ack_1), which reaches $Node_1$ at t_2. The corresponding RTT is hence calculated as $t_2 - t_1$. Note, however, that other nodes in the network also listen to all these messages, since it is a diffusion network. Thus, $Node_2$ hears the $Data_1$ message at t_3 and the reply to that message, i.e., Ack_1, at t_4. Therefore, a TDOA measurement is generated as $t_4 - t_3$. The same process is followed by $Node_1$ to range with $Anchor_2$ and $Anchor_3$. Based on the assumption that $Node_2$ is only covered at $Anchor_1$ and $Anchor_2$, $Node_2$ is able to calculate two TDOAs: $t_4 - t_3$ and $t_7 - t_6$. These two measurements are enough to position $Node_2$ using a multilateration TDOA algorithm. Note that the TDOA position calculated at $Node_2$ involves hearing just two access points, which makes it possible for positioning to take place where TOA techniques would be ineffective. The only datum needed by MS_2 in addition to the TDOA measurements is the position of $Node_1$. This information can be supplied by the unknown node once it becomes settled (e.g., by broadcasting), or it can be estimated in the passive-TDOA node. Simulation analysis demonstrates that, under line-of-sight (i.e., visibility between nodes), the positioning error achieved by this algorithm is often below 1.4 times the error achieved by the 2-way TOA. Better results are achieved if the technique is deployed under non-line-of-sight conditions, providing figures similar to those achieved by the 2-way TOA technique (Martin-Escalona & Barcelo-Arroyo, 2008). This behaviour is especially relevant for location since non-line-of- sight is the usual condition for location-system operation; hence, the best performance is desired in such scenarios.

5.2 Autonomous passive TDOA: TOA position estimated

One of the most constraining requirements of the passive-TDOA algorithm is the position of the 2-way TOA node. Supplying this information in location procedures where position has been requested by a third party should not involve additional changes in the 2-way TOA algorithm and could be considered the final step for the passive-TDOA algorithm. However, the same does not apply to services in which the user requests his or her own position.

Although the impact of supplying the 2-way TOA positions on the capacity of the network is expected to be small, it does become necessary to define a protocol that guarantees the supply of TOA positions once they have been computed, so that passive-TDOA nodes can figure out their own locations. This protocol could involve some modifications in the 2-way TOA algorithm, which is not a desirable fact. OMA SUPL (OMA, 2008) can be used for such purposes, but security issues need to be addressed before its implementation (e.g., positions should not identify users).

The algorithm initially proposed for passive-TDOA has been modified to cope with TOA position supplying. Accordingly, two operational modes have been defined: *assisted* and *autonomous*. The former consists of the algorithm as defined in the previous sections. The *autonomous* operational mode allows positions of TOA and passive-TDOA nodes to be jointly-computed in the passive-TDOA node, in a passive fashion.

There are several benefits to computing the TOA and passive-TDOA positions jointly. The first one is that the passive-TDOA algorithm does not depend on supplying the TOA position. Accordingly, any 2-way TOA algorithm could be used together with the passive- TDOA algorithm with only slight changes. Furthermore, the passive-TDOA nodes will compute their own position and the position of the 2-way TOA nodes, which gives way to approaches for improving accuracy. The autonomous passive-TDOA algorithm becomes especially interesting in scenarios in which an application needs to locate all the users in the network. Nodes report their positions, as well as the positions of 2-way TOA nodes estimated in the passive-TDOA nodes, and then the application can use the redundancy of positions to improve the accuracy of the 2-way TOA nodes.

The *Autonomous* mode of the passive-TDOA algorithm is based on a usual feature of 2-way TOA algorithms: the redundancy on RTTs. These algorithms tend to measure several RTTs involving the same landmark in order to reduce errors caused by the measurement system and radio channel, hence improving the accuracy. *Autonomous* mode uses two consecutive RTTs on the same landmark to estimate two TDOAs (as defined in the case of the *normal* operational mode), as well as the RTT being measured at the TOA node. As expected, the RTT estimate in the passive-TDOA node will be noisier than the ones made in the TOA node, but it is expected to be accurate enough to allow the passive-TDOA algorithm to compute its own position.

Fig. 4 shows the procedure that constitutes the *autonomous* operational mode of the passive- TDOA algorithm. The explanation is based on the scenario proposed in Fig. 3, but reduced to one 2-way TOA node (i.e., $Node_1$), a landmark (i.e., *Landmark*), and a passive-TDOA node (i.e., $Node_2$). As explained for the case of the *assisted* operational mode, $Node_1$ starts a ping- fashion procedure to compute the range between the landmark and itself. As a result, the RTT_1 (i.e., $t_2 - t_1$) is measured. Consequently, $TDOA_1$ is deducted from the ping procedure as $t_4 - t_3$. Until this point, the procedure is exactly the same as that presented in the case of *assisted* mode.

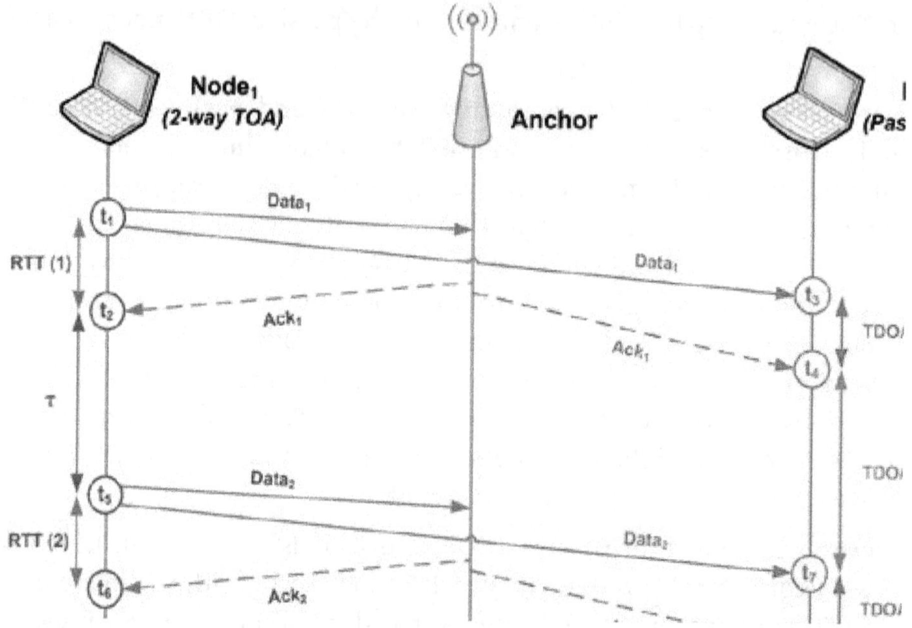

Fig. 4. Flow diagram for the *autonomous* **operational mode of passive-TDOA algorithm**

Then, it is assumed that $Node_1$ starts a new 2-way TOA procedure involving the same entities (i.e., *Landmark* and $Node_2$) after a predefined time (T), which is known by all nodes in the network. This new procedure provides new estimates for $Node_1$ and $Node_2$, i.e., RTT_2 and $TDOA_2$, respectively. Furthermore, *autonomous* mode benefits from this redundancy in the measurements by using it to estimate the ranging between *Landmark* and $Node_1$ in $Node_2$. This can be done by simply measuring a new time-difference in $Node_2$: *TDOA'*. This time- difference corresponds to the difference between the arrival time to $Node_2$ of the first *TOA response* and the second *TOA request* messages, subtracting the time elapsed between the two ping processes (i.e., $t_7 - t_4 - T$ in Fig. 4), which is assumed to be known by all nodes in the network. This information, together with the $TDOA_1$ and $TDOA_2$ measurements, allows the network to deduce the ranging information concerning $Node_2$ and the *Landmark*. The formulation starts from

$$T\langle i,j\rangle = R\langle i,j\rangle + R\langle j,k\rangle - R\langle i,k\rangle, \tag{6}$$

which computes the TDOA from the ranging information. *R* in Equation (6) computes the distance between two nodes, *T* stands for the distance-difference, and subscripts *i*, *j*, *k* stand for the TOA node, the landmark, and the passive-TDOA node, respectively (as in the rest of the document). According to Equation (6) and the scenario presented in Fig. 4, two TDOAs are computed as

$$T\langle i,j\rangle^1 = R\langle i,j\rangle^1 + R\langle j,k\rangle^1 - R\langle i,k\rangle^1 \qquad (7)$$

and

$$T\langle i,j\rangle^2 = R\langle i,j\rangle^2 + R\langle j,k\rangle^2 - R\langle i,k\rangle^2, \qquad (8)$$

where the superscript indicates the ping procedure involved in the measurement. These two TDOAs (in distance) are then averaged (under the assumption of providing the same QoS) as

$$T\langle i,j\rangle = \frac{1}{2}\left(T\langle i,j\rangle^2 + T\langle i,j\rangle^2\right). \qquad (9)$$

According to its definition, *TDOA'* is computed as

$$TDOA' = T\langle j,i\rangle = R\langle i,j\rangle^1 + R\langle i,k\rangle^2 - R\langle j,k\rangle^1. \qquad (10)$$

Under the assumption of noiseless measurements, TOA ranging can be estimated in the passive-TDOA node as

$$R\langle i,j\rangle = \frac{1}{2}\left(T\langle i,j\rangle + T\langle j,i\rangle\right). \qquad (11)$$

Finally, once *R<i,j>* is estimated, the same algorithm as used in the *assisted* mode is used to compute the position of the passive-TDOA node.

Simulation results indicate that estimating the ranging of the 2-way TOA node results in less accurate positions, as expected. However, under non-line-of-sight conditions, which are the usual case, passive-TDOA provides positions with only 20% more error than the 2-way TOA, with the benefit of no traffic injection. This is especially relevant for group location, i.e., those applications that involve more than a single location process.

5.3 Applications of the passive-TDOA algorithm

The passive-TDOA algorithm has multiple applications in the field of location. The main one has been discussed above and consists of allowing an unknown node to be positioned without injecting traffic into the network. Therefore, the load due to positioning is reduced, and the network throughput remains available for other services. This feature is essential for location algorithms since it improves scalability, which is especially essential for the location platform in the ad hoc environment.

Another application of passive TDOA is the capability of the algorithm to position unknown nodes in environments where TOA techniques cannot. For instance, Fig. 3 shows how passive-TDOA is able to position a customer who only has two access points in sight. Under the same conditions, the TOA technique is not able to provide a location, since this technique requires at least three transmitters (even more depending on the algorithm) to perform a 2D trilateration. The passive-TDOA algorithm would be able to go further in positioning under constrained scenarios. In fact, this technique would be able to compute the position of a station with just one access point in sight, whenever enough settled nodes are in sight and their positions are known. This makes the passive-TDOA algorithm a very interesting solution for positioning under extreme conditions (e.g., scenarios in which there is interference), eventually mitigating the impact of some access points being down (e.g., due to maintenance, fire damage, etc.). Since passive-TDOA can work with fewer landmarks, it helps the system continue to offer location-based services in those circumstances where TOA is not able to provide some positions.

Passive-TDOA can also be used to improve the accuracy of TOA positions. The passive- TDOA node is able to estimate its position and the positions of other TOA nodes involved as long as enough measurements are available. Subsequently, these positions can be coupled to reduce the noise and improve the final accuracy. Furthermore, this operational mode can be used to locate unknown nodes with no location capabilities at all, as explained in more detail previously in this document.

All these applications of the passive-TDOA algorithm give rise to dramatic improvements in the scalability of the system, since more customers can be located while only a few TOA positioning processes are running. Note, however, that all the applications of the passive- TOA algorithm depend on their expected accuracy, since a large error in the positions computed by passive-TDOA will make these positions useless, and, therefore, system scalability will not increase at all. This work analyses the accuracy expected from passive- TDOA under several conditions and compares it with the positioning error achieved by a regular 2-way TOA algorithm.

It must be noted that, even though the algorithms are addressed to ad hoc networks, they can be implemented in other networks based on infrastructure, such as those operating under the standard IEEE 802.11. In these networks, the anchors would be the access points, and the terminal nodes would be the 802.11 clients. This demonstrates the capabilities of the algorithm presented and the wide range of applications for which it can be used.

6. CONCISE SUMMARY

This chapter addresses the positioning issue within the ad hoc framework. Current literature indicates that ad hoc algorithms primarily concentrate on this subject, as location techniques employed in other cellular technologies are applicable in the ad hoc context. The primary algorithms suggested for ad hoc placement are outlined, with particular emphasis on passive-TDOA. This technique is designed to enhance the scalability of two-way Time of Arrival (TOA) solutions while simultaneously ensuring satisfactory accuracy metrics. Two operational modes are elucidated comprehensively, and the primary applications of this method are examined.

FOOTNOTES

1. "Ad hoc" is actually a Latin phrase that means "to this (thing, purpose, end, etc.)"

REFERENCES

1. Stojmenovic, I. (2002). Position-based routing in ad hoc networks, *IEEE Communications Magazine*, vol. 40, July 2002, pp. 128-134, ISSN: 0163-6804.
2. Bourkerche, A.; Oliveira, H.; Nakamura, E. & Loureiro, A. (2007). Localization Systems for Wireless Sensor Networks, *IEEE Wireless Communications*, Vol. 14, December 2007, pp. 6-12, ISSN: 1536-1284.
3. Seidel, S.Y. & Rapport, T.S. (1992). 914 MHz path loss prediction Model for Indoor Wireless Communications in Multi-floored buildings. *IEEE Trans. on Antennas & Propagation*, vol. 40, no. 2, February 1992, pp. 207-217, ISSN: 0018-926X.
4. Wang, Y.; Jia, X. & Lee, H.K. (2003). An Indoors Wireless Positioning System Based on Wireless Local Area Network Infrastructure, *Proceedings of the 6th International Symposium on Satellite Navigation*, pp. 1-13, University of New South Wales, Melbourne (Australia), July 2003.
5. Lassabe, F.; Canalda, P.; Chatonnay, P. & Spies, F. (2005). A Friis-based calibrated model for WiFi terminals positioning, *Proceedings of 6th IEEE International Symposium on a World of Wireless Mobile and Multimedia Networks (WOWMOM)*, pp. 382-387, ISBN: 0-7695-2342-0, Giardini Naxos, Messina (Italy), June 2005.
6. Bahl, P. & Padmanabhan, V. (2000). Radar: An In-Building RF-based User Location and Tracking System, *Proceedings of the 19th IEEE Conference on Computer Communications (INFOCOM)*, vol. 2, pp. 775-784, ISBN: 0-7803-5880-5, Tel Aviv (Israel), March 2000.
7. Kotanen, A.; Hannikainen, M.; Leppakoski, H. & Hamalainen, T.D. (2003). Positioning with IEEE 802.11b wireless LAN. *Proceedings of the 14th IEEE International Sympossium on Personal, Indoor and Mobile Radio Communications (PIMRC)*, vol. 3, pp. 2218-2222, ISBN: 0-7803-7822-9, Beijing (China), September 2003.
8. Ciurana, M.; Barcelo-Arroyo F. & Izquierdo, F. (2007). A ranging system with IEEE 802.11 data frames, *Proceedings of the 1st IEEE Radio and Wireless Symposium*, pp. 133-136, ISBN: 1-4244-0445-2, Long Beach, California (USA), January 2007.

9. Ibraheem, A. & Schoebel, J. (2007). Time of Arrival Prediction for WLAN Systems Using Prony Algorithm, *Proceedings of the 4th Workshop on Positioning, Navigation and Communication (WPNC)*, pp. 29-32, ISBN: 1-4244-0871-7, Hannover (Germany), March 2007.

10. Reddy, H. & Chandra, G. (2007). An improved Time-of-Arrival estimation for WLAN-based local positioning, *Proceedings of the 2nd International Conference on Communication Systems software and middleware (COMSWARE)*, pp. 1-5, ISBN: 1-4244-0613-7, Bangalore (India), January 2007.

11. 3GPP. (2004). Functional stage 2 description of LCS; Technical Specification Group Services and System Aspects, *3GPP TS 23.271*, version 6.8.0, June 2004.

12. 3GPP. (2002). Location Services (LCS); Functional description; Stage 2, *3GPP TS 03.71,* version 8.7.0, September 2002.

13. Pages-Zamora, A., Vidal, J. & Brooks, D.H. (2002). Closed-form solution for positioning based on angle of arrival measurements. *Proceedings of the 13th IEEE International Symposium on Personal, Indoor and Mobile Radio Communications (PIMRC)*, vol. 4, pp. 1522-1526, ISBN: 0-7803-7589-0, Pavilhão Atlântico, Lisbon (Portugal), September 2002.

14. Savvides, A.; Han, C.C. & Srivastava, M.B. (2001). Dynamic Fine-Grained Localization in Ad-Hoc Wireless Sensor Networks. *Proceedings of the 7th ACM International Conference on Mobile Computing and Networking*, pp. 166-179, ISBN: 1-58113-422-3, Rome (Italy), July 2001.

15. Sun, G.; Chen, J.; Guo, W. & Ray-Liu, K.J. (2005). Signal processing techniques in network- aided positioning: a survey of state-of-the-art positioning designs, *IEEE Signal Processing Magazine*, vol. 22, no. 4, July 2005, pp. 12-23, ISSN: 1053-5888.

16. Doherty, L.; Ghaoui, L.E. & Pister, K.S.J. (2001). Convex Positioning Estimation in Wireless Sensor Networks. *Proceedings of the 20th IEEE Conference on Computer Communications (INFOCOM)*. vol. 3, pp. 1655-1663, ISBN: 0-7803-7016-3, Anchorage, AK (USA), April 2001.

17. Bulusu, N.; Heidemann, J. & Estrin, D. (2000). GPS-less low cost outdoor localization for very small devices, *IEEE Personal Communications,* vol. 7, October 2000, pp. 28-34, ISSN: 1070-9916.

18. Römer, K. (2003). The Lighthouse Location System for Smart Dust, *Proceedings of the 1st* ACM/USENIX *international conference on Mobile systems, applications and services,* pp. 15-30, San Francisco, California (USA), May 2003.

19. Niculescu, D. & Nath, B. (2003). DV based positioning in ad hoc networks. *Springer Journal of Telecommunication Systems*, vol. 22, no. 1-4, January 2003, pp. 267-280, ISSN: 1018- 4864.

20. Capkun, S.; Hamdi, M. & Hubaux, J. (2001). GPS-free positioning in mobile ad-hoc networks. *Proceedings of the Hawaii International Conference on Systems Sciences (HICSS)*, pp. 1-10, ISBN: 0-7695-0981-9, Maui, Hawaii (USA), January 2001.

21. Niculescu, D. & Nath, B. (2003). Localized Positioning in Ad Hoc Networks. *Elsevier Ad Hoc Networks*, vol. 1, no. 2-3, September 2003, pp. 247-259.

22. Nagpal, R.; Shrobe, H. & Bachrach, J. (2003). Organizing a Global Coordinate System from Local Information on an Ad Hoc Sensor Network. *International Workshop on Information Processing in Sensor Networks (IPSN).* Published as Lecture Notes in Computer Science, LNCS 2634, pp. 333-348. ISSN 0302-9743.

23. Fu, Y.; Liu, H.; Qin, J. & Xing, T. (2006). The localization of wireless sensor networks nodes based on DSSS. *Proceedings of the IEEE International Conference on Electro/Information Technology*. pp. 465-469. ISBN: 0-7803-9592-1, East Lansing, MI (USA), May 2006.

24. He, T.; Huang, C.; Blum, B.; Stankovic, J. & Abdelzaher, T. (2003). Range-Free Location Schemes for Large Scale Sensor Networks, *Proceedings of the 9th annual international conference on Mobile computing and networking (MOBICOM)*, pp. 81-95, ISBN: 1- 58113-753-2, San Diego, CA (USA), September 2003.

25. Yang, S; Kang, D.; Namgoong, Y.; Choi, S. & Shin, Y. (2008). A simple asynchronous UWB position location algorithm based on single round-trip transmission. *IEICE Transactions on Fundamentals of Electronics, Communications and Computer Sciences.* vol. E91-A, no. 1, January 2008, pp. 430-432, ISSN:0916-8508.

26. Martin-Escalona, I. & Barcelo-Arroyo, F. (2008). A New Time-Based Algorithm for Positioning Mobile Terminals in Wireless Networks, *EURASIP Journal on Advances in Signal Processing*, Hindawi Publishing Corporation, vol. 2008, pp. 1-10. ISSN: 1687-6172.

27. OMA (2008), Secure User Plane Location Architecture (SUPL), Open Mobile Alliance, *[Online]*, http://www.openmobilealliance.org.

Chapter 32 LOCATION TRACKING SCHEMES FOR BROADBAND WIRELESS NETWORKS

1. INTRODUCTION: AN OVERVIEW

The IEEE 802.16-2004 standard for wireless metropolitan area networks (WMAN) is meant to facilitate last mile wireless broadband access by addressing the requirements for increased capacity, elevated data rates, and enhanced multimedia capabilities. The IEEE 802.16e standard (IEEE Std 802.16e-2005, 2006) improves the earlier IEEE 802.16-2004 specification by resolving mobility concerns for mobile stations (MSs). The IEEE 802.16-2009 standard (IEEE Std 802.16-2009, 2009) has recently been designated as a consolidated version of the IEEE 802.16 specification by the IEEE 802.16 maintenance work group. The IEEE 802.16-2009 standard is recognized as the version of IEEE 802.16-2004 and integrates content from IEEE 802.16e-2005, IEEE 802.16-2004/Cor1-2005, IEEE 802.16f-2005, and IEEE 802.16g-2007. To meet the E911 Phase II mandate established by the Federal Communications Commission, location-based services (LBSs) (Perusco & Michael, 2007) are regarded as a fundamental component of the IEEE 802.16-2009 standard. Furthermore, to achieve effective resource management, location updates are crucial for various other activities, including paging processes.

The IEEE 802.16 standard mandates the provision of adequate location estimation capability throughout a broad spectrum of mobile station velocities. Location tracking is intended as a method to deliver accurate estimations for monitoring the movement patterns of the mobile station. Nevertheless, some concerns must be addressed prior to using the position tracking mechanism within the IEEE 802.16 system. It is observed that timing information, specifically the time-difference-of-arrival (TDOA) measurements, from a minimum of four base stations (BSs) is necessary to execute a two-dimensional location estimation and tracking for a mobile station (MS). The rigorous synchronization requirements of the IEEE 802.16 OFDMA-based system render frequent Time Difference of Arrival (TDOA) measurements with neighboring (non-serving) base stations a time-consuming and unrealistic endeavor for location estimation and tracking. Frequent scanning for neighboring base stations is an inefficient use of bandwidth, particularly in broadband wireless communication.

This chapter proposes two position tracking strategies to mitigate the issue of frequent connections between the mobile station and neighboring base stations. The kinematics-assisted location tracking (KLT) scheme employs kinematic relationships to estimate the mobile station's location at a specific time when neighboring base stations are unavailable, whereas the geometry-assisted location tracking (GLT) algorithm leverages geometric constraints for predicting the mobile station's position. The two techniques are designed to interpolate the position of a mobile station (MS) between two direct location estimations from the MS to the neighboring base stations (BSs). The simulations will demonstrate that both proposed systems may deliver viable performance with markedly less communication overhead.

2. TDOA MEASUREMENTS OF IEEE 802.16 NETWORK

To illustrate for the TDOA measurement scheme, the procedures related to the basics of IEEE 802.16 network operations are introduced first. The IEEE 802.16 adopts OFDMA based tech- nique, which implies the MS and the serving BS should synchronize in both time and fre- quency domain in order to receive the data correctly. Providing that an MS intends to join an IEEE 802.16 network, it conducts initial ranging with the serving BSs to obtain the synchro- nization parameter. In order to indicate which time slots for the MS to receive and transmit data, the downlink map (DL-MAP) and the uplink map (UL-MAP) are designed respectively. First the MS should listen to the BS's broadcast message to capture the ranging opportunity in the UL-MAP. The MS conducts contention based initial ranging to obtain related parameter and then is granted to join the network. After the MS establishes the link with serving BS, the MS performs periodic ranging in order to maintain the synchronization property while the MS may move to different place or the channel condition may vary at different time. It is noted that the periodic ranging is one of the routine process which is not considered as an overhead in this work. The ranging scheme is conducted by the MS sending assigned CDMA codes to serving BS to measure the distance related parameter, e.g. timing advance value. It is noticed that the timing advance value is the round trip time between the MS and the serving BS. The timing advance information is utilized to reserve the proper timing for the uplink transmission. By performing the ranging scheme, the serving BS measures the timing adjustment according to previously recorded timing advance information to update the distance between MS and serving BS. In order to support for the MS's mobility, the scanning scheme is specified for the MS to perform ranging with neighbor BSs. With the negotiation between serving BS and neighbor BSs, the scanning scheme can directly obtain ranging opportunity without contention. However, the MS is unavailable to serving BS while it performs scanning schemewiththeneighborBSs.

In the IEEE 802.16-2009 standard, two types of TDOA are specified as the downlink TDOA (D-TDOA) and the uplink TDOA (U-TDOA) where the measurements are performed at the MS and the BS respectively. These two schemes are based on ranging and scanning scheme to obtain time difference between the serving BS and the neighbor BSs. Due to the superior timing resolution obtained from the U-TDOA measurement at the BS (i.e., around 25 to 50 nanoseconds measured at the BS compared to microseconds at the MS), the U-TDOA mea- surement is chosen in this paper for achieving better location estimation accuracy. Moreover, as described in the standard, the general U-TDOA method is adopted while the frequency reuse factor is not equal to one which is considered as a more general case. Several assump- tions are specified as follows: (a) both the serving and neighbor BSs are operating with the same frame size; (b) the frames at both the serving and the neighbor BSs are synchronized; and (c) the MS can communicate with both the serving and the neighbor BSs.

Fig. 1 illustrates the timing diagram of the general U-TDOA measurement in IEEE 802.16- 2009. The MS ranges sequentially with the serving BS and neighbor BSs. It is noted that the second frame of the MS is operating on the same frequency with the serving BS and the third is the same with the neighbor BS. The serving BS (i.e., the 1st BS) and the neighbor BS (i.e., the 2nd BS) measure the timing adjustment t_adj1 and t_adj2 respectively, and the neighbor BS reports t_adj2 to the serving BS. The timing advance value t_adv remains the same since the MS does not make any timing adjustments while conducting ranging with both the serving and the neighbor BSs. Therefore, serving BS calculates the time difference *t*21 = (*t_adj*2 *t_adj*1)/2 and the difference of the MS's distance to the serving BS and neighbor BS is obtained by multiplying this difference by the speed of light.

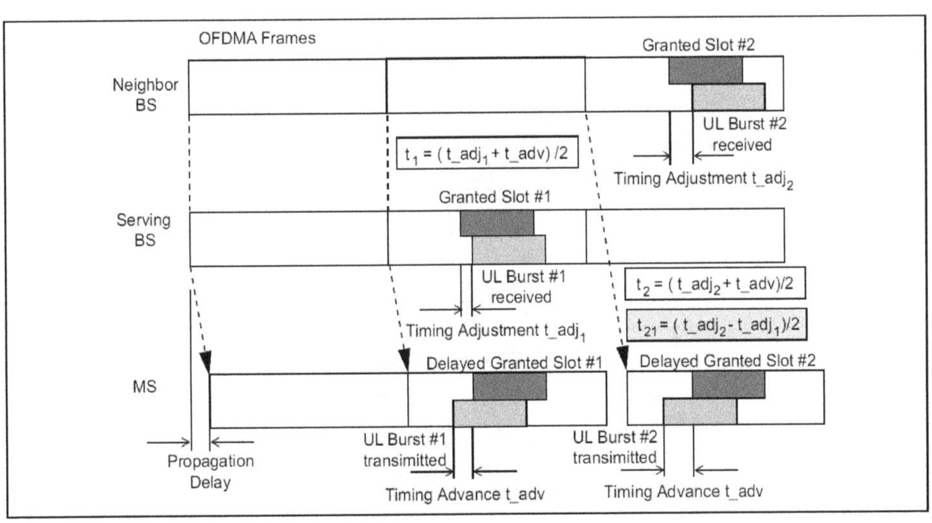

Fig. 1. Timing Diagram of the general U-TDOA measurement proposed in the IEEE 802.16- 2009 standard.

Fig. 2 illustrates the message exchange sequences for the general U-TDOA measurement. The serving BS requests neighbor BSs to assign a dedicated ranging opportunity for the MS. The MS will first conduct ranging with the serving BS in order to perform the U-TDOA measurement. Through the ranging response (RNG-RSP) message, the serving BS will assign a Rendezvous time, a CDMA code, and a Tx opportunity offset for the MS. It is noted that the Rendezvous time specifies the frame in which the BS transmits an UL-MAP containing the definition of the dedicated ranging region. As the Rendezvous time is expired, the MS will transmit the allocated CDMA code within the regular ranging region. The time-of-arrival (TOA) measurement t1,k performed at the serving BS (BS1) is obtained as an average value of both the timing adjustment $t\_adj_{1,k}$ from the measurement and the timing advance t_adv_k acquired from the periodic ranging, i.e., $t_{1,k} = (t\_adj_{1,k} + t\_adv_k)/2$ where the subscript denotes the *k*th time step.

Moreover, the dedicated ranging process is repeated through the neighbor BS (e.g. BS2) by sending the mobile scanning response (MOB_SCN-RSP) message. The neighbor BS measures *t_adj2,k* and reports the value to the serving BS. The TOA measurement for BS2 can therefore be acquired as *t2,k* = (*t_adj2,k* + *t_advk*)/2. As a result, the U-TDOA measurement calculated at the serving BS is obtained as *t21,k* = (*t_adj2,k* - *t_adj1,k*)/2. Similar process can be performed to obtain the timing information from the other neighbor BSs. Nevertheless, with the TDOA measurements, at least four BSs should be involved to perform a 2-D location estimation. There is a significant overhead to perform location tracking scheme as depicted in Fig. 2. In the following section, the proposed location tracking schemes are proposed to alleviate the overhead of frequent ranging with neighbor BSs.

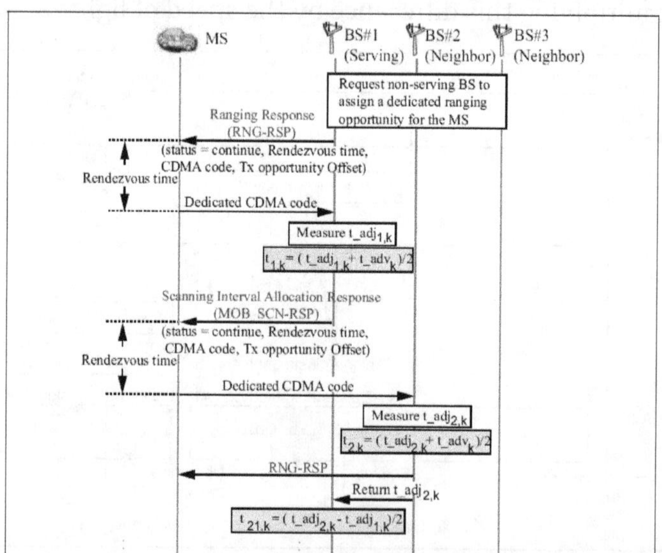

Fig. 2. The message exchange sequences of the general U-TDOA measurement method pro- posedintheIEEE802.16-2009standard.

3. PROPOSED LOCATION TRACKING SCHEMES

3.1 Mathematical Modeling of Signal Measurements

In this subsection, the mathematical models for both the TOA and the TDOA measurements are presented to facilitate the location estimation of the two-dimensional coordinates for the MS. The measured relative distance ($r_{i,k}$) between the MS and the ith BS (obtained at the kth time step) can be represented as

$$r_{i,k} = c \cdot t_{i,k} = \zeta_{i,k} + m_{i,k} + n_{i,k} + s_{i,k} \quad (1)$$

where $t_{i,k}$ denotes the TOA measurement obtained from the ith BS at the kth time step, and c is the speed of light. $r_{i,k}$ is contaminated with the TOA measurement noise $m_{i,k}$ due to the imprecision of the measuring device. The non-line-of-sight (NLOS) error $n_{i,k}$ is assumed to be existent in the considered environments, which is inherently a parameter with positive value.

$s_{i,k}$ denotes the unknown asynchronous clock time offset between the MS and the BS. The noiseless relative distance $\zeta_{i,k}$ between the MS and the ith BS can be obtained as

$$\zeta_{i,k} = [(x_k^\circ - x_{i,k})^2 + (y_k^\circ - y_{i,k})^2]^{\frac{1}{2}} \quad (2)$$

where $\mathbf{x}^\circ_k = [x_k^\circ \ y^\circ_k]^T$ represents the MS's true position at the kth time step, and $\mathbf{x}_{i,k} = [x_{i,k} \ y_{i,k}]^T$ is the location of the ith BS. On the other hand, the relative distance $r_{ij,k}$ from the TDOA measurement $t_{ij,k}$ can be obtained by computing the time difference between the MS w.r.t. the ith and the jth BSs as

$$\begin{aligned} r_{ij,k} &= (r_{i,k} - r_{j,k}) = c \cdot (t_{i,k} - t_{j,k}) = c \cdot t_{ij,k} \\ &= (\zeta_{i,k} - \zeta_{j,k}) + (m_{i,k} - m_{j,k}) + (n_{i,k} - n_{j,k}) \end{aligned} \quad (3)$$

It is noted that in IEEE 802.16-2009 standard each BS equips a GPS in order to achieve time synchronization. Therefore, the relationship $s_{i,k}\, s_{j,k} = 0$ is true since the frames at the serving and the neighbor BS are synchronized. As depicted in the previous section for the general U-TDOA method, the TOA measurement (in (1)) is acquired for the purposed of obtaining the TDOA measurement (in (3)).

3.2 Location Estimation and Tracking Algorithms

The main concept for the proposed schemes is to maintain the accuracy for location estimation with a reduced number of dedicated ranging (i.e., the general U-TDOA measurement in Figs. 1 and 2) between the MS and the BSs. The increased number of dedicated ranging with the neighbor BSs can result in unsatisfactory communication performance between the MS and its serving BS, e.g. with degraded scheduling performance for realtime applications. It is noted that the dedicated ranging state indicates the state for the MS to conduct the general U-TDOA method with the serving and the neighbor BSs as shown in Fig. 2. Without communications between the MS and the BSs, on the other hand, the non-dedicated ranging state (i.e., the gen- eral U-TDOA measurement is not available) is defined as the state in which the MS's location information is estimated and predicted by the proposed KLT and GLT schemes, which will be explained in the next two subsections.

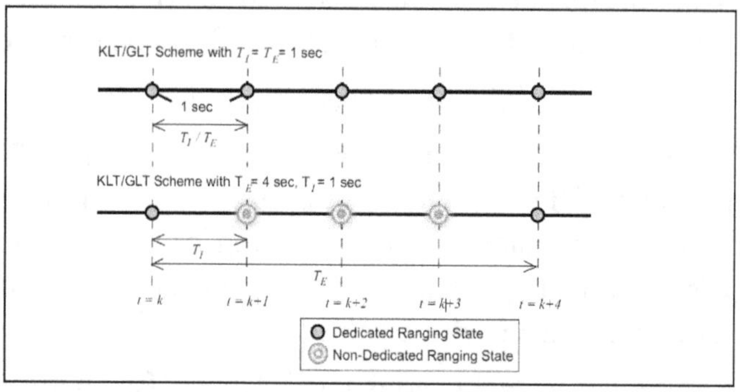

Fig. 3. The timing diagram for the relationship between the dedicated and non-dedicated rangingstates.

Fig. 3 illustrates the relationship between the dedicated and the non-dedicated ranging states. The location estimation period (T_E) is defined as the time duration between two dedicated ranging states. On the other hand, the location information period (T_I) is designed as $T_I = T_E / m$ with $m \geq 1$, which represents the time interval either between two non-dedicated ranging states or between a dedicated and a non-dedicated states. In other words, T_I is de- fined as the interleaved period where the MS's location information becomes available, either obtained from the general U-TDOA method of the proposed KLT/GLT scheme. In other word, the U-TDOA method is utilized at the dedicated ranging state; while the KLT/GLT scheme interpolates the position information at the non-dedicated ranging state. Moreover, the sampling time Δt is denoted as the time interval between the kth and the (k 1)th time steps as in (1) to (3) It is selected the same as the location information period, i.e. $\Delta t = T_I$.

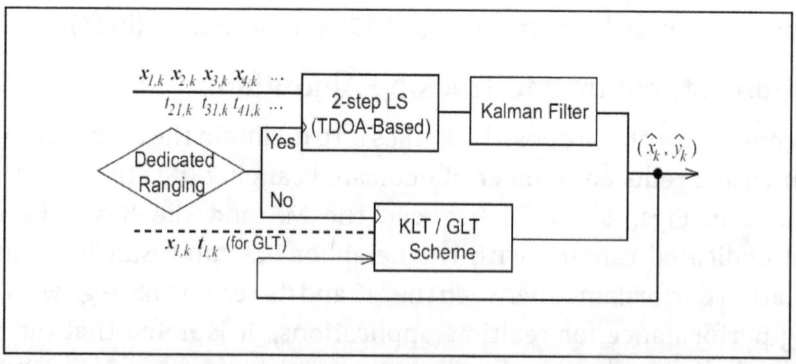

Fig. 4. The schematic diagram of the proposed KLT and GLT algorithms.

Fig. 4 illustrates the schematic diagram of the proposed KLT and GLT algorithms. Either the dedicated or the non-dedicated ranging can happen for obtaining the MS's estimated position $\hat{x}_k = [\hat{x}_k \, \hat{y}_k]^T$. For the dedicated ranging case, the cascaded location tracking (CLT) scheme as proposed in (Chen & Feng, 2005) is exploited. The CLT algorithm is cascaded by two functional components, i.e. the two-step least square (LS) method for location estimation and the Kalman filtering technique for location tracking. The two-step LS method obtains the initial location estimation $\hat{x}_k^{LS} = [\hat{x}_k^{LS} \, \hat{y}_k^{LS}]^T$ from the TDOA measurement input $t_{ij,k}$ (in (3)) within two computing iterations. Furthermore, the Kalman filter is utilized to smooth out and trace the estimation errors and finally acquires the MS's estimated location $\hat{x}_k = [\hat{x}_k \, \hat{y}_k]^T$. On the other hand, since the TDOA measurements are not available during the non-dedicated ranging state, two schemes are proposed to substitute the functionality of the two-step LS method as follows.

With the unavailability of the TDOA measurements during the non-dedicated state, the KLT scheme is utilized to adopt the predicted information from the output of the Kalman filter. Considering a three-states linear model, the MS's position, velocity, and acceleration can be estimated via the Kalman filter as $\hat{z}_k = [\hat{x}_k \, \hat{v}_k \, \hat{a}_k]^T$, where $\hat{x}_k = [\hat{x}_k \, \hat{y}_k]^T$, $\hat{v}_k = [\hat{v}_{x,k} \, \hat{v}_{y,k}]^T$, and $\hat{a}_k = [\hat{a}_{x,k} \, \hat{a}_{y,k}]^T$. Assuming that the state vector $\hat{z}_k$ is available either via the dedicated or non-dedicated ranging, the next non-dedicated states $\hat{z}_{k+1}$ at the $(k+1)$th time instant can be acquired by utilizing the feedback information from the output of the Kalman filter at time k.

3.2.1 Kinematics-Assisted Location Tracking (KLT) Scheme

By adopting the updates from the kinematic relationship, the MS's predicted position $\hat{x}_{k+1}$ at the $(k+1)$th time step can by acquired as

$$\hat{x}_{k+1}^{KLT} = \hat{x}_k + \hat{v}_k \cdot \Delta t + \frac{1}{2} \cdot \hat{a}_k \cdot \Delta t^2 \tag{4}$$

where Δt is the sampling interval as $\Delta t = T_I$. The location estimation and tracking at the non-dedicated ranging state can therefore be performed.

3.2.2 Geometry-Assisted Location Tracking (GLT) Scheme

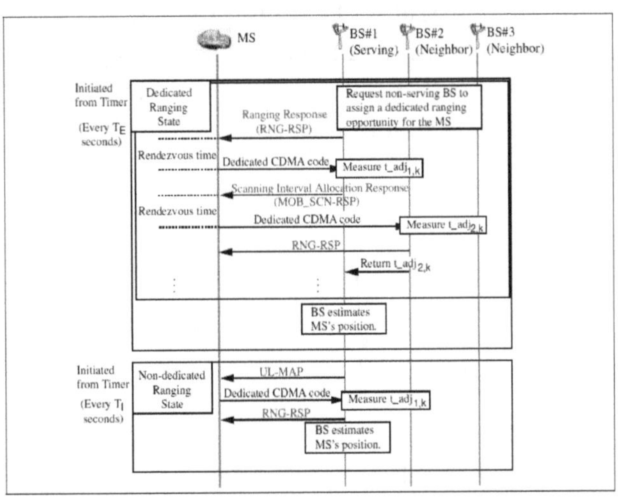

Fig. 5. The message exchange sequences of propose GLT schemes.

Similar to the KLT algorithm as described in the previous subsection, the proposed GLT scheme is utilized to provide location estimation during the non-dedicated ranging state. The concept of the GLT algorithm is to utilize the frequent periodic ranging between the MS and the serving BS. Based on the periodic ranging, the relative distance $r_{1,k}$ between the serving BS and the MS can be obtained from the corresponding TOA measurements $t_{1,k}$. Fig. 5 depicts the message exchange sequences of the proposed GLT schemes within the IEEE 802.16-2009 network. It is noticed that the flowchart is the same as the general U-TDOA scheme as in Figs. 1 and 2 at the dedicated ranging state. However, at the non-dedicated ranging state, the TOA measurement is obtained through periodic ranging scheme as shown in Fig. 5.

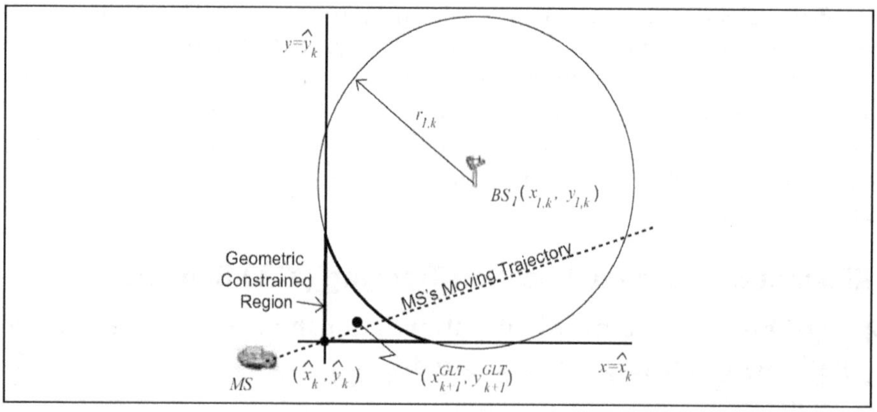

Fig. 6. The schematic diagram of the geometric constraints for the proposed GLT scheme.

$\hat{x}_k, y = \hat{y}_k$ As shown in Fig. 6, the circular region can be formed according to the center point $\mathbf{x}_{1,k} = [x_{1,k} y_{1,k}]^T$ with radius of $r_{1,k}$. Meanwhile, two additional linear equations can be acquired from the feedback of the Kalman filter at the kth time instant, i.e. $x =$. As a result, the two linear and one circular equations can be utilized to provide the geometric constraints for obtaining the MS's position estimation. Based on the constrained region, the LS method is employed to minimize the sum of the square errors for the MS's position. Therefore, the MS's estimated position by adopting the GLT scheme is acquired as

$$\hat{x}_{k+1}^{GLT} = \mathbf{G} \cdot (\mathbf{H}^T \mathbf{H})^{-1} \mathbf{H}^T \mathbf{J} \tag{5}$$

where

$$\mathbf{G} = \begin{bmatrix} 1 & 0 & 0 \\ 0 & 1 & 0 \end{bmatrix} \tag{6}$$

$$\mathbf{H} = \begin{bmatrix} -2x_{1,k} & -2y_{1,k} & 1 \\ 1 & 0 & 0 \\ 0 & 1 & 0 \end{bmatrix} \tag{7}$$

$$\mathbf{J} = \begin{bmatrix} r_{1,k}^2 - x_{1,k}^2 - y_{1,k}^2 \\ \hat{x}_k \\ \hat{y}_k \end{bmatrix} \tag{8}$$

4. PERFORMANCE EVALUATION

Simulations are performed to show the effectiveness of the proposed KLT and the GLT schemes. Different noise models (Greenstein et al., 1997) are considered in the simulations in order to represent various environments, including the urban, the suburban, and the rural cases. In the cellular-based network, an exponential distribution is assumed for the NLOS model with the distribution of $p_{n_{i,k}}(\upsilon)$ as where $\upsilon_{i,k} = c \cdot T_{i,k} = c \cdot T_m \zeta_{i,k}^{\varepsilon} \omega$ is the RMS delay spread between the ith BS to the MS at the kth time step; T_m is the median value of $T_{i,k}$ whose value depends on various environments, i.e. $T_m = 0.4$, 0.3, and 0.1 for urban, suburban, and rural respectively. ε is the path loss exponent which is assumed to be 0.5. The shadow fading factor ω is a lognormal random variable with zero mean and standard deviation σ_ω chosen as 4 dB in the simulations. Moreover, the measurement noises (i.e. $m_{i,k}$ in (1)) is considered Gaussian-distributed as $N \sim (0, \sigma_m^2)$ with $\sigma_m = 10$ m. The asynchronous offset (i.e. $s_{i,k}$ in (1)) between the MS and the BS clock time is also assumed to be Gaussian-distributed with $\sigma_s = 7.5$ m.

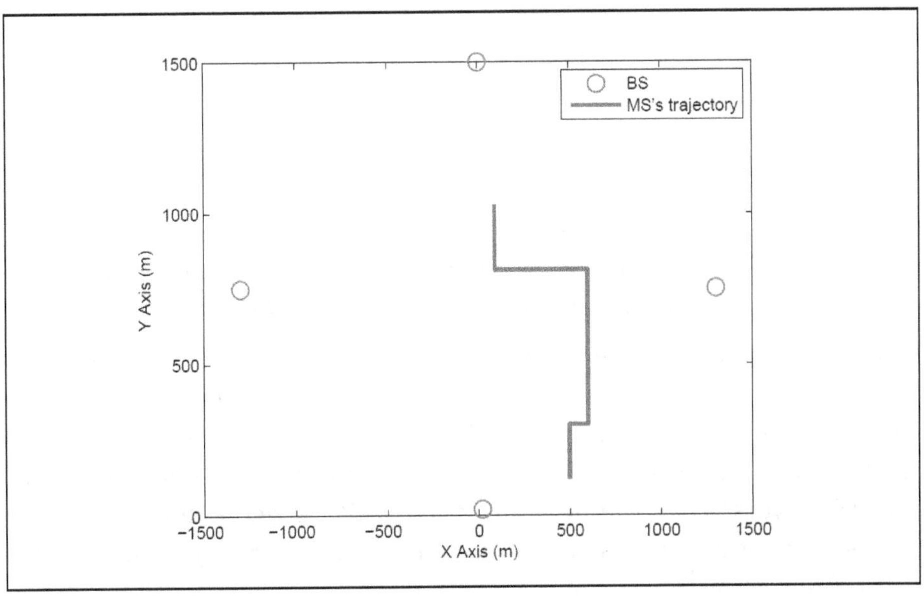

Fig. 7. The geometric layout of the simulation (Green Line: MS's True Trajectory; Red Empty Circles: thePositionoftheBSs)).

Fig. 7 illustrates the MS's trajectory with the Manhattan street scenario in the simulation. The MS's true trajectory is illustrated via the green lines; while the locations of the BSs are represented by the red empty circles as in Fig. 7. The acceleration is designed to vary at time $t = 21$, 26, 31, 47, 63, 76, and 89 sec from $a_k = (a_{x,k}, a_{y,k}) = (0, -1)$, (4, 0), (-4, 0), (0, 2), (0, -2), (-3, 0) to (3, 0) m/sec^2. The corresponding MS's velocity lies between (0, 70) km/hr.

Fig. 8 shows the performance comparison between the proposed KLT and GLT schemes under the urban environment (with *TI* = 1 sec and *TE* = 1, 2, and 4 sec). It is noted that the position error is defined as $P_e = \|\hat{x}_k - x_k^{\circ}\|$. The case with *TI* = *TE* = 1 sec indicates that the non-dedicated ranging does not exist, which is served as the lower bound of the estimation errors. As shown in the figure, comparably inferior performance is observed with larger values of *TE*, which indicates that the dedicated ranging with the TDOA measurement is not frequently available. Moreover, the proposed GLT algorithm outperforms the KLT scheme for each specific case, e.g. around 50 m less of the position error under the case of *TE* = 4 sec with 67% of position errors.

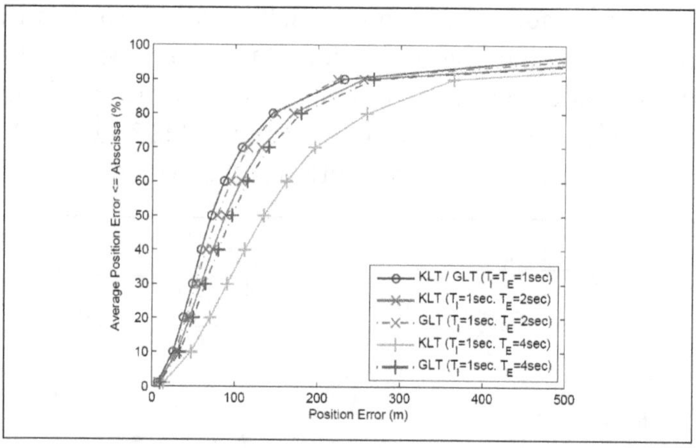

Fig. 8. Performance comparison between the proposed KLT and GLT schemes under the urban environment (T_I = 1sec).

Fig. 9 shows the performance comparison with 67% of position errors between the proposed KLT and GLT schemes under the different noise environment. It is noticed that the KLT scheme performs similar to GLT scheme at the smaller NLOS environment, e.g. Tm = 0.1 (rural environment). However, the performance of KLT is comparably worse than the per- formance of GLT scheme under the excessive NLOS errors. The effectiveness of adopting the periodic ranging in GLT scheme can be observed in the case.

In order to evaluate the overhead of the frequent location tracking, serving BS unavailable time (i.e. T_U) is defined for the percentage of the frame communicating between the MS and the neighbor BSs. In the dedicating ranging period, the MS should synchronize with other BSs and therefore the ongoing transmission should be buffered in serving BS. Although the more frequent the dedicating ranging performed brings higher location estimation accuracy, the total usage in the serving BS's point of view would decrease. In the Fig. 2, the MS needs to synchronize to the neighbor BSs first and then performs the ranging process. The following parameter is defined to perform a dedicated ranging with the other BSs:

- *Tsyn*: average time to synchronize with the new BS
- *Trng*: average time to perform range process with a BS

The values for *Tsyn* and *Trng* are chosen as 20 millisecond (msec) and 30 msec in average as reported in (Jiao et al., 2007). As the dedicated ranging specified for the LBS, the time of *Trng* might be shorter. In terms of the *Tsyn* and *Trng*, the serving BS unavailable time counts in percentageis:

$$T_U = \frac{3 * (T_{syn} + T_{rng})}{T_E} \tag{10}$$

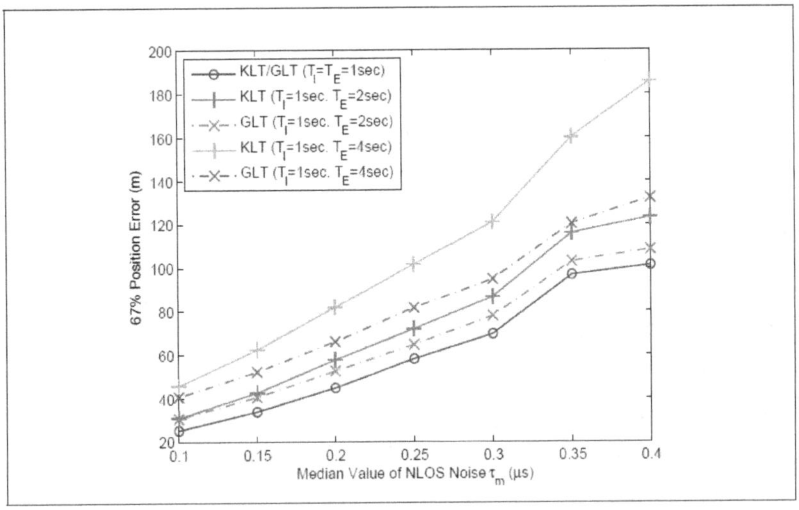

Fig. 9. Performance comparison between the proposed KLT and GLT schemes under different NLOS noise (T_I = 1 sec).

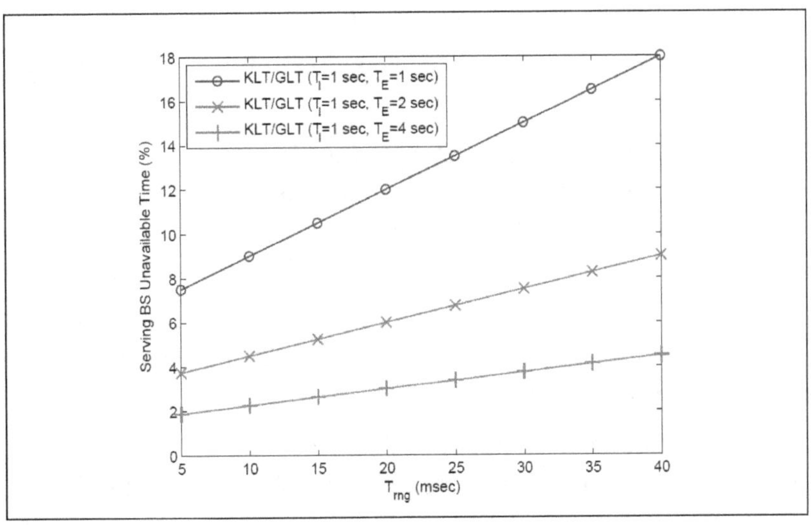

Fig. 10. Serving BS unavailable time via the average time to perform range process.

It is noted that at least three neighbor BSs participate a dedicated ranging. Fig. 10 shows the percentage of the BS unavailable time via the *Trng* from 5 to 40 msec. As the curves shows that the KLT/GLT scheme with T_E = 2*sec* has half unavailable time than T_E = 1*sec*. While the overhead of the serving BS is considered as the important factor, comparing to the per- formance of location estimation in Fig. 9, the KLT/GLT scheme with T_E = 2*sec* is a better solution with a tradeoff.

5. CONCISE SUMMARY

Two assisted location tracking schemes are proposed in this paper. The schemes are capable of estimating the position, velocity, and acceleration of the MS during the dedicated ranging state. With the non-dedicating ranging state, the assisted methods utilizing the tracking information and the periodic ranging information are proposed. It is shown in the simulation results that the proposed location tracking schemes provide consistent performance and reduces the overhead of the serving BS.

REFERENCES

1. Chen, C.-L. & Feng, K.-T. (2005). Hybrid location estimation and tracking system for mobile devices, *Proc. IEEE 61st Vehicular Technology Conferencec 2005-Spring*,Vol.4.
2. Greenstein, L. J., Erceg, V., Yeh, Y. S. & Clark, M. V. (1997). A new path-gain/delay-spread propagation model for digital cellular channels, *IEEE Trans. Veh. Technol.* 46: 477 – 485.
3. IEEE Std 802.16-2004 (2004). IEEE standard for local and metropolitan area networks - part 16: Airinterferenceforfixedbroadbandwirelessaccesssystems.
4. IEEE Std 802.16-2009 (2009). IEEE Standard for Local and metropolitan area networks Part 16: Air Interface for Broadband Wireless Access Systems, pp. 1–2082.
5. IEEE Std 802.16e-2005 (2006). IEEE Standard for Local and Metropolitan Area Networks - Part 16: Air Interference for Fixed Broadband Wireless Access Systems, Amendment 2: Physical and Medium Access Control Layers for Combined Fixed and Mobile Oper- ationinLicensedBandsandCorrigendum1.
6. Jiao, W., Jiang, P. & Ma, Y. (2007). Fast handover scheme for real-time applications in mobile wimax, *Proc. IEEE International Conference on Communications*,pp.6038–6042.
7. Perusco, L. & Michael, K. (2007). Control, Trust, Privacy, and Security: Evaluating Location- basedServices,*IEEE Technol. Soc. Mag.* 26:4–16.

33 Chapter

WIRELESS MULTI-HOP LOCALIZATION GAMES FOR RECREATIONAL COMPUTING

1. INTRODUCTION: AN OVERVIEW

Ad-hoc networking capabilities offer the ability to establish diverse network types without reliance on infrastructure base stations. Innovative solutions for sensor networks, such as Zigbee, utilize ad-hoc networking capabilities to establish networks. These sensor nodes can effortlessly establish networks in outside fields and indoor environments without the need for extensive base station setup, while also monitoring neighboring information in areas often inaccessible for human observation. The Internet Engineering Task Force (IETF) has deliberated on the method of ad-hoc networking through the Mobile Ad-hoc Network (MANET) Working Group. MANET is a possible method for establishing alternative network infrastructure in scenarios where conventional networks are compromised due to disasters such as fires and earthquakes. The wireless terminals equipped with radio capabilities transmit data to a specified destination. Recently, businesses such as Nintendo and Sony Computer Entertainment have manufactured mobile game consoles equipped with ad-hoc networking capabilities. Networking capabilities are crucial for facilitating the collaboration of several participants in gaming. The ad-hoc networking technology, being independent of infrastructure networks, facilitates a player's seamless entry into a game via a wireless network. To employ this functionality, several games utilizing ad-hoc networking capabilities have been created. Nevertheless, the games released to far exclusively utilize ad-hoc networking functionalities for game participation.

We have created two wireless multi-hop localization games with ad-hoc networking capabilities and have shown various preliminary results in (29). The suggested games, a war game and a tag game, are derived from traditional field games. Players utilize mobile gaming consoles equipped with ad-hoc networking functionalities to navigate a field. The games employ wireless multi-hop localization to ascertain node placements. Members of one team collaboratively create an ad-hoc network to ascertain their whereabouts and vie for positional precision against the opposing team. We employed an established multi-hop localization method known as ROULA (28). We employed simulation to assess the multi-hop localization games and examine their attributes. Node velocity and obstacle position determined the win rate of the games, whereas preserving connectivity and adhering to local regulations resulted in elevated win rates. The findings indicated that the suggested games functioned effectively as localization apps utilizing ad-hoc networking capabilities.

This study aims to introduce novel localization applications utilizing ad-hoc networking capabilities. The notion of multi-hop localization games is introduced. Wireless multi-hop localization games are assessed to determine the performance of localization-based games with ad-hoc networking capabilities in a simulated environment. The principal findings derived from the simulation are encapsulated as follows.

- The win rate for the games depends on node velocity and obstruction position.
- A higher connectivity constraint leads to a higher win rate for the games.
- Enforcing the local rule of the death penalty enables the win rate to be controlled for the games.

2. LOCALIZATION AND MOBILE GAMES

2.1 Multi-hop localization

Multi-hop localization techniques have been discussed for wireless multi-hop networks such as sensor and ad-hoc networks. The motivation behind developing multi-hop localization is wanting to know where the node position is in wireless multi-hop networks by using a small fraction of the anchor nodes. An anchor node is one whose position is known in advance through means such as global positioning system (GPS). Much research has been conducted on how to estimate node positions in wireless multi-hop networks (9–15; 28). Most localization techniques can be categorized into two types. The first is localization by using extra ranging devices, such as ultra sound devices, and the second is localization without using extra ranging devices.

In AHLoS (11), an iterative multilateration by using time-of-arrival (TOA) measurements was proposed to estimate large numbers of node positions with a small number of anchor nodes. The basic idea behind iterative multilateration is that at least three anchor nodes carry out the multilateration to estimate unknown nodes. Once the positions for unknown nodes are estimated by anchor nodes, the nodes are configured as pseudo-anchor nodes. Then, pseudo- anchor nodes join to estimate unknown nodes that remain in the network. Another distance-measurement approach have been extensively discussed in the literature. In (16), robust trilateration using the rigidity of graph theory for flipping avoidance has been proposed. In sweeps (17), algorithms to identify global rigidity were employed to estimate the node positions without flipping for sparse node networks. In (18), an error control algorithm was formulated to mitigate against the error propagation for iterative localization. The distace measurement approach normally achieves precise positioning accuracy. However it requires extra ranging devices, increasing the cost for all nodes.

The localization scheme without using extra ranging devices has been developed for large- scale sensor networks, and it basically exploits connectivity information of multi-hop net- works. In GPS-less (9), anchor nodes first flood beacon packets containing their anchor lo- cation information, and unknown nodes estimate their positions by using anchor location information with a Centroid formula. In DV-Hop (10), the positions for unknown nodes in a network are estimated by using average hop-count distances from anchor nodes. First, an- chor nodes flood their location information to all other anchor nodes, and calculate the aver- age 1-hop distance. Next, anchor nodes carry out a trilateration to unknown nodes by using hop-count distances. In AFL (15), the positions of unknown nodes are estimated without us- ing anchor nodes. The basic idea behind AFL is to utilize reference nodes that represents the relative axis in a network. The five reference nodes are automatically selected in the manner described in (15), and they determine relative node positions based on the hop-counts from their reference positions. In REP (19), the hop-count distance in a network with holes is calculated by using boundary detection (20). Boundary detection is a technique that can detect the network boundary with only information on network connectivity. In (21), boundary detection and a Delaunay graph were jointly used to prevent node positions from flipping. The localization scheme without using ranging devices enables nodes to estimate node positions while only using the radio capabilities of a sensor node. Hence, it has great flexibility to enable nodes to be applied to localization in the network.

We previously developed optimized link state routing-based localization (ROULA) (28). ROULA does not require the use of extra ranging devices for any nodes and precisely estimate the node distance by using multipoint relay (MPR) nodes. We thus used ROULA in our proposed games to enable the nodes to estimate their positions. ROULA is described in Section 3.

2.2 Mobile games

Let us now present a brief history of mobile games and discuss different aspects of the pro- posed multi-hop localization games from these. A number of game consoles have been developed for the entertainment computing market. These game consoles have two basic types: home game consoles and mobile game consoles. The Nintendo Entertainment System™ ("Famicom" in Japan) is the iconic home game console and was introduced in 1983 by Nintendo (3). A user plays the games by using a wired hand-held controller. Famicon supports capabilities for multiplayer games. Two users can play games using two controllers connected by cables to the console.

Mobile game consoles have been developed with ad-hoc networking capabilities, such as Nin- tendo DS™ in 2004 by Nintendo (3) and Play Station Portable (PSP)™ in 2004 by SCE (4). Many video games on mobile game consoles have been released by game software companies. Hot shots golf™ (6) ("minna no golf" in Japan) is one of popular portable video games for PSP. Hot shots golf supports multiple players by using ad-hoc networking capabilities. However, hot shots golf only uses ad-hoc networking capabilities for joining the game.

Mobile games for ubiquitous computing environments have recently attracted a great deal of attention (23; 26; 27). Many varieties of mobile games have been developed thus far. Geo- caching (22) is a GPS-based treasure hunting game for outdoor environments. The basic idea behind geocaching is that players hide and seek out containers called "geocaches". A player hides a geocache and registers the positions provided by the GPS receiver. Once the geocache is registered and released on the geocaching web site, another player finds the geocache based on the positions. Geocaching is being carried out in the actual field, and everyone can get started by using a GPS receiver and mobile console with Internet capabilities.

Human Pacman (24) is a multiplayer field game using a GPS receiver and wireless networking capabilities. Pacman is a video game for Famicon and was originally developed by Namco (5) in 1980. Human Pacman is real field version of Pacman. Palyers are assigned to either the Pacman team or the Ghost team. Each team has at least two helpers to assist its own team. Virtual cookies are placed on the map and their positions correspond to a real field. The goals are for the Pacman team to collect all virtual cookies and for the Ghost team to catch all the Pacman players. Can You See Me Now? (CYSMN) (25) is a chase game based on location information with GPS. Three runners are visible to players' locations through an virtual online map and they run through actual city streets. Players avoid the runners and compete for the time elapsed since joining the game. If a runner gets within five virtual meters of a player, the player is seen and is excluded from the game.

Table 1. Comparisons of conventional mobile games with proposed games.

Game names	Scoring metrics	Player's behavior for game win	Networking capabilities	Real field use	No. of participants, Np	Required equipment
Hot shots golf™ (6)	Golf game score	Individual	Used to connect to other players	No	$1 \le NP \le 8$	Mobile console
Classical war game	Hitting with model gun	Individual	Not used	Yes	$2 \le NP$	Model guns and goggles
Classical tag game	Avoiding oni and elapsed time	Individual	Not used	Yes	$2 \le NP$	None
Geocaching (22)	Collecting geocaches	Individual	Used to display locations of geocaches	Yes	$1 \le NP$	Mobile console and GPS receiver
Human Pacman (24)	Collecting virtual cookies	Individual or group	Used to record player's trajectory	Yes	$8 \le NP$	HMD, mobile console and GPS receiver
CYSMN (25)	Avoiding runners and elapsed time	Individual	Used to display locations of players	Yes	$4 \le NP$	Mobile console and GPS receiver
Proposed games	Increasing positioning accuracy and elapsed time	Group	Used for ad-hoc connections and position estimations	Yes	20 NP	Mobile console and GPS receiver

Table 1 summarizes the features of current mobile games and the proposed multi-hop localization games. Our proposed game has novel distinct aspects from the other works. First, our proposed games use ad-hoc networking capabilities. Conventional mobile games use net- working capabilities such as wireless local area network (WLAN) to access the game server that provide the players' location information or a virtual map through the Internet. Our pro- posed games have novel uses for ad-hoc networking capabilities to conduct multi-hop localization in mobile games. Second, the scoring metric for the game is based on the positioning accuracy of the multi-hop localization technique. In some of the literature, localization is described as being "cooperative" (8). Nodes in the wireless network help to connect with one another to establish their relative positions. The positioning accuracy depends on the number of nodes in the network. Hence, nodes are required to cooperate to achieve higher positioning accuracy. Players must cooperative with their own team in the games.

Finally, let us discuss the number of participants in the proposed games. The proposed games require large numbers of participants compared with other games. This is because multi-hop localization without ranging devices requires a large number of nodes to estimate the positions of the nodes (28). ROULA is guaranteed to estimate all node positions when connectivity is about 20 (28). Connectivity indicates how many nodes are connected to other nodes in 1-hop on average. The least number of participants can be reduced further by using localization with ranging devices although improving the performance of the localization algorithm is beyond the scope of this paper.

3. OPTIMIZED LINK STATE ROUTING-BASED LOCALIZATION

3.1 Overview of ROULA

In our two wireless multi-hop localization games, the players used ROULA (28) to enable them to estimate their positions. Let us briefly describe the ROULA technique. A more detailed description of ROULA and its performance are described in (28).

Figure 1 has a conceptual representation of ROULA in a non-convex network topology. The basic idea behind ROULA is that each node matches regular triangles that form exactly convex curves, and makes them into global coordinates by merging overlapping regular triangles iteratively. ROULA is independent of anchor nodes and can determine the correct node positions in a non-convex network topology. In addition, ROULA is compatible with the optimized link state routing (OLSR) network protocol (30) and uses the inherent distance characteristic of MPR nodes.

A non-convex network topology can occur when nodes cannot be deployed in some areas because of obstructions, e.g., buildings or natural features such as trees or mountains. A non- convex network topology appears to be a non-convex curve if the network is seen from a global point of view. However, if the network is viewed locally, each small set of the network appears to be a convex curve. In other words, a non-convex network topology is composed of partially convex curves. To find these convex curves, nodes in ROULA search for nodes that are arranged into regular triangles.

Nodes in ROULA are assumed to use the OLSR protocol in the network layer. Using the OLSR protocol has two advantages. First, the MPR selection used in OLSR has the inherent characteristic of reducing distance errors in localization without using ranging devices. Second, nodes in OLSR always hold and update the latest 2-hop node information and MPR nodes in a proactive action that periodically floods hello packets. Node in ROULA localize MPR nodes as their 1-hop nodes without having to make any modifications to the MPR selection. Flood- ing hello packets and the computational task of MPR selection can be integrated by using the underlying network layer processes.

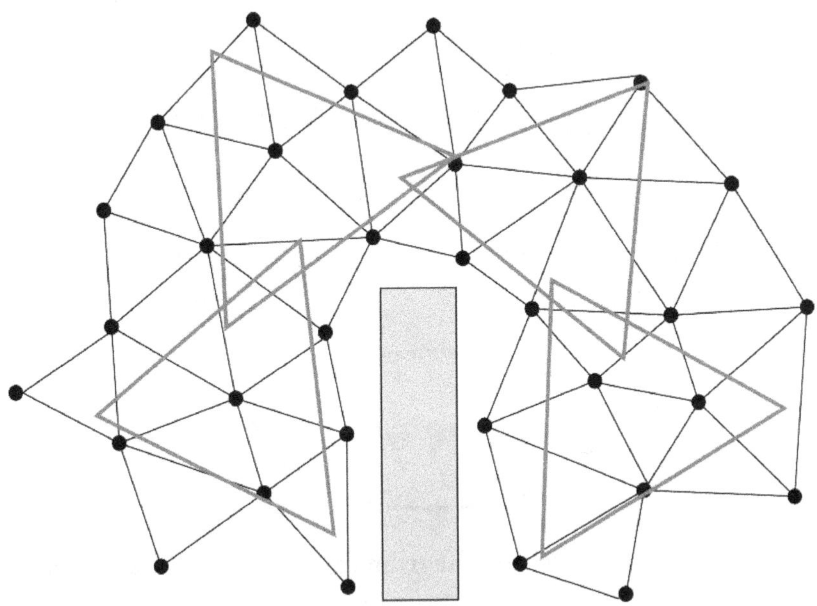

Fig. 1. Conceptual representation of ROULA in non-convex network topology.

3.2 Algorithm

The four operations for ROULA are summarized below (28).

1. **Estimating MPR node distances:** Nodes flood hello packets containing their own 1- hop nodes list to their 1-hop nodes. Once a node has a 2-hop nodes list, it selects MPR nodes and estimates the distances between them.
2. **Estimating farthest 2-hop node distances:** Each node selects the farthest 2-hop node for each MPR node and estimates the distances between them.

3. **Estimating relative node positions on regular triangles:** Nodes flood TRI_NOTICE packets to their farthest 2-hop nodes with their farthest 2-hop nodes list. Then, nodes that received TRI_NOTICE packets match regular triangles by using the received far- thest 2-hop nodes lists. Nodes then obtain sets of local coordinates by merging their overlapping regular triangles.
4. **Estimating one set of relative coordinates of network:** Sets of relative coordinates are collected and merged into one set of relative coordinates for the network. After that, nodes that have not estimated their positions estimate these by using the Centroid formula (28). If at least three anchor nodes are in the network, the relative coordinates can be converted into absolute coordinates that have the correct network orientation.

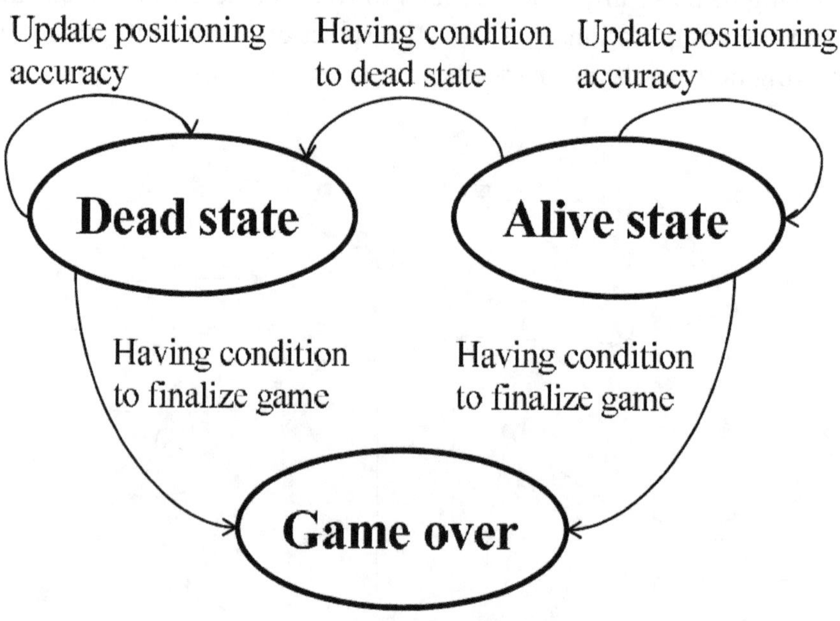

Fig. 2. Principle state transition diagram for multi-hop localization game.

We assume that nodes are deployed in a two-dimensional plane, and a sink node for the network merges all sets of local coordinates in the network. Routing protocol operations are assumed to be done without requiring additional time.

4. WIRELESS MULTI-HOP LOCALIZATION GAMES

4.1 Overview

The fundamental concept underlying wireless multi-hop localization games is that players on a team establish an ad-hoc network to estimate their positions and then compete for positioning accuracy with the other team by using a multi-hop localization technique. The players use mobile game consoles, called “nodes”, with ad-hoc networking capabilities and play the game on a field.

Figure 2 presents a principle state transition diagram for a multi-hop localization game. Each node is either in a “dead” or an “alive” state. The initial state is alive. Nodes periodically send hello packets and update their positions by multi-hop localization. The condition for transition to a dead state is based on positioning accuracy. The more accurate the positioning obtained by a node, the lower the probability of it transitioning to a dead state. When an alive node satisfies the condition to transition to a dead state, it makes the transition. The condition for finalizing the game is different for each game’s goal.

Two objectives in using ad-hoc networking capabilities are to connect nodes within a limited communications range and to estimate node positions. Once a node is connected to other nodes, it can specify the number of 1-hop nodes. ROULA can estimate node positions by using the number of 1-hop nodes.

Here, we have simplified the mobility characteristics of human motions to win a game as random motions.

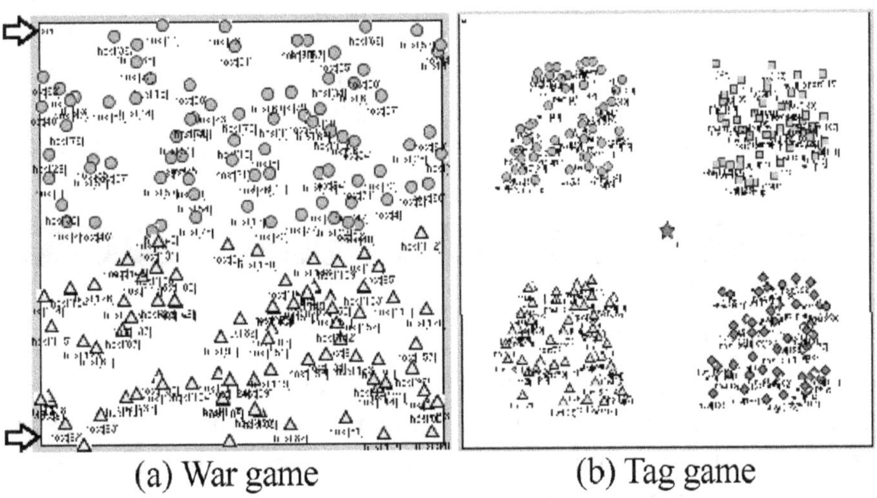

Fig. 3. Initial node placements of (a) war and (b) tag games. Teams 1, 2, 3, and 4 correspond to circles, triangles, squares, and diamonds. Oni is represented by star. Arrows indicate locations of enemy lines.

S.no	Algorithm 1 When node i senses hello packet of node j
1.	if node i is on same team as node j then
2.	receive packet.
3.	else
4.	drop packet.
5.	if ei == ej && U (0, 100) ≤ 50 then

6.	transition to dead state.
7.	else if ei > ej then
8.	transition to dead state.

4.2 War game

Let *Ntm* denote the number of teams and *Ng* denote the number of nodes required to finalize the war game. Each team has an equal number, *Nn*, of players. The goal of the war game is for *Ng* alive nodes on a team to reach the enemy line. *Ntm* |*Ntm* > 1, *Ng* |*Ng* > 0, and |*Nn Nn* |*Ng* can be varied. *Ntm* was consistently set to 2 and *Ng* was set to 1 for the war game discussed here.

Let us consider the case of *Nn* = 80. Figure 3(a) shows the node placement at the beginning of the war game. The field is divided in half, and each team initially occupies one of the two areas. Each team has the same number of nodes. The nodes for team 1 are represented by circles, and those for team 2 are represented by triangles. The arrows in Fig. 3(a) indicate the locations of the enemy lines, which were set 10 [m] from the back end of each team's area. The mobility of each node was modeled as a random waypoint constrained to proceed toward the enemy line. The velocity of each node was determined by using a random variable with an exponential distribution, ε(*v*), with a mean of *v*. If a node reaches the enemy line, its team is declared the winner. The nodes on each team periodically run multi-hop localization to estimate their positions. The nodes cannot communicate with the nodes on the other team.

S.no	Algorithm 2 When node i senses hello packet of oni
1.	if (0, 100) ei κ then
2.	Node i transitions to dead state.

We used the positioning error obtained by multi-hop localization as the metric to determine whether a node transitions to a dead state. In the proposed game, all nodes are assumed to be anchor nodes to enable relative coordinates to be converted into absolute coordinates and obtain the positioning error. The positioning error, *ei* , is normalized by the communication range, *R*:

$$e_i = \frac{\sqrt{(\hat{x}_i - x_i)^2 + (\hat{y}_i - y_i)^2}}{R}, \quad i = 1 \ldots N, \tag{1}$$

where *N* is the total number of nodes, (*xi* , *yi*) represents the true position of node *i*, and $(\hat{x}_i, \hat{y}_i)$ is the estimated position. The true position can be obtained by using GPS. When a node cannot estimate its own position, it is assigned a positioning error of 100%. A node transitions to a dead state depending on its positioning error. State transitions algorithm for node *i* is described in Algorithm 1. In the proposed games, nodes periodically flood hello packets. When a node senses a hello packet, the node receives the packet only if it has arrived from a node on the same team. Otherwise, the node drops the packet and decides whether to transition to the dead state on the basis of positioning errors (lines 5–8 of Algorithm 1). The u (a, b) represents a random variable with a uniform distribution in the interval $[a, b)$. If the node has the same positioning error, it transitions to a dead state with a probability of 50% (line 5 of Algorithm 1). Otherwise, the node transitions to a dead state if it has a greater positioning error. Once the node transitions to the dead state, it stops moving and receiving packets for localization. If all the nodes on a team transition to dead states, the other team is declared the winner.

4.3 Tag game

Let *Noni* denote the number of demons ("oni" in Japanese). Each team has the same number of players. The goal of the tag game is for players on each team to survive *Noni* oni attacks. Play- ers belong to one of the *Ntm* teams. The *Noni* oni move around the field and never transition to dead states. $Ntm \mid Ntm > 0$, $Noni > 0$, and $Nn > 0$ can be varied. Here, we have consistently considered the case where $Ntm = 4$, $Noni = 1$, and $Nn = 50$ for the tag game.

Figure 3(b) shows the node placement at the beginning of the tag game. Four teams are located in four equal areas. Teams 1, 2, 3, and 4 correspond to the circles, triangles, squares, and diamonds. The oni is located at the center of the field, and is represented by the star. The mobility of the oni and nodes was modeled as a random waypoint. The velocity of each node was chosen by using a random variable with an exponential distribution, $\varepsilon(v)$. The nodes periodically run multi-hop localization to estimate their positions.

Algorithm 2 gives the algorithm for node i to transition to a dead state. When node i receives a hello packet from the oni, it transitions to a dead state according to a probability based on its own positioning error. The basic operation of this metric is that if the positioning error is 60%, the probability to transition to the dead state is 60%. In line 1 of Algorithm 2, we introduced design parameter κ to mitigate the impact of positioning error. Our evaluation of the impact of κ is discussed in Section 5.3. We defined *max_step*, which denotes the maximum length of time for the tag game. The conditions to finalize the tag game are cases where only one team survives or *max_step* time is up. When *max_step* is out of time, the winner is the team that has the maximum survival time. The survival time is defined as

$$T_{survive} = \sum_{t=0}^{\text{max\_step}} \text{number of alive nodes.} \tag{2}$$

In our evaluation, we set *max_step* to 1000.

Table 2. Simulation parameters for war game

Field	500 × 500 [m]
Communication range	100 [m]
Node mobility	Random waypoint constrained to advance toward enemy line
Node velocity	E (v), v = 1, 2, 4 [m/step]

5. EVALUATION

5.1 Simulation setting

The simulation environment we used was a discrete event simulation environment, OM- NeT++ (31) with Mobility Framework (32). Existing network simulators do not have localization functionality. We implemented localization functionality into OMNeT++. Our localization simulation platform enables to test the localization performance with discrete event simulation. The simulation trials were conducted 30 times with random seeds, and the results were averaged.

5.2 War game

5.2.1 Impact of number of nodes

Table 2 lists the simulation parameters for the war game. The communication range was fixed and we have ignored packet loss in this paper. Hello packets were periodically sent by 5 time step.

Figure 4 shows snapshots of the war game at time steps of 500 and 1000 for 160 nodes. We set the mean node velocity (*v*) of all nodes to 1 [m/step]. A cross on a node represents a dead state. As we can see from Fig. 4(a), the nodes proceeded toward the enemy lines. As time went by, the nodes got closer to the enemy lines, and more and more nodes died, as seen in Fig. 4(b).

Figure 5 plots the positioning error, ratio of estimated nodes, and number of alive nodes against the time step when each team (T) had 120 nodes. The variance in the positioning error increased as the number of alive nodes decreased, which is consistent with the finding that the number of nodes contributes to positioning accuracy in multi-hop localization (28). As time went by, the number of nodes that could participate in localization decreased. Hence, the variance in positioning accuracy increased. We defined the ratio of estimated nodes as the percentage of nodes that could estimate their positions out of all alive nodes. The number of alive nodes decreased over time. A small number of nodes makes it difficult to estimate node positions using multi-hop localization. Therefore, the ratio of estimated nodes decreased as the number of nodes decreased. The number of alive nodes on both teams remained approximately the same over time. This is because all the nodes had the same velocity and used the same strategy to proceed to the enemy lines.

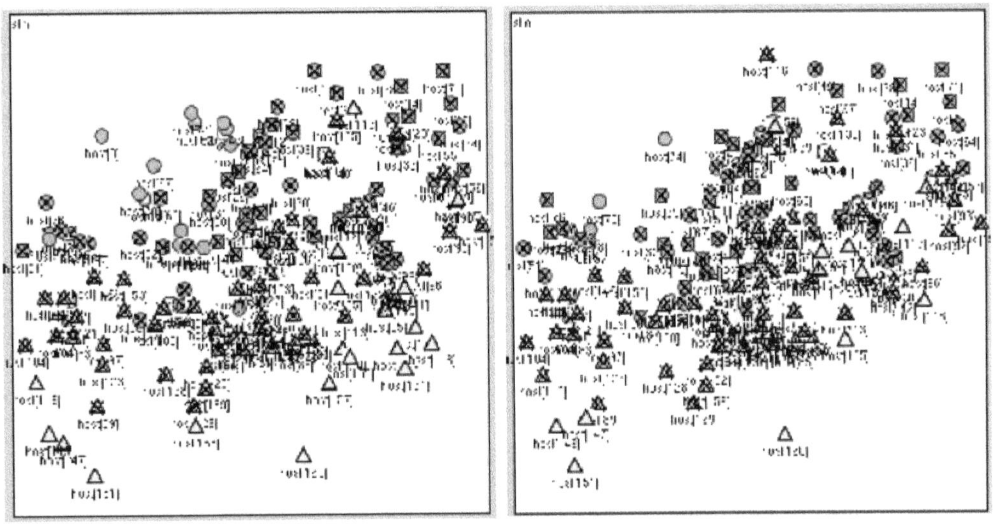

(a) t=500 (b) t=1000

Fig. 4. Snapshots of war games for time steps (a) 500 and (b) 1000 (*N*=160, *v*T1,*T*2={1,1}). Nodes for team 1 are represented by circles, and those for team 2 are represented by triangles. Cross on node represents dead state.

Figure 6 plots the results for 160 nodes. Compared with the results for 120 nodes, the ratio of estimated nodes was better, confirming that the number of nodes contributed to the ratio of estimated nodes.

Table 3 lists the number of wins by team for 30 trials with the different parameter settings. The row for scenario A in Table 3 shows that the number of wins for teams 1 and 2 for 120 and 160 nodes, corresponded to 16 and 14, and 15 and 15. The number of nodes did not significantly affect the number of wins.

Although the results presented here were for basic scenarios, we observed that the multi-hop localization game using ROULA worked well as a game with ad-hoc networking capabilities.

5.2.2 Impact of velocity

We evaluated the impact of velocity by varying the velocities of nodes on each team. Figure 7 shows snapshots of war games at time steps of 250 and 500 for 160 nodes and the mean node velocities of 1 [m/step] for team 1 and 4 [m/step] for team 2. As seen in Fig. 7(a), the nodes on team 2 were closer to the enemy line than those on team 1. Figure 7(b) shows that many nodes on team 2 died on their enemy's side, and that many nodes on team 1 died on their own side.

Figure 8 plots the positioning error, ratio of estimated nodes, and number of alive nodes when the velocities of nodes on team 1 were 1 and those on team 2 were 2. The ratio of estimated nodes of team 2 was slightly lower than that on team 1. This is because the nodes on team 2 were more spread out because they moved more quickly, making it more difficult to estimate their node positions using multi-hop localization.

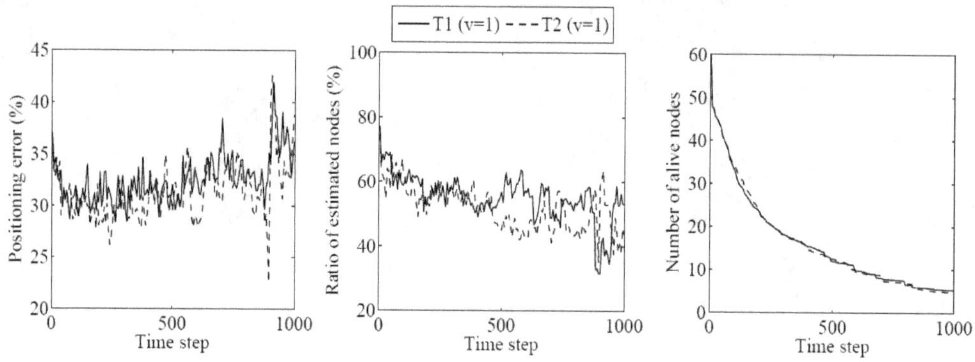

Fig. 5. Positioning error, ratio of estimated nodes, and number of alive nodes (*N*=120,*vT*1,*T*2={1,1}).

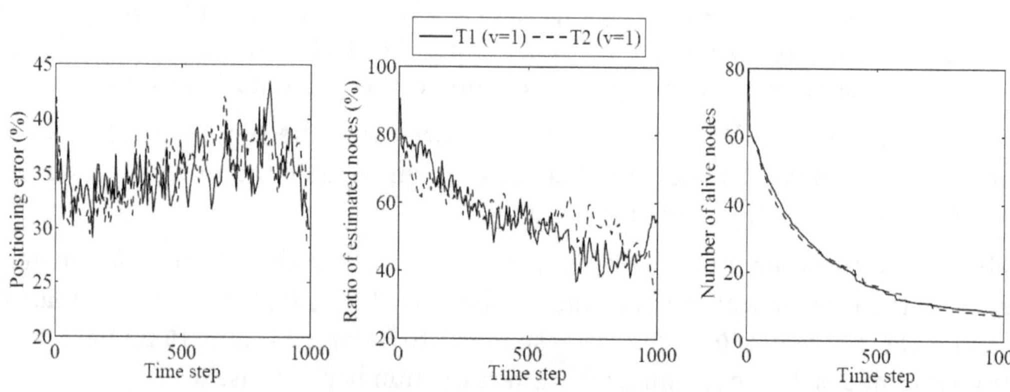

Fig. 6. Positioning error, ratio of estimated nodes, and number of alive nodes (*N*=160, *vT*1,*T*2={1,1}).

However, the goal of the war game was to reach the enemy line. The row for scenario B in Table 3 indicates the number of wins for teams 1 and 2 for velocities of 1 and 2 [m/step]. Although the ratio of estimated nodes on team 2 was slightly lower than that for team 1, team 2 had more wins. This is because the condition for finalizing the war game was reaching the enemy line; the team with the higher average node velocity had the greater number of wins.

Figure 9 plots the positioning error, ratio of estimated nodes, and the number of alive nodes when the velocities of nodes on team 1 were 1 [m/step] and those on team 2 were 4 [m/step]. The ratio of estimated nodes on team 2 was lower than that on team 1. However, team 2 had more wins as can be seen from the scenario B results in Table 3. This result suggests that the win rate for the war game depends on the node velocity of nodes.

Table 3. Number of team wins in war game. In scenario A, number of nodes N was varied and for $vT1,T2$ = {1, 1}. In scenario B, the velocity $vT1,T2$ was varied for N=160. In scenario C, y coordinate of obstruction was varied for N=160 and $vT1,T2$ = {1, 1}.

		Team1	Team2
Scenario A: N	120	16	14
	160	15	15
Scenario B: $v_{T1,T2}$	{1,2}	12	18
	{1,4}	9	21
Scenario C: y coord. of obst.	250	15	15
	100	29	1

5.2.3 Impact of obstruction position

We evaluated the impact of obstruction position by adding an obstruction to the field and varying its position. Figure 10 shows snapshots of war games assuming that there is an obstruction at position (250, 100). The height and width of the obstruction were 200 and 200 [m], respectively. No node could enter the portion with the obstruction. Figure 10 shows that nodes had trouble moving forward even though the velocities of the nodes on both teams were the same.

To evaluate the impact of the obstruction's position, we fixed its x-axis position at 250 and varied its y-axis position. As seen in Fig. 11, the positioning accuracy and ratio of estimated nodes were almost the same when the obstruction's position was (250, 250). As we can see from in Fig. 12, when the obstruction's position was (250, 100), the ratio of estimated nodes on team 2 was lower than that on team 1. This is because the obstruction made the network topology non-convex, making it difficult to estimate the node positions using multi-hop localization (28). Although the positioning accuracy for team 2 was better than that for team 1, the ratio of estimated nodes was lower. Hence, many nodes were assigned a 100% positioning error. Consequently, the number of alive nodes on team 2 was less than that on team 1.

Not surprisingly, the row for scenario C in Table 3 reveals that the number of team wins was closely related to the obstruction's position. This is because the scoring metric is based on positioning accuracy. The result proved that the win rate for the war game depends on obstruction positions.

Since multi-hop localization increases the positioning error in a non-convex network, the characteristics of an obstruction's position can be considered in team strategies. For example, players can collaborate to move to avoid making a non-convex network in a team's topology. The characteristics of multi-hop localization open the door to creating various game strategies.

5.3 Tag game

5.3.1 Impact of local rule on connectivity constraint

We evaluated the impact of two local rules, i.e, connectivity constraint and death penalty, in the tag game. The connectivity constraint is a rule where the nodes have to avoid situations where the current connectivity becomes less than or equal to a specified connectivity. The connectivity is defined by the number of nodes connected by 1-hop. Thus, nodes have to keep moving to prevent the current connectivity from being violated. The rule of the connectivity constraint can be easy to accomplish in an actual game, because each node can know the cur- rent connectivity due to the use of mobile game consoles with ad-hoc networking capabilities. First, we evaluated the impact of local rule of the connectivity constraint.

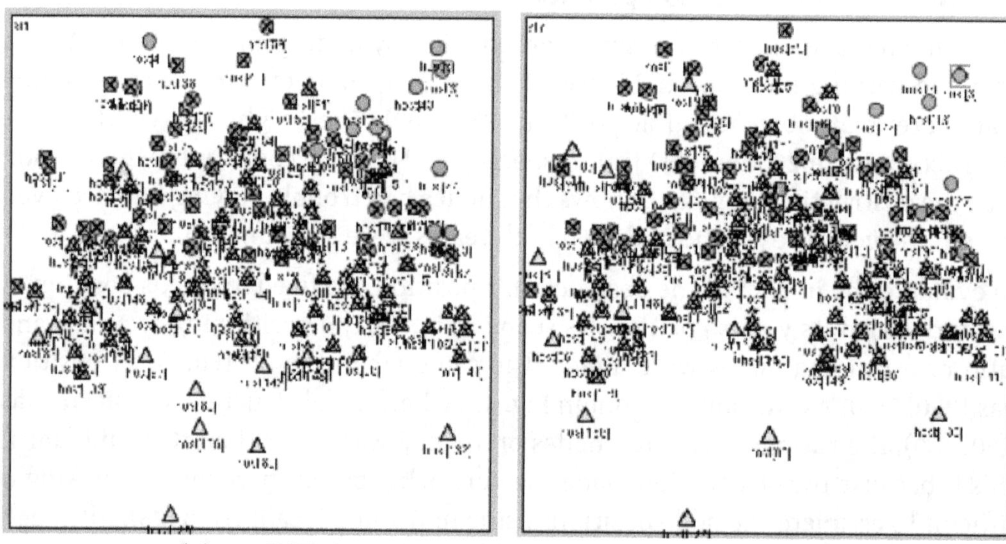

(a) t=250 (b) t=500

Fig. 7. Snapshots of war games for time steps of (a) 250 and (b) 500 (*N*=160, *vT1,T2* = {1,4}). Nodes for team 1 are represented by circles, and those for team 2 are represented by triangles. Cross on node represents dead state.

Table 4 presents the simulation parameters for the tag game. Figure 13 shows snapshots of a tag game with the local rule of the connectivity constraint (C). Teams 1, 2, 3, and 4 are located at the top left, bottom left, top right, and bottom right, respectively. The connectivity constraints correspond to 0 (not applied), 2, 5, and 8. As shown in Fig. 13(a), the nodes on team 1 spread over the field while those on team 4 are bunched together. Those on teams 3 and 4 spread gradually, as shown in Fig. 13(b).

Table 4. Simulation parameters for tag game.

Field	700 × 700[m]
Communication range	100[m]
Number of nodes	200
Node mobility	Random waypoint
Node velocity	E (v), v =1[m/step]
Connectivity constraint	$C_{T1,T2,T3,T4}$={0 (not applied), 2, 5, 8}

Figure 14 plots the results for positioning error, ratio of estimated nodes, and number of alive nodes. The higher the connectivity constraint, the lower the positioning error. This is because the positioning accuracy using multi-hop localization depends on the connectivity (28). The greater the connectivity constraints, the higher the ratio of estimated nodes.

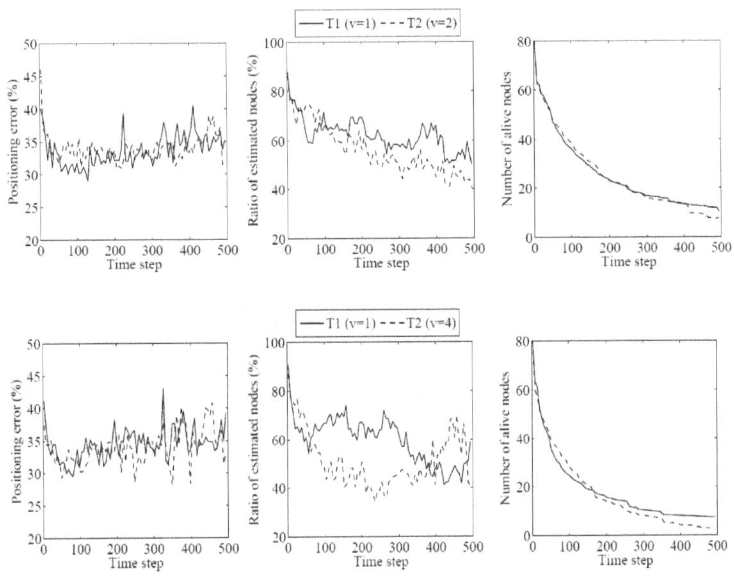

Fig. 8. Positioning error, ratio of estimated nodes, and number of alive nodes (N=160, $vT1,T2$={1,2}).

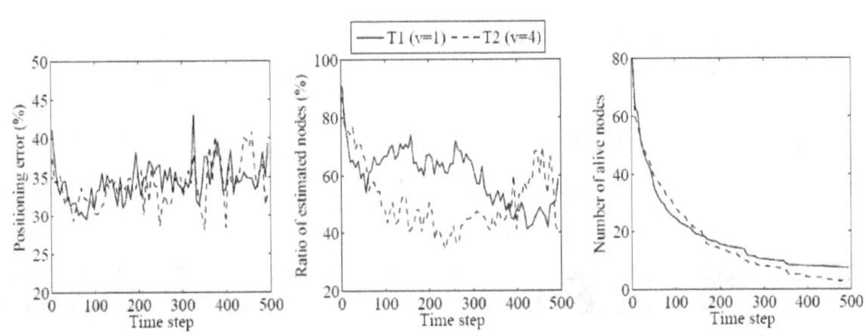

Fig. 9. Positioning error, ratio of estimated nodes, and number of alive nodes (N=160, $vT1,T2$={1,4}).

Table 5 summarizes the survival time for the tag game. As seen from the row for scenario D in Table 5, team 1 with a connectivity constraint of 0, had the longest survival time even though it had the lowest localization rate. This is because nodes with a lower connectivity constraint could more readily move around the field. Since the probability of their encountering an oni was lower, nodes with a lower connectivity constraint could survive longer. This result is not suitable for playing the game, because there is no advantage to cooperate for localization, and it does not support the fairness of the game. We thus examined the introduction of a design parameter and a local rule to control the win rate for the game.

5.3.2 Impact of local rule on death penalty

We next evaluated the local rule of a death penalty to impose a penalty for moving alone. The local rule of the death penalty was to impose transition to a dead state when the node could not estimate its own position ω times, consecutively. In addition, we introduced a design parameter κ to mitigate transition to a dead state by using multi-hop localization. The parameter κ encourages the longer survival time in the tag game. κ was introduced in Algorithm 2.

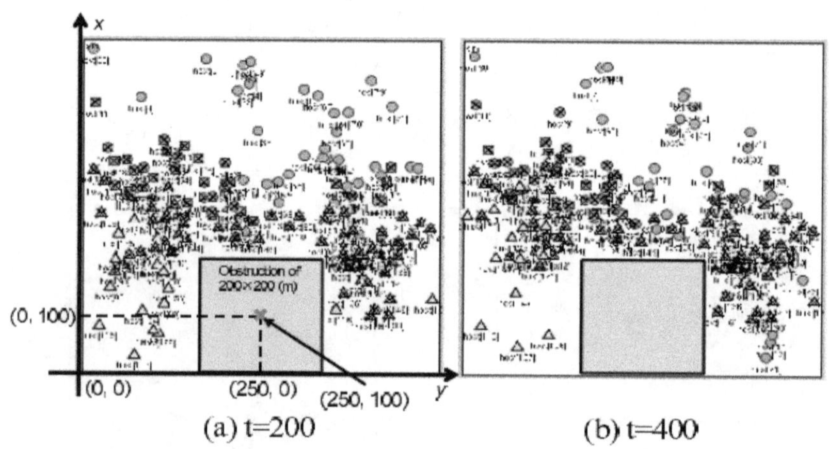

Fig. 10. Snapshots of war game for time steps (a) 200 and (b) 400 with obstruction at (250, 100) (*N*=160, *vT*1,*T*2={1,1}). Nodes for team 1 are represented by circles, and those for team 2 are represented by triangles. Cross on node represents dead state. Obstructions are drawn as large gray squares.

Table 5. Survival time in tag game for *CT*1,*T*2,*T*3,*T*4={0,2,5,8}. Scenario D enabled the rule of connectivity constraint. Scenario E enabled the rule of death penalty.

	Team 1	Team 2	Team 3	Team 4
Scenario D	6429.4	5460.9	5855.8	6001.9
Scenario E	2237.2	2739.4	2937.4	3454.3

Figure 15 shows snapshots of the tag game with the local rule of the death penalty enabled. Nodes on team 1 with a connectivity constraint of 0 are still widely spread out, however, their death rate is higher due to the local rule of the death penalty.

Figure 16 plots the results for positioning error, ratio of estimated nodes, and number of alive nodes with the local rule of the death penalty. The κ was set to 0.5, and ω was set to 2. The number of alive nodes on team 1 decreased over time, because nodes with a lower connectivity constraint had wider dispersion. As we can see from the row for scenario E in Table 5, the higher the connectivity constraint, the longer the survival time. This result demonstrates that the local rule of the death penalty and the design parameters κ, ω effectively maintained the fairness in the tag game.

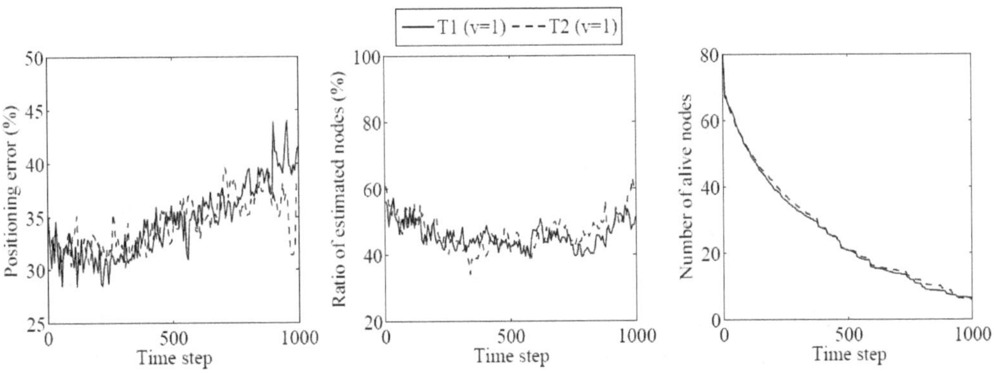

Fig. 11. Positioning error, ratio of estimated nodes, and number of alive nodes with obstruction at (250, 250) (N=160, $v_{T1,T2}$={1,1}).

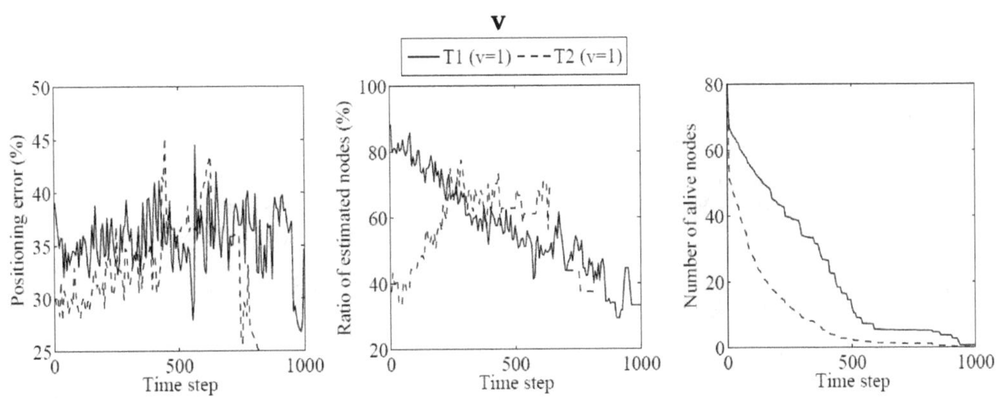

Fig. 12. Positioning error, ratio of estimated nodes, and number of alive nodes with obstruction at (250, 100) (N=160, $v_{T1,T2}$={1,1}).

6. CONCISE SUMMARY

We created two wireless multi-hop localization games: a war game and a tag game, derived on traditional field games. The suggested games utilize mobile gaming devices equipped with ad-hoc networking functionalities. The core principle of a wireless multi-hop localization game is that team members create an ad-hoc network to ascertain their locations and thereafter vie for positional precision against other teams via a multi-hop localization method. Through simulation, we determined that node velocity and blockage locations were parameters influencing the win rate in the war game. In the tag game, the elevated connection constraint resulted in prolonged survival. The simulations indicated that the victory rate for the suggested games is contingent upon obstruction placements and connectivity limitations. We also established that the incorporation of a design parameter and the enforcement of local regulations were necessary to regulate the win rate for the game. The findings indicated that the proposed games functioned effectively as games with ad-hoc networking capabilities.

This study presupposed that nodes exhibited random mobility to examine the fundamental operations of the proposed wireless multi-hop localization games. In reality, players would collaborate to reduce their location inaccuracies, or oni would implement a system to monitor active nodes. These motions can be integrated into node mobility in simulations to get more authentic game outcomes. The study exclusively addressed several application approaches for integrating ad-hoc networking and multi-hop localization, indicating a necessity for additional research about their suitability and efficacy in gaming contexts. Our forthcoming endeavors encompass comprehensive assessments of games employing diverse location-based strategies with positioning inaccuracies, empirical game testing in real-world environments, and the validation of user satisfaction levels during actual gameplay of the suggested games..

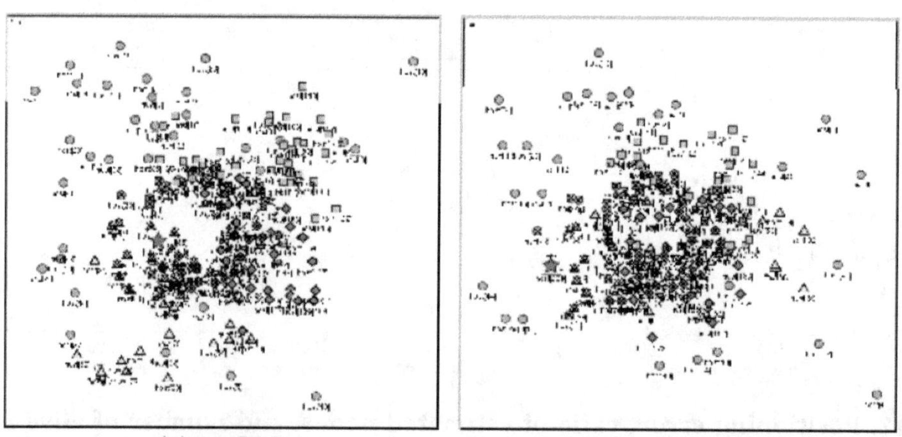

(a) t=500 (b) t=1000

Fig. 13. Snapshots of tag game for time steps (a) 500 and (b) 1000 (N=200, $CT1,T2,T3,T4$={0,2,5,8}). Teams 1, 2, 3, and 4 correspond to circles, triangles, squares, and di- amonds. Oni is represented by star. Cross on node represents dead state.

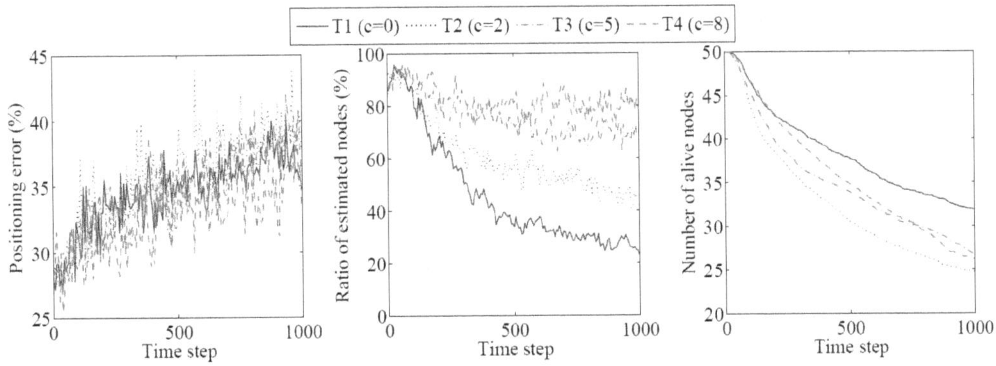

Fig. 14. Positioning error, ratio of estimated nodes, and number of alive nodes (*N*=200)

Fig. 15. Snapshots of tag game for time steps (a) 500 and (b) 1000 with local rule of death penalty enabled (*N*=200, *CT*1,*T*2,*T*3,*T*4={0,2,5,8}). Teams 1, 2, 3, and 4 correspond to circles, triangles, squares, and diamonds. The oni is represented by a star. A cross on a node represents a dead state.

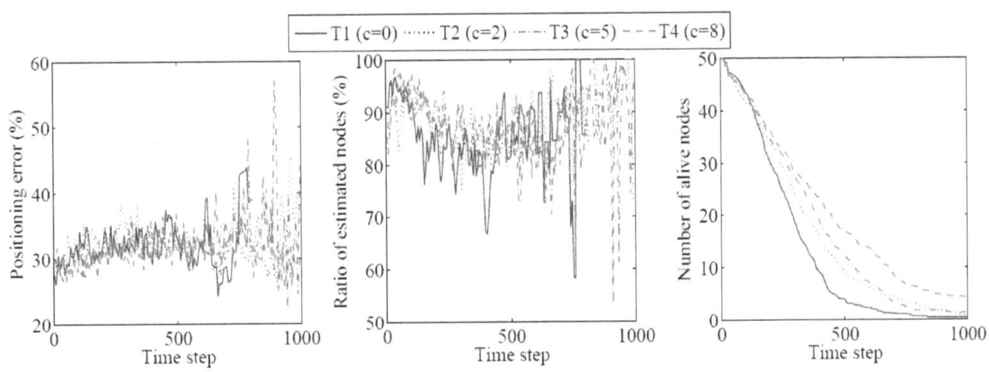

Fig. 16. Positioning error, ratio of estimated nodes, and number of alive nodes with local rule of death penalty (*N*=200, κ = 0.5 and ω = 2).

REFERENCES

1. Zigbee Alliance, http://www.zigbee.org/.
2. MANET Working Group, http://www.ietf.org/html.charters/manet-charter.html.
3. Nintendo Co.,Ltd, http://www.nintendo.com/.
4. Sony Computer Entertainment Inc., http://www.scei.co.jp/index_e.html.
5. Namco Limited, http://www.namco.co.jp/.
6. Hot Shots Golf: Open Tee, http://www.us.playstation.com/PSP/Games/Hot_Shots_Golf_Open_Tee.

7. J. Navas and T. Imielinski, "GeoCast - Geographic Addressing and Routing," *Proc. ACM/IEEE Mobicom*, pp. 66–76, 1997.
8. N. Patwari, J. N. Ash, S. Kyperountas, A. O. Hero III, R. L. Moses, and N. S. Correal, "Locating the Nodes–Cooperative Localization in Wireless Sensor Networks," *IEEE Signal Processing Magazine*, vol. 22, pp. 54–69, 2005.
9. N. Bulusu, J. Heidemann, and D. Estrin, "GPS-less Low Cost Outdoor Localization For Very Small Devices," *IEEE Personal Communications Magazine*, vol. 7, no. 5, pp. 28–34, 2000.
10. D. Niculescu and B. Nath, Ad Hoc Positioning System (APS), *Proc. IEEE Globecom*, vol. 5, pp. 2926–2931, 2001.
11. A. Savvides, C. Han, and M. B. Strivastava, "Dynamic Fine-grained Localization in Ad- hoc Networks of Sensors," *Proc. ACM/IEEE Mobicom*, pp. 166–179, 2001.
12. C. Savarese, J. Rabaey, and K. Langendoen, "Robust Positioning Algorithms for Dis- tributed Ad-hoc Wireless Sensor Networks," *Proc. USENIX Technical Annual Conference*, pp. 317–327, 2002.
13. T. He, C. Huang, B. M. Blum, J. A. Stankovic, and T. Abdelzaher, "Range-free Localization Schemes for Large Scale Sensor Networks," *Proc. ACM/IEEE Mobicom*, pp. 81–95, 2003.
14. D. Niculescu and B. Nath, Ad Hoc Positioning System (APS) Using AoA, *Proc. IEEE Infocom*, vol. 3, pp. 1734–1743, 2003.
15. N. B. Priyantha, H. Balakrishnan, E. Demaine, and S. Teller, "Anchor-free Distributed Localization in Sensor Networks," *Technical Report TR-892*, MIT LCS, 2003.
16. D. Moore, J. Leonard, D. Rus, and S. Teller, "Robust Distributed Network Localization with Noisy Range Measurements," *Proc. ACM Sensys*, pp. 50–61, 2004.
17. D. K. Goldenberg, P. Bihler, M. Cao, J. Fang, B. D. O. Anderson, A. S. Morse, and Y. R. Yang, "Localization in Sparse Networks using Sweeps," *Proc. ACM Mobicom*, pp. 110–121, 2006.
18. J. Liu, Y. Zhang, and F. Zhao, "Robust Distributed Node Localization with Error Man- agement," *Proc. ACM Mobihoc*, 2006.
19. M. Li and Y. Liu, "Rendered Path: Range-free Localization in Anisotropic Sensor Net- works with Holes," *Proc. ACM Mobicom*, pp. 51–62, 2007.
20. Y. Wang, J. Gao, and J. S.B. Mitchell, "Boundary Recognition in Sensor Networks by Topological Methods," *Proc. ACM Mobicom*, pp. 122–133, 2006.

21. S. Lederer, Y. Wang, and J. Gao, "Connectivity-based Localization of Large Scale Sensor Networks with Complex Shape," *Proc. IEEE Infocom*, pp. 13–18, 2008.
22. Geocaching, http://www.geocaching.com/.
23. S. Bjork, J. Holopainen, P. Ljungstrand, and K. Akesson, "Designing Ubiquitous Com- puting Games – A Report from a Workshop Exploring Ubiquitous Computing Entertain- ment," *Personal and Ubiquitous Computing*, vol. 6, pp. 443–458, 2002.
24. A. D. Cheok, K. H. Goh, W. Liu, F. Farbiz, S. W. Fong, S. L. Teo, Y. Li, and X. Yang, "Human Pacman: A Mobile, Wide-area Entertainment System Based on Physical, Social, and Ubiquitous Computing," *Personal and Ubiquitous Computing*, vol. 8, pp. 71–81, 2004.
25. S. Benford, R. Anastasi, M. Flintham, A. Drozd, A. Crabtree, C. Greenhalgh, N. Tanda- vanitj, M. Adams, and J. Row-Farr, "Coping with Uncertainty in a Location-based Game," *IEEE Pervasive Computing*, vol. 2, no. 3, pp. 34–41, 2003.
26. C. Magerkurth, A. D. Cheok, R. L. Mandryk, and T. Nilsen, "Pervasive Games: Bringing Computer Entertainment Back to the Real World," *ACM Computers in Entertainment*, vol. 3, 2005.
27. C. Schlieder, P. Kiefer, S. Matyas, "Geogames: Designing Location-Based Games from Classic Board Games," *IEEE Intelligent Systems*, vol. 21, no. 5, pp. 40–46, 2006.
28. T. Takenaka, H. Mineno, Y. Tokunaga, N. Miyauchi, and T. Mizuno, "Performance Anal- ysis of Optimized Link State Routing-based Localization," *Information Processing Society of Japan (IPSJ) Journal*, vol. 48, no. 9, pp. 3286–3299, 2007.
29. T. Takenaka, H. Mineno, and T. Mizuno, "Evaluation of Wireless Multi-hop Localiza- tion Game for Entertainment Computing," *Proc. IEEE International Symposium on Personal, Indoor and Mobile Radio Communications (PIMRC)*, 2008.
30. T. Clausen and P. Jacquet, "Optimized Link State Routing Protocol (OLSR)," *IETF RFC 3626*, 2003.
31. OMNeT++ Descrete Event Simulation System, http://www.omnetpp.org/.
32. Mobility Framework for OMNeT++, http://mobility-fw.sourceforge.net/.

34 Chapter ASSESSING NETWORK SECURITY

1. INTRODUCTION: AN OVERVIEW

The impetus for this research is encapsulated in Lord Kelvin's renowned assertion: "You cannot improve what you cannot measure." The contemporary information era has redefined this, highlighting the necessity to quantify abstract concepts like Information Security. Numerous sources, including academic studies and industrial publications, such as (Danahy, 2004), (Fisher, 2009), and (Sonnenreich et al., 2006), concur on the significance of assessing security in the realm of Information Technologies.

This chapter supplies essential information and appropriate methods to assess the security of IT systems and business services reliant on IT systems. The primary objective of the stated techniques is to enhance the management of IT systems and infrastructure security.

2. THE NEED FOR SECURITY MEASUREMENT

According to the American dictionary of Princeton the general definition of measurement is "*the act or process of assigning numbers to phenomena according to a rule*". Measurement has a very close relationship with metric which, according the same source, is a "*a system of related measures that facilitates the quantification of some particular characteristic*".

Focusing on the research area of IT (Maizlitsh, 2005) distinguishes between metrics that are used to quantify values that act as a control of proper functionality and those that act as a performance indicator. Security measurement is a topic that falls under the first category of controlling the proper functionality of security processes.

Although IT Security measurement is very interesting and useful topic in both academic and industrial environments, it deals with the quantification of an abstract concept. Similarly to any other abstract concept, security measurements tend to have rather vague implementations. This is justified by the fact that is hard to provide a figure that could express the current level of security. Thus, the difficulty of measuring security leads to the research of proper methodologies that could define the appropriate metrics as well as describe the necessary measurement process.

The expected benefits from the measurement of security are:

- **Enable business strategy:** IT Security is essential for the development and the support of trust between organizations, partners, customers and employees. This implies that there measuring the current level of security can held the alignment of business and technology strategies with security aspects and requirements.
- **Support the daily business activities:** Security measurement can accommodate the increases of the value of information and thus the increased risk levels related to each organizational asset.
- **Facilitate risk management:** The provision of a better toolset for managing risks can improve decision making as well as taking advantage of business opportunities.
- **Reduce costs:** A limited understanding of security status could lead to a high-cost operation of IT Systems and business processes, as well as to increased marketing and promotion expenses in order to "protect" the reputation of the products and the services of an organisation.
- **Comply to regulatory and legal requirements:** Being able to present and report the current status of security and risks is the basic condition for compliance.

A standardized approach of security measurement should aim to enable the operation of an organization without uncertainties or doubts, within a framework that could quantify the probability of a threat occurring, estimate the cost a potential damage, depict the performance overhead of the security processes and evaluate the effectiveness of security measures.

3.REQUIREMENTSOFSECURITYMEASUREMENTMETHODOLOGIES

Having described the expected benefits of security measurement, this paragraph presents the necessary attributes of the security measurement methodologies, by interpreting business requirements in terms of IT Security. The adoption of those requirements if essential in order to make the measurement results utilizable.

A basic requirement is to enable envision to management in the section of security. Each measurement methodology should primarily intend to provide information that would depict the current status as well as the future trends from the security point of view. Additionally, the analysis of the security measurement should:

- Aid an analyst to diagnose the issues that are related to security and evaluate the performance of the existing mechanisms and processes.
- Quantify specific security characteristics and parameters.
- Easy the investigation of hypothetical and "before and after" scenarios.

- Focus the measurement interest to the causes, the media and the meaning of the results instead of the methodologies that were used.

According to (Jaquith, 2007) each measurement methodology should have as many of the following characteristics as possible:

- Consistently measured
- Cheap to gather
- Expressed as a number
- Uses at least one unit of measure
- Contextually specific
- Partial weight
- Repetitiveness
- Comparability

3.1 Consistently measured

The measurement methodologies provide reliability when they can be calculated with a reliable way. Different persons should be in position to apply the method and result the same answers using same set of data. The condition which is required to verify this, is expressed as follows: "Will two different individuals in which is submitted the same question give the same answer with regard to the measurement of some size?". These measurements should be differentiated from the "measurements" that they depend on the subjective crises of researchers and analysts that are reported as classifications, gradations or estimations.

A measurement methodology can ensure its consistence by recording the individual steps of measurement using a way that will be transparent and explicit to the person that will be asked to measure. Each measurement methodology should explain "how" each step should be applied and "why" it is applied with this particular way.

A particularly efficient way of maintaining consistence is the usage of questions of partial ignorance, that is to say questions that can be answered with "yes" or "no". Another way is the use of automated processes that would follow each time the same process of measurement without procedural divergences.

3.2 Cheap to gather

Each measurement methodology needs time in order to calculate the results. All measurement methodologies begin row data and afterwards, following the precise steps of each model, generate some useful information. Hence, initially, somebody or something should collect the data from a suitable source, convert them to the desirable form, and finally calculate and format the results.

An efficient measurement methodology should collect those steps of transformation and format using a unified and fast process. If the process of measurement is insufficient, the method of collection of data can cost time and money to the organisation, which could have been spent in the analysis of results.

The high cost of measurement methodology can be caused by a series of factors such as the frequency of measurements, the complexity of process and its non automated nature.

It is therefore reasonable for a model of measurement to also make proposals on the most optimal candidate sources of data, in the light of saving time and money.

3.3 Expressed as a number

All measurements should be expressed as an absolute number or percentage, which represents something that measures a quantity of size. Gradations such as "high, intermediate, low" or "1, 2, 3" (from a third degree scale) represent relative grades but do not also measure any size, therefore they cannot be used in a proper model of measurement. Thus, "expressed as an absolute number" implies the number of total elements and not the number that expresses the order of total elements.

Thus, measurement methodologies that are not expressed as numbers are not suitable for the measurement of security. Indicators such as traffic lights with the three possible values "red, yellow, green" they do not constitute some type measurement since they do not include some kind of numerical scale.

It should be noted that the colors of traffic lights can be used as depiction or presentation of the current state but in a more abstract level accompanying the necessary numerical data that should remain the main objective of security measurement.

3.4 Uses at least one unit of measure

Another basic requirement of measurement models of security is that all the related measurements should also include a relative unit of measurement, which will characterize the sizes that are been measured. For instance, the measurement "number of natural invasions in the IT building" uses as a unit of measurement the invasions. With the use of units of measurement, the researcher knows how to express similar measurements using the same way.

In certain cases it is better to use more than one measurement units aiming to facilitate the comparison of different applications. In the previous example the more general measurement unit can be also mentioned as the "number of individuals that tried to invade in the IT building", which is also another unit of measurement. The use of this unit can be more suitable for the comparison with another measurable size, that of "total number of individuals that enters in the IT building".

Another requirement for the good measurement methodologies is that they mean something to the persons that examine them. They could reveal issues of infrastructure or service under review improving or demonstrating the value of persons and processes for the organisation. Even if the close relation to the general context does not constitute a main requirement for a good measurement, it helps to maintain measurement results inside the framework of the organisation under discussion while making the results more useful. This should benefit the end recipients (which are usually the management executives of organisation) to comprehend the current security status and decide with rational way based on results of the measurements.

As an example it can be mentioned the use of measurement as "the mean number of attacks" for the entire organisation. This measurement can have the all above characteristics (consistence, numerical price etc.) but it does not help anyone to improve his work. If this measurement is differentiated and connected with the enterprising services that it offers, as the servers of an electronic trade service, it will be a much more important tool for the decision-making process of more specific sectors, such as the protection of specific servers but also the physical protection of personnel.

3.5 Partial weight

The quantification of an individual factor that influences security is without a doubt very useful. Nevertheless, another important issue is the effect of these individual factors to the security of an entire organisation.

This characteristic is related with the previous paragraph ("Contextually Specific") due of the relativity that is implied between measurable sizes and the overall security of the organisation. It differs however in the fact that the requirement of overall estimation includes the way and the size with which a specific measurement influences the security and the operation of organisation.

As an example, the measurement of "numbers of power failures" is precise and relative to security. However, the way with which this measurement influences the operation of organisation can become also the weight of this particular size. Thus, in the case where there is no way to tackle a power failure (eg. A power generator) the weight of this measurement concerning the total estimate of security should be a large figure.

It should also be clarified that the requirement of an overall estimate could also be considered an extension of measurements, which could even require some form of calculation.

3.6 Repetitiveness

The requirement of repetitiveness includes the measurement of same factors while applying the same measurement methods in different time periods. This repetition aims in the verification of previous measurements as well as in the observation and recording of the evolution of a particular size.

Thus, this repetition should not constitute measurement from one only person but be also verified from the measurements of different persons.

Regarding the evolution of factors that are measured, the measurements should be performed periodically, in order to detect unexpected changes, or immediately after a particular known change which will probably influence security.

So, the measurements should be calculated with a frequency proportional with the rate of change of process. The methodologies that use samples at regular time intervals can help the organisations to analyze the effectiveness of security in precise time intervals and prepare them to be in the position to react in time in case of a new security incident. As expected, in a decision for whether a measurement should be calculated often, the cost of measurement should be taken into account in terms of time and money. Alternatively measurements could be performed only before and after each change.

3.7 Comparability

Also, it is very important that one should measure and observe the improvement or the deterioration of security as time advances. For this reason, the results of measurements should comparable to corresponding results of other organisations or different situations for the same organisation so that they can be contrasted to the current security status.

As reported above, a way to do that is to use common sizes and units of measurement. Additionally, is possible to measure in equivalent or relevant time periods points that share common characteristics, such as measurement of number of robberies during the last and first day of each month.

4. TAXONOMY OF EXISTING SECURITY METHODOLOGIES

Currently, there are several approaches for Security measurement. Most of them tend to emphasize on different aspects of security than objective measurements. There are very few approaches that focus on providing the means for quantifying security. The most noticeable solutions are:

- Solutions based on Vulnerability analysis
- Solutions based on Penetration testing
- Solutions based on Baseline comparison

- Solutions based on Best-practice and standards
- Solutions based on Risk management

4.1 Solutions based on vulnerability analysis

Solutions based on Vulnerability Analysis such as Microsoft Security Analyzer are connecting the security status of a networked system to the number its network-related vulnerabilities. Unfortunately vulnerability analyzers can not be used to measure security of an entire organization because they do not take into account many factors such as operational flaws and personnel security. Moreover, the results are not related at all to the number of actual security incidents.

4.2 Solutions based on penetration testing

Solutions based on penetration testing such as Corsaire Testing, are following the exact same patterns of the attackers without causing real damage to the systems. However the presented outcomes of these approaches are more like subjective ratings and gratings than objective measurements. Additionally, they always focus on the technology related aspects of the organization and neglect other important factors such as operational and physical security.

4.3 Solutions based on baseline comparison

The baseline comparison solutions contain standard security controls, which are applicable to the great majority of IT systems providing basic security. The basis for the decision of whether the organization or specific service fulfils the security requirements is based on the Auditor's personal judgment.

The main issues regarding this kind of approach are that it is very subjective and tends to change every time the Auditor changes. Again the outcome is more like a rating than a proper measurement.

4.4. Solutions based on best-practice and standards

These solutions (e.g. ISO/IEC 17799, BS 7799 and NIST SP 800-33) refer to several suggestions for security countermeasures and controls to improve an organization's information security. Although these are approaches are quite thorough and explanatory, they are more useful when developing new infrastructures and services. So far the aspects of quantification and measurement have not been dealt with the same zeal.

4.5 Solutions based on risk management

These solutions assess security by describing, analyzing and evaluating single scenarios. Again, since the estimation of the risk is based on the Auditor's personal judgment, such solutions tend to be very subjective.

4.6 Combining the security's basic elements

Apart from the above categories two more categories of security measurement methodologies can be proposed. The first is concerned with the combination of security's basic elements. These basic elements are Integrity, Availability and Confidentiality. Other additional elements of IT Security are Non-Repudiation as well as Authentication.

An effort that could be included in this category is that of (Knorr, 2000). Within its framework, is proposed a structured approach for the analysis of metrics of security and for the quantification of the overall security of Electronic Business Applications. It uses a table that represents "overall security" and divides it to smaller parts. These parts correspond to sites, potential targets and mechanisms of application security and are connected with the participating parts of an Electronic Business Application (customer, tradesman, means of communication). This process aims to the calculation of a quantifier of an Electronic Business Application, which functions as a means for the analysis, planning and comparison tool of similar applications.

Another approach that falls under this category is the one by (Serrelis, 2007) that aims to offer the foundation for a model that could help security analysts to quantify and measure security. Comparing to the requirements that were initially set, the suggested model has supported the consistency requirement throughout the document by the use of questions with objective answers. The questions also aimed to answers which would be cheap to gather, since the answers could come from automated systems such as IPSs. Additionally the model has managed to express security as a number (percentage). Security calculation has used at least one unit of measure (such as blocked spam emails) satisfying another requirement of a proper quantification model. The last requirement has also been covered since the level of security of the overall enterprise or the individual services makes a lot of sense to management people. Thus the model can also claim to be contextually specific. On the downside, it should be pointed out that the model is not considered so much with the new products, but with the existing services. Other type of questions should be posed to calculate the security level of new services and/or products.

4.7 Combining factors that are related to security

The second category of security measurement methodologies is concerned with the combination of factors that are related indirectly to security. Approaches of this type, even if of limited number, can be grouped together if they measure or calculate elements which are not directly related to security unlike the previous category. They aim to describe the relation between security and factors that are easily and objectively measured.

A typical example of this category is the approach that is presented in (Campbell, 2003), where the economic impact of incidents of security it is examined. The economic impact is translated in fall of the stock prices of an organisation, as a result of the negative image that is created in the investment public. Thus the stock price constitutes a factor which can indirectly be related to the level of security of organisation.

This approach has been an important factor for the development of the approach proposed and presented in paragraph 6, which also aims in the development of methodology for the objective measurement of security using factors that are related indirectly to security.

5. FROM MEASUREMENT TO CALCULATION

As it is defined by Webster dictionary, calculation is "deliberate process for transforming one or more inputs into one or more results, with variable change". The term calculation is used in numerous sciences, from the precisely defined arithmetic calculation to the calculation of abstract concepts which is implemented with the use of special algorithms and suitable combination of factors.

Another, alternative way of calculation of sizes is also the statistical analysis, eg. the calculation of likely results of an electoral result.

In every case the calculation of a factor is advisable in cases where his direct measurement or the quantification of its size is not feasible. These cases mainly include abstract concepts that are not straightly measurable, with security being a very representative example.

The calculation of security is differentiated from the measurement of security. While the measurement is based on the collection and representation of primary data, the calculation uses primary data with a combinational way so that it produces a result which represents security.

Because of the abstract nature of IT security, a direct measurement will not have real and usable results since it will be based on the limitations of the methods reported in the previou chapter. The calculation of however of security can be more efficient by overcoming these limitations using measurable sizes.

There are various methods for the calculation of security. These can depend on the judgments and estimates of researchers thus they are labelled as classifications or gradations. A second category of methods can be based on statistical methods, which could lead to an estimate of the level of security. Other methods can combine the measurement of values with the co-calculation of which the value of security could be deduced.

The optimum method of calculation of security is differentiated depending on the specific needs of each organisation, service, infrastructure or system. However, in all cases, it should be selected with a process that will be based on well defined factors that should also have well defined relations between them.

It should be also clarified that the methods of calculation and the methods of measurement of security do not constitute alternative solutions from each other, but complementary. Precise measurement of security should not be considered feasible, due to its abstract nature, but due to the fact that calculation of security cannot be reliable if it is not based on measurable factors. The researcher of security should therefore use measurement methodologies that would result measurable factors. From the combination of these sizes the value of security will also be deduced.

It becomes easily understood that the calculation of security can be realised with two ways. These are the quantification of non measurable factors and abstract significances, such as security and the use of measurable factors that are measured with the appropriate security measurement methodologies. The latter involve measurable factors and are applied as a type of quantitative analysis. Also, the level of security can result as an estimate of the researchers which is applied as a type of qualitative analysis.

6. A NEW QUANTIFICATION METHODOLOGY

Within the framework of the current research, a new approach of calculation of security was also created, which manages security quantification methodology as a value which is calculated with the combination of certain easily measurable factors. These factors are related indirectly with security as well as with the level of security of specific business services.

This approach is based on the principle that the abstract concepts can be calculated with the combination of factors that is related indirectly with them and themselves can be easily measured. At the same time it seeks the satisfaction of following general requirements:

- Appreciation of security as factor that is an important part of the business production environment and not a collateral issue with minimal or no operational interest.
- Usage and combination of factors that can be measured or be quantified with objective ways.
- Connection of results of calculation of security with the business decisions.

For the application of the particular methodology of calculation of security, the sources of primary data should be determined in order to be combined for security calculation. This particular methodology considers that the value of security can result from the combination of parameters that are related with it. The factors that were selected are five and they all concern certain business, functional or commercial value. These five factors are mentioned as CARLS from initial their names in the English language. These are:

- **Compliance:** It expresses the percentage of conformity with the legal and regulatory framework that is applicable to the business service.
- **Availability:** It expresses the percentage of uptime of service in comparison its mission time.
- **Return:** It expresses the size of profits that results from the particular service.
- **Liabilities:** It expresses the size of economic losses due to the particular service.
- **Stock price:** It expresses the price of stock of the company that offers the service.

All factors are essentially different aspects of business services and should be available in order be composed in a value that would represent the level of security for each of the business services. The usage of these specific factors has two basic advantages, which are the main reasons for their choice in this model.

The first advantage is the fact that all factors are already have been measured by organisations for reasons of operational evaluation. This means that there is no need for additional effort in order to assemble the information required. The second advantage is the fact that each factor provides an objective image of the organisation and its particular business services, which objectivity can not disputed.

The measurement and monitoring of all factors is considered essential for the development, viability and proper operation of each organisation. It is exceptionally usual, in the great majority of organisations, to monitor and collect all the above factors. In many cases these factors are also measured for each business service separately. This fact makes the collection of the necessary elements a simple, easy and feasible process. Moreover, the CARLS factors have a lot more meaning for the persons that are found in not technical positions and their mentality is directed form the operational needs of their organisations. Compared to other approaches this can be seen as an advantage because using this methodology the understanding but also the usability of the value of security is facilitated which is based on familiar notions and no on technical terms as "integrity" and "confidentiality".

The main objective remains the calculation of the value of security of a specific service. This is implemented with the determination, the quantification and the combination of factors that can be measured easily and that is related indirectly with the security. This value portrays the level of security of specific service. The following paragraphs present the arguments in favour the choice of the particular factors, sating why CARLS factors are considered suitable for the calculation of security as well as an analysis for each one from them.

Compliance: The impact of non-compliance is profound. While many small issuers can operate with inconsistent compliance processes, problems eventually arise. Instead of focusing on the regulatory and punitive aspects of incomplete or ineffective compliance, this white paper will examine the functional impact of not remaining compliant with security regulations. Compliance can impact liquidity, which can affect your ability to raise funds for growth. The difficult aspect of compliance is knowing everything you have to do, when and how. Ongoing compliance requires an investment – for the same reasons as the initial compliance work you did when going public. The liquidity opportunities that initially attracted your company to the publicly traded arena are the same reasons for remaining compliant.

Availability: Government organizations and businesses of all sizes need to create and implement comprehensive business and operations continuity plans. Most organizations understand that they need to protect their data and systems -an activity known as disaster recovery. The disaster recovery is only half the battle-enterprises need also be prepared to quickly and seamlessly restart business processes in order to continue operations.

Return: The owners of a company and the company's creditors share a similar goal: to increase wealth. They are thus very concerned about profitability in all phases of operations. Creditors are specifically concerned that the company use its resources profitably so that it can pay interest and principal on its debt. Owners are concerned that the company be profitable so that stock values will increase. Company managers must show they can manage the owners' investment and produce the profits that owners and creditors demand. Because top management must meet the profit expectations of company owners, it passes down to the lower levels of management those profitability goals, which are then spread throughout the company. All managers, therefore, are expected to meet profitability goals, which are often increased and tightened as each level of management seeks a margin of security.

Liabilities: Most health related businesses would agree that securing insurance is one of the basic costs of doing business. As responsible business owners, they have budgeted for the appropriate coverages as a precautionary measure in the event of a loss— especially a catastrophic loss. However, there are a few optimistic souls who think of business insurance as an option. These risk takers appear perfectly content to operate their salons with little or no coverage in place. Unfortunately, most financial experts agree that this is a very dangerous practice, as those who gamble and lose usually pay a much higher price in the long run. The bottom line is, while none of us ever expects to get sued, we've all got to accept that even the most adept operator may face litigation for any number of reasons. While there are a wide variety of insurance coverages available for protecting yourself and your business, one of the most essential is liability. Liability is an especially important issue for those in the tanning industry, whose business is providing customers a service which may pose some risk of injury to them. Liability risks come in many more forms than might be expected. In addition to liability arising specifically from the use of tanning equipment, salon owners also may be held accountable for a variety of other kinds of business liabilities, such as a customer slipping and falling.

Stock Market: By using a stock market return framework to examine the economic implications of information security breaches, [3] study contributes to the literature examining the economic effects of information security breaches. We find there evidence of an overall negative stock market reaction to announcements of information security. The economic cost of publicly announced information security breaches 445 breaches in major newspapers, although this finding is not robust across all specifications. Nevertheless, these results provide some support for the argument that information security breaches adversely affect the future economic performance of affected firms.

The choice of the above factors satisfies the two of the three basic requirements that had been placed within framework of the current approach of for the calculation of security, that is to say to appreciate security as a factor that is part of the business production environment as well as to use and combine measurable factors that can be quantified with objectively.

Based on the ideas described in the previous paragraph, a figure that would represent the level of security for a specific service should take into account all security factors presented. In order to mathematically express a formula that calculates security, several assumptions have been made.

Firstly, the notion of Target level for each factor is introduced. The target level is set by the upper management who is responsible for the overall operating constrains, such as security, of each business service offered. Within this context, the target level of Compliance, Availability, Returns and Stock Price are set. The target level of compliance can be the compliance to a specific industry directive or governmental law or even an international standard. Similarly, the target level of Availability should be defined taking into account the business needs of each service.

The Current level of Compliance will be represented as a "Yes" or "No" factor in order to keep the model as simple as possible. A future extension to that model can express the current compliance level as a percentage, signifying that a service does or does not cover all compliance needs (e.g. covers a law but not a specific international standard).

So, the Security figure for each service can expressed as a function of independent variables by the use of following formula:

$$S_S = \frac{C}{C_T} \times \frac{A}{A_T} \times \frac{R-L}{R_T} \times \frac{S}{S_T} \quad (1)$$

Where:

- S_s = Security level of a Specific Business Service
- C = Current Level of Compliance [0|1]
- C_T = Target Level of Compliance (0-1]
- A = Current Level of Availability [0...1]
- A_T = Target Level of Availability [0...1]
- R = Current Return of the Service (in a monetary value)
- L = Current Liabilities of the Service (in a monetary value)
- R_T = Target Return of the Service (in a monetary value)
- S = Current Stock Price (Represents the company brand) (in a monetary value)
- S_T = Target Stock Price (in a monetary value)

Having expressed security using the formula above, a proper usage of the results could be to a financial motivated one. Our target is to balance the spending in Security for each Business Service in order to maximize the organisation's Return on Investment:

$$\max ROI\,(S1\,, S2\,, ..., Sn\,) \quad (2)$$

subject to

$$\sum_{i=1}^{n} (R_i - I_i - L_i) > 0 \quad (3)$$

Where:

- S_n = Security level of a Business Service
- R_i = Revenues of a Business Service
- I_i = Total Investments in a Business Service (Part of which is Security spending-investments)
- L_i = Total Liabilities of a Business Service

Using the last formula another objective is achieved. This is the connection of results of calculation of security with the business decisions that are related to security investments. In other words this formula aims to answer the question whether a security investment would cost more than the expected benefits.

7. CONCISE SUMMARY

This chapter examines if and how the principles of security measurement methodologies can be utilized to produce an objective assessment of the security of commercial services. The rationale for this inquiry centers on the justification of expenditures and investments associated with security. Consequently, while security management is intricately linked to both technical and organizational dimensions, it frequently proves challenging to delineate a quantifiable "version" of security that is more accessible and applicable at the operational level.

This chapter provides a critical assessment and classification of the needs for measurement and computation methods of security, which underpin the limitations of existing methodologies. A novel security computation method has been created that seeks to quantify security using aspects indirectly associated with it.

The fundamental premise adhered to is that the research emphasis should shift from the assessment of security to the quantification of security.. Other principles were:

- Appreciation of security as factor that is an important part of the business production environment and not a collateral issue with minimal or no operational interest.
- Usage and combination of factors that can be measured or be quantified with objective ways.
- Connection of results of calculation of security with the business decisions.

The methodology for quantifying security is executed by computation. The variables utilized for the calculation are the CARLS factors: Compliance (C) with the legal and regulatory framework, Availability (A) of business services, Return (R) of each business service, Liabilities (L) associated with specific services, and Stock price (S) of the organization, which reflects its reputation and public image. The methodology indicates that security is reflected in each of these elements, hence establishing an indirect relationship among them. This relationship is articulated by a mathematical formula that regards the factors as equivalent.

A significant benefit of the process is that it enables management executives to more readily understand the generated values and more effectively assess where to concentrate and bolster security efforts. This is particularly significant because security is an abstract term that is not easily articulated as a quantifiable value.

One limitation of the method is that all factors are regarded as equivalent during the computation of security. Future research could examine the extent to which security is affected by various parameters and how this is modified according to service, organization, or market type..

REFERENCES

1. Danahy, J. (2004) The Need for Metrics and Measurement in Application Security, OWASP Metrics and Measurement Standards
2. Fisher, D. (2009) Experts call for better measurement of security, Blog, recovered: 14/6/09, http://www.threatpost.com/blogs/experts-call-better-measurement-security
3. Sonnenreich, W.; Albanese, J. & Stout, B. (2006) Return On Security Investment (ROSI) – A Practical Quantitative Model, Journal of Research and Practice in Information Technology, Vol. 38, No. 1, February 2006
4. Maizlitsh, B. & Handler, R. (2005) IT Portfolio Management: Step by Step, John Wiley & Sons, ISBN: 978-0-471-64984-7, US
5. Sommerville, I. (1996) Software Engineering, Fifth Edition, Addison-Westley, ISBN: 978- 0201427653, UK
6. Tipton, H. & Krause, M. (2008) Information Security Management Handbook, Sixth edition, Auerbach Publications, ISBN 978-1420067088
7. Olzak, T. (2007) The Pros and Cons of Security Risk Management, Tech Republic, recovered: 14/6/09, http://blogs.techrepublic.com.com/security/?p=180
8. Parker, D. (2007) Risks of risk-based security, Communications of the ACM, Volume 50, Issue 3 , March 2007, pp 120.
9. Jaquith, A. (2007) Security Metrics: Replacing Fear, Uncertainty, and Doubt, Addison- Wesley Professional, ISBN 978-0321349989
10. Campbell, K.; Gordon, L. A.; Loeb, M. P. & Zhou L. (2003) The economic cost of publicly announced information security breaches: empirical evidence from the stock market, Journal of Computer Security, Volume 11, Issue 3 (March 2003) pp 431– 448
11. Serrelis, Em. & Alexandris, N (2007) An Empirical Model for Quantifying Security Based on Services, IEEE Computer Society, Proceedings of the International Multi- Conference on Computing in the Global Information Technology, pp 30
12. Knorr, K.; Rohrig, S. (2000) Security of Electronic Business Applications: Structure and Quantification, Proceedings of the 1st International Conference on Electronic Commerce and Web Technologies EC-Web 2000, pp 25-37

35 Chapter

A TESTING PROCEDURE FOR THE INTEROPERABILITY AND CONFORMANCE OF SECURE WEB SERVICES

1. INTRODUCTION:AN OVERVIEW

The design, development, and deployment of electronic (e-) services utilizing XML and Web Service (WS) technologies is the prevailing trend in attaining interoperability. E-services may be provided as independent Web Services or integrated into Service Oriented Architectures (SOAs) (High et al., 2005).

In this setting, whereas applications with same business objectives utilize identical technical standards, their interaction capabilities are frequently severely constrained. Consequently, application developers are increasingly focused on assessing compatibility among common services provided either independently or via a Service-Oriented Architecture (SOA). The establishment of an effective framework (EIF) is crucial for assessing the interoperability of these services, achieved through the exact delineation of the applicable standards and norms that ensure service interaction. Current testing procedures established by various organizations (e.g., ISO/IEC 9646, ESTI) address the interoperability of services as a generalized issue. They solely offer guidelines and outline overarching testing techniques applicable for assessing the compatibility of diverse telephony, software, and data communication systems. Many Web Service-oriented approaches (e.g., WS-I, ebXML IIC framework) exhibit deficiencies as they fail to assess all necessary components of an interoperability framework, particularly the security elements of message content.

Furthermore, literature identifies distinct testing methodologies (Saglietti et al., 2008) that categorize applications under examination as white boxes, possessing complete insight into the software; black boxes, lacking any comprehension of their internal workings; or grey boxes, with partial awareness of their internal structure. The characteristics of the WSs (e.g., geographic spread of the analyzed WSs and dependence on external trustworthy third parties) significantly influence the selection of the most suitable testing type, as they provide distinct issues that must be emphasized and considered.

Consequently, there exists a distinct necessity for specialized techniques and frameworks that assess and ensure the comprehensive application interaction capabilities of prevalent Web Services, while implementing the most suitable testing strategies that encompass all parts of WSs. Identifying this need, this study provides a well-formed gray box testing methodology termed ICoM, able to evaluate if diverse services achieve communication effectively based on the chosen standards. It delineates the exact framework of the participating entities, outlines specific procedures to adhere to, details explicit tests to be conducted, and facilitates the implementation of certain testing suites. ICoM has been utilized to assess the interoperability of the current autonomous SELIS e-invoicing service (Kaliontzoglou et al., 2006) and the SWEB e-invoicing service integrated into a SOA-based platform (SWEB). (Karantjias et al., 2008).

2. PRIOR WORK

This section presents the existing testing methodologies and frameworks illustrating their weaknesses and indicating the need for a more holistic methodological framework. Widely used types of testing are also described identifying the most appropriate method that should be applied to WSs due to their inherent characteristics.

2.1 Existing Testing Methodologies and Frameworks

Traditionally, interoperability testing methodologies for the Internet Protocols have been used extensively in the telecommunication industry and in the Internet world. For example the Open Systems Interconnection - Conformance Testing Methodology and Framework (ISO/IEC 9646) (OSI, 1997) is a widely spread and successfully applied conformance testing methodology which has evolved over the years. Nevertheless, it is considered as overly generic framework that allows a high degree of freedom and gives little practical guidance (ETSI, 1998).

The European Telecommunications Standards Institute (ETSI), acknowledging the importance of the testing methodologies, has also contributed towards this direction. ETSI defined a more integrated framework that consists of two primitive types of tests, the conformance and the interoperability testing. The ETSI conformance testing (Moseley et al., 2003), (ETSI, 1995) is based on the ISO/IEC 9646 using its principles as a basis, but not as strict guidelines. It focuses mostly on making easier, more applicable and more readable the use of test suites in the proposed methodology. Therefore, ETSI defined a core language the Testing and Test Control Notation TTCN-3 (ETSI, 2002), (Dibuz & Kremer, 2003) that can be used for the specification of test suites which are independent of test methods, layers and protocols.

On the other hand, ETSI interoperability testing (ETSI, 2007) constitutes a generic approach merely providing guidance on the specification and execution of the interoperability tests. These guidelines are in the form of recommendations rather than strict rules. The TTCN-3 can also be used in this kind of testing offering a higher level of flexibility.

Despite the independent operation of both types of testing, they are closely connected satisfying different objectives (Kulvatunyou et al., 2003). Conformance Testing checks to what extent a solution conforms to the corresponding specification or standard. Interoperability Testing proves the end-to-end functionality between the solutions. It should be noted that the use of either type of test does not guarantee interoperability.

A significant limitation of both abovementioned methodologies is that they treat the interoperability of the WS-based services as a generic problem providing generic testing practices.

Currently, there are only two widely used WSs testing methodologies, WS-I and ebXML: The Web Service Interoperability Standardization Organization (WS-I) (Seely & Lauzon, 2005), (Ehnebuske, 2003) is an industry consortium chartered to promote WS interoperability across platforms, operating systems, and programming languages. It has released a number of profiles and testing tools that compose a scalable testing environment. The shortcomings of this methodology are the following:

1. WS-I does not support the definition of specific and discrete test cases that should be followed during the tests.
2. WS-I tools achieve to monitor only the message flow, without being able to control the testing execution.
3. WS-I tools do not achieve to support a wide range of evaluation criteria (interoperability areas or multiple types of testing). They achieve to test only the conformance of the exchanged messages and the defined services' descriptions against the appropriate standards. They fail to cover criteria regarding the interoperability and the conformance of the applied security features of the message content and the transformation of the exchanged documents between different formats.

OASIS ebXML (ebXML, 2001) is an end-to-end B2B XML framework that provides concrete specifications for dynamic B2B collaborations. It has specified the Implementation, Interoperability, and Conformance (IIC) test framework (OASIS, 2003), (Lee, 2005), (Kim & Yun, 2003) describing the required architecture and providing the necessary test material to be processed by the architecture, a mark-up language and format for representing test requirements, and test suites (set of Test Cases). This approach has the following shortcomings:

4. ebXML IIC is intended to support conformance and interoperability testing only for ebXML specifications and implementations.
5. ebXML IIC does not impute the responsibility of a communication failure to the corresponding system.
6. ebXML IIC does not cover criteria regarding the interoperability and the conformance of the applied security features of the message content and the transformation of the exchanged documents between different formats.

Despite their weaknesses, the above frameworks can be used as the basis for the development of enhanced and more targeted methodologies to test and guarantee the inter- working of common WS-based applications.

2.2 Testing Types Existing Testing

Software testing, including interoperability testing, may take place at different levels of depth, depending on the actual known technical details of the application under test. The bibliography acknowledges three main types of testing: black box, white box and grey box testing (Peyton et al., 2008).

- Black box testing treats the software as a black-box where only the inputs and outputs of the black box are tested without any understanding of the internal behaviour or the adopted specifications. It aims to test the functionality according to the requirements. Thus, the tester inputs data and only sees the output from the test object based on the objects published and known interfaces.
- In White box testing, the tester has access and knowledge of the internal data structures, code, and algorithms of the software. A White Box tester typically analyzes source code, derives the corresponding test cases and targets specific code paths to achieve a certain level of code coverage.
- In recent years the term Grey Box testing has come into common usage and it refers to a technique of testing the system with limited knowledge of its internal architecture. The tester usually has access to specification documents (beyond simple requirements) and generates tests based on information such as state-based models or architecture diagrams.

The selection of the most appropriate testing type relies on the nature of the application under test. Web Services (WSs) are composed by a set of related and integrated services (High et al., 2005). The main characteristics of these services are the following (Rizwan & Mamoon, 2007):

- They can be distributed in the sense that they are located in different geographic areas, having independent capabilities and are accessible only via specific interfaces that are described by WSDL documents.

- They can be implemented in diverse programming languages and support independent operating systems.
- They can be chained with dependencies on other trusted third parties such as PKI and timestamp authorities.

The business design of WSs is essentially a composition of these repeatable services which represents and forms the desired business logic. The above features of the WSs introduce several challenges with respect to testing. White box testing especially in a SOA environment is quite impractical to perform due to the nature of the WSs that make access to source code or binaries very difficult. On the other hand, the WS interoperability testing methodologies (WS-I, ebXML IIC) adopted in the frameworks analyzed in the previous paragraph only enable black box testing of WS, leading to limited and inefficient test coverage due to the "blind" nature of that type of testing.

The distributed nature of Web Services makes Grey Box testing ideal for detecting interoperability flaws on the communication channels between WSs, mostly by leveraging the rich information contained in the descriptions of the services interfaces (WSDL documents). A Grey Box Tester is able to identify at a high level the internal structure of the tested WSs, defining the composed services and accessing the provided interfaces having limited or even no access to the actual code. Additionally, several test cases regarding the deployment of the security features and the communication protocols can be performed covering all the aspects of the WSs. Therefore grey box testing has been adopted as the most appropriate type to use in the methodology proposed in this paper.

3. THE ICOM METHODOLOGY

In this Section, we will describe the structure of the proposed methodology. Before presenting its main features and implementation steps, it is imperative to present the requirements it satisfies which overpass the weaknesses of the existing frameworks. The requirements that ICoM satisfies are:

- **Clarity**: The methodology specifies concisely the evaluated entities and the required information items for the testing process (e.g. test cases and test data).
- **Adaptability & Extensibility:** The methodology is extensible in the sense it may easily evaluate new aspects of the WSs and adopt and integrate new testing tools and libraries.
- **Flexibility**: The methodology is parameterizable in the sense that different parts of the methodology can be adopted for the realization of specific sets of test suites.

- **Structural**: The methodology is structured and comprises a definite and precise set of implementation steps.
- **Independency & scalability**: The methodology offers a high level of independency from testing technologies, the number of entities involved and the platforms hosting systems under test. This fact will offer the possibility of testing interoperability on several different WSs.

In order for the methodology to accomplish its objective goals comprises of four district phases:

- *Phase 1* "Entity identification and setting": the entities involved are identified and their specific setting and order for the tests is defined. The involved entities are the Systems under Test (SuTs) being evaluated for interoperability and conformance and the Test Coordination Infrastructure (TCI) which monitors the testing suites applied by the SuTs in order to identify any erroneous behaviour.
- *Phase 2* "Entity structure definition": the structure of the involved entities is identified. This includes the SuTs, which consist of the actual WS under evaluation and the specific structural additions of the testing infrastructure that are required in the testing procedure. The internal structure of the WS is immutable and an analysis of the available services is carried out. This phase also includes the specification of the precise structure of the TCI.
- *Phase 3* "Conformance testing": the definition and generation of the executed conformance test cases for each SuT, based on which the parameterization of the SuTs structural additions and the TCI is completed. Each SuT is evaluated against the adopted standards.
- *Phase 4* "Interoperability testing": the formulation and the derivation of the interoperability test cases, performing the necessary parameterization of the the SuTs structural additions and the TCI. The actual interoperability testing between all SuTs' communications takes place during this phase.

The following section describes these four phases in detail.

3.1 Phase 1: Entity Identification and Setting

As shown in the Figure 1, the initial step is the identification of the exact number, order and setting of all entities participating in the testing suite. The full methodology deployment demands the execution of the following process:

- *Entities (SuTs) definition*: defining the entities (SuT 1... SuT N (Figure 1), TCI) that participate in the test.
- *Web Service (WS) declaration*: declaring the Web Service that will be tested.

- *Testing Scenario*: specifying a testing scenario. A testing scenario consists of a sequence of actions described at a high level which must be performed by the SuTs in order to execute a specific electronic transaction.
- *Role determination*: defining the entities' role based on the specified testing scenario. Specifically, the entity that initializes the execution of the testing suite and the sequence of the other entities, as this is described in the testing scenario.

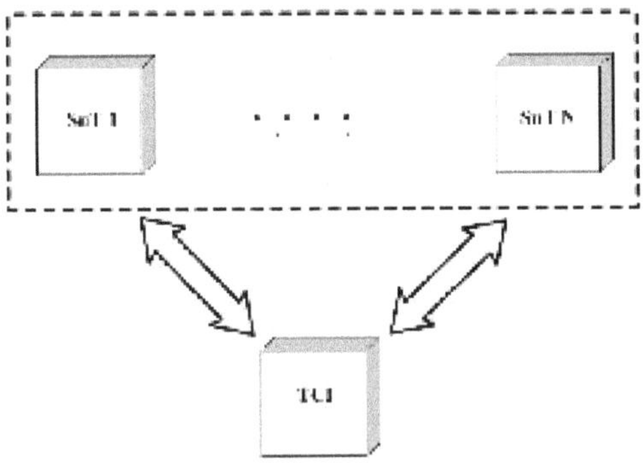

Fig. 1. General Entity Setting

The TCI, as presented in Phases 3 and 4 of the proposed methodology, acting as the initiator and an intermediate entity of the testing suite analyzes the testing results and indicates the conformance and the interoperability of the entities under test.

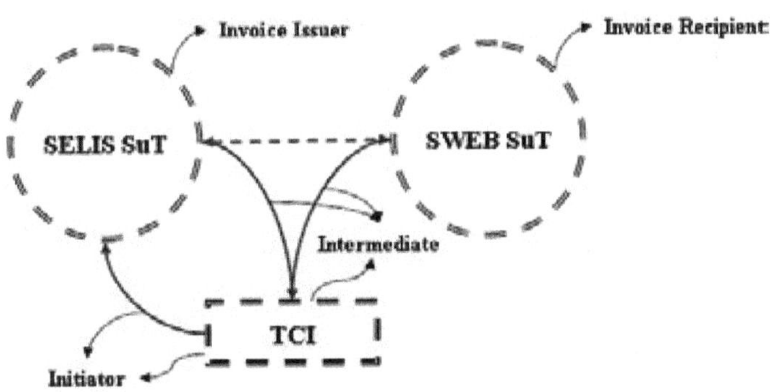

Fig. 2. Example Entities Identification

In this paper, we will use ICoM to test the interaction capabilities of two existing and fully operational WS-based solutions for e-invoicing, the autonomous SELIS service (Papastergiou et al., 2007b) and the SOA-based SWEB service (Papastergiou et al., 2007a). These services shall be used as demonstration material (case study) throughout the methodology presentation to better show its capabilities with specific examples. A case study example that imprints the main steps of the current phase is the following:

Example 1

The involved entities that participate in the test, Figure 2, are the SELIS SuT and the SWEB SuT while the provided invoicing service constitutes the Web Service that will be tested. The testing scenario we shall be following involves a communication initiated by SELIS SuT, acting as the Invoice Issuer (*role: Issuer*) that invokes SWEB SuT, which acts as the Invoice Recipient (*role: Recipient*) handling the dispatched invoice and responding with an acknowledgment. This scenario covers specific aspects of an invoicing transaction such as the issuance, dispatch and receipt of an invoice document. The TCI triggers, monitors the execution of the applied testing suites.

3.2 Phase 2: Entity Structure Definition

During this phase, the actual structure of the involved entities, TCI and SuTs, should be defined and shaped precisely by the responsible operators, indicating their constituent parts. The final form of each entity depends upon the tests that will be performed and the suites that will be followed.

3.2.1 Definition System under Test (SuT)

A SuT primarily contains the WS to be tested (WSuT). A common WSuT, as depicted in Figure 3, includes a set of primary services $\{S_1,...,S_n\}$ that are combined to form and execute the WS's business logic. Each service encapsulates an explicit function having a number of Inputs and producing a specific Output. It may also interact with other services in order to complete its objective goal.

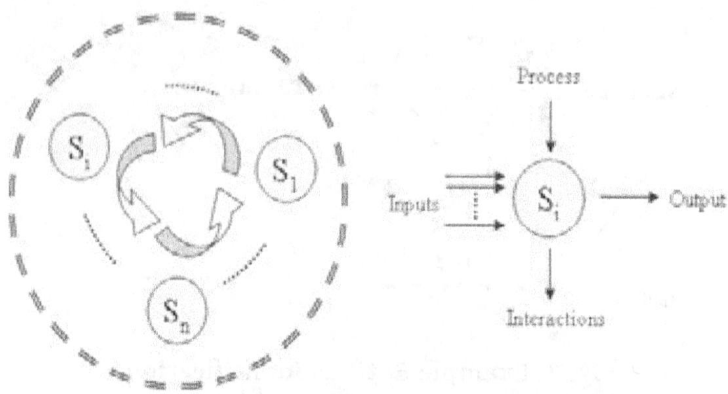

Fig. 3. Web Service under Test (WSuT)

A representative example of an advanced WSuT (Papastergiou et al., 2009), (Karantjias et al., 2008) may include a set of primary services such as the following:

- communication with legacy systems and proper data transformation,
- document management and application of digital signatures and / or encryption as a secure mechanism on the business level, and

- messaging formulation, processing and application of security mechanisms on the messaging level.

All these services, following concrete procedures, manage and derive data that are based on specific standards. The factual conformance of these data to the individual requirements specified by the corresponding specifications and the ability of other systems to handle these data correctly constitute factors that are able to leverage and infer the interoperability and the conformance capabilities of a WSuT. Take for example the case where the security service of a "WSuT A" signs a XML document according to the W3C XML Digital Signature `standard. Initially, the produced signed document should be tested for compliance with the principles of this standard and then there should be test that another "WSuT B" is able to successfully verify that signature. The conclusion that comes from this example is that the "WSuT A" produces signed documents that conform to the W3C XML Digital Signature standard and is able to interoperate successfully with the "WSuT B" on the application of signature at the business level.

Thus, in order for a WSuT to derive the required evaluation data, it should perform a certain number of activities as represented and indicated by specific test cases. A test case comprises a set of conditions and variable and depicts the test control logic which is sufficient for the execution of a testing suite.

ICoM deals with the execution of test cases and the collection of the respective data defining two structural components the *Service Orchestration Engine* and the *Report Engine* as seen on the following figure. These components are part of the testing infrastructure and along with the WSuT compose an integrated SuT.

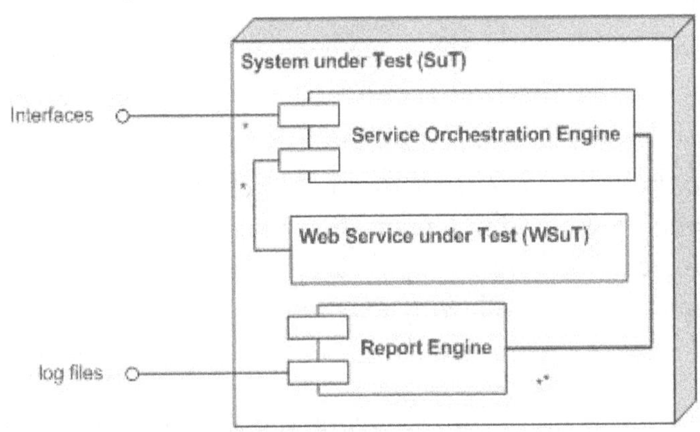

Fig. 4. System under Test (SuT)

The Service Orchestration Engine is responsible to coordinate the available WSuT's services to perform specific workflows. Each workflow is represented by a predefined BPEL process which imprints the logic of an executed test case. The BPEL test cases that will be adopted and executed are designed during phases 3 and

4 where the actual conformance and interoperability testing is performed. In these phases, the Engine undergoes the appropriate parameterization in order to run the defined BPEL processes. The parameterization includes also the provision of specific interfaces that can be invoked by the TCI in order to initiate the execution of a BPEL test case promoting the concept of automation of the testing procedure. Thus, the Service Orchestration Engine provides a thorough control of the testing suite and enables the effective accumulation of the evaluated data by adopting BPEL processes as forms to represent and execute test cases. The nature of the accumulated data depends on the type and the purpose of the executed test case and varies from simple XML documents and documents with security features to secure or not SOAP messages and supported XSLT files used for document transformation.

The second structural component of the SuT, the Report Engine acts as the collector of the evaluated data. Its main responsible focuses on gathering and consolidating them in log files.

Concluding, ICoM defines four major steps that lead to the definition of a SuT.

1. *service identification*: Identification of the primary services of the WSuT.
2. *interface analysis*: Analysis of the services' interfaces and data types used per service, extracting the messages types of the inputs and outputs as described in the WSDL documents. This may include an extensive analysis of several WSDL documents.
3. *standards definition*: definition of the standards that each WSuT adopts and implements.
4. *testing components adaptation*: adaptation of the two structural testing components, the Service Orchestration Engine and the Report Engine to the WSuT.

It should be noted that the above steps are completely independent of the underlying infrastructure and the WSuT implementation language and do not bind ICoM to a specific technological solution. The application of these steps in our demonstrated case study is depicted in the following example:

Example 2

The SELIS and SWEB SuTs are setup following the aforementioned four basic steps. In SELIS, we have identified three specific areas of services with diverse functions. These services are divided into:

- *Basic services,* which provide the basic functions used to perform primitive tasks. SELIS includes document management services, message and document transformation services, message forwarding services, publication and query services and notification services.

- *Security mechanisms and services* that address the security requirements of SELIS- invoicing. It supports the following security mechanisms: digital signatures, advanced electronic signatures, encryption, timestamping and credential management.
- *Infrastructure support services*, which manage the connection with the back-office systems such as databases, wrapper software on top of legacy systems, existing ERPs etc.

Each of these services has specific known interfaces as described by the corresponding WSDL documents having concise inputs and giving a concrete output. The standards that adopted in the services implementations are the following:

- the XML common business library version 4.0 (xCBL 4.0) and the Exact ERP XML schema, for the representation of the invoice information,
- the Extensible Stylesheet Language (XSL) Transformations, for the transformation of the invoice documents,
- several security standards such as W3C XML Encryption, W3C XML Digital Signature and XML Advanced Electronic Signature (XAdES) for the application of the appropriate security features on the business level and
- SOAP and the WS-Security standard for Web Services invocation and
- the Web Services Description Language (WSDL) for the description of invoked services.

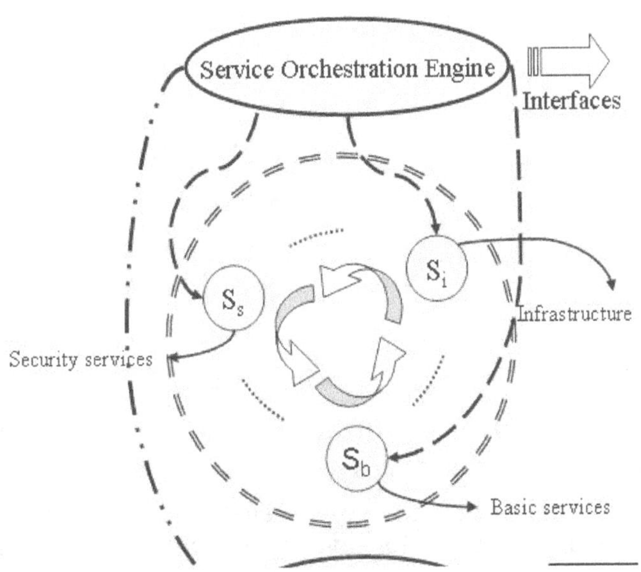

Fig. 5. SELIS SuT

Figure 5 depicts the overall form of the defined SELIS SuT which is composed by the two proposed structural testing components, the Service Orchestration Engine and the Report Engine and the SELIS WSuT. The process is similar in the case of SWEB.

3.2.2 Test Coordination Infrastructure (TCI)

The logical and organizational structure of the TCI is independent of the nature of the SuTs. On the contrary, technologically, it offers significant flexibility and scalability allowing the upgrade of already adopted testing tools and libraries and the integration of new more advanced ones. This upgrade enables the testing of different systems in various aspects.

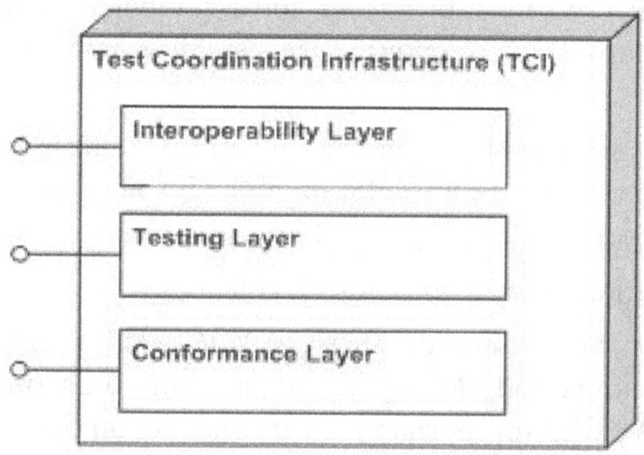

Fig. 6. Test Coordination Infrastructure

The general structure and functionality of the TCI is depicted in the Figure 6. Three fundamental layers, the *Testing Layer*, the *Interoperability Layer* and the Conformance Layer compose the TCI at a high level.

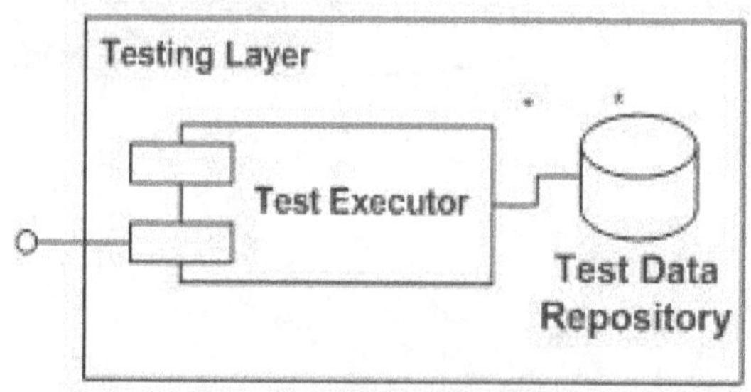

Fig. 7. Testing Layer

The Testing Layer (Figure 7) consists of the *Test Data Repository* and the *Test Executor*. The Test Executor orchestrates the execution of the deployed BPEL test cases in ICoM phases 3 and 4, based on a predefined schedule formed during these phases. Following this schedule, the Executor invokes sequentially the interfaces provided by the SuT Service Orchestration Engine in order to initiate the execution of the corresponding BPEL process. The invocation of the interfaces may require as input specific parameters (test data) which are retrieved from the Test Data Repository. As we will see in the following Section, the required test data rely on the nature of the deployed BPEL processes and are created along with the definition of the test cases.

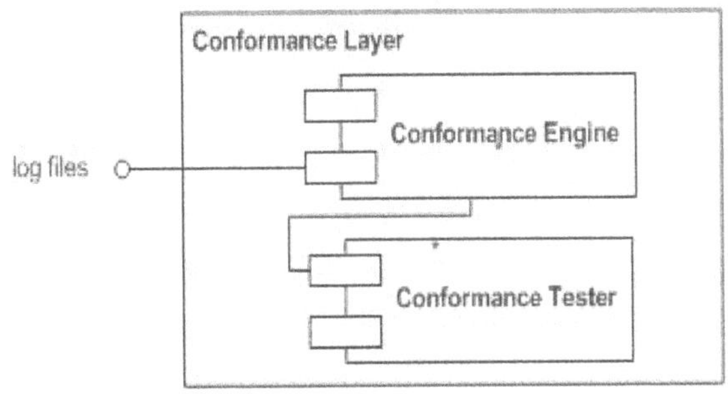

Fig. 8. Conformance Layer

The next layer of the TCI is the Conformance Layer (Figure 8) its main responsibility is to evaluate the conformance of each SuT against the adopted standards in phase 3. The evaluation process is performed based on the data produced by the SuT during the execution of the BPEL test cases. This layer contains two sub-components, the *Conformance Engine* and the *Conformance Tester*.

The Conformance Tester consists of a set of testing tools and libraries that actually assess the conformance of these data to the corresponding standards. The exact tools and libraries that should be adopted depend on the SuT's standards that have been defined during the formulation of a SuT (step 3). These range from tools that verify the conformance of a XML document to the corresponding XML schema and libraries that validate the security features of the XML documents to tools that check the conformance of the exchanged SOAP messages and message descriptions against the respective standards. Therefore, ICoM as methodology is quite extensible allowing the integration of new more updated tools/libraries in the Conformance Tester.

In the current phase, the steps that should be performed are the following:

the identification and the integration of the required tools in the Conformance Tester, the implementation of the appropriate tools' interfaces that enable Conformance Engine to invoke them. In case that the required interfaces can not be implemented due to the nature of the testing tools, a manual process is performed for the communication of these components.

In this layer, the Conformance Engine acts as the recipient and the analyzer of the log files that are produced by the SuTs in order to specify the tools that should be used for the evaluated data respectively.

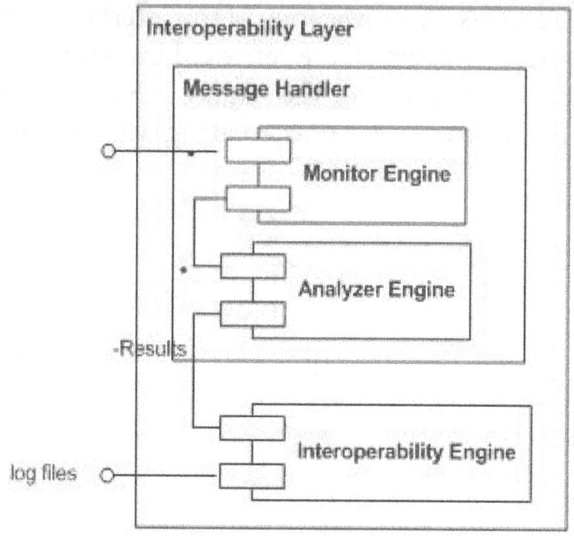

Fig. 9. Interoperability Layer

The Interoperability Layer (Figure 9) is the last but equally important layer comprising the *Message Handler* and *Interoperability Engine.* The Message Handler operates as the intermediate node during Interoperability testing (phase 4) that intercepts and delegates the exchanged messages to the SuTs. It comprises the Monitor Engine which intercepts the SOAP messages exchanged among the SuTs and the Analyzer Engine that determines whether these messages conform to their corresponding message descriptions.

The second subcomponent of the layer, the Interoperability Engine, is the actual interoperability consolidation point. It obtains as input the log files that are produced by the SuTs and the Analyzer Engine's conformance results providing them to the test operator. Based on these results, the test operator is able to do the following:

- notify the SuTs' interaction possibilities,
- detect the inaccurate points and
- impute the responsibility of the communication failure to the corresponding SuT.

Deductions are made by carrying out a process that consists of three main steps. The first one is to verify that the SuTs possess and handle the evaluated data without the detection of any erroneous behaviour. This means that the evaluated data are valid for all the SuTs. The second step includes a comparison process. During this process the exchanged data (e.g. exchanged SOAP messages and documents) are compared in order to acknowledge that the SuTs possess the same data. In the last step, the test operator confirms that the exchanged messages are part of the business processes that the SuTs have defined in their service descriptions. These steps enable the operator to identify whether the SuTs are interoperable and to what extent during the last phase of the proposed methodology.

In the following example we present the form of the TCI in our working example.

Example 3

The TCI has been shaped as presented in Figure 10. All the layer's components, Conformance Engine, Test Executor and Interoperability Engine have been implemented in Java technology. In the Testing Layer, a native XML Database, eXist has been adopted as the Test Data Repository enabling the storage of XML-based test data. The Conformance Tester of the Conformance Layer is shaped based on the SELIS and SWEB standards adopting testing tools that perform the conformance evaluation. Representative tools include testing environment and libaries for XML signature validation (IBM XML security suite (IBM XML), IAIK XML signature library (IAIK XML), IAIK XAdES toolkit (IAIK XAdES)) and tools for XML Schema document conformance (Altova XMLSpy).

The WS-I Tools (Brittenham, 2003), monitor (Brittenham et al., 2005) and analyzer (Brittenham, 2005), have been used in order to operate as the two subcomponents of the Interoperability Layer's Message Handler, Monitor and Analyzer Engine correspondingly. These tools provide an unobtrusive and automated way to log and analyze Web Service messages producing the respective conformance results that will be used for the interoperability evaluation.

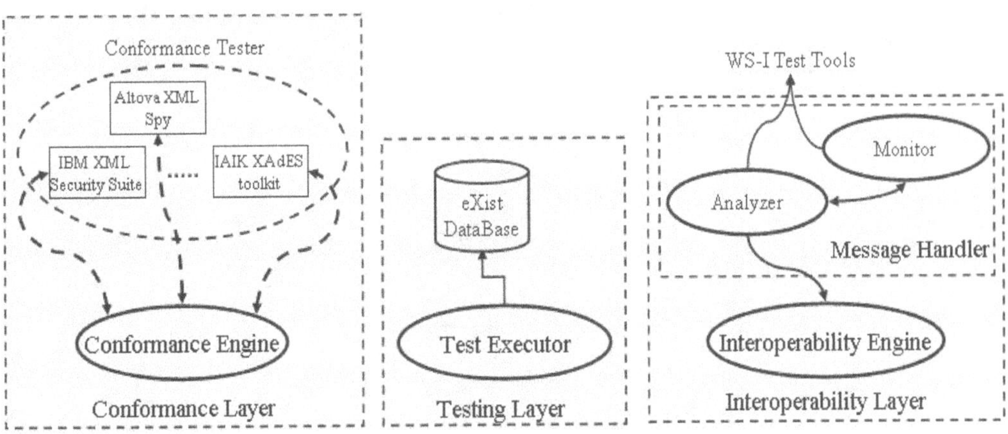

Fig. 10. TCI Working Example

Based on the above mentioned form of the TCI, the SELIS and SWEB SuT are able to be assessed taking into account the corresponding evaluation results that are derived from the execution of the defined test case in phase 3 and 4 of the proposed methodology.

3.3 Phase 3: Conformance Testing

Conformance testing has the primary goal of testing a WS against the standard it implements. This testing type involves a single SuT plus the TCI. The main steps that ICoM proposes are:

- *Definition of Conformance Test Cases*: In Section 0, we specified that ICoM adopts a BPEL representation of the deployed test cases. Our decision was based on the identification of a number of limitations (Pentafronimos et al., 2008) that the existing test case languages present and the nature and features of the BPEL language.

Generally, BPEL allows the definition and the representation of specific business flows in a XML format. It has unique features in both syntax (e.g. flow with activity synchronization, join condition) and semantics (e.g. dead-path-elimination) that make BPEL a highly compact and expressive language. In literature, there is intensive research on providing precise semantics for BPEL and verification of BPEL models (Fostre et al., 2006), (Xu et al., 2006). Additionally, there exist frameworks and models (Zheng et al., 2007), (Sinha & Paradkar, 2006), (Yuan et al., 2006), (Yan et al., 2006) that enable the automatic generation and definition of BPEL-based test cases.

Currently, most of the derived BPEL test cases are generated to test whether the implementation of a WS conforms to the BPEL behaviour and WSDL interface models. In ICoM, the BPEL processes specified and adopted depict activity flows that produce the appropriate evaluated data based on which the conformance and the interoperability capabilities of a WSuT are assessed.

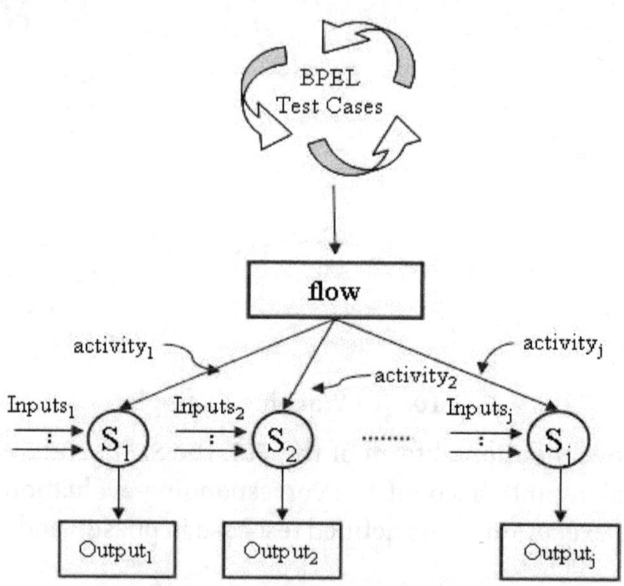

Fig. 11. BPEL Test Case

As depicted in Figure 11, a BPEL test case is a partially-ordered list of basic activities that that should be executed during a specific test run. The structural definition of a BPEL test case is as follows:

BPEL test case = {$Activity_j$, S_j, $Input_j$, $Output_j$}.

- $Activity_j$ is a set of activities that should be performed.
- S_j is a set of primary WSuT services that are invoked and orchestrated for the execution of a test case. Each service is associated with the realization of a specific activity.
- $Output_j$ is the result that each S_j derives. These results are gathered as the evaluated data of the SuTs.
- $Input_j$ is set of parameters that each service S_j requires according to the provided functionality in order to complete a defined process. The inputs can be:
- test data that are fed by the TCI during the initiation of a BPEL process,
- outputs of other primary services,
- parameters that have been defined and are included in the BPEL process.

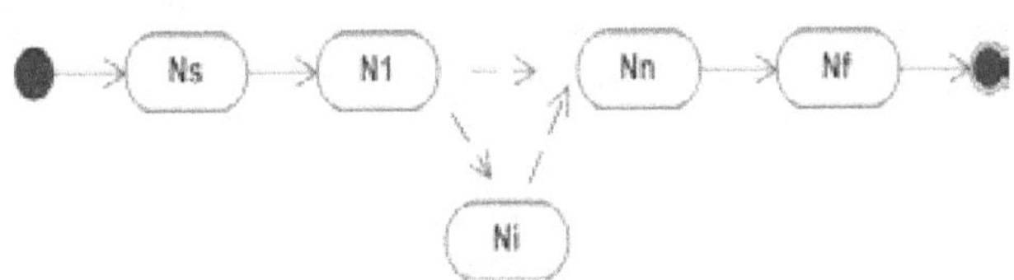

Fig. 12. Test Case Activity Graph Diagram

An activity graph diagram is also able to provide a visualization of the BPEL test cases (Figure 12). It illustrates and reflects the activity flow of the BPEL process in an effective manner. A test case activity diagram is composed by {N, E, N_s, N_f} where N is a set of nodes {N_1, ..., N_n} that correspond to the applied activities, E is a set of edges {E_1, ..., E_n} that are the implicit sequence concatenations as defined by the performed workflow, N_s is the Start Node and N_f is the Final Node of the workflow.

In conformance testing, the designed (conformance) test cases include only internal activities. This means that merely the services of the examined SuT interact with each other in order to derive the evaluated data. Usually, in this type of test these data come from the final node of the test case.

The main objective of the current step focuses on the definition of the deployed BPEL processes based on the standards evaluated against. In this sense, the ICoM is quite adaptable since it is able to evaluate different aspects of the WSuT.

The test operator is able to create these processes utilizing existing BPEL test case generation frameworks or any other BPEL creation engine (ActiveBPEL, 2006).

The processes are embedded in the SuT Service Orchestration Engine and the appropriate interfaces are implemented. During the BPEL generation phase, the required test data for each test case are specified and produced by the conformance evaluated tools of the TCI or by any other process.

Additionally, the test operator constructs a test case execution schedule taking into account the complexity of the applied processes. The schedule is a XML document that consists of the URLs of the BPEL processes interfaces and the corresponding required test data. This schedule along with the test data is stored in the Test Data Repository of the TCI. The steps that follow present and include the actual conformance testing sequence of the proposed methodology.

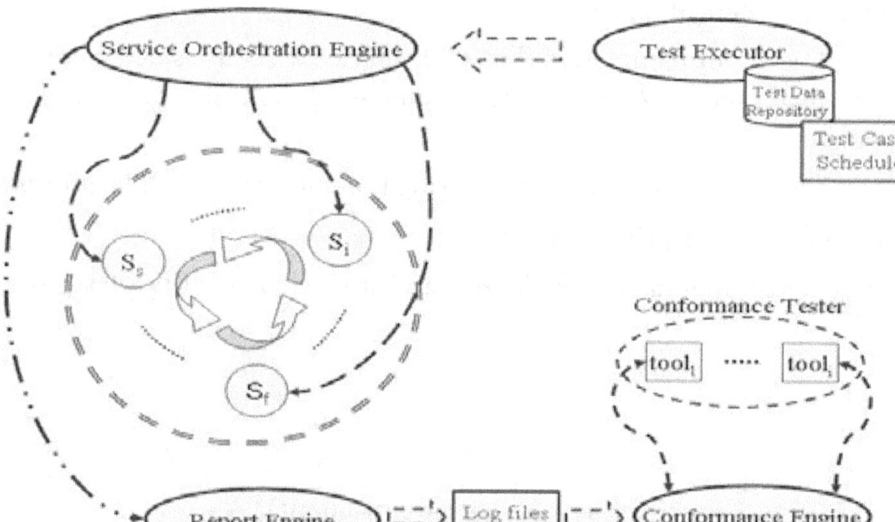

Fig. 13. Conformance Testing suite

- *Execution of test cases*: In this step, the TCI Test Executor automatically initiates the testing procedure by invoking the interface of the Service Orchestration Engine following the execution schedule. This action triggers the execution of the corresponding BPEL process running the defined test case. In Figure 13, the S_s is the initial service that is invoked and S_i is a set of services that contribute to the derivation of the evaluated data by the S_f.
- *Collection of results*: At the end of the test case, the Service Orchestration Engine has accumulated the evaluated data that are produced as outputs by the involved service of the WSuT. The Report Engine collects and consolidates these data in log files which are prepared for evaluation.
- *Results analysis*. Initially, the Conformance Engine analyzes the log files and extracts the produced data. Then, the Engine specifies the tools (tool1, ... ,tooli) of the Conformance Tester that should be used based on the nature

of these data. The Engine feeds the data via the implemented interfaces to the corresponding tools, which in turn infer the conformance of the implementation to the respective standard. Suggestions concerning any corrections to the implementation are also provided to the SuT, enabling the deployment of a fine-tuning process that will correct discrepancies.

- *Corrective actions*: Corrective actions by the WSuTs' developers may include both re- design and re-implementation or only updates of specific services within the WSuT.
- *Re-execution of failed tests*: When the corrective actions are complete, the SuT undergoes a new test round to check if the previously failed tests are now successfully passed.

At the end of the last step, the process begins again from "Execution of test cases" step in subsequent iterations until all tests are successful.

In the example that follows, it is illustrated an instance of the execution of the current phase's steps in our demonstrated case study.

Example 4

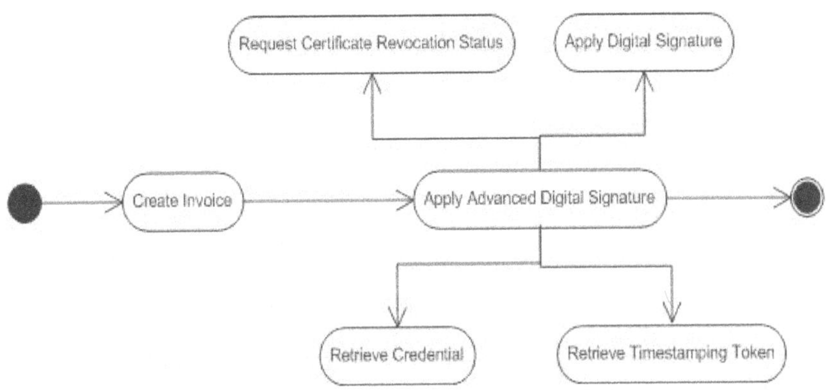

Fig. 14. Activity Diagram of the XAdES conformance test case

Figure 14 depicts an activity diagram representing an example test case for the conformance testing of the SELIS XAdES implementation against the XAdES standard. The actions that compose the test case are the following:

1. creation of a XML Invoice Document based on the xCBL standard,
2. application of Advanced Digital Signature on the produced document. This process includes four separate sub-processes which occur transparently:
   - certificate retrieval of the certificate that will be used for the signature process,
   - digital signing of the invoice and certain other properties according to the W3C XML Digital Signature standard,

- time stamping by requesting, and embedding a time stamp token on the generated signature according to the IETF 3161 standard, and finally
- revocation information inclusion by embedding certificate revocation status data after requesting them on-line from the server of the Certification Authority that has issued the signer's certificate.

The above test case is to be used as follows: initially the TCI Test Executor initiates the execution of the corresponding BPEL process of the SELIS Service Orchestration Engine invoking the appropriate interface. The choreography of the required WSuT services derives an xCBL invoice document signed according to the XAdES standard as illustrated in Figure 15. The Report Engine embeds the signed document to a log file which is retrieved by the TCI's Conformance Engine. The Engine delegates the document to the integrated IAIK toolkit to validate the applied signature.

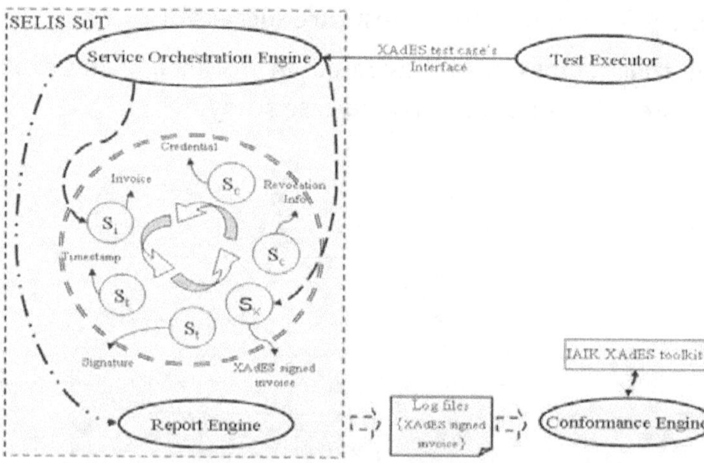

Fig. 15. SELIS Conformance XAdES Testing Suite

During our testing effort, in the actual first execution of this test case the toolkit indicated an incompatibility of the produced signature to the corresponding XML schema. This discrepancy was pointed out to the developers of the SELIS-invoicing which performed the necessary corrections. The re-execution of the test case denoted the conformance of SELIS with the XAdES standard.

3.4 Phase 4: Interoperability Testing

Interoperability testing is a more complex process than conformance testing because it usually involves at least two SuTs wishing to intercommunicate (Figure 16). The interoperability steps proposed by ICoM are not different from the corresponding conformance steps described in the previous section with regards to the logic and the sequence of the performed steps. On the contrary, the objective goals and the operation of these steps present significant differentiations. Thus, interoperability testing includes:

- *Definition of Conformance Test Cases*: The nature and the structure of the (interoperability) test cases that are designed and used in this phase are almost similar with the conformance ones, presented in Section 0. These test cases apart from internal activities include also and external activities. This means that the primary services of a SuT do not interact only with each other, but also with the services of other SuTs (Figure 16). Thus, the complexity of the BPEL processes that should be adopted to represent the logic of a test case is increased at a significant level.

The definition of the interoperability test cases takes into consideration two parameters. The first one is the testing scenario and the role assignment to the SuTs which was defined in the phase I of ICoM. The second parameter is the standards that the SuTs have adopted and are evaluated against. The specified interoperability test cases should constitute instance of this scenario taking into account the variants of this scenario based on the adopted standards.

BPEL processes should be formulated merely for the SuTs that initiate the execution of a testing suite. For example, the specified scenario, as depicted in Figure 16, is that the "SuT A" interacts with the "SuT B" retrieving a response. Therefore, based on a defined test case, the "WSuT A" orchestrates its corresponding services e.g. As and Ak to execute a specific process that enables service Ai to communicate with the service Bj of the "WSuT B" expecting a reply which is handled it appropriately. The BPEL process that corresponds to the above test case includes merely the actions which are executed by the "WSuT A". "WSuT B" reacts to this interaction creating the reply according to the logic that is included in the implementation.

Identically to the conformance testing, the BPEL processes are created via BPEL generation framework or any other available BPEL engine and are embedded in the Service Orchestration Engine of the respective SuT. The execution of the test cases is defined by a testing schedule that is prepared.

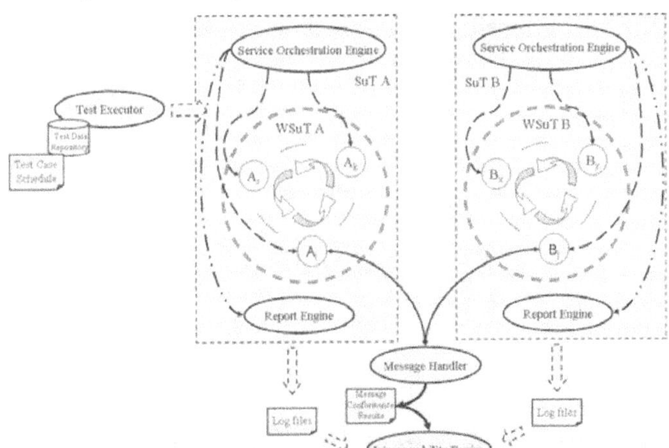

Fig. 16. Interoperability Testing Suite

- *Execution of test cases*: As presented in Figure 16, this step is completed following a similar process with the corresponding of the conformance testing. The execution of the external interactions among the involved WSuTs introduces an additional factor that should be taken into account and concerns the conformance of the exchanged messages to the defined business process. Thus, the TCI's Message Handler participates in the external interactions intercepting and analyzing the exchanged messages, and checking that they belong to the proper message domain.
- *Collection of results*: The Service Orchestration Engines of the SuTs taken part in the test case accumulate the whole of the evaluated data that are produced by all the involved WSuTs' services. Then the corresponding Report Engines collect and consolidate them in log files.
- *Results analysis*. The test results are analyzed and conclusions are made on the interoperability capabilities of the SuTs, as presented in Section 0.
- *Corrective actions*: Corrective actions may include both re-design and re-implementation or only updates of specific areas within the SuT.
- *Re-execution of failed tests*: As soon as the corrective actions have finished, the SuTs undergo a new test round to check if the previously failed tests are now successfully passed.

At the end of last step, the process begins again from second one in subsequent iterations until all tests are successful. In the Example 5 that follows the operation of the interoperability testing is described in detail.

Example 5

Figure 17 represents the activity diagram of an interoperability test case that is an instance of our working demonstration scenario, as implemented by the SELIS and SWEB SuTs. This test case includes only the actions performed by SELIS which is the actual initiator of the testing procedure.

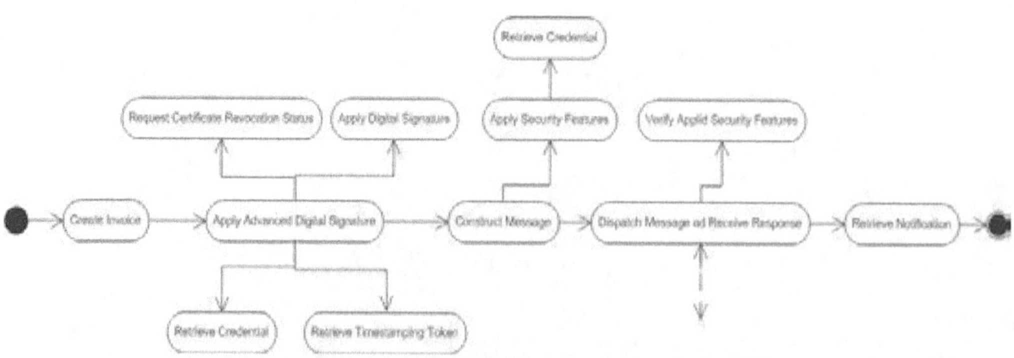

Fig. 17. Activity diagram of an Interoperability Test Case

As depicted in Figure 18 the process begins from the service A_1 of SELIS WSuT that creates a xCBL invoicing document (I_1). The document is signed by service A_2 according to the XAdES standard (SI_1) gathering the required time stamps and related certificate revocation status information data from their respective sources. Service A_4 packages the signed invoice in a SOAP message (M_1) where the WS Security features are applied (SM_1) using the service A_3. Finally, the service A_5 dispatches the message to the to the SWEB.

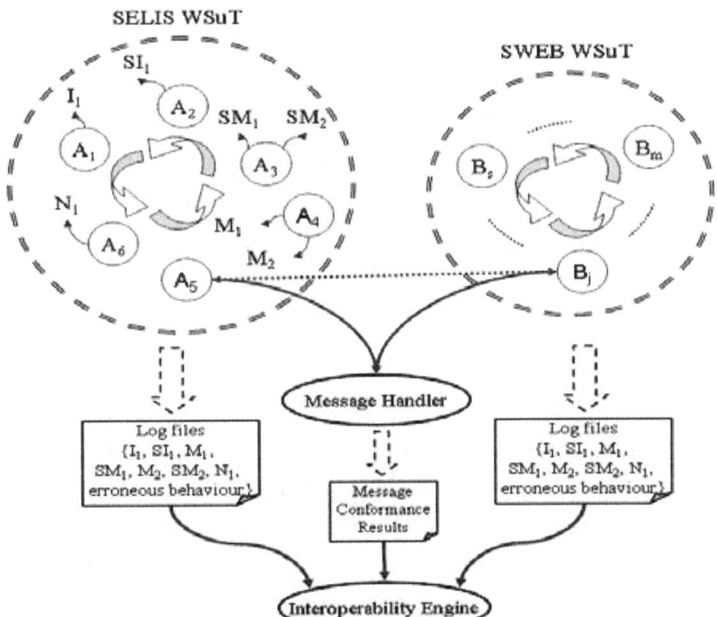

Fig. 18. SELIS and SWEB-invoicing Interoperability Testing Suite

SWEB handles the received SOAP message according to its predefined internal processes without following any steps specified by the test operator. Thus, SWEB receives the SOAP message, decrypts it and verifies the WS Security features. Then, the invoice document is extracted and the XAdES signature is verified (along with the rest of the cryptographic information it encompasses like any time stamps). A notification (N_1) is created that is packaged in a new SOAP message (M_2) where the WS-Security extensions are applied (M_2) and is sent to SELIS.

The latter as soon as receives the response, handles it according to the test case actions. Service A_5 retrieves the SOAP message and using the service A_3 validates the applied security features. Finally, the service A_6 manages the notification.

It should be noted that, the exchanged SOAP messages (SM_1 and SM_2) are intercepted by the TCI Message Handler. The Handler analyzes them checking that these messages conform to the defined SuTs' WSDL documents and produces the appropriate conformance results. The SuT Report Engines of both SuTs collect all the evaluation results and import them in log files. These consist of the exchanged SOAP messages (M_1, SM_1, M_2, and SM_2), the exchanged documents (I_1, SI_1, N1) and any erroneous behaviour that was reported during the whole process e.g. the application and validation of the applied security features of the invoice document.

The TCI Interoperability Engine receives the SuTs' log files and the Message Handler conformance results that are provided to the test operator which is responsible to analyze them and indicate the SuTs communication capability. The analysis we have performed in our demonstration systems verified that:

- the SuTs possess the same documents (I_1, SI_1, N_1) and messages (M_1, SM_1, M_2, SM_2) that were created either form the one or form the other system,
- no erroneous behavour has been detected during the interaction e.g. the validation of all message and document security features was successful,
- the exchanged messages (SM_1, SM_2) are part of the SuTs' business processes.

Therefore, according to the abovementioned analysis the two systems are interoperable.

4. CONCISE SUMMARY

The establishment of an interoperability framework relies on two elements: the exact definition of the employed standards and the delineation of a stringent set of principles to be adhered to. The testing approaches ensure the framework's development. However, the current testing approaches and frameworks fail to encompass all interoperability facets of a Web Services-based environment.

This work introduces an improved well-formed testing approach called ICoM, capable of testing and ensuring the end-to-end application interaction capabilities of WS-based services provided independently or through a SOA. ICoM successfully addresses the deficiencies of current approaches while meeting diverse criteria. ICoM is founded on established interoperability methodologies and frameworks, utilizing commonly employed testing types to address various interoperability and compliance aspects of web services, ultimately creating a framework that is adaptive, expandable, and versatile. ICoM was exemplified through an e-invoicing service provided as an independent web service (SELIS) and through the service-oriented architecture (SOA) platform SWEB.

Future endeavors in this domain encompass the incorporation of novel testing methodologies, including integration, performance, and stress testing, into the proposed framework. The introduction of these additional testing kinds will augment ICoM by facilitating the assessment of several dimensions of the assessed services and fostering the development of a more cohesive and advanced testing framework.

REFERENCES

1. High, R.; Kinder, S. & Graham, S. (2005). *IBM's SOA Foundation - An architectural Introduction and Overview.*
2. European Interoperability Framework for Pan-European eGovernment Services (EIF), available at http://europa.eu.int/idabc/
3. Kaliontzoglou, A.; Boutsi, P. & Polemi, D. (2006). eInvoke: Secure e-Invoicing based on Web Services. *Electronic Commerce Research*, vol 6, Numbers 3-4, pp. 337-353, Springer.
4. Papastergiou, S.; Karantjias, A. & Polemi, D. (2007a). Innovative, Secure and Interoperable E/M-Governmental Invoicing. *18th Annual IEEE International Symposium on Personal, Indoor and Mobile Radio Communications (PIMRC)*, Athens.
5. Secure, interoperable, cross border m-services contributing towards a trustful European cooperation with the non-EU member Western Balkan countries (SWEB), IST-2006- 2.6.5, 6th Framework Programme, Priority 2, Information Society Technologies (2007), www.sweb-project.org/.
6. OSI - Open System Interconnection, Conformance testing methodology and framework (1997), ISO/IEC 9646.
7. European Telecommunications Standards Institute (ETSI), available at http://portal.etsi.org/mbs/Testing/testing.htm
8. Moseley, S.; Randall, S. & Wiles, A. (2003). Experience within ETSI of the combined roles of conformance testing and interoperability testing. *Standardization and Innovation in Information Technology*, pp 177- 189, IEEE Press.
9. ETSI 300 406 (1995). Methods for testing and Specification (MTS); Protocol and profile conformance testing specifications; Standardization methodology.
10. ETSI ES 201 873 (2002): The Testing and Test Control Notation version 3, v2.2.0.
11. Dibuz, S. & Kremer, P. (2003). Interoperability Testing - Framework and Model for Automated Interoperability Test and Its Application to ROHC. *TestCom 2003*, LNCS vol 2644, pp. 243–257, Computer Science.
12. ETSI EG 202 237 V1.1.2 (2007-04): Methods for Testing and Specification (MTS); Internet Protocol Testing (IPT); Generic approach to interoperability testing.
13. Kulvatunyou, B.; Ivezic, N.; Martin, M. & Jones, A.T. (2003). A Business-to-Business Interoperability Testbed: An Overview. *The Fifth International Conference on Electronic Commerence*, Pittsburg, PA October.
14. Seely, S. & Lauzon, D. (2005). *WS-I monitor tool functional specification*, ver. 1.1. Technical report, WS-I.

15. Ehnebuske, D. et al. (2003). *WS-I Overview.* Available at www.ws- i.org/docs/20021003.wsi.introduction.pdf ebXML Technical Architecture Project Team, (2001). ebXML Technical Architecture Specification v1.0.4, February 16.
16. OASIS ebXML Implementation, Interoperability and Conformance Technical Committee:, (2003). ebXML Test Framework v0.3, 07 March.
17. Lee, Y. (2005). ebXML Test Framework on Dually Coupled Asynchronous MSH. *Fourth Annual ACIS International Conference on Computer and Information Science (ICIS'05)*, pp. 198-203, IEEE Press.
18. Kim, D. & Yun, J.H. (2003): Development -of an ebXML Conformance Test System for e- Business Solutions. *EC-Web 2003*, LNCS, vol 2738, pp. 145-154, Springer-Verlag Berlin Heidelberg
19. IBM XML security suite, available at http://www.alphaworks.ibm.com/tech/xmlsecuritysuite.
20. IAIK XML signature library, available at http://jce.iaik.tugraz.at/sic/products/ xml_security.
21. IAIK XAdES library, http://jce.iaik.tugraz.at/sic/products/xml_security/xades
22. Papastergiou, S.; Kaliontzoglou, A. & Polemi, D. (2007b) Interoperability issues of a Secure ELectronic Invoicing Service (SELIS). *18th Annual IEEE International Symposium on Personal, Indoor and Mobile Radio Communications (PIMRC 2007)*, 3-7 September, Athens.
23. ETSI Technical Report 266 (1996): Methods for testing and Specification (MTS); Test Purpose style guide.
24. Saglietti, F.; Oster, N. & Pinte, F. (2008).White and grey-box verification and validation approaches for safety- and security-critical software systems. Information Security Technical Report, Vol. 13, *Elsevier Advanced Technology*, ISSN 1363-4127, p. 10 – 16.
25. Peyton L.; Stepien, B. & Seguin, P. (2008). Integration Testing of Composite Applications, *Proceedings of the Proceedings of the 41st Annual Hawaii International Conference on System Sciences*, IEEE Computer Society.
26. Rizwan M.; Mamoon Y., (2007). SOA Testing using Black, White and Gray Box Techniques, White paper Crosscheck Networks, available at http://www.crosschecknet.com/ resources/articles/soatesting-v2.htm.
27. Brittenham, P. (2003). Understanding the WS-I Test Tool, available at http://www- 128.ibm.com/developerworks/webservices/library/ws-wsitest/.
28. Brittenham, P.; Durand, J.; Kleijkers, L. & Stobie, K. (2005a). WS-I Monitor Tool Functional Specification, WS-I Testing Work Group.

29. Brittenham, P., et al. (2005b). WS-I Analyzer Tool Functional Specification WS-I Testing Work Group.

30. Pentafronimos G.; Papastergiou S. & Polemi D. (2008). Definition and representation of test cases for e-government Web Services, *2nd International Conference on Theory and Practice of Electronic Governance (ICEGOV2008)*, 1 - 4 December, 2008, Cairo, Egypt.

31. Fostre, H.; Uchitel, S.; Magee, J. & Kramer, J. (2006). Model based analysis of obligations in web service choreography, *Proc. of AICT-ICIW*. IEEE Computer Society.

32. Xu, K.; Liu, Y. & Pu, G., (2006). Formalization, verification and restructuring of bpel models with pi calculus and model checking, IBM, Tech. Rep.

33. Zheng, Y.; Zhou, J. & Krause, P., (2007). An Automatic Test Case Generation Framework for Web Services. *Journal of Software*, vol. 2(3), pp. 64-77.

34. Sinha, A. & Paradkar, A. (2006). "Model based functional conformance testing of web services operating on persistent data," in Proc. of TAV-WEB. ACM Press, pp. 17–22.

35. Yuan, Y.; Li, Z. & Sun, W., (2006). A graph-search based approach to bpel4ws test generation, *Proc. of ICSEA*. IEEE Computer Society, p. 14.

36. Yan, J.; Li, Z.; Yuan, Y.; Sun, W & Zhang, J. (2006). Bpel4ws unit testing: Test case generation using a concurrent path analysis approach, *Proc. of ISSRE. IEEE Computer Society*, 2006, pp. 75–84.

37. ActiveBPEL Engine Architecture (2006), available at http://www.activebpel.org/ docs/architecture.html.

38. Karantjias A.; Papastergiou S. & Polemi D. (2008). Holistic Electronic & Mobile Government Platform Architecture. *8th Joint Conference on Knowledge - Based Software Engineering 2008 (JCKBSE 08)*, IOS Press, August 25-28, Athens, Greece.

39. Papastergiou, S.; Polemi, D. & Douligeris, C., (2009). SWEB: An advanced mobile Residence Certificate Service, *3rd International Conference on e-Democracy "Next Generation Society: Technological and Legal Issues"*, Lecture Notes of ICST (LNICST), Springer, ISBN 978-963-9799-54-7, Athens, Greece.

INDEX

D

E

O

P

Q

R

S

T

U

V

W

Z

www.ingramcontent.com/pod-product-compliance
Lightning Source LLC
LaVergne TN
LVHW081940200926
848484LV00009B/2478
* 9 7 8 1 7 8 7 1 5 6 7 3 9 *